POLITICAL MODERNIZATION

**A READER
IN COMPARATIVE
POLITICAL CHANGE**

SECOND EDITION

POLITICAL MODERNIZATION

A READER
IN COMPARATIVE
POLITICAL CHANGE

SECOND EDITION

edited by
Claude E. Welch, Jr.
State University of New York at Buffalo

103566

Duxbury Press, a division of Wadsworth Publishing
Company, Inc., Belmont, California

Duxbury Press
A Division of Wadsworth Publishing Company, Inc.

© 1971 by Wadsworth Publishing Company, Inc.

L.C. Cat. Card No.: 72-142149

Printed in the United States of America

3 4 5 6 7 8 9 10—74 73

Preface

In preparing the second edition of this reader, I have benefited from comments and queries by several scholars. Their most frequent critique focused on the exclusion from *Political Modernization* of articles dealing particularly with Latin America. Such an omission requires a note of explanation.

The editor of a reader inevitably is constrained by the material available. As of this date, few social scientists—Apter, Cardozo, Germani, Inkeles, Lipset, Scott, and Silvert being notable exceptions—have systematically analyzed political modernization in Latin America. The tendency of social scientists to concentrate on recently independent states in their studies of modernization results from a fundamental historical and social fact. Despite the presence of many American Indians (especially in the Andean and Central American states), the basic social, economic, and political contours of Latin America derive from Portuguese and Spanish conquest and rule and from extensive European immigration. The development of *haciendas*, the distinctive role of the Catholic church, and the looming presence of military *caudillos*, especially in the nineteenth century, distinguish Latin American states from most Asian and tropical African states. Independent a century or more before the great wave of decolonization hit other parts of the Third World, Latin America has made changes significantly different from those typical of the countries described in the subsequent pages. What I have lost in geographic scope, I hope to have gained in analytic clarity.

I wish to express particular thanks to John Hammond and Mary Karen Delmont, research assistants *par excellence*. More broadly, however, I wish to compliment students of the State University of New York at Buffalo, whose questions, whether naive or sophisticated, led me to explore paths I might otherwise have left to others.

Claude E. Welch, Jr.

CONTENTS

POLITICAL MODERNIZATION

A READER
IN COMPARATIVE
POLITICAL CHANGE

SECOND EDITION

THE COMPARATIVE
STUDY OF POLITICAL
MODERNIZATION

Many so-called revolutions become revolutionary only in retrospect. Few persons in the late eighteenth century would have spoken of the "industrial revolution" then starting in England. The impact of technology, mass production, factory-centered life, and the like was slowly realized: not until 1884 was Arnold Toynbee's *The Industrial Revolution* published, placing the phrase in common circulation. An equally profound revolution, the "revolution of modernization," now affects almost all parts of the globe and may have equally great consequences.

The systematic study of modernization is a recent phenomenon. It can be attributed to the demise of colonialism, particularly since the end of World War II. New states have emerged from the cocoon of European administration with a speed that has astounded many observers. The membership of the United Nations has burgeoned—51 members in 1945, and, at the end of 1969, 125 members, half of which had been under European rule when the organization was founded.

The independence of these formerly dependent territories has spurred many types of scholarly investigation. Economists investigate patterns and means of economic development in order to discover how these newborn states might reach self-sustaining growth. Sociologists seek to identify the means of inculcating among the peoples of the new nations a new sense of identity that rises above the time-honored bonds of village, caste, or ethnic group. The study of non-Western politics has burst into prominence as political scientists look beyond the confines of Western Europe and European-settled states. Yet, despite the widespread academic interest in the former colonial territories, relatively few comparisons of the process of change have been published. Are the new states unique in their patterns of development, or do they follow paths similar to those of Western countries? Can we identify stages of growth through which all states and societies must pass? Among what policies can political leaders choose in their quest for development?

The alterations visible in the newly independent states—the economic, social, and political changes—may be studied as part of the revolution of modernization. To understand this revolution we must first place modernization in its widest context. Modernization is a *process*, based upon the rational utilization of resources and aimed at the establishment of a "modern" society. A modern society is characterized by the application of technology (as shown by wide-ranging control of the environment and the utilization of inanimate sources of energy), by extensive social interdependence, by urbanization, literacy, social mobility, and a host of similar factors. Popular identification with the history, territory, myths, and national identity of the state become reasonably effective.[1] The old social units (tribe, caste, village) are subordinated to, though not necessarily destroyed by, the national community and lose many of their functions of social integration.[2] In other words, the process of modernization undermines traditional society as an inevitable part of change.

There are very few countries today that do not aspire to modernization.[3] Dynamism, change, industrialization, independence, influence, power, internal unity: these are some of the attributes of modern societies sought by the political elites of the recently independent states. These elites seek to refashion old societies and to pattern the changes (in part, at least) on the successful experiences of other countries. In

---

[1] Robert E. Ward, "Political Modernization and Political Culture in Japan" (*World Politics*, XV, 4, July 1963), p. 570. Professor Ward's article is reprinted in this reader, p. 100.

[2] Charles A. Micaud, et al., *Tunisia: The Politics of Modernization* (New York: Praeger, 1964), p. x.

[3] Edward Shils, *Political Development in the New States* (The Hague: Mouton, 1962), p. 7.

Burma as in Burundi, in Cyprus, Ceylon, and Costa Rica, in Mali as in Malawi, the revolution of modernization has started. Time-honored customs and styles of life are being changed in response to seemingly irresistible forces. Kemal Ataturk, the dominant figure in the modernization of Turkey between the World Wars, eloquently described these irresistible forces:

> Before the impetuous torrent of civilization resistance is futile: it is quite without mercy towards the heedless and refractory. In the face of the might and superiority of civilization, which pierces mountains, flies in the sky, sees everything from the atoms invisible to the eye to the stars, and which enlightens and investigates, nations striving to advance with a medieval mentality and primitive superstitions are condemned to perish or at least to be enslaved and humiliated.[4]

To trace these patterns of change and their political ramifications is the task of the readings in this book. By presenting evidence from many parts of the world, though primarily from the states of Africa and Asia that have become independent since World War II, we can see more clearly the directions of alteration. No revolution can be fully comprehended in mid-course. Yet, by examining the broad implications of the revolution of modernization in several settings, we can enhance our understanding of the global changes—worldwide, as well as all encompassing.

This book grew from a conviction that, all too often, the comparative study of political change has been artificially divided, whether on geographic grounds (books on Africa, for example, rarely draw comparisons with Latin America), on grounds of purported institutional similarities (parliamentary governments, presidential systems, one-party states, and the like), or on other bases open to criticism. Many studies rest upon an essentially static method of analysis and neglect the dynamic factors that sparked the revolution of modernization. The following pages rely upon different assumptions—that the agents that upset the traditional way of life deserve central attention; that these agents of change have touched all but the most inaccessible regions of the world; that the resultant revolution seems to follow certain paths, which can be fruitfully analysed.

WHAT IS POLITICAL MODERNIZATION?

Modernization is a universal and complex phenomenon. Wherever, whenever, and under what auspices it has occurred, modernization is

---

[4]Quoted in Manfred Halpern, *The Politics of Social Change in the Middle East and North Africa* (Princeton: Princeton University Press, 1963), p. 36, n. 12.

characterized by a core belief in rational or scientific control. This belief is the most important characteristic. Modernization, in the words of Benjamin Schwartz, depends upon the "systematic, sustained and purposeful application of human energies to the 'rational' control of man's physical and social environment for various human purposes."[5] In a similar vein, Robert Ward views modernization as the movement toward a modern society, characterized "by its far-reaching ability to control or influence the physical and social circumstances of its environment, and by a value system which is fundamentally optimistic about the desirability and consequences of this ability."[6]

Put in somewhat different terms, modernization involves the diffusion of what one expert calls the "world culture"—"based on advanced technology and the spirit of science, on a rational view of life, a secular approach to social relations, a feeling for justice in public affairs, and, above all else, on the acceptance in the political realm of the belief that the prime unit of the polity should be the nation-state."[7] Whether introduced by external force, internal innovation, or conscious imitation, the world culture has made a strong impact on traditional ways of life.

Historically, the first instances of modernization occurred in Western Europe after the Renaissance and the Reformation. The emergence of the scientific outlook—the willingness to revise long-standing concepts, to utilize experiments—brought a fundamental alteration.

> Men came to believe for the first time that it would be possible to rearrange society on rational principles . . . All these social, economic, political and cultural revolutions helped to break the 'cake of custom' of traditional society, and to create our modern world of incessant change and innovation and of enduring achievements.[8]

The forces unleashed by this transformation soon spread far beyond Western Europe. Other societies were affected either by the direct imposition of colonial rule or by the indirect threat of such imposition. Colonialism had far-reaching effects, though these were initially confined to relatively small areas and groups of people. Administrative organs based on Western institutions were established; large trading firms introduced new manufactured goods; missionaries offered education and medical care, as well as generous doses of an alien religion.

---

[5]Quoted in Marius B. Jansen, ed., *Changing Japanese Attitudes Toward Modernization* (Princeton: Princeton University Press, 1965), pp. 23–24.

[6]Ward, "Political Modernization and Political Culture in Japan," p. 570.

[7]Lucian W. Pye, *Aspects of Political Development* (Boston: Little, Brown, 1965), p. 8.

[8]I. R. Sinai, *The Challenge of Modernisation* (London: Chatto and Windus, 1964), pp. 18–19.

Long-standing patterns of social organization were weakened, as illustrated in the readings of Section 2. New social classes—an urbanized labor force, a growing number of local entrepreneurs, and, above all, a new group of intellectuals whose understanding and aspirations extended far beyond their traditional social groupings—arose through the impact of external rule. Aspects of European civilization thus could be found in colonies all around the world.

For lands that did not fall directly under colonial administration, the impact, though indirect, was nevertheless substantial. A major impetus for change in nineteenth-century Japan, for example, was fear of intervention by Western states. Unless the Japanese adopted scientific techniques and industrial advances—in short, until they created the hallmarks of modernization in their own country—they were prey for external encroachments and interference. The revolution of modernization thus came to affect the entire world. Its ramifications could not be escaped.

Change occurs in all societies—indeed, it is unavoidable. All analysts agree, however, that modernization requires a thoroughgoing transformation, of polity as well as society. The revolution of modernization, as Manfred Halpern has argued, "involves the transformation of all systems by which man organizes his society—the political, social, economic, intellectual, religious, and psychological systems."[9]

For analytical clarity, modernization is studied in three ways: (1) as a primarily economic phenomenon, bound up with the process of industrialization; (2) as a series of interconnected social and psychological changes that alter both traditional patterns of behavior and individuals' perceptions; (3) as a variety of political changes, such as the differentiation of new political structures, widened political participation, the growth of "nationalism," and the like. Of course, no sweeping revolution can be so readily compartmentalized; the economic, social, and political changes are intertwined, perhaps mutually reinforcing. The creation of a new industry—or even the introduction of a metal-tipped rather than a wooden plow—is likely to have an immediate social impact as significant as the economic impact and possibly a long-range political effect as well. However, to encourage further research and deeper understanding, we must impose possibly artificial distinctions upon otherwise elusive concepts.

One school of research—the "growth economists"—address themselves to the study of modernization as a primarily economic phe-

---

[9]Manfred Halpern, "Toward Further Modernization of the Study of New Nations" (*World Politics*, XVII, 1, October 1964), p. 173.

nomenon. Can the historical patterns of economic change in the "developed" countries recur in the states emerging from colonial rule? How might the vicious circle of low productivity, low investment, and a subsistence level of living be broken? Will industrialization provide a panacea to the multitude of problems facing the new nations? Tentative answers to these problems—and detailed analyses of the obstacles to rapid, large-scale, industrial development—appear in a number of books.[10]

It is tempting to define the process of modernization as, simply, the process of industrialization. Leaders of recently independent states believe that industrialization is the key to future progress. Many scholars, pointing to the central importance of industrialization in the modernization of Western states, also tend to equate the two processes.[11] They believe that modernization *is* industrialization and the concomitant effects of industrialization upon social structure, communications, world view, and the like. However, a simple equation between modernization and industrialization is unwarranted. Traditional social patterns may persist side by side with the most modern factory.[12] It is more accurate to view industrialization as a necessary, but not sufficient, condition for the emergence of a modern society. Modernization clearly involves more than economic change. A factory can readily be established, if sufficient funds are available; but changes in cultural patterns are far more difficult to bring about.

---

[10]See among many others, the following studies: P. T. Bauer and B. S. Yamey, *The Economics of Underdeveloped Countries* (Cambridge: Cambridge University Press, 1957); Robert L. Heilbroner, *The Great Ascent: The Struggle for Economic Development in Our Time* (New York: Harper & Row, 1963); Albert Hirschman, *The Strategy of Economic Development* (New Haven: Yale University Press, 1958); Bert F. Hoselitz, *et al.*, *Theories of Economic Growth* (New York: Free Press of Glencoe, 1963); Simon Kuznets, Wilbert E. Moore and Joseph J. Spengler, eds., *Economic Growth: Brazil, India, Japan* (Durham: Duke University Press, 1955); W. Arthur Lewis, *The Theory of Economic Growth* (London: George Allen & Unwin, 1955); G. M. Meier and R. E. Baldwin, *Economic Development: Theory, History, Policy* (New York: Wiley, 1957); David E. Novack and Robert Lekachman, eds., *Development and Society: The Dynamics of Economic Change* (New York: St. Martin's Press, 1964). A useful bibliography compiled by Arthur Hazlewood, *The Economics of Underdeveloped Areas* (Oxford: Institute of Commonwealth Studies, 1959, second edition), covers the basic literature published to 1958.

[11]Wilbert E. Moore, *Social Change* (Englewood Cliffs, N. J.: Prentice-Hall, 1963), p. 91. Industrialization is defined as "the extensive use of inanimate sources of power for economic production, and all that that entails by way of organization, transportation, communication, and so on." Moore, pp. 91-92.

[12]James G. Abegglen, *The Japanese Factory* (New York: Free Press of Glencoe, 1958), pp. 127–129. I take issue with Apter, who asserts that industrialization is, in effect, a universal leveller of social institutions: "Industrialization is that aspect of modernization so powerful in its consequences that it alters dysfunctional social institutions and customs by creating new roles and social instruments, based on the use of the machine." David E. Apter, *The Politics of Modernization* (Chicago: University of Chicago Press, 1965), p. 68.

The social and psychological aspects of modernization similarly represent an important part—but not the totality—of the process we are describing. With the weakening of traditional social restraints, popular awareness of other groups and active participation in politics increase. The psychological transformations that typify modernization are equally dramatic. Modernization involves "psychic mobility" or "empathy"—"the capacity to see oneself in the other fellow's situation."[13] Other psychological aspects include a greater tendency to use "rational" or pragmatic norms in deciding issues (rather than traditional or religious-magical norms) and a more optimistic outlook concerning the utility of change. The readings in Sections 2 and 3 illustrate the social and psychological transformations involved in modernization.

But it is with the political aspects of modernization that we are primarily concerned. The goal of political modernization is the development of an institutional framework that is sufficiently flexible and powerful to meet the demands placed upon it. In short, the government must become fully capable of performing a wide variety of duties. Its capacities must increase, so that change can be accommodated within political channels. Political modernization is linked with economic growth and with social and psychological changes—for the obvious reason that the capacity of a government to deal with demands is affected by economic and cultural factors.

The process of political modernization has three major characteristics:

1. an increased centralization of power in the state, coupled with the weakening of traditional sources of authority;
2. the differentiation and specialization of political institutions;
3. increased popular participation in politics, and greater identification of individuals with the political system as a whole.

Political modernization thus involves a dramatic shift in the locus of authority. Tribal chiefs, petty princes, and the like gradually lose their power. Religious, traditional, familial, and ethnic authorities are supplanted, as Samuel P. Huntington notes, by a single, secular, national political authority.[14]

A modernized political system is highly complicated. Political modernization multiplies the volume, range, and efficiency of official decisions. To meet the complex tasks placed upon them, the organs of government become (as the jargon would have it) "highly differen-

---

[13]Daniel Lerner, *The Passing of Traditional Society: Modernizing the Middle East* (New York: Free Press of Glencoe, 1958), pp. 50–51. Also see K. H. Silvert, ed., *Expectant Peoples: Nationalism and Development* (New York: Random House, 1963), pp. 21–24.
[14]Samuel P. Huntington, "Political Modernization: America vs. Europe" (*World Politics*, XVIII, 3, April 1966), p. 378.

tiated" and "functionally specific." A brief comparison of the tasks performed by the government of the United States with the political duties of a traditional chief in Africa would make this point obvious. The difficulties of changing the structure and operation of governmental institutions are discussed in the readings of Section 5.

The third aspect of political modernization is perhaps the most difficult to achieve. Popular attitudes must be transformed, the nature of political participation changed. Widespread awareness of and participation in national politics characterizes a modern society, not a traditional society. This participation comes in part through the growth of political parties and interest groups. Traditional social institutions, such as caste, can be subtly transformed into vehicles of participation. The result (hopefully) is a society in which popular identification with the state as a whole—its history, territory, myths, and national identity— tends to supplant identification with traditional social units.

Historically speaking, centralization of control and the differentiation of political institutions preceded popular participation in politics. The recently independent states, however, are following a different path from Western Europe, where participation grew over many centuries. In the post-colonial countries, participation may be relatively high and the possibility of political instability correspondingly great. There is no greater challenge to political modernization than meeting the demands brought by increased popular participation in politics. As Sidney Verba comments, orderly patterns of change are unlikely in the recently independent states unless individuals who are physically and legally members of the political system also feel themselves to be members of that system.[15] Orderly patterns of political modernization thus presuppose a transformation of attitudes—a dramatic shift away from traditional social and political practices. Let us turn now to the difficulties of such a change.

TRADITIONAL SOCIETIES AND THE IMPACT OF MODERNIZATION

When traditional attitudes and practices seem to impede the course of modernization, their transformation can be approached in two ways: (1) by legislating against manifestations of communalism or tribalism (as in many African one-party states) in order to implant national unity as rapidly as possible; or, (2) by exploiting favorable aspects of traditional beliefs in order to change these beliefs in a gradual fashion. The first method is a head-on attack against tradition, which is seen by governmental leaders as a retrograde force; the sec-

---

[15]Lucian W. Pye and Sidney Verba, eds., *Political Culture and Political Development* (Princeton: Princeton University Press, 1965), p. 529.

ond, a gradual accommodation with tradition, in which tradition itself is eventually undermined and transformed.

The disengagement from traditionalism sought by political leaders in new states is by no means an easy, straightforward, or short-run task. Social norms and customs are deeply ingrained; they pervade and regulate most aspects of daily life. Yet traditional mores are likely to impede the social transformations associated with modernization. To weaken the hold of traditionalism is the primary problem confronting recently independent states—for it is the unresolved tension between "national" loyalty and "communal" loyalty that substantially determines the course of political modernization.

The noted French sociologist Gustave LeBon described the problem in this way: "To respect tradition is a condition of existence for a people; to know how to disengage from it, a condition of progress."[16] In Moslem countries, as Richard H. Pfaff demonstrates in his comparative study of Turkey and Iran, the disengagement from traditionalism involves a continual redefinition of the relationship between Islam and society—a redefinition that results from the subordination of Islam to the state and the development of secularly defined nationalism. The feeling of religious community must be supplemented by political loyalty.[17]

The process of disengagement from traditionalism does not imply that traditional social divisions can, will, or should disappear. Particularism is not confined to recently independent states—it is a universal phenomenon. But a fundamental distinction exists between political systems in which local affiliations tend to define the most enduring political relationships for the bulk of the population, and political systems in which individuals share a distinct loyalty to the system as a whole. Edward Shils outlines the problem of particularism in these terms:

> The constituent societies on which the new states rest are, taken separately, not civil societies, and, taken together, they certainly do not form a single civil society... They lack the affirmative attitude toward rules, persons, and actions that is necessary for consensus. They are constellations of kinship groups, castes, tribes, feudalities— even smaller territorial societies—but they are not civil societies. The sense of identity is rudimentary, even where it exists. The sense of membership in a nation-wide society, and the disposition to accept the legitimacy of the government, its personnel, and its law are not

[16]Quoted in Micaud, *Tunisia: The Politics of Modernization*, p. 33.
[17]Richard H. Pfaff, "Disengagement from Traditionalism in Turkey and Iran" (*Western Political Quarterly*, VI, 1, March 1963), pp. 79–98.

great. Society-wide institutions, other than the state, are scant in the societies we are discussing.[18]

A paradox of modernization is that social change and participation may increase rather than diminish the scope and intensity of communal conflicts. It has often been assumed that the erosion of traditional values (as through increased personal mobility, urbanization, literacy, and the like) entails a corresponding development of modern values. The process shows many more complexities, however. The inculcation of new values requires two steps: (1) the weakening of longstanding norms of social conduct through the uprooting of old settings, habits, and commitments; and (2) the induction of individuals into relatively stable new patterns of group membership, organization, and commitment.[19] But the result of social change may be a reincarnation and expansion of communal solidarity rather than an integration of diverse groups. Increased consciousness of group antagonisms and cultural differences—not increased sentiments of national unity—can be the initial result of modernization. In Ceylon, for example, the replacement of ethnic by national loyalties was farther away in 1961 than a decade earlier. Modernization increased tensions between the Sinhalese-speaking and Tamil-speaking groups; the unifying purpose of the independence struggle faded away, leaving behind a host of contradictions and cleavages.[20] Comparable events have taken place in many other new states.[21]

The reason for the persistence of primordial sentiments is relatively simple. An individual's perceptions and loyalties are shaped substantially during his childhood and adolescence through the process of socialization.[22] Cultural change in new states has not as yet brought a

---

[18]Edward Shils, "On the Comparative Study of the New States," in Clifford Geertz, ed., *Old Societies and New States: The Quest for Modernity in Asia and Africa* (New York: Free Press of Glencoe, 1963), p. 22.

[19]Karl W. Deutsch, "Social Mobilization and Political Development" *(American Political Science Review*, LV, 3, September 1961), pp. 493–514. Professor Deutsch's article is reprinted in this reader, pp.153.

[20]W. Howard Wriggins, "Impediments to Unity in New Nations: The Case of Ceylon *(American Political Science Review*, LV, 2, June 1961), pp. 313–320. Professor Wriggins' article is reprinted in this reader, p. 219.

[21]"Predominant identification with one's own ethnic group, accompanied by hostility to out-groups, appears to have increased in some African states since independence." William John Hanna, ed., *Independent Black Africa: The Politics of Freedom* (Chicago: Rand McNally, 1964), p. 22.

[22]In the United States, for example, it has been suggested that political socialization occurs substantially between the ages of three and thirteen. David Easton and Robert D. Hess, "The Child's Political World" (*Midwest Journal of Political Science*, VI, 3, August 1962), pp. 229–246.

substantial change in long-standing patterns of socialization for the majority of the populations. A child born in Western Nigeria, for example, will in all probability grow up speaking the Yoruba language; time-honored folk tales and legends will implant in him a sense of Yoruba cultural identity; in a conflict pitting Yoruba against members of another tribe, he will be advised to support his ethnic "brothers." In short, this child will come to share the outlooks characteristic of his own ethnic group. Lucian W. Pye bases much of his analysis of Burma's political oscillations upon family relationships that appear to produce "an odd combination of optimism and distrust, a combination which in varying degrees seems to be present in many transitional societies having difficulties in modernizing."[23] These deeply rooted sentiments cannot be readily altered. It would be unrealistic to expect a drastic change in social attitudes without a transformation of the patterns of socialization. Hence, for the overwhelming proportion of the inhabitants of recently independent states, the attitudes implanted in childhood—the stress upon group solidarity in particular—continue to influence social and political action.[24]

It cannot be doubted that social change uproots old settings, habits, and commitments. Although traditional values of solidarity may be weakened, they are likely to continue affecting political loyalties. The "relatively stable new patterns of group membership" might well be *Sinhalese* solidarity rather than *Ceylonese* solidarity. Social change does not lead directly or automatically to a deeply implanted sense of national identity. To transform a sentiment of group unity into a fact of national integration is extremely difficult—and the course of political modernization will be directly affected.

Although traditional political structures are often gravely weakened by social change, many deep-rooted cultural values may remain substantially unaltered. During the period of European rule, the collaboration of traditional rulers with the colonial administration undercut the social support of the rulers.[25] Chiefs in many parts of Africa became simply cogs in the administrative machinery; the relationship of mutual trust and responsibility between chiefs and subjects was transformed as the chiefs increasingly owed their power to support from the colonial government. For analytical purposes, however, let us distinguish between traditional political structures (in this case, the

---

[23]Lucian W. Pye, *Politics, Personality, and Nation Building: Burma's Search for Identity* (New Haven: Yale University Press, 1962), p. 184.
[24]Robert LeVine, "Political Socialization and Culture Change," in Geertz, *Old Societies and New States*, pp. 284–85.
[25]See, for example, David E. Apter, *Ghana in Transition* (New York: Atheneum, 1963), p. 122.

chiefs) and traditional values of group solidarity. The imposition of colonial administration likely led many Africans to reject long-standing patterns of authority because of the identification of chiefs with European rulers; it does not follow, however, that the Africans tossed overboard their ethnic identity, that they rejected their belief in the value of solidarity with their "brothers" in the same communal group.

After independence, friction between ethnic groups often increased. No longer could the colonial government serve as the scapegoat for all domestic difficulties. When Africans (and, by extension, other races or groups under alien political rule) "find themselves associated with other Africans of different tribes in opposition to Europeans, they express their unity in racial terms and ignore the tribal differences; [but] when Africans find themselves associated with fellow tribesmen in opposition to other groups they express their unity in tribal terms."[26]

The persistence of group loyalties in the post-independence period and in the face of efforts at national integration explains why leaders in many new states have turned to authoritarian forms of government. These men place greatest emphasis upon the would-be national community and its transcendence and supersession of traditional communities. Their commitment is to national unity "as the supreme value and goal."[27] Discipline—not recognition or encouragement of diversity or individuality—is seen as perhaps the most important step in social modernization. As Jose Arsenio Torres points out, "Freedom is freedom to involve the community, be it by means of traditional or modern symbols and goals, in the tasks of the government: the nation or the community is the unit of effective action ... Unity, at any price, becomes the emblem of national endeavor."[28]

Is there an inherent contradiction between communal solidarity and national unity? Does ethnocentrism seriously jeopardize the prospects for modernization? Reading the harsh criticisms of "tribalism" made by African leaders, for example, one would be tempted to conclude that ethnocentrism automatically works against modernization. Yet the relationship is much more complex. Since modernization requires fundamental changes in cultural values, patterns of authority, consensus, and the like, an appeal to ethnocentric values can some-

[26]Michael Banton, "Race Relations in ... South Africa of the Sahara" (*International Social Science Bulletin*, XIII, p. 209), quoted in Hanna, *Independent Black Africa*, p. 22.

[27]James S. Coleman and Carl G. Rosberg, Jr., eds., *Political Parties and National Integration in Tropical Africa* (Berkeley and Los Angeles: University of California Press, 1964), p. 663. A selection from Professors Coleman and Rosberg's book is reprinted in this reader, p. 330.

[28]Jose Arsenio Torres, "The Political Ideology of Guided Democracy," (*Review of Politics*, XXV, 1, January 1963), p. 57.

times make these changes easier and more comprehensible. The example of Meiji Japan illustrates how traditional values and institutions can be invoked to hasten change. In Japan after 1868, reverence for the Emperor was inculcated systematically to bring rapid industrialization while ensuring the tranquility, obedience, and loyalty of the countryside. As Robert E. Ward notes, "the control devices utilized were almost without exception traditional . . . the rapid development of Japan . . . rested ultimately on the effective enlistment of traditional institutions and appeals in the service of the modernizing process."[29] Communal solidarity eased modernization by providing a stable social framework within which change could occur.

Two obvious difficulties exist in this example of orderly change. Are other groups as receptive to change as the Japanese, or might traditional values (including group solidarity) of other peoples pose insuperable obstacles to modernization? Secondly, assuming that a heightened sense of *national* identity characterizes modernization, might not an aroused sense of *communal* identity within a particular region militate against national identity?

The answer to the first question is relatively simple. Societies differ in their speed and ease of adaptation; many of the distinctions among societies can be traced back to the nature of traditional beliefs, particularly the acceptance of change. But in almost all societies, the pains of transition can be eased by the astute utilization of tradition. The second question leads to the complex problem of social and political integration, to which the readings in Section 4 are devoted. Primordial sentiments do not disappear overnight but rather after a long and often acrimonious period of transition. The authoritarian and single-party regimes in many new states draw their *raison d'être* from persistent group loyalties. Until a sense of identity with the state as a whole—not merely with one's group—becomes widespread, orderly patterns of change are unlikely. In short, the forecast for most recently independent countries is continued instability and uncertainty. What revolution as sweeping as that of modernization has ever been accomplished without upheaval?

MODELS AND METHODS OF MODERNIZATION

There are many roads to modernization. As we have suggested, modernization is a *process* directed toward the establishment of a modern society. Methods differ; the time available differs; the priorities differ. In Great Britain, the process was gradual. Social, economic,

---

[29]Ward, "Political Modernization and Political Culture in Japan," p. 580.

and political alterations were not concurrent: the "cake of custom" changed over many centuries. In the Soviet Union, by contrast, modernization was much more compressed: industrialization, forced collectivization of agriculture, a turning away from the West typified the Stalinist period. Social, economic, and political change—all under the strict control of the Communist Party—raised the U.S.S.R. from a relatively weak state to a leading world power. The modernization of Japan did not occur under the auspices of a revolutionary political party but under the benevolent guidance of an aristocratic bureaucracy. Many examples thus exist and are examined in the reprinted selections in this book. Three points deserve particular attention: the role of intellectuals, the uneven nature of change, and the active role of government in promoting modernization.

One characteristic of modernization is leadership by a small group of intellectuals, who are usually influenced by Western education and whose knowledge and outlooks are far broader than those of their compatriots. The Meiji bureaucrats and the leaders of most anticolonial movements in Africa and Asia had in common a deep-seated belief, derived from their education, of the necessity for change. Their control of the governmental apparatus gave them tremendous power with which to guide the process of modernization. As Edward Shils has noted, "In no state-formations in all of human history have intellectuals played such a role as they have in these events of the present century."[30] Upon their shoulders has been placed the responsibility for leadership: the intellectuals take major responsibility for developing a sense of nationalism "when there was little sense of nationality among the peoples whose nationality the intellectuals were proclaiming";[31] they demand industrialization, dynamism, a scientific outlook, a better way of life; they transmit new political ideas to the populace; they utilize political resources for wide-ranging change.

A second hallmark of modernization in new states is its partial character. Economic and political changes, for example, may precede social alteration, or vice versa. A Bedouin nomad may follow a way of life substantially unchanged for centuries while his brother may work in a highly complex oil refinery, as modern as any in the world. To reiterate a point: traditional cultural patterns can persist side by side with modern technology. Economic change may outpace social

---

[30]Edward Shils, "The Intellectuals in the Political Development of the New States," (*World Politics*, XII, 3, April 1960), p. 329.

[31]Shils, "The Intellectuals," p. 342.

and cultural change. Independence for a country might come long before the population fully accepts or understands its new responsibilities.

Thus there are great discontinuities—and consequent tensions—in development. While the British people gradually adjusted to a series of alterations, the peoples of new states must assimilate much more quickly the overlapping social, economic, and political changes of modernization. The time span is compressed. Kwame Nkrumah exclaimed, "What other countries have taken three hundred years or more to achieve, a once dependent territory must try to accomplish in a generation if it is to survive. Unless it is, as it were, 'jet-propelled,' it will lag behind and thus risk everything for which it has fought."[32] This "jet-propelled" character, on the other hand, risks serious maladjustments. In Western states, development was relatively " 'natural' ... [in that] political change had a close interrelation with socioeconomic advance."[33] In the so-called developing countries of the present day, however, change is uneven, discontinuous, and marked by lags, leads, and uncertainties.

The final noteworthy aspect of modernization is the extensive reliance upon the centralization, governmental initiation of, and government leadership of the modernization process. Here the link between modernization and politics becomes most apparent. In the twentieth century, governments are both endowed with the technological capability to carry out sweeping changes in wide realms of social life and willing, as well as able, to attempt fundamental transformations. It is under the direct auspices of the state that modernization is carried out.

The interest of leaders of new states in the Soviet Union results from the apparent rapidity with which the U.S.S.R. was transformed, through totalitarian methods, from a predominantly agricultural country of secondary importance to one of the two major world powers. Modernization—like ideology—is shaped by the times. Monarchical absolutism and constitutional democracy no longer seem apt ways of achieving modernization;[34] the contemporary emphasis is upon strong, centralized governmental leadership of the process of modernization.

---

[32]Kwame Nkrumah, *Ghana: The Autobiography of Kwame Nkrumah* (Edinburgh: Thomas Nelson, 1957), p. x.

[33]Robert A. Scalapino, "Ideology and Modernization—The Japanese Case," in David E. Apter, ed., *Ideology and Discontent*, (New York: Free Press of Glencoe, 1964), p. 99.

[34]Scalapino, "Ideology and Modernization," p. 108.

The important role of intellectuals, an uneven pace of change, extensive reliance upon the state: these are the common factors of the revolution of modernization. Modernization is doubtless the most important phenomenon affecting the societies of contemporary states.

What may we conclude from this brief preview of modernization? First, we must be aware of the complexity of modernization. It must be viewed as a process that results in a fundamental transformation of society, economy, and polity. The nature and extent of change are bound to differ from one setting to the next; however, certain common themes and patterns can be analyzed in a comparative fashion.

Secondly, modernization, as a process, is subject to disruption. Modernization entails the capability of institutionalizing change and providing for continuous alteration of society and the political system. As Samuel P. Huntington suggests, there is no guarantee that new states can reach such a stage of political development. The possibility of stagnation—of political "decay" or communal sentiments precluding national unity—must always be kept in mind.

Thirdly, we cannot assume that the wide-ranging changes will occur peacefully. Revolution is no stranger to excess—and modernization represents a revolution. The breakdown of traditional values, views, and groups creates tensions whose solution is extremely difficult under the best of circumstances There is no justification in believing that modernization, as if by the wave of a wand, can insure a peaceful transition to new ways of life.

Finally, the comparative study of modernization provides fruitful insights into the nature of political, economic, and social change. Yet political scientists find themselves in a quandary; they must describe a process of central significance with neither a general theory of change nor widely accepted propositions. To paraphrase what Maurice Duverger said in a related context, it is, at the present time, impossible to give a valid description of the comparative aspects of political modernization—yet it is essential to do so. This book of readings is intended to help clarify several approaches to political modernization in the hope that broader understanding and a clearer theoretical formulation will eventually emerge.

2

THE SETTING FOR MODERNIZATION: TRADITIONAL SOCIETIES AND THE PROCESS OF TRANSFORMATION

Social modernization underlies political modernization. A convenient way to begin our analysis of modernization is by examining the societies of recently independent states. These are new states—with old societies. To the casual observer from an industrialized country, such societies may seem unchanging, backward, parochial, traditional. Daily life appears harsh and constricted. Arduously produced subsistence crops provide but a meager surplus at each harvest. Time-honored customs pervade and regulate most aspects of the daily routine. Wisdom is often equated with age and knowledge of the past rather than with youth or education or a vision of future improvement. An inherent conservatism—a deep-seated distrust of change unless its value is convincingly demonstrated—characterizes traditional societies. How does change come about?

Many scholars have posited simple dualities to explain social change: traditional versus modern; "mechanical solidarity" versus "organic solidarity" (Durkheim); *Gemeinschaft* versus *Gesellschaft*

(Tönnies) ; ascription versus achievement.[1] Like all dichotomies, these highlight essential features, but obscure basic complexities—particularly the ability of traditional societies to change. For example, many regard the American Indian tribes of the seventeenth century as static and resistant to alteration. But, when Spanish *conquistadores* introduced horses, the Plains Indians altered their basic life style in less than a generation. Faced with new opportunity, they quickly achieved a new foundation for subsistence and culture, based on pursuit of the buffalo.

In most African and Asian societies, the scramble for colonies and the resulting imposition of Western administrations had revolutionary effects. As the M.I.T. study group notes in the first selection, colonialism started the processes of social, economic, and political modernization in these societies. The idea of progress—the belief that a better way of life can be obtained through accepting rather than rejecting change—eroded traditional customs. Literacy and urbanization became prime agents of modernization.[2] The apathy, fatalism, and constricted outlook typical of traditional societies were partially supplanted by a more optimistic, wider-ranging view of life. The transitional process began; traditional society could never be the same again.

We must not assume, however, that the impact of modernization automatically destroys traditional outlooks, ways of life, or perceptions of group solidarity. Weakens, yes—destroys, no. The "pull of the past" inevitably influences modernization. In a sense, tradition mediates between the forces of change and the acceptance of change. We must study the content of existing traditions, examining the interpenetration of "old" and "new" to avoid what Professor Gusfield calls "misplaced polarities" in the study of social modernization.

Social, economic, and political modernization interact in complex ways. Focusing on the *Vanniyar* caste of southern India, Professors Lloyd and Susanne Rudolph illustrate how caste, a traditional social institution, is being modified in response to the forces of modernization. Caste does not represent an impassible barrier to change; in fact, it facilitates some types of alteration by linking them to the past. Caste associations have helped to expand political participation, building on long-established social ties to give villagers greater acquaintance with democratic practices and economic betterment.

In most African and Asian societies, political awareness and action developed through opposition to colonial administration. In soci-

---

[1]For a penetrating critique of such dualities, see C. S. Whitaker, Jr., "A Dysrhythmic Theory of Political Change" *(World Politics,* XIX, 2, January, 1967), pp. 190–217.

[2]Daniel Lerner, *The Passing of Traditional Society: Modernizing the Middle East* (New York: Free Press, 1958), p. 61.

eties less touched by the European presence, political awareness has not been as readily transformed into political action. Professor Hindley, in the concluding selection, explores the apparent political passivity of the Thais. Lacking an alien presence, the Thai political system has remained essentially undisrupted and slow to change. A limited degree of social and political modernization has not—as yet—fundamentally changed the "traditional" value of deference to authority.

THE TRANSITIONAL PROCESS

M.I.T. Study Group

According to a group of M.I.T. scholars, the impact of colonial rule "set the static traditional societies in motion." The authors examine the basic characteristics of traditional societies and the forces that start the "transitional process"—physical intrusion by a more advanced society, economic example, and the communication of skills and ideas. Modernization need not bring democracy; in fact, it may bring about an explosive sense of frustration if the growing demands encouraged by popular participation cannot be satisfied.

THE TRADITIONAL SOCIETY

A. The Range of Cases

The nature of the transitional process which we are considering here—and which American policy confronts in many parts of the world—takes its start from the character of the traditional societies which are in the process of being superseded. We begin, therefore, with an effort to sketch briefly the major features of the traditional society.

History offers us a wide range of such societies. Some were relatively primitive tribes living within a narrow region, on a self-sufficient base, with tribal rather than territorial political and economic organization, and tenuously connected if at all with other tribes and regions. In parts of Africa and in small areas elsewhere we can still find such isolated and primitive forms of social, political, and economic organization.

From *United States Foreign Policy: Economic, Social and Political Change in the Underdeveloped Countries and Its Implication for United States Policy.* A report submitted to the United States Senate Committee on Foreign Relations (Study No. 12) by the Center for International Studies, Massachusetts Institute of Technology, Cambridge, Mass. (Washington, D.C.: Government Printing Office, 1960).

Other traditional societies have been made up of loosely organized regions, with fairly elaborate structures of political and social organization and quite sophisticated agricultural techniques, but weak or nonexistent central governments. Medieval Europe, for example, could be described in some such terms, as well as India before the arrival of the European colonial powers.

But some traditional societies were very substantial empires with quite powerful centralized governments, manipulating a corps of civil servants and a military establishment, capable of collecting taxes and maintaining public works over large areas, capable of conquering and administering other regions and of generating a framework for elaborate patterns of trade and even significant industrial development. The Roman and Mayan Empires were such elaborate traditional organizations, as were certain of the Chinese dynasties at the peak of their effectiveness and some of the Middle Eastern empires at various stages of history.

B. Basic Features of the Traditional Society

What did these traditional societies have in common? One essential fact about them was that they developed within a limited technology. They sometimes exhibited high proficiency in certain directions, but they were incapable of generating a regular flow of inventions and innovations and of moving into a sustained growth process. It followed directly from this limitation that the bulk of their economic activity was taken up with acquiring food. Typically, some 75 percent or more of the working force was in agriculture.

However, the history of traditional societies—notably those which had reasonably strong centralized governments—was not static. In times of peace, acreage would be expanded, trade would increase, the population would rise; the government would collect taxes efficiently, maintain the irrigation works, and expand the opportunities for commerce. But the traditional society could not break through into sustained economic growth.

The periodic breakdowns in traditional societies were brought on by various immediate causes: population pressure, wars, the disintegration of central rule, etc. But behind these lay more fundamental facts. Basically, these societies lacked the adaptability to adjust their behavior to new circumstances. In the absence of a modern scientific attitude and a corps of inventors and technological innovators, for example, they could not produce the flow of new technology necessary to overcome the pressure of population and the natural limitation of arable land.

It followed from the preponderant role of agriculture that the ownership and control of land was a decisive factor in social prestige and, usually, in political influence. In some, the bulk of the land was owned by a relatively small number of nobles and the king, and it was worked by peasants who stood in a feudal, hierarchical relationship to these owners. This condition still exists, for example, in parts of the Middle East. In other cases land ownership was quite widely spread, as it was in China, resulting in an endless struggle by the peasants to acquire more land, to establish an economic position relatively independent of the luck of the harvests, and thus to rise in the society. In many of the African tribes, land was owned communally, with no concept of individual tenure and thus little incentive for systematic investment in improvements.

In traditional societies, face-to-face relationships were extremely important, as were the ties to family and clan. Men tended to be bound together and be valued by one another in terms of such intimate connections rather than because of their ability to perform specific functional tasks.

Although traditional societies sometimes provided a channel for able men of the lower economic classes to rise in power and prestige (often through the civil service and the military establishment), there was a tendency for people to assume that the status of their children and grandchildren would be similar to that of their parents and grandparents. A kind of long run fatalism pervaded traditional societies despite the ebb and flow of family fortunes and despite the slow evolution of the society as a whole.

The cultural and religious life of traditional societies, and the values they elevated, varied widely. Generally, however, they formed a coherent pattern, giving men a reasonably orderly rationale for the relatively stable round of life they faced, at whatever level in the society they found themselves. They provided a set of relationships of men to one another and to the world about them which gave them a degree of security in facing their appointed destiny within the traditional structure.

C. Disequilibrium in Traditional Societies

Well before some traditional societies moved into an active phase of modernization, they began to develop men, institutions, and attitudes which helped prepare the way for modernization. The requirements of conducting war, for example, led the central government to enlarge the military caste, which in some cases proved to be more willing to face the consequences of modernization of the society than the traditional landowners. This was true, for example, of Prussia before 1793, Japan before 1868, China in the second half of the 19th century, and Turkey before 1914. War also increased the requirements for credit and trade, tending to elevate somewhat the status of moneylenders and those who managed domestic and foreign commerce—men whose formal place in the traditional hierarchy was usually low. And in those traditional societies which assumed imperial responsibility, the management of empire itself strengthened the role and status of the civil servant and the technician.

Thus some traditional societies had undergone substantial changes toward modernization, out of their internal dynamics, before they were actually confronted with the shock of full-scale intrusion by more advanced societies. In other cases, however, more advanced nations moved in on traditional societies which were extremely primitive, with virtually no elements initially prepared to deal with the values and methods of modern life.

WHAT BREAKS UP TRADITIONAL SOCIETIES AND MOVES THEM TOWARD MODERNIZATION?

Leaving aside the gradual evolutions of Great Britain, Western Europe, and the United States, what forces have in the past broken up traditional societies? The broad answer is that they have been disrupted, their cohesion and prestige shattered by contact with societies which were more advanced economically and as social and political units.

The impact of more advanced societies took at least three distinguishable forms: physical intrusion, including in many instances colonial rule; economic example; and the communication of skills and ideas. We shall examine briefly the role of each in unhinging traditional societies and launching the modernization process.

A. Intrusion

Intrusion by a more advanced society most commonly was accompanied or followed by occupation and the setting up of colonial administrations, actions which had revolutionary effects on the traditional society in two ways.

First, in pursuit of its own interests (and often, too, in response to an impulse to spread the values and advantages of modern civilization) the colonial power executed specific policies which directly affected the economic, social, political, and cultural life of the traditional society. Ports, docks, roads, and, in some places, railroads were built. These were usually designed primarily for the economic or military advantage of the colonial power, but they had wider effects in creating national markets, commercializing agriculture, helping cities to grow, and bringing to backward areas contact with elements of modern life. Forms of central administration and centralized tax systems were usually set up, providing in some instances the initial framework for a modern government. Some colonials were drawn into the modern economic and administrative activities necessary to execute the purposes of the colonial power. Some modern goods and services were diffused, altering the conception of the level of life which men could regard as attainable. To at least a few colonials the opportunity for a Western education was opened. Perhaps most important, the colonial power usually brought to the traditional society some version of the Western tradition of law, a version of those rules and procedures for the dispensation of justice which transcend and limit the powers of the individuals who exercise political authority.

In short, it was of the nature of the colonial experience that at every level of life it brought to the traditional society contact with some degree of modernization.

The character and extent of modernization varied with the concept of colonial rule that each power brought to its various colonies. In India, for example, the British made special efforts to train men for both the civil service and the army: the Moslems on the whole opted for military training, the Hindus for the civil service, reflecting in that choice underlying differences in the culture of the two groups in the Indian peninsula. In Burma, on the other hand, the British did relatively little to train either soldiers or civil servants. The French, in their empire, made great efforts to bring a thin top layer of the indigenous leaders as fully as possible into French cultural, intellectual, and political life. The Belgians in the Congo concentrated, for economic reasons, on literacy and vocational training for the lower levels of the labor force and did nothing to prepare an elite for leadership. The Dutch in Indonesia and the Portuguese in East Africa by and large adopted policies designed to limit the extent and the pace of modernization.

But however colonial policy might vary, colonialism nevertheless had one first and universal direct effect. It set the static traditional societies in motion, so to speak, moving them into transitional status. That is, they lost the cohesion and integrity of the traditional system, but by no means did they attain the full status of modern societies.

The second effect of colonialism was indirect but perhaps even more profound than the direct infusion of modern elements. As time passed, and an increasing number of men in the colonial society became acquainted with the methods and ideas of the West, they reacted against the human and collective humiliation that inevitably accompanied colonial rule, and they sought independence. Many, it is true, were drawn imitatively toward the manners and mores of the colonial power (for example, colonials who were educated abroad or who had positions of privilege within colonial rule), and others found their positions strengthened by colonial rule (for example, African tribal chiefs and the Indian princes). But in the end a reactive nationalism emerged, spreading through elements in the colonial elite, catching up the urban populations, and reaching back even into the countryside. Of all the forces which have helped bring about the modernization of traditional societies, this reactive nationalism has probably been the most powerful.

Colonial rule was not the only form of intrusion that helped unhinge traditional societies. The defeat of the traditional society in war against a more advanced power often played an important role. This was so, for example, in Germany after the Napoleonic occupation; in Russia after the Crimean War; in Japan after its imposed opening to trade by the West in the shadow of modern naval cannon; in Turkey after the First World War; in China after the defeats by the British in the 1840's and by the Japanese in the 1890's. The demonstration that the traditional form of organization was incapable of maintaining the physical integrity of the nation tended to lower the prestige of the traditional rulers, their values, and their institutions. And it tended to strengthen the hand of those groups in the traditional society—soldiers, intellectuals, men of commerce, civil servants, lesser nobility—who for various, often differing reasons were already interested in moving toward some form of modernization.

B. Economic Example

Quite aside from the multiple impacts of colonialism and superior military power, contact with more advanced societies sometimes led to a spreading awareness of what modernization could do in terms of human welfare. Such contact demonstrated, for example, that public health could be improved; that food output could be increased; and that cheaper textiles could be provided to the peasant and the worker. In the 20th century the intimacy of communications, including the fact that modern armies have been based in many of these transitional societies, has peculiarly heightened an awarenss of the gap between modern and traditional standards of life. Any awareness of this kind, creating as it does an increasing pressure for a rapid rise in popular welfare, undermines the traditional society.

The contrast between the traditional and the modern economy was not solely, or perhaps even most significantly, a contrast in standards of living and levels of consumption. The employment opportunities and the modes of life available in the new cities gave people new images of the roles they could play in society. In traditional societies the normal thing was to accept one's status and frequently one's occupation as determined by inheritance and custom. Modern economic activity, whether colonial or indigenous, has taken people out of their conventional roles and put them in new situations both of work and of life which have greatly broadened their perception of the range of alternative activities in which they might engage. This increased mobility and widened perception of alternatives has markedly weakened the most stabilizing elements in traditional society.

C. The Communication of Skills and Ideas

Contact with the more modern societies brought about, for some, a training in new skills. Those trained usually formed part of the transitional society's elite, with some access to instruments of political power. But until the local society was transformed in quite fundamental ways, these trained men found it difficult to exercise effectively their skills as, for example, doctors, engineers, economists, and soldiers. The problem of unemployed intellectuals troubles many parts of contemporary Asia and the Middle East. A part of the force which has tended to disrupt the transitional societies has been the frustration of those with modern training who found that they lacked adequate scope for the exercise of their newly developed talents and opportunities to play newly perceived roles.

Moreover, the more advanced societies of the West communicated not only skills but also ideas. Among these ideas were the quite revolutionary Western notions that all men stood equal before the law, that they should have equal opportunity to develop their talents, and that policies should be determined and political leadership selected on a one-man, one-vote basis. It is easy to forget how powerful and disruptive these long-accepted foundations of modern Western life still are in traditional or only partly modernized societies.

In addition to these democratic ideas, many of the new intellectuals from the transitional societies have been exposed during their formative years in the West to Marxist and other socialist notions. These have often had a great appeal because they purport to explain the forces at work in transitional societies. The theory of the class struggle, Lenin's theory of imperialism, and Communist doctrine on the organization of revolutionary movements have gained considerable currency and influence, and have helped generate dissatisfaction with traditional attitudes and values.

Although the traditional societies or those early in the transitional process were not technically prepared to install modern democratic processes, the disruption of the traditional society and the infusion of these new ideas sometimes led to strong movements toward increased popular participation in the political process. Among the peasants the spread of these ideas encouraged powerful movements for land reform, in which the peasant's ageless hunger for his own plot of land at last expressed itself. The modernization of Mexico, for example, took its start with just such a primitive agrarian drive.

The new ideas have not by any means been uniquely responsible for the pressure of the peasantry for land reform, for peasant revolts have been a periodic feature of the history of traditional societies. But from the French Revolution, through the Taiping Rebellion in China and the Russian revolution, down to the pressure for land reform in contemporary Egypt and Iran, the spread of egalitarian ideas has played a catalytic role of some importance. The impact of new ideas, moreover, is vastly heightened today by the existence of the mass media and the instrumentalities of mass organization. Revolutionary ideas can be diffused with extraordinary rapidity, reaching groups throughout the society.

D. The Dynamics of Modernization

Contact with more advanced societies has been, then, the principal force which has eroded the structure and values of traditional societies. Through physical intrusion, economic example, and the communication of skills and ideas, this contact has pushed the traditional societies into a transitional process. After a certain point, the energies of those colonial people who had acquired some modern skills have tended to focus around the goal of independence; and this objective has helped to unify elements in the society which in fact held quite differing views of the modernization process. Where the colonial problem did not exist, the transitional process has been furthered in different degrees by a sense of military inferiority and national danger; by the pressure of the peasants for their own land; by the pressure of the educated elite for a chance to exercise their new skills; by the spreading perception that higher standards of welfare were attainable.

But the process has also been advanced by the fact that the breakup of the traditional society opened the way for men who enjoyed the exercise of power to contend for the vacated or weakened places of authority. Transitional societies which did not experience colonial rule, or newly independent ex-colonial states, have generally experienced a period of unstable rule in which various individuals and groups have sought to seize and consolidate power. These struggles for power have often been just that: the contention of men for positions of prestige and authority, quite unrelated to movements toward or away from modernization. But over substantial periods of time these struggles for power have reflected and become suffused with the views and objectives of various specific groups in the society who wished to achieve, or forestall, various aspects of the modernization process. The raw struggle for power in succession to the traditional leaders or the colonial power, or both in combination, has thus been in itself an active element in the transitional process.

WHAT RETARDS AND DISTORTS THE PROCESS OF MODERNIZATION?

A. The Scope of Change

It is one thing for a traditional society to experience the intrusion of modern elements which set in motion new dynamic trends. It is quite a different matter for such a society to achieve a working modern system which moves toward peaceful objectives by increasingly democratic means. Before a modern society can be achieved—before the modern elements within a traditional society can become not only dominant but constructive—a succession of profound changes must take place at every level; for any established society has deeply rooted characteristics which yield only reluctantly, with pain and the passage of time, and only to strong and persistent pressure for change. And along the way there are many possibilities for distortion, frustration, and situations disruptive to world order and the American interest.

Historical experience indicates that modernization does not require the destruction of a traditional culture. On the contrary, the old culture almost always leaves permanent and significant marks of continuity on the fully modernized society. Nevertheless, the traditional culture must undergo drastic alteration.

Psychologically, men must transform the old culture in ways which make it compatible with modern activities and institutions. The face-to-face relations and warm, powerful family ties of a traditional society must give way to more impersonal systems of evaluation in which men are judged by the way they perform specialized functions in the society. In their links to the nation, to their professional colleagues, to their political parties, men must find a partial alternative for the powerful, long-tested ties and symbols of the traditional life centered on family, clan, and region. And new hierarchies, based on function, must come to replace those rooted in land ownership and tradition.

Politically, the people must come to accept new forms for the organization of political power. The balance of social and political power must shift from the village to the city, from the tasks and virtues of agricultural life to those of commerce, industry, and modern administration. And they must come to accept new forms for the transfer of political power. They must begin—in a process with many difficult stages—to judge politics and politicians in terms of policies rather than merely inherited status or even personality; and they must develop forms for transferring power by registering consent.

Economically, they must achieve a situation where the society regularly saves and productively invests a sufficient volume of its resources, and incorporates regularly new ways of doing things, so that the growth of the national economy outpaces population increase and continuing economic growth becomes the normal condition of the society—a process which, in itself, involves every dimension of the society and many sectors of the economy.

To achieve these conditions requires the passage of time: time for the social structure to be altered; time for new political attitudes and institutions to be created and consolidated; time for the creation of the skills and habits and institutions on which capital formation depends. Above all, time must pass for new generations to succeed one another, each finding the environment, techniques, and goals of modernization a bit more familiar and acceptable.

Moreover, there is nothing which decrees that the forces of modernization will win eventual or automatic victory. It is of the very nature of the transitional process that at every step of the way the impulses making for modernization live in active contention with powerful forces tending to retard and to frustrate the transformation of the traditional society into full constructive modernity.

The interplay between the new hopes and the old ways may yield bloody civil conflict susceptible to exploitation by external powers; there may be efforts to channel the modernization process into disruptive foreign adventures; there may be a seizure of the society's politics by dictators who exploit popular frustrations and the inevitable looseness of the transitional period for their own or for other purposes.

There are four principal areas in which elements of resistance must be overcome if the modernization of a traditional society is to be carried through successfully: human attitudes, politics, economics, social structure. . . .

B. The Pull of the Past

The modernization process requires that fundamental human attitudes must change in such ways as to make the efficient operation of a modern society not only possible but also psychologically congenial; and it may well be that, especially in the first generations of the transition, the commitment of men to the goal of modernization is more apparent than real.

Modern man is psychically mobile, his distinctive characteristic being the ability to imagine himself performing all manner of tasks and roles. Traditional man was so inhibited by the barriers of status that he believed it wrong and dangerous even to move mentally out of his place in the social order. Transitional man can imagine and hope for change, but in his mind the exciting possibilities are balanced against old doubts and fears. And so the literate elite in transitional societies may be quite skilled, and they may talk the language of modernization with fluency and apparent conviction; but latent within them is a conflict between the modes of action and the values which modernization requires and the ingrained habits and attachments of the traditional society.

The latent power of the traditional society—the pull of the past—may take many forms. It may lead men to gather around them in authority not the most competent colleagues but those most personally loyal, often members of their family. It may lead them to talk of industrialization while in fact harboring a profound reluctance to engage in the homely pursuits of production and the marketplace, which in the traditional society enjoyed so low a status. It may prevent them—as in contemporary India—from treating cattle as part of the material stock of agricultural capital rather than as religious symbols. It may lead them to continue to concentrate their attention and emotions on old familiar issues and feuds—sanctioned by the values and history of the traditional society—rather than on the new issues and tasks of modernization.

No matter how passionately in one part of their beings men may want to see their societies and themselves enjoy the benefits of modernization, they are capable of sustaining in tolerable psychological order only a limited rate of change; and they may cling more tenaciously than they are aware to elements in the traditional society as a source of security in a transitional situation where much else about them is changing.

C. Political Resistance

A society freed from colonial rule or one which has overthrown a traditional government must create a minimally effective national government, a task which confronts such problems as these:

It is almost certain to be the case that much energy and attention must be devoted to overcoming the residues of political authority derived from the traditional society which cannot be harnessed constructively to the purposes of the new modern national government. Examples are the sects in southern Vietnam, the Indian princes, the Chinese war lords, the African tribal leaders.

The new government must also develop a minimum core of technically trained men capable of maintaining order, collecting taxes, and organizing the staff work required for the inevitably substantial role of the government in the economy and in the educational process.

Modernization develops aspirations in the minds of various groups of citizens for progress toward many new goals, economic, educational, and cultural, which are not regarded by traditional governments as within their responsibilities. The new government must demonstrate effective leadership in establishing programs to promote these new objectives if it is to survive. Means of communication must be developed between the government and its citizens to convey to them a sense that the national goals being pursued are ones which they would sanction.

Political development thus must contend with vested power derived from the traditional society; the lack of trained men; the low literacy rate and the lack of other facilities permitting persuasive mass communication; and the absence of a widespread popular conviction that the new national government is an appropriate vehicle for furthering popular goals.

In the process of contention there are many occasions for frustration and backsliding, many ways in which political life may be diverted to sterile or disruptive goals. The Communist appeal to the underdeveloped areas is designed to exploit precisely these possibilities.

D. Lack of Basic Capital

The resistance to modernization also takes the form of certain basic initial economic weaknesses. A very considerable expansion must take place in the number of modern men and institutions, as well as in physical capital, before sustained growth is possible at rates which substantially outstrip population increase.

Regular growth requires that men learn to apply systematically and progressively to the production of goods and services that modern science and technology have created. It is this ability to absorb and to in opposition to some external power or threat. By their very nature apply modern technology (to agriculture and raw materials as well as industry) which distinguishes a modern growing economy from a traditional economy.

In one sense, the most basic economic change required is, therefore, psychological. Men must cease to regard the physical world as fixed. They must learn that it is capable of being understood and manipulated in terms of stable and logical rules which men can master. But such a change in attitude is not enough. Before a society's economic capabilities can grow regularly at a rate higher than its population increase, large numbers of men must be trained in specialized techniques; and the economic institutions of the society, public and private, must be effectively geared to the process of regular innovation. The society must learn to mobilize and to use its surplus above minimum consumption not for high living for a few nor for war nor for traditional monuments but for productive investments. Moreover, the industrial process itself requires that important nonindustrial sectors be developed: notably, social overhead capital, agriculture, and foreign exchange earning sectors.

It will already be evident from this analysis that such wide-ranging economic change cannot occur unless there is prior or concurrent change in the social, political, and psychological dimensions of the society. But even on narrow economic grounds it is clear that a time interval will be required before the transitional society can acquire sufficient basic capital in human, institutional, and material forms to gather momentum. . . .

E. Social Conflict

The small elite groups who dominate the political process in a transitional society will at first be united in motives and purpose only in opposition to some external power or threat. By their very nature they will be of many minds as to the evolution of their own society. Some, in fact, may be primarily concerned not with modernization but with the maintenance of their own economic and social prerogatives, granted by the traditional society, the colonial powers, or both. Some may seek to divert the national sentiment and the energies of the new national government into external adventure in hope of redressing old humiliations or exploiting newly perceived opportunities for national aggrandizement. Still other groups may strive primarily to consolidate the power of the new central government as against contending regional authorities. Others may be interested primarily in seeing quickly installed the political and legal forms of modern democracy; and still others—initially usually a minority of the elite—may be anxious to get on with the concrete tasks of economic and technical modernization of the economy.

The confusions and cross-purposes which result from this diffusion of objectives inevitably retard the process of modernization. They may tempt men to seek escape from the frustrations of internal differences and to unite in aggressive attitudes or action toward the outside world. Or they may tempt men to accept in desperation the unity and discipline which Communist or other totalitarian forms hold out to them.

Although the small westernized and literate elites play a disproportionately powerful role in the early stages of the modernization process, in the end the mass of citizens must be brought into the mainstream of change. Each person must begin to assume new functions and new relations to the economic and political process.

The transition to modernization usually begins with more than 75 percent of the population in the countryside and less than 10 percent literate. The round of life is tied to the rhythm of the harvests and to the narrow local scene; to a traditional system of land tenure and the assumption that life for the children and grandchildren is likely to be much as it is and has been in living memory. Social life is built around a close family; traditional political and social relations, long sanctioned by custom, tend to be passively accepted. The government— and the nation itself—is likely to seem a remote and distant entity, associated with the extraction of taxes and the arbitrary recruitment of sons for military service.

In the end all this must alter. There must be a radical shift in balance to urban life; literacy must increase; agricultural methods must change; and the markets must widen and become increasingly commercial. Land tenure arrangements are likely to require alteration. The idea must spread that the physical environment can be understood and controlled in ways which permit higher standards of welfare. The government must come to be identified with activities and objectives which conform to popular interests. And in the end, if democracy is to emerge, the citizen must come to accept the responsibilities as well as the power to determine who shall rule and in what direction public policy shall go.

Merely to list this array of fundamental changes is to suggest the massiveness of what is involved in modernization for the many hundreds of millions of human beings whose lives now are caught up at various intermediate points between the traditional society and one version or another of modern society. The scale and profundity of change suggest also why time must pass and the generations succeed each other. Even more important for an understanding of the policy problems we confront, this array suggests why we must expect inner conflict, frustration, and outbursts of violent popular feeling as modernization proceeds.

As the traditional society loses its authority and sanctions, men are made both insecure and at the same time more hopeful that their lot may be improved. The rapid spread of modern communications, including international communications, begins to make vivid what the fruits of successful modernization might be in material, social, and political terms. But the process of modernization intrinsically requires a long time, even if the society's leaders give to its constructive dimensions all their energy and attention. It is not surprising, therefore, that popular moods may at times turn backward, in an effort to recapture some of the lost security and order of the traditional society. In Burma, for example, U Nu recently waged a successful campaign to return to power on the basis of an appeal to Buddhism. It is not surprising that men and women caught up in the process of modernization can easily be led to turn their frustrations against foreigners. And it is not difficult to understand why, if frustration and chaos persist, communism may be accepted, in apathy or with eagerness, as a promised resolution of these conflicts and dilemmas.

But there is also evidence from the distant and recent past that if the processes of modernization are steadily extended, if the loss of elements from traditional life is balanced by evident, even if limited, progress, these multiple changes can take place without irreversible damage to the society and without its seizure by totalitarian dictatorship.

F. Strategic Dimensions of Modernization

It follows directly from the concept of modernization as a process of contention between modernizing and retarding elements, with many possibilities of frustration, diversion, and even regression, that the societies we call underdeveloped stand at various stages along the way from traditional to modern status.

It is, moreover, central to this analysis that every dimension of these societies is involved in the modernization process; that the progression cannot be defined simply in terms of psychological change or politics or social structure or popular attitudes or economics.

Nor do these elements in the process of modernization all move by some common law. In some societies the modernizing influence was initially felt in the realm of government and administration through colonial rule. In other societies the commercial, the educational, or the religious spheres were the first to be changed. There is thus no uniform pattern of development for all transitional societies.

Our knowledge about the uneven character of social change also suggests that not all changes will contribute equally to a general advance toward a more modern system. On the contrary, some innovations can create situations which make it more rather than less difficult for subsequent changes to occur in a smooth fashion. Improvements in public health standards, for example, can readily alter the death rate and produce a rapid growth in population, which will subsequently become a drain on all efforts to raise per capita incomes. Similarly, the expansion of educational facilities at a grossly faster rate than the openings of new career opportunities can produce well-recognized tensions and frustrations.

We can at this point reach certain broad conclusions: powerful and persistent forces are pressing all the transitional societies in the direction of modernization. Among these forces are the challenge of population pressure; the spread of literacy and modern skills; and the intensity of modern national and international communications. But while the direction of change is toward modernization in all these societies, the pace of movement will vary greatly, and so will their vulnerability to dangerous diversions—notably, aggressive behavior or acceptance of totalitarian government. . . .

SOME FACTORS IN SOCIAL CHANGE

A. Social Evolution in Transitional Societies

In the early period of transition, when a society begins to break out of its traditional structure, the most powerful social class generally consists of the men who own or control the land, a group likely to be deeply conservative in every respect. Feeling a deep attachment to the old ways of life, and sensing that social and technological change threatens their hegemony, they tend to resist all efforts to modernize.

Where their strategy has been to resist by partial incorporation of the new, the landowners often have survived as individuals while their power as a class waned. Where they have resisted all efforts at modernization, the landed class and its members have gone down together. The basic shift to urban and industrial life, which is the core process of modernization, must spell the end of hegemony by landowners as a class.

The traditional society is characterized by the absence of any indigenous middle class large enough or strong enough to challenge the landowners' power. In the early stages of transition, therefore, the decisive challenge to the landlords' supremacy generally comes not from any one social class but from a coalition, a group which varies considerably in specific composition from one country to another but whose leadership is almost invariably made up of men deeply affected by Western ways of thought and action.

In colonial countries those at the forefront of independence movements have often received a university education in the West, sometimes being trained for one of the professions like law or medicine, or they have been introduced to Western patterns of thought and organization through military corps, administration, and industrial and trade union organizations. In countries without colonial histories, such as Turkey, leadership has often been assumed by military officers whose sense of power combined with a strong sense of national pride created in them a desire to lead the way to modernity.

Whatever their particular background, those who lead the fight for independence, or in noncolonial societies the struggle to displace the landowning class, are likely to be more skilled in the political and military tasks of achieving power than in the arts of governing and modernizing a traditional society. Depending on the circumstances and problems of achieving independence, they may become skilled in communicating with and organizing peasants and workers for disruptive activity, in writing revolutionary tracts and editing revolutionary journals, or in conducting guerrilla warfare. Once independence or power is achieved, they often find it difficult to turn their minds and convert their skills to the tasks of modernization. As a result, the first generation of new leaders is often inadequately prepared by experience and training to deal with the problems confronting them when responsibility is attained. Thus progress toward modernization is inevitably slow in the early transitional period. Groups within the governing elite are likely to contend in an erratic and unstable manner, with frequent shifts of power from one to another. Moreover, the elite groups tend to rally around individuals, the substance of whose programs may be ambiguous and unclear even to themselves. Political activity revolves around issues of power and personality rather than around alternate national policies.

Nevertheless, during this period certain dynamic forces are at work in the society which tend to move the social structure and the political debate into a new phase. First, contacts with more modern societies are likely to increase the number of persons trained in the West or otherwise introduced to modern ideas and skills. Second, the very responsibility of managing a national government, even if conducted without great skill and purpose, tends to enlarge the number of men with modern attitudes and commitments. Third, even if sustained economic growth is unlikely at this early stage, commercial activity is apt to increase, cities to grow, and some experiments in industrialization to be undertaken. Finally, because progress is slow and the high hopes and optimistic slogans that accompanied the arrival of independence (or the proclamation of a modern-style government) remain still largely unfulfilled, there is a dynamic created by the sense of frustration on the part of members of the younger generation of the westernized elite.

This combination of forces may bring into being a new coalition determined to push forward with a more purposeful program of modernization. The balance of the social elements in such a coalition varies widely according to the initial structure of the traditional society and its experience during transition. In some instances the coalition has contained a large percentage of men from the military; in others (e.g., the Congress Party in India) the military has played no significant role. At some stage in the process, though not necessarily at the beginning, intellectuals and professionally trained men have been influential; occasionally men of commerce and industry have been in the forefront; and in a few cases landowners, drawn for one reason or another into a commitment to modernization, have played a constructive role. We can, then, make the general observation that the social basis for the modernizing coalition lies in the city and in the essentially urban skills of the elite, both military and intellectual, who have adopted Western attitudes.

We shall deal particularly with two of the groups which often join in the modernizing coalition. The first is the military, which is playing a decisive role in many transitional societies today. The second is the intelligentsia, the manipulators of symbols who shape the slogans and doctrines by which the new ways of life are rationalized and justified.

B. The Special Potential of the Military

The likely social origins of the military group in a transitional society, the nature of their profession, and the context in which they operate contribute important elements to their potential for leadership toward modernization.

The top officer group was traditionally from the landowning class and committed to the preservation of old privileges and social relationships. But lower officers sometimes came from other classes; their social status was not high, and they were not so firmly committed to defend the old social order. Moreover, in recent times, because the military has had to be expanded and thus officers have had to be recruited more widely, in many armies officers have increasingly come from less elite classes—even from craftsmen or peasant groups—and sometimes reflect dissatisfaction with the old order.

Moreover, a contemporary military organization is by its nature a modern rather than a traditional structure. In concept at least, men are arrayed according to function and advanced according to skill and reliability in the execution of their function. They are judged by individual performance rather than by their connection with other persons, family group, or clan. While these objective norms have not been fully and promptly recognized in all the armies that have emerged in transitional societies, they have exercised a powerful modernizing influence.

This influence has been strengthened by the care and resources often devoted by professionals from Western societies to the training of the military, and by traditional pride in military prowess, which has made it easy for restless individuals to find satisfaction in a military career. It is no accident that competent and distinguished military units have emerged in transitional societies well before modern institutions in the civil service, politics, or the economy; for example, the Indian Army, the Malay Regiments, the Philippine Scouts, the Arab Legion, the Gurkha Regiments and the King's Own African Rifles. As long as these forces were controlled by foreign powers they were naturally conservative—or at least their feelings of rebellion at colonial policies were suppressed. But once independence was achieved, the military could acquire only through the national government the equipment and the professional stature they sought. It is of the nature of the military profession that something like patriotism in modern terms be accepted.

Finally, the officer corps is likely to face an easier set of problems in the transitional period than their civilian counterparts within the new leadership. They may have to undertake military operations, either against the colonial power or against residual traditional elements; but where successful, these exercises arouse confidence in their strength. Aside from combat itself, their tasks are to acquire new equipment, to train men in their use, and to maintain in tolerable order the peacetime round of military life—inherently an easier job than to get political, social, and economic programs organized on a wider basis in the society. Thus it is possible for the army to develop a group of confident officers with modern attitudes and modern skills, operating within a reasonably orderly modern institution administered on relatively modern lines.

Supplementing these broad influences on the officer corps is the fact that those who are recruited into the army are given with their training a certain minimum technical education for modern life. Historically, armies in transitional societies have been a vehicle for expanding literacy; and the handling of motor transport, guns, and other military equipment has spread—and usually quickly spread—elements of basic training in industrial skills. The Burmese Army, for example, in addition to the standard engineer corps and signal corps, has special chemical warfare and psychological warfare sections and even a historical and archeological section. In all the new armies attempts have been made to introduce specialized training schools and advanced techniques of personnel and procurement. Inevitably, then, a certain number of officers and men are being trained in industrial skills more advanced than those common to the civilian economy.

It is by no means foreordained—as the history of the military in Latin America amply demonstrates—that their potentials for modernization will automatically and constructively harness the military to the modernization process. The military leadership may for long periods build and maintain their modern units in a vacuum, drawing important resources from the society but keeping aloof from its civilian problems and making little contribution to their solution. The officer corps may develop a hypernationalism and throw its inevitably substantial political weight toward external adventure, diverting the society from modernizing tasks. It may exploit its unity and high degree of organization to seize power but bring to power little insight and sympathy for the complex civil tasks of modernization. In some instances its political weight has been used to preserve the status of groups rooted in the traditional society who conceived it to be in their interest to forestall the course of modernization.

But history has also demonstrated in numerous instances from the Samurai and the Prussian Army of the 19th century down through Ataturk and Magsaysay that the military can play a thoroughly constructive part in modernization.

A striking example is the unbroken maintenance of civilian supremacy in the Turkish Republic over the past 35 years despite the important role which the military played in founding that Republic.* A major condition in this case was Ataturk's establishment and effective maintenance of a clear division between military and civilian leadership. The corps of officers who with him made the revolution and founded its republican institutions were obliged, like Ataturk himself,

---

*[This analysis was completed before the Turkish army overthrew the elected government of Premier Menderes on May 27, 1960.—Ed.]

to resign their commissions when they took up posts of political authority; as a corollary, no officer who remained in uniform was permitted
to be active in political life. An important consequence, once the principle and practice of civilian supremacy were firmly established, was that
the Turkish Army could perform major functions in the modernization
of Turkish society without compromising the civil authority.

At present, the Turkish Army recruits some 200,000 young civilians into its training program each year. These young men (and women)
are often illiterate villagers, whose induction into the Army represents
their first sustained exposure to other Turks in other areas of Turkey.
They are taught to read and write, to handle tools and equipment; they
are taught the fundamentals of personal hygiene and public health;
they are taught the symbols and institutions of modern political life
in a republic. As they complete their training and return to their villages, these young people become a permanent asset in the modernization of Turkey. They put their new knowledge to work; they teach
other villagers at home some of what they have themselves learned;
they remain a "relay point" for information and opinion emanating from
the modernized section of Turkish society. Thus they speed the process
of modernization while helping to stabilize it.

In summary, then, the military—the one traditional social order
likely to survive the process of social change—may be able to play a key
role in promoting mobility while maintaining stability, in facilitating
change while preventing chaos. Upon the efficiency with which the
military sector can be made to perform this role may hinge the successful outcome of the transition in many societies.

C. The Secular Intelligentsia

While the military are strong in their capacity to manage violence, in their commitment to rational institutions based on functional
criteria and efficient performance, in their sense of nationhood as a
supreme value, they are often weak in other skills and attitudes needed
in a modernizing society. Consider, for example, the basic process of
economic growth. Military men are not generally trained economists, and
their economic programs are likely to be inspirational rather than productive. In the Middle East, where military takeover has been virtually
continuous over the past few decades, instances have multiplied in
which new military regimes rapidly foundered on their own well-meant
land reform programs. Virtually every new regime made some more
or less serious gesture in the direction of land reform which won it
popular plaudits for a time but which failed to solve the basic problem
of raising agricultural productivity.

Military elites are liable to make dangerous errors in framing and administering laws, instituting and operating schools, devising and sustaining a communication network, unless they are guided by people with professional knowledge and experience in these activities. These people are the "secular intelligentsia"—the economists and engineers and agronomists, the lawyers and administrators, the doctors and public health officers, the deans and professors, the "communicators" who manage the flow of public news and views that no modernizing polity can do without. They are an "intelligentsia" because it is they who acquire and apply modern knowledge to the manifold tasks of running an urban, industrial, participant society efficiently. They are "secular" because their public roles and social functions are independent of, and usually hostile to, the sacred symbols and institutions of the traditional society.

Their first task as a class is to win preeminence over the sacred intelligentsia, who traditionally performed most of the legal and judicial, teaching and counseling, healing and helping, soothsaying and certifying functions that the secular intelligentsia now seeks to perform. In societies moving toward a modern division of labor—with increasing urbanization, industrialization, participation—the new men of knowledge steadily gain strength. But there are continuous frustrations. The doctor is unhappy when people go to the *shaman* for medical therapy, the lawyer when people go to the *shariya* for adjudication, the teacher when people go to the *imam* for learning, the agronomist when people go to their neighbor for weather forecasts, the communicator when people go to the village elder for guidance on moral judgment of public issues.

These frustrations mount as the number of modern specialists expands in an environment that remains highly traditionalized. The men of the secular intelligentsia become individually impatient and as a group extremist in their views of what must be done. They may form alliances of various sorts—with each other, with foreign agents, even with "deviants" among the traditionalist sectors of landowners and sacred intelligentsia. But ultimately, if they are to make more than a short splash, the secular intelligentsia ally themselves with the military sector.

The historical logic is clear. The military possess the coercive power needed to maintain stability; the secular intelligentsia have the knowledge needed to effect change. Military leadership alone usually has foundered because its perspective is too narrow to cope with the variety of problems that arise in modernizing societies; the secular intelligentsia alone usually has failed because its ideas outrun its capacity to develop institutions that are operational. Neither can manage the transition without the other, and so forms the "unholy alliance," which Western social scientists have described (and decried) since Pareto, Mosca, Michels, Lasswell.

D. Social Change Under a Modernizing Coalition

If the modernizing coalition we have described meets with some success, and modernization actually begins to make a dent upon the society, the pace of social change steps up rapidly. New people begin to take over the shaping of public policy—people with the attitudes and technical skills needed to perform the manifold tasks of urbanization, industrialization, and monetization as well as the complex tasks produced by the rationalization of work and the secularization of beliefs.

In general, and with deference to the variety of specific forms which modernization has taken historically and in the contemporary scene, the central tendency of sociological change appears to be the multiplication of key social roles, in part new roles, in part adaptations of old ones. As life becomes more technically oriented, power and prestige shift away from the few dominant men in the traditional structure—the wealthy pasha, the wise priest, the village elder—toward men equipped to perform more specific functions in the modern division of labor. Professional and technical skills are required for the roles associated with the growth of cities and the spread of industries, the technical advances and modernization of agriculture, the growing dependence of public policy upon an informed and participant citizenry. The banker and the economist tend to replace the landowner and moneylender as sources of cash and managers of credit; the industrialist and manager replace the merchant and trader; the civil servant, the engineer, the agronomist, and others take over special functions that earlier were concentrated in village elders and other men of hereditary wealth or wisdom.

Significant for the long run is the replacement of the sacred intelligentsia by the new secular intelligentsia; as the importance of traditional religious outlook diminishes, attention shifts to new professions skilled in the secular learning demanded by people caught up in modernization. Especially important among these are the teachers, since every society undergoing modernization exhibits a great increase in the numbers of people who go through formal public education as a way of learning their new careers. Another important group are those who manage the mass media of communication. Through these channels the bulk of the population, including the illiterate elders as well as the younger people destined for new lives, are brought into contact with the new ways and the new words by which these ways are rationalized. Involved here is the important process of increasing popular participation in a modernizing society.

E. The Peasants and Urban Workers

Our analysis thus far has focused on narrow elites—on men who acquire certain Western skills and are in a position to contend for power and to direct the course of events within their nation. We turn now to the evolution of attitudes and skills among the people as a whole, and to their slow change from a passive to an active role in the modernization process.

Here again the course of events depends substantially on the kind of traditional structure that existed; on whether the society underwent a period of colonial tutelage and on the kind of colonial policy that was pursued; on the particular setting and impulses that led to the overthrow of the traditional society, colonial rule, or both. Without excessive distortion, however, we can draw a general picture of the changing horizons of the peasant and the urban worker as modernization proceeds.

In the traditional society and in the early stages of transition something like 75 percent of the population lives in rural areas and up to 90 percent of the population may be illiterate. Mass media, if they exist at all, reach only a small number of people. There are no institutions which permit genuine popular participation in the political process. The peasants are likely to appear apathetic, accepting their traditional lot, but their apathy may well conceal extremely complex feelings. They may harbor, for example, a deep hunger to own their own land, or to see their children healthy, educated, and advanced, aspirations which find expression only when a realistic opportunity for change presents itself. On the other hand, as we have previously noted, they may simultaneously feel great reluctance to abandon the familiar way of life, which offers psychic security as well as a familiar protection from some of the crushing burdens of poverty.

In the early period of transition, as urban activity increases, the attractions of the city draw men away from the countryside, even though urban life itself is often impoverished and demands an almost revolutionary shift in social and cultural adjustments. In the cities the unskilled worker is generally left on his own, but in the trades of higher skill unions are organized at a relatively early stage of the modernization process. Literacy and technical training begin to spread. And so fairly early in the transitional stage the cities often develop a quite modern way of life, standing as advanced enclaves in a society still predominantly rural and primitive.

The coming to power of the modernizing coalition has direct effects on both the urban worker and the peasant. Their political role begins to change, for the new leadership feels impelled to make a direct appeal to the mass of citizens. The legitimacy of the new leadership, which has often won out by revolution against the colonial power or the old order, rests in large measure on a real or pretended commitment to advance the interests of the people as a whole and to achieve for all the citizens of the nation the fruits of modernization. At a minimum, the modernizing coalition is likely to take steps to establish means of communication between the government and the people as a whole. This is the stage at which politicians are likely to take to the airwaves and a popular press is apt to be created.

Whatever the substantive accomplishments of the modernizing coalition in its early period of power, and however deep or shallow its commitment to furthering popular interests, its very existence will probably increase the demand for modernization and for an increasing degree of participation in the society's decisions.

This is a point of maximum danger for the developing society. The mass media, bringing news and views of the world to illiterates in their urban slums and remote villages, introduce a new element into the process of modernization. People learn for the first time about the world outside their immediate environs, and their sense of life's possibilities begins to expand. We recall Nasser's statement: "Radio has changed everything.... Leaders cannot govern as they once did. We live in a new world."

One danger is that people will learn the fashions of popular participation long before the institutions of representative government are properly functioning. Then "pseudoparticipation" takes command, i.e., plebiscites that offer the form of public election without its substance, mob politics of the street in which "popular will" can destroy people and property without constructing better public policy. When exposure to the mass media overstimulates a people to this point, the leadership is pressed to give radio propaganda primacy over political economy. While oratory resonates, development is likely to be shunted to the side and growth impeded. The result, for people led to impose demands which their transitional society cannot yet supply, may be a potentially explosive and spreading sense of frustration.

Whereas the West achieved a participant society as an outcome of the slow growth of physical, social, and psychic mobility over many centuries (the centuries our history textbooks now summarize as age of exploration, renaissance, reformation and counterreformation, industrial revolution, rise of democracy), the new societies seek to accomplish this sequence in decades. In this desire for rapid progress lies the danger that the effect of mass media will be to increase popular desires and demands faster than they can be satisfied by economic and social growth. Mossadegh in Iran fell victim to this imbalance, as did Shishakli in Syria.

To analyze such dangers is easier than to prescribe ways of overcoming them. What the new governments must do is to create institutions through which individual citizens can begin to take part in the decisions of the community. Fully as important as plebiscites, representative assemblies, and other instruments of participation on the national scale—indeed probably a vital prerequisite for the successful operation of national institutions—are local organizations of many sorts which can engage people actively in matters of immediate concern to them.

In the villages, community development and other programs for agricultural cooperation and reform; in the towns, trade unions and other organizations; in both town and country, institutions of local government which engage the interest and support of the people—such activities as these help to bridge the gap between government and people, help to introduce content into the forms of democracy which most of the underdeveloped societies have eagerly accepted.

In terms of social change the problems confronting the transitional societies which are led by modernizing coalitions are those posed by the very nature of democracy. Democracy is not adequately summed up in the formula of universal suffrage; the individual requires something more than a vote to guarantee that his interests will be taken into account in the society's decisions. A sound democracy depends heavily on the strength and number of the institutions which stand between the individual and the national government, defending his individual rights in the process of defending institutional interests. And, while the process of modernization creates some of the preconditions for democracy, its emergence is by no means foreordained. Democracy is a purposeful human achievement, not an automatic reflex of modernization.

FOR FURTHER READING

GABRIEL A. ALMOND AND JAMES S. COLEMAN, eds., *The Politics of the Developing Areas* (Princeton: Princeton University Press, 1960)

DAVID E. APTER, *The Politics of Modernization* (Chicago: University of Chicago Press, 1965)

JAMES S. COLEMAN, ed., *Education and Political Development* (Princeton: Princeton University Press, 1965)

RUPERT EMERSON, *From Empire to Nation: The Rise to Self-Assertion of Asian and African Peoples* (Cambridge: Harvard University Press, 1960)

CLIFFORD GEERTZ, ed., *Old Societies and New States: The Quest for Modernity in Asia and Africa* (New York: Free Press of Glencoe, 1963)

MANFRED HALPERN, *The Politics of Social Change in the Middle East and North Africa* (Princeton: Princeton University Press, 1963)

SAMUEL P. HUNTINGTON, *Political Order in Changing Societies* (New Haven: Yale University Press, 1968)

JOHN H. KAUTSKY, ed., *Political Change in Underdeveloped Countries: Nationalism and Communism* (New York: Wiley, 1962)

JOSEPH LA PALOMBARA, ed., *Bureaucracy and Political Development* (Princeton: Princeton University Press, 1963)

JOSEPH LA PALOMBARA AND MYRON WEINER, eds., *Political Parties and Political Development* (Princeton: Princeton University Press, 1966)

DANIEL LERNER, *The Passing of Traditional Society: Modernizing the Middle East* (New York: Free Press of Glencoe, 1958)

MARION J. LEVY, JR., *Modernization and the Structure of Societies* (Princeton: Princeton University Press, 1966)

WILLIAM MCCORD, *The Springtime of Freedom: The Evolution of Developing Societies* (New York: Oxford University Press, 1965)

A. F. K. ORGANSKI, *The Stages of Political Development* (New York: Knopf, 1965)

LUCIAN W. PYE, *Aspects of Political Development* (Boston: Little, Brown, 1966)

LUCIAN W. PYE, ed., *Communications and Political Development* (Princeton: Princeton University Press, 1963)

LUCIAN W. PYE AND SIDNEY VERBA, eds., *Political Culture and Political Development* (Princeton: Princeton University Press, 1965)

DANKWART A. RUSTOW AND ROBERT E. WARD, eds., *Political Modernization in Japan and Turkey* (Princeton: Princeton University Press, 1964)

EDWARD SHILS, *Political Development in The New States* (The Hague: Mouton, 1962)

K. H. SILVERT, ed., *Discussion at Bellagio: The Political Alternatives of Development* (New York: American Universities Field Staff, 1964)

K. H. SILVERT, ed., *Expectant Peoples: Nationalism and Development* (New York: Random House, 1963)

I. R. SINAI, *The Challenge of Modernisation* (London: Chatto and Windus, 1964)

TRADITION AND MODERNITY: MISPLACED POLARITIES IN THE STUDY OF SOCIAL CHANGE[1]

Joseph R. Gusfield

"Traditional" and "modern" are neither incompatible nor internally consistent terms. No single, uniform set of processes brings modernity, Professor Gusfield comments. Instead of simple, opposed dichotomies, we must analyze the heterogeneity and interpenetration of "tradition" and "modernity."

While riding the Kodama express from Tokyo to Kyoto several years ago, I saw what might be taken as a symbolic expression of transitional development. The Japanese passenger in the seat across from mine had made himself comfortable during his nap by unlacing his shoes and pulling his socks partly off. Half in and half out of both shoes and socks, he seemed to make a partial commitment to the Western world which his clothing implied. One could only wonder about his future direction either back into his shoes and socks or out of them and into sandals and bare feet.

This particular example has been chosen because it accentuates the idea of change in contemporary new nations and economically growing societies as one which entails a linear movement from a traditional past toward a modernized future.[2] A significant assumption in this model of change is that existing institutions and values, the content of tradition, are impediments to changes and are obstacles to modernization. It is with this assumption that our paper is concerned. We wish to call attention to

---

From *The American Journal of Sociology*, Vol. LXXII, No. 4 (1966), pp. 351-362, by permission of the University of Chicago Press and the author.

[1] Presented at the annual meeting of the American Sociological Association, Chicago, September 2, 1965.
[2] There is a wide literature analyzing concepts of tradition and modernity or development. Leading efforts to conceptualize these societal types of W. W. Rostow, *The Stages of Economic Growth* (Cambridge: Cambridge University Press, 1960); Gabriel Almond and James Coleman, *The Politics of Developing Areas* (Princeton, N.J.: Princeton University Press, 1960), chap. i; Daniel Lerner, *The Passing of Traditional Society* (Glencoe, Ill.: Free Press, 1958), chaps. ii, iii.

the manifold variations in the relation between traditional forms and new institutions and values, variations whose possibilities are either denied or hidden by the polarity of the traditional-modern model of social change. We want, further, to explore the uses of tradition and modernity as explicit ideologies operating in the context of politics in new nations. Our materials are largely drawn from modern India, although we shall refer to other Asian and African countries as well.

The concepts of economic development and of economic modernization have now been generalized to many areas of national life by social scientists. There is now a discussion of communication development, educational development, and, most widely used, of political development.[3] While these are sometimes used to relate specific institutions to economic growth and development as possible correlative influences or effects, they are also utilized as independent concepts. Some writers have viewed political modernization as implying the necessary framework within which nationhood can be achieved and operate. Others have seen certain institutions and political values as inherently valuable and legitimate perspectives toward change.[4]

At the same time that the concept of development has become generalized, a large number of specific studies of new nations (many to be discussed here) have made us aware of the wide variety of outcomes and possibilities for change and continuity. These have led to a more critical appreciation of the many possible interrelations between new and old aspects of social, economic, and political life. The view that tradition and innovation are necessarily in conflict has begun to seem overly abstract and unreal.

In the study of economic growth we have come to be aware that Weber's conception of traditional versus rational economic behavior is a great distortion of the realities of many concrete situations. In the study of political alternatives and possibilities we have become sensitive to

---

[3] See the various volumes published by Princeton University Press under the series title "Studies in Political Development." Also see A. F. K. Organski, *The Stages of Political Development* (New York: Alfred A. Knopf, Inc., 1965).

[4] "We can distinguish several different uses of the concept "political development." Sometimes it is used as functional to economic development. Here the writer seeks to determine the political conditions essential to support effective economic change. For one example, see Wilfred Malenbaum, "Economic Factors and Political Development," *Annals*, CCCLVIII (March, 1965), 41–51; in the same volume, Lucien Pye uses the concept as independent of economic forms but gives it a substantive content (see Pye, "The Concept of Political Development," *Annals*, CCCLVIII [March, 1965]). Shils gives the concept of "modernity" a meaning closer to that of a goal toward which political elites aspire. This makes concern for a given state of society a perspective rather than an empirical theory and is thus closer to the use we make of it in the last section of this paper. "Our central concern will be with the vicissitudes of the aspiration toward the establishment of a political society" (Edward Shils, "On the Comparative Study of the New States," in C. Geertz [ed.] *Old Societies and New States* [New York: Free Press, 1963], pp. 1–26, at p. 6).

the reifying effect of unilinear theories. They make Anglo-American political forms either inevitable or necessarily superior outcomes of political processes in new nations. Functional theories of political and economic development now seem less viable.[5] An emphasis on what Shils calls the issue of consensus at the macrosociological level leads to a concern for how pre-existing values and structures can provide bases for identification with and commitment to larger social frameworks than those of segmental groups and primordial loyalties.[6] Here traditional symbols and leadership forms can be vital parts of the value bases supporting modernizing frameworks.

In exploring the concepts of tradition and modernity we shall discuss the assumptions of conflict between them. These assumptions are inconsistent with recent studies which will reveal a wide range of possible alternatives and show that "tradition" is a more specific and ambiguous phenomenon than usually realized.

FALLACIES IN THE ASSUMPTIONS OF THE TRADITIONAL-MODERN POLARITY

In assuming that new economic and political processes face an unchanging and uniform body of institutional procedures and cultural values, the linear theory of change greatly distorts the history and variety of civilizations. In this section we will examine seven assumptions of this theory and indicate the difficulties in its use.

FALLACY 1: DEVELOPING SOCIETIES HAVE BEEN STATIC SOCIETIES

It is fallacious to assume that a traditional society has always existed in its present form or that the recent past represents an unchanged situation. What is seen today and labeled as the "traditional society" is often itself a product of change. The conquests of foreign powers and the growth of social and cultural movements deeply influenced the character of family life, religious belief and practice, and social structure in India over many centuries.[7] Islamic civilization provided vital alternatives to caste and to political groupings. The impact of British culture and institu-

---

[5] Moore has suggested that we now know that a variety of political forms are capable of both congruence and conflict with economic development (Wilbert Moore, *Social Change* [Englewood Cliffs, N.J.: Prentice-Hall, Inc., 1963], p. 112).
[6] This is a major problem discussed in Clifford Geertz (ed.), *op. cit.* See especially papers by Shils, Geertz, D. Apter, and M. Marriott.
[7] For a critical analysis and refinement of those views of India based on Hindu scriptures, as were those of Max Weber, see M. N. Srinivas, *Caste in Modern India* (Bombay: Asia Publishing House, 1962), especially Introduction and chaps. i and xii. A similar point is made in Harold Gould, "The West's Real Debt to the East," *Quest* (January–March, 1962), pp. 31–39.

tions has been immense.[8] Even India's caste system has by no means been a fixed and invariant system.[9] The conception of India as a non-industrial and agricultural society, only now opened to industrialism, also needs revision. The decline of native Indian industries in the late eighteenth and early nineteenth centuries was a consequence of the protection of British textile manufacturers, then spearheading the Industrial Revolution in England. The shift of both rural and urban artisans to the land was an important ingredient in the buildup of an agricultural surplus population. Even the system of land tenure in existence just before independence was the product of fairly recent changes.[10] To speak of the traditional feudal structure of India is to confuse recent history with past history. Tradition has been open to change before its present encounters with the West and with purposeful, planned change.

FALLACY 2: TRADITIONAL CULTURE IS A CONSISTENT BODY OF NORMS AND VALUES

In elaborating the distinction and interaction between the "great tradition" of urban centers and the "little tradition" of village communities, anthropologists have called our attention to the diversity and the existence of alternatives in what has been supposed to be a uniform body of rules and values. We must avoid accepting the written and intellectualized versions of a culture as only the literate form of a common set of beliefs and behavior patterns. The distinction between "popular" religion and the religion of the literati elite has long been a recognition of this difficulty in characterizing the "religion" of a society.[11]

Even within the literate forms of a tradition, inconsistency and opposition are marked; the Sermon on the Mount and *The Wealth of*

---

[8] Percival Spears, *India* (Ann Arbor: University of Michigan Press, 1960); Charles Heimsath, *Indian Nationalism and Hindu Social Reform* (Princeton, N.J.: Princeton University Press, 1964), chap. i; Srinivas, *op. cit.*, chap. v; Gould, *op. cit.*
[9] Srinivas, *op. cit.;* Bernard Cohn, "Power, Land and Social Relations in 19th Century Banaras" (Paper presented at meeting of the American Asian Studies Society, Washington, D.C., 1964).
[10] R. C. Dutt, *Economic History of India* (London: Routledge & Kegan Paul, 1908), pp. 32, 261; S. Bhattacharya, *East India Company and the Economy of Bengal* (London: Luzac, 1954), pp. 158–59; Vikas Misra, *Hinduism and Economic Growth* (London: Oxford University Press, 1962), chap. iii; Milton Singer, "Changing Craft Traditions in India," in W. Moore and A. Feldman (eds.), *Labor Commitment and Social Change in Development Areas* (New York: SSRC, 1960), pp. 258–76; Neil Smelser, *Social Change in the Industrial Revolution* (Chicago: University of Chicago Press, 1959), pp. 109–16; Robert Frykenburg, "Traditional Processes of Power: Land Control in Andhra" (Paper presented to the meeting of the Association for Asian Studies Society, Washington, D.C., 1964); Daniel Thorner, *The Agrarian Prospect in India* (Delhi: University Press, 1956).
[11] In a study of religious behavior among low-caste sweepers, Pauline Kolenda has recently presented a vivid picture of the differences in the Hinduism of higher and of lower social levels ("Religious Anxiety and Hindu Fate," *Journal of Asian Studies*, XXIII [June, 1964], 71–82).

Nations are both part of Western culture. Catholicism and Protestantism are Christian religions, and even within the single Church of Peter, diverse monastic orders have expressed a catholicity of values. Hindu philosophical and religious teaching is consistent with a number of diverse orientations to life. The doctrine of the four *ashramas*, for example, conceives of the good life as one in which men pursue different values at different stages in the life cycle.[12]

The importance of this diversity is that it provides legitimizing principles for a wide set of alternative forms of behavior. This point has been rather convincingly made in the recent discussion of economic development and cultural values in India.[13] Neither the behavior of popular religion nor teachings of the scriptures are devoid of moral bases for materialistic motivations or for disciplined and rational pursuit of wealth. Everyone need not be a *sadhu* (holy man) at all times.

FALLACY 3: TRADITIONAL SOCIETY IS A HOMOGENEOUS SOCIAL STRUCTURE

Like other societies, Indian society has institutionalized different styles of life in different groups, both within and without the caste system. Such divisions of labor make it possible for specific communal and status groups to be the bearers of traditions which differ from the dominant streams yet enable valued social functions to be performed. While Weber referred to "the Protestant ethic," the specific sects who carried the ethic were by no means typical of all Protestant groups.[14] The role of foreign and pariah peoples has often been commented upon as a source of economic growth, innovation, and entrepreneurial behavior.[15] The Jews in Europe, the Muslims in West Africa, the Chinese in Indonesia, and the East Indians in East Africa are examples of groups whose marginality has rendered them able to engage in the impersonality of market behavior and to remain aloof from the status consumption demands of the indigenous population. In India, the Parsees and the Jains

---

[12] For a description of the doctrine of Ashramas, see K. M. Sen, *Hinduism* (London: Penguin Books, 1961), chap. iii.
[13] Milton Singer, "Cultural Values in India's Economic Development," *Annals,* CCCV (May, 1956), 81–91. See the clash of viewpoints among Goheen, Singer, and Srinivas in the discussion of "India's Cultural Values and Economic Development," *Economic Development and Cultural Change,* VIII (October, 1958), 1–13. Vikas Misra (*op. cit.*), similarly to Singer and Srinivas, does not see the cultural elements of Hinduism as an impediment to economic growth.
[14] For an account of the atypicality of Quaker economic rationality among American colonials, see F. B. Tolles, *Meeting House and Counting House; The Quaker Merchants of Colonial Philadelphia, 1682–1763* (Chapel Hill: University of North Carolina Press, 1948).
[15] Sheldon Stryker, "Social Structure and Prejudice," *Social Problems,* VI (1959), 340–54; Bert Hoselitz, "Main Concepts in the Analysis of the Social Implications of Technical Change," in Hoselitz and Moore, *Industrialization and Society* (New York: UNESCO, 1963), pp. 11–29, especially pp. 24–28.

have been potent carriers of economic innovation and the development of large-scale industrial production.

Generalizations about the anti-economic character of the Hindu traditions lose sight of the provision for specific groups which are ethically capable of carrying a logic of economic growth and change. Within the caste system of Hinduism, the untouchables have been able to perform tabooed occupations necessary to the economy. Other castes have developed traditions of business and commerce which, although dishonored in Hindu "tradition," are permissible and even obligatory for the Marwari, the Chettiar, and the Baniya. It is their very legitimation within existing structure that permits their acceptance and implementation of innovating economic behavior.

FALLACY 4: OLD TRADITIONS ARE DISPLACED BY NEW CHANGES

The capacity of old and new cultures and structures to exist without conflict and even with mutual adaptations is a frequent phenomenon of social change; the old is not necessarily *replaced* by the new. The acceptance of a new product, a new religion, a new mode of decision-making does not necessarily lead to the disappearance of the older form. New forms may only increase the range of alternatives. Both magic and medicine can exist side by side, used alternatively by the same people.

The syncretism of inconsistent elements has long been noted in the acceptance of religious usages and beliefs. Paganism and Catholicism have often achieved a mutual tolerance into a new form of ritualism drawn from each in Spanish-speaking countries.[16] The "great tradition" of the urban world in India has by no means pushed aside the "little tradition" of the village as they made contact. Interaction has led to a fusion and mutual penetration.[17] We have become increasingly aware that the outcome of modernizing processes and traditional forms is often an admixture in which each derives a degree of support from the other, rather than a clash of opposites.

FALLACY 5: TRADITIONAL AND MODERN FORMS ARE ALWAYS IN CONFLICT

The abstraction of a "traditional society" as a type separate from a specific historical and cultural setting ignores the diversity of content

---

[16]For one account of such syncretisms, see Robert Redfield, *The Folk Culture of Yucatan* (Chicago: University of Chicago Press, 1941), chap. ix.

[17]"While elements of the great tradition have become parts of local festivals, they do not appear to have entered village festival custom 'at the expense of' much that is or was the little tradition. Instead we see evidence of accretion in a transmutation form without apparent replacement and without rationalization of the accumulated and transformed elements" (McKim Marriott, "Little Communities in an Indigenous Civilization," in M. Marriott [ed.] *Village India* [Chicago: University of Chicago Press, 1955], p. 196).

in specific traditions which influence the acceptance, rejection, or fusion of modernist forms. Japan is unlike the Western societies in the ways in which "feudalism" and industrial development have been fused to promote economic growth.[18] Commitment to emperor and to family, a collectivistic orientation, and a high degree of vertical immobility have been factors supporting social and economic change in the Japanese context while they appear to have been factors producing resistance in the individualistic culture of the West. In this context the hardened commitment of labor to a specific employer operated to promote economic growth while the same process appeared an impediment in the West.[19]

Traditional structures can supply skills, and traditional values can supply sources of legitimation which are capable of being utilized in pursuit of new goals and with new processes. In one Indonesian town, Geertz found the sources of economic expansion largely among the *prijaji*, the Muslim group representing new forces in religion as well as in business. In another town, the source of economic innovation and business expansion was in the traditional nobility. The *prijaji* could build on, but were also hampered by, the characteristics of the bazaar modes of trading and the closed social networks of a pariah group. The traditional nobility, however, was well equipped to form a business class through the wide social networks and the strength of their authority, which rested on a traditional base.[20]

Anthropologists have made the same point in connection with problems of selective culture change. One traditional culture may possess values more clearly congruent with modernization than another; another may cling more tenaciously to its old ways than another. Ottenberg's study of tribes in West Africa found them able to accept and utilize the British culture in Nigeria to a much greater extent than was true of the other major Nigerian tribes. The Ibo's system of voluntary associations, coupled with their values of individualism and achievement, adapted them well to the kinds of opportunities and demands which British colonialism brought. In contrast, the Masai in East Africa are a notorious case of resistance to

---

[18]For some analyses of this phenomenon in Japan, see Reinhard Bendix, *Nation-Building and Citizenship* (New York: John Wiley & Sons, 1965), chap. vi; Robert Scalapino, "Ideology and Modernization: The Japanese Case," in D. Apter (ed.), *Ideology and Discontent* (New York: Free Press, 1965), pp. 93–127; Everett Hagen, *On the Theory of Social Change* (Homewood, Ill.: Dorsey Press, 1962), chap. xiv.

[19]For a description and analysis of labor commitment in Japan, see James Abegglen, *The Japanese Factory* (Glencoe, Ill.: Free Press, 1958); Solomon B. Levine, *Industrial Relations in Post-war Japan* (Urbana: University of Illinois Press, 1958), chap. ii. Richard Lambert describes a similar process operating in western India but sees it as a possible impediment to economic growth (Lambert, *Workers, Factories and Social Change in India* [Princeton, N.J.: Princeton University Press, 1963], especially chap. iii and pp. 214–21).

[20]Clifford Geertz, "Social Change and Economic Modernization in Two Indonesian Towns," in Hagen, *op. cit.*, chap. xvi.

culture change, fiercely upholding existing ways with very little accommodation.[21]

FALLACY 6: TRADITION AND MODERNITY ARE MUTUALLY EXCLUSIVE SYSTEMS

A given institution or cultural system contains several aspects or dimensions. Each dimension does not function in the same way in response to new influences on a society. Tradition and modernity are frequently mutually reinforcing, rather than systems in conflict.

Earlier theories of economic growth viewed extended family systems and caste structure as impediments to economic growth.[22] We now recognize, however, that such relations are complex and can vary from one context to another. Caste as an unalloyed impediment to economic growth has been much exaggerated through failing to balance its role in the division of labor and in caste mobility (one dimension) against its tendencies toward status demands as limitations on desire to accumulate capital (a second dimension).[23] Efforts on the part of castes to become mobile, to attempt improvements in their material as well as their ritual position are by no means new to Indian life. The expanded scope of regional castes, the development of caste associations, and the importance of castes in politics are not impediments to economic growth.[24] They enable credit facility, occupational sponsorship and training, and political influence to be made available on a basis of segmental, traditional loyalties. This brings an element of trust and obligation into an economic context where suspicion and distrust are otherwise frequently the rule between persons unconnected by other ties than the "purely" economic.

Studies of the impact of industrialization on family life in preindustrial and primitive societies similarly indicate the compatibility of extended family forms with industrialism.[25] In the context of Indian economic

---

[21]Simon Ottenberg, "Ibo Receptivity to Change," in M. Herskovits and W. Bascom, *Continuity and Change in African Culture* (Chicago: University of Chicago Press, 1959), pp. 130–43; Harold Schneider, "Pakot Resistance to Change," *ibid.*, pp. 144–67. Also see the description and analysis of labor commitment in East Africa in A. Elkin and L. Fallers, "The Mobility of Labor," in W. Moore and A. Feldman, *op. cit.*, pp. 238–54.

[22]For a generalized statement of this view, stressing an open system of social mobility as a prerequisite for economic growth, see Kingsley Davis, "The Role of Class Mobility in Economic Development," *Population Review*, VI (July, 1962), 67–73.

[23]This is a major conclusion of V. Misra, *op. cit.*

[24]Caste associations and caste loyalties appear to be important sources of social support in urban India and are growing in size and number (see Srinivas, *op. cit.*; M. Weiner, *The Politics of Scarcity* (Bombay: Asia Publishing House, 1962), chap. iii; Bernard Cohn, "Changing Traditions of a Low Caste," *Journal of American Folklore*, LXXI (July–September, 1958), 413–21; Lloyd and Suzanne Rudolph, "The Political Role of India's Caste Associations," *Pacific Affairs*, XXXIII (March, 1960), 5–22. [Reprinted in this reader, p. 63.]

[25]William Goode, "Industrialization and Family Change," in B. Hoselitz and W. Moore, *op. cit.*, chap. xii; Jean Comhaire, "Economic Change and the Extended Family," *Annals*, CCCV (May, 1956), 45–52; Manning Nash, *Machine Age Maya* (Glencoe, Ill.: Free Press, 1958).

growth, the large extended families of the Tatas, Birlas, and Dalmias are among the most striking instances of major industrial organizations growing out of and supported by traditional family units. Berna's study of entrepreneurship in Madras provides additional information, among small businesses, of the extended family as a major source of savings and capital accumulation.[26]

The role of traditional values in the form of segmental loyalties and principles of legitimate authority are of great importance in understanding the possibilities for the occurrence of unified and stable polities at a national level. The contemporary Indian political process utilizes caste, village, and religious community as basic segmental groups through which the individual and the family are drawn into modern political institutions. Primary ties of kinship and clan are in process of fusion to centralized structures of national, participative politics.[27]

The "stuff" of much modern politics in India is itself drawn from the pre-existing struggles between caste, religion, region, and economic groupings. We have become aware that much of what appears to be ideological and economic conflict in Indian politics is actuated and bolstered by struggles for social and economic position among the various caste groups.[28]

The setting of traditional and pre-existing conflicts in the context of new institutions is crucial to understanding Indian educational change. Critics of Indian education often point to the intensive desire for humanistic curriculums among both educators and students, contrasting this with the presumed necessities of technical and agricultural skills in economic development. They fail to see that the politics of egalitarianism revolves around the quest for status in traditional terms. Groups that have not been part of the educational structure in the past now utilize it to gain status increases as well as jobs. This is of great importance in a nation attempting to draw formerly isolated groups into a national identity.[29]

---

[26] James Berna, "Patterns of Entrepreneurship in South India," *Economic Development and Cultural Change*, VII (April, 1959), 343–62.

[27] This is a dominant theme in contemporary discussion of Indian politics (Joseph Gusfield, "Political Community and Group Interests in Modern India," *Pacific Affairs*, XXXVI [Summer, 1965], 123–41, and the literature cited there).

[28] "The 'revolution of rising expectations' is in reality an explosion of social competition . . . not aimed at American, British or Russian living standards, but are demands by one group for improvement . . . vis-à-vis another group within India" (Weiner, *op. cit.*, p. 71).

[29] The social composition of university students in India shows a very high preponderance of high castes in the student bodies, although leveling processes are at work. This situation, and its significance are described in my forthcoming "Equality and Education in India," in Joseph Fisher [ed.], *Social Science and the Comparative Study of Educational Systems* (Scranton, Pa.: International Textbook Publishers, 1967). For a general analysis of Indian higher education, see Allen Grimshaw, "National Goals, Planned Social Change and Higher Education: The Indian Case," in R. Feldmesser and B. Z. Sobel, *Education and Social Change* (New York: John Wiley & Sons, in press).

FALLACY 7: MODERNIZING PROCESSES WEAKEN TRADITIONS

This discussion of Indian education suggests that new institutions and values may, and often do, fuse and interpenetrate the old. In his influential paper on caste mobility, M. N. Srinivas has shown that, while higher social levels appear to be "westernizing" their life styles, when lower and middle levels seek mobility they do so by becoming more devotedly Hinduistic, following more Brahminical styles, and otherwise Sanskritizing their behavior.[30] The fluidity introduced by political competition under independence and democracy becomes harnessed to a more traditional orientation.

The technological consequences of increased transportation, communication, literacy, and horizontal mobility, in furthering the spread of ideas, also intensifies the spread and influence of the "great tradition" into more and more communities and across various social levels.[31] Pilgrimages to distant shrines become easier and enable the conception of a unified, national religion to take firmer root. Caste groups can now be formed on regional and even national lines, buttressed by associational life and written journals. The spread of community development and of educational facilities brings in its wake new, semiurban personnel who carry the Sanskritic traditions fully as much, if not more so, than they do the westernizing influences.[32] The communities of the "little tradition" are, in fact, more open to such traditional winds of change than to wholly new movements. The holy men and the wandering players who carry religious messages and dramas drawn from the Hindu great traditions are more likely to effect attention than the movies.[33]

TRADITION, IDEOLOGY, AND NATIONHOOD

Tradition is not something waiting out there, always over one's shoulder. It is rather plucked, created, and shaped to present needs and aspirations in a given historical situation. Men refer to aspects of the past as tradition in grounding their present actions in some legitimating principle. In this fashion, tradition becomes an ideology, a program of action in which it functions as a goal or as a justificatory base. The concern for tradition as an explicit policy is not an automatic response to change but is itself a movement capable of analysis.

---

[30] "Sanskritization and Westernization," in Srinivas, *op. cit.*
[31] McKim Marriott, "Changing Channels of Cultural Transmission in Indian Civilization," in L. P. Vidyarthi (ed.), *Aspects of Religion in Indian Society* (Meerut: Kedar Nath Ram Nath, 1961), pp. 13–25.
[32] The schoolteacher, in these decades of expanding primary education, is a source of Sanskritic as well as Western influences. See David Mandelbaum's account in "The World and the World View of the Koda," in M. Marriott (ed.), *Village India*, pp. 223–54, especially pp. 239 ff.
[33] John Gumperz, "Religion as a Form of Communication in North India," *Journal of Asian Studies*, XXIII (June, 1964), 89–98.

In similar fashion, to be "modern" appears in many new nations as an aspiration toward which certain groups seek to move the society. "Modern" becomes a perceived state of things functioning as a criterion against which to judge specific actions and a program of actions to guide policy. In Scalapino's apt phrase, intellectuals in new nations utilize "teleological insight"—the assumed ability to read the future of their own society by projecting it in accordance with the experience and trends of "advanced" nations.[34] Such insight operates as a crucial determinant in developing goals, but it too is a creation of choice among possibilities, not a fixed and self-evident set of propositions.

The desire to be modern and the desire to preserve tradition operate as significant movements in the new nations and developing economies. It is our basic point here that these desires, functioning as ideologies, are not always in conflict; that the quest for modernity depends upon and often finds support in the ideological upsurge of traditionalism. In this process, tradition may be changed, stretched, and modified, but a unified and nationalized society makes great use of the traditional in its search for a consensual base to political authority and economic development.

TRADITION AND NATIONAL UNIFICATION

Writing about African intellectuals in the formerly French colonies, Immanuel Wallerstein remarks that these parts of Africa are the chief centers for the ideological development of "Negritude"—the preservation and development of a uniquely indigenous African culture.[35] Here, where the intellectuals were trained in the French language and where they fully accepted the French culture, it is necessary to identify and discover a national cultural tradition and to self-consciously aid its development. In a similar fashion, an Indian colleague of mine once remarked that "Indians are obsessed with Indianness."

Many observers have noted the phenomenon of the revival of indigenous tradition as a phase of nationalistic and independence movements, especially where intellectuals had come to look to some other country as a basic source of new values.[36] Such reactions have set in among Russian intellectuals against France in the nineteenth century, among the Indonesians against the Dutch, among the Japanese against Europe; and against the British among the Indians both during and after the struggle for independence. The Indian intellectuals, westernized and European in cultural orientation, underwent a renaissance of traditional Hinduism as one aspect

---

[34] Scalapino, *op. cit.*, p. 106.
[35] Immanuel Wallerstein, *Africa—the Politics of Independence* (New York: Vintage Books, 1961), pp. 75–76.
[36] *Ibid.*, chap. vii; John Kautsky, *Political Change in Underdeveloped Areas* (New York: John Wiley & Sons, 1962), pp. 53–54; Heimsath, *op. cit.*, chap. xii; Mary Mattosian, "Ideologies of Delayed Industrialization," *Economic Development and Cultural Change* (April, 1958), pp. 217–28.

of the struggle against colonial dominion.[37] Despite their general commitment to modernization (often against the British post-Sepoy rebellion policy of maintaining native custom), a recrudescence of Indian national identity was partially fostered by explicit adoption of customs and styles which were both traditional and closer to popular behavior. It was this ideology which Gandhi gave to the movement, even as he sought the abolition of many features of that tradition.

The issue of the nationalist movement is not abated in its victory. For the new elites of newly independent nations, the issue is not so much that of overcoming tradition but of finding ways of synthesizing and blending tradition and modernity. While it is now possible for the urbanized and intellectual elite to wear Saville Row and avoid the clothes of Chowri Bazaar without being a traitor, the issues of personal integrity and of political functions still remain.

Those who depict the elites in India as cut off from roots in an indigenous civilization ignore the ways in which Hinduism and Indian family life exert strong pulls as continuing aspects of Indian life, even where highly westernized. Almost always the Indian intellectual speaks a regional language as his mother tongue, is steeped in classic Sanskrit literature, and is deeply tied to an extended family. Parental arrangement is still the very dominant mode of marital selection, and he is often married to a highly traditional wife.[38]

Independence, even within the westernized circles, has given continuing support to a movement toward the recapturing of Hindu folklore and the furtherance of tradition as a source of national unity in a common culture. What Indian book or journal does not have its section that links modern thought or institutions to analogues in Hindu scripture? How often is the romanticization of the village and the rejection of the city not found among vigorous exponents of political democracy and economic change? This ideological construction of Indian tradition is offered as a "great tradition," and this Indian populism is found among intellectual and urbanized elites as it is in the provincial and peasant villages.

Nationalism is deeply committed to both horns of the dilemma of tradition and modernity. The effort to define a national heritage in the form of a set of continuing traditions is also a way of coping with the wide gap that separates elite and mass, city and village, region and region

---

[37]This "revivalist" stream was only one of the major themes in Indian nationalism, but it had a great impact throughout the movement (Heimsath, *op. cit.;* A. R. Desai, *Social Background of Indian Nationalism* [Bombay: Popular Book Depot, 1959], chaps. xiii, xviii).

[38]Shils has made this point in his study of Indian intellectuals (Edward Shils, *The Intellectual between Tradition and Modernity* [The Hague: Mouton & Co., 1961], especially pp. 60–67).

in the Indian context. It is a complement to the modernizing processes which are involved in the aspiration toward a unified nation. A common culture that cuts across the segmental and primordial loyalties is a basis for national identity and consensus. Without it, the modernization based on nationhood lacks a foundation for legitimating central authority.

In describing these movements we are not referring to efforts to pit tradition against modernity. This is certainly to be discovered in populist and aristocratic movements which call for the rejection of economic growth and the resistance or abolition of imported institutions and values. In India this can be seen in the xenophobic and militant Hinduism which characterized the RSS and still is a potent political force in the Hindu Mahasabha and, to a lesser degree, in the Jan Sangh party.[39] This appeal to an undisturbed society avoids the dilemma fully as much as does the ideology based on a linear theory of change.

The synthesis of tradition and modernity is evident in Gandhian influence. Was Gandhi a traditionalist or a modernizer? Asking the question poses the immense difficulty in separating the various streams in reform and social change blowing over the Indian subcontinent. Certainly his genius lay in uniting disparities, in utilizing the traditional authority of the holy man for social reforms and for political union. His leadership of the independence movement gave India a common experience which has been one of the crucial legacies of the independence movement to its present national existence and to the authority of the Congress Party.

The Gandhianism of the neo-Gandhians, such as Vinoba Bhave and Jayaprakash Narayan, represents an important ideological development in the search for political institutions which will cope with the problems of nationhood within indigenous cultural forms.[40] But Gandhian Socialism represents only one form in which this drive toward a synthesis is manifest. The recent movement toward the development of local autonomy and participation in India rests both on the growing political power of village communities and the ideological force which has recreated a tradition of Indian village democracy. In the various proposals for a system of Panchayati Raj (movement toward greater local power in economic decisions at the village level), Indian government and politics are wrestling with the

---

[39] See Richard Lambert "Hindu Communal Groups in Indian Politics," in R. Park and I. Tinker (eds.), *Leadership and Political Institutions in India* (Madras: Oxford University Press, 1960), pp. 211–24. Even in the Swatantra Party, a movement led by an antitraditionalist set of ideologies, its anti-Congress character has drawn to it strong forces of antimodernism (see Howard Erdman, "India's Swatantra Party," *Pacific Affairs* [Winter, 1963-64], pp. 394–410).

[40] This quest for an indigenous form of political democracy is marked in Narayan's writings, as well as in conversation (see Jaya Prakash Narayan, *The Dual Revolution* [Tanjore: Sarvodaya Prachuralaya, 1959]; *Swaraj for the People* [Varanasi: Ahkhih Bharat Sarva Seva Sangh, 1961]).

problem of creating a consensus for developmental policies which will have the legitimating support in tradition, even if the tradition is newly discovered.[41]

THE MEDIATING ELITES

Elsewhere we have analyzed the growing political power of new, less westernized, and more localistic political elites and subelites in India.[42] Such people, with sources of power in state and region, mediate between the westernized elites and the mass of the Indian society in ways which bring a greater degree of traditional commitments and styles, of caste and other primordial ties, into the political and cultural arena.

The very process of political egalitarianism and modernization contains the seeds of new ideologies of tradition. Literacy in India not only stimulates a common cultural content but has also led to ideologies of regionalism, extolling the virtues of regional languages and cultures.[43] While such movements impede the development of an all-Indian cultural consensus, they are neither antimodern nor specifically anti-India. They do, however, presage the decline of that form of national elite that has been associated with colonial cultural influences. India appears to be approaching and entering a phase in which modernization will be directed and implemented by persons whose loyalties and ideologies are considerably more traditionalized than has been true in the past decades.

THE AMBIGUITIES OF MODERNITY

Just as "tradition" is renewed, created, and discovered, so too "modernity" as a goal toward which men aspire appears in some specific historical guise. The post-colonial elites owed much to the cultures of the colonial powers in India. Through travel, through language and literature, through colonial educational institutions, they had absorbed a picture of modernity as it was practiced in one country at one time. It is not a random selection that led the Indian elites to conceive of politics in the British mode or led Nehru's political pronouncements and judgments of the 1950's to echo the liberalism of Harold Laski in the 1920's.

---

[41] See the analysis of the Panchayats in my paper on Indian political community, cited above (n. 27); and in Reinhard Bendix, "Public Authority in a Developing Political Community: The Case of India," *Archives Europeennes de Sociologie*, IV (1963), 39–85, especially 61 ff.

[42] Gusfield, "Political Community and Group Interests in Modern India," *op. cit.*

[43] Witness the rise of self-conscious rediscovery of Hindi literary tradition. The linguistic and cultural renaissances in many parts of India are post-independence phenomena (see Selig Harrison, *India: The Most Dangerous Decade* (Princeton, N.J.: Princeton University Press, 1960).

But being modern is far more ambiguous than being British. The disappearance of the postcolonial elites carries with it an increase in the range of alternatives ideologically open to the new, more traditionalized political groups. The possible routes to economic wealth and political nationhood are considerable, as we have shown in the earlier section of this paper. As countries come onto the scene of self-conscious aspiration toward the modern, they are presented with more and more successful models of the process. England, Germany, the United States, Japan, the Soviet Union are highly diverse in political institutions and histories. In the sense of having achieved high standards of living and egalitarian societies, they are all reasonably "developed."

THE CULTURAL FRAMEWORK OF MODERNITY

We cannot easily separate modernity and tradition from some *specific* tradition and some *specific* modernity, some version which functions ideologically as a directive. The modern comes to the traditional society as a particular culture with its own traditions. In this respect it has been impossible to divorce modernization from some process of westernization. McKim Marriott has made this point most vividly in analyzing the reasons for villagers' rejection of Western and westernized doctors. The role of the doctor, as a technical expert, grants him authority in modern culture but not in the Indian village where technical and commercial skills have a low approval. Efficiency and thrift, those two great Western virtues, are not such in the eyes of the peasant in Utter Pradesh.[44]

The social scientist's designation of specific institutional forms as modern may also function as ideology and as aspiration, specifying what it is in a particular culture which is emulative. The concept of political development is far more difficult and culture-bound than is that of economic development. Even with the latter, we clearly recognize a diversity of institutional routes to industrialization and higher incomes. To label, apart from a specific context, either a capitalistic, socialistic, or communistic approach to economic growth as antithetical to economic growth would certainly seem fallacious to the economist. Similarly, the industrialized and

---

[44]"It is important to note that a distinction can be made between 'Western' and 'scientific' medicine. Westerners conceive of a Western medicine as a system of curing based on 'rational' techniques and 'scientific' concepts of cause and effect. But this characteristic . . . only partly determines the total range of practices involved in treatment and cure. Treatment is bedded in a social as well as a scientific matrix, and many practices of the Western doctor are based on cultural values and ideas of personal relationships that are peculiar to Western society" (McKim Marriott, "Western Medicine in a Village of Northern India," in S. N. Eisenstadt [ed.], *Comparative Social Problems* [New York: Free Press, 1964], pp. 47–60, at p. 59).

egalitarian societies of the West have by no means demonstrated either a uniform or an unchanging form of polity. The Soviet Union, France, Germany, and the United States (and we might well include Japan) are hardly a single form of political structure, and each of these has in turn undergone many changes during its history. They are all national polities, to be sure, and all ones in which the population is mobilized, to a degree, to political participation and loyalty. These facts, however, state problems in a wider fashion, without specific institutional directives.

To conclude, the all too common practice of pitting tradition and modernity against each other as paired opposites tends to overlook the mixtures and blends which reality displays. Above all, it becomes an ideology of antitraditionalism, denying the necessary and usable ways in which the past serves as support, especially in the sphere of values and political legitimation, to the present and the future. We need a perspective toward change which does not deny the specific and contextual character of events.

I do not know much about the total style of life of that passenger on the Kodama express. To think of him as fixed on a continuum between tradition and modernity (as well as between Kyoto and Tokyo) hides the immense variations and possibilities, the capacity for blending opposites, which human beings and nations possess. In the concepts of the traditional and the modern, we are certainly wrestling with a feature of social change. We need to recognize that there is a variety of events on the wrestling program and that the outcomes, unlike many wrestling matches, are quite in doubt.

FOR FURTHER READING

EDWARD C. BANFIELD, *The Moral Basis of a Backward Society* (New York: Free Press, 1958)

REINHARD BENDIX, "Tradition and Modernity Reconsidered" *(Comparative Studies in Society and History,* IX, 3, April 1967, 292–346)

OSCAR LEWIS, *Village Life in Northern India* (Urbana: University of Illinois Press, 1958)

BRONISLAW MALINOWSKI, *The Dynamics of Cultural Change: An Inquiry into Race Relations in Africa* (New Haven: Yale University Press, 1945)

ROBERT REDFIELD, *The Primitive World and Its Transformations* (Ithaca: Cornell University Press, 1953)

D. WEINTRAUB AND E. BERNSTEIN, "Social Structure and Modernization: A Comparative Study of Two Villages" *(American Journal of Sociology,* LXXI, 5, March 1966, 509–521)

THE POLITICAL ROLE OF INDIA'S CASTE ASSOCIATIONS

Lloyd I. Rudolph and Susanne Hoeber Rudolph

Caste is a unique feature of the culture of India. Does this deeply engrained way of dividing society automatically preclude change? By focusing upon caste associations, the Rudolphs show how a long-standing social framework is adapted to the forces of modernization. Caste associations expand political participation and appear to be bringing democratic practices to the attention of the population.

It is one of the paradoxes of Indian politics that India's *ancien régime*, surely one of the oldest and most deeply rooted in the world, produced no reaction. In three-fifths of India the nationalist middle classes which emerged out of the British colonial experience aimed not only at independence but also at the transformation of Indian society. The Rebellion of 1857 is the only historical event in which the old order attempted to preserve itself, but its causes and objectives were so ambiguous that its meaning remains open to serious dispute even today. At Independence, the vestigial political expression of the *ancien régime*, the princely states, which covered two-fifths of India's territory, swiftly collapsed. This event was as much the result of the atrophied condition of the institutions and wills of the ruling order as of the skill with which the Indian Government (through Sardar Patel) managed the negotiations. Only a few minor local parties today stand for a full return to the rule of Brahmans and *Kshatryas** according to the precepts of *dharma* or traditional duty, and they are ineffectual.[1]

From *Pacific Affairs*, Vol. XXXIII, No. 1 (1960), pp. 5–22, by permission.
*[Traditionally, these are the two highest castes, which provided the priests and scholars and the warriors and rulers.—Ed.]

[1]Not even the *Jan Sangh*, strongest of the right-wing parties, espouses such a program. It is much more a rightist radical party than a traditionalist one.

There is one perspective in which the absence of a reaction in the European sense is not surprising: within Hinduism, conflict (at the level of theology, philosophy and law) has generally been dealt with less by confrontation of adversaries, struggle and decision, than by compartmentalization, absorption or synthesis. And absorption appears likely to be the fate of the *ancien régime's* most central and durable institution—caste. Within the new context of political democracy, caste remains a central element of Indian society even while adapting itself to the values and methods of democratic politics. Indeed, it has become one of the chief means by which the Indian mass electorate has been attached to the processes of democratic politics.

The appeal of India's relatively weakly articulated voluntary associations is confined to the urban-educated who are more or less attuned to the modern political culture. Caste, however, provides channels of communication and bases of leadership and organization which enable those still submerged in the traditional society and culture to transcend the technical political illiteracy which would otherwise handicap their ability to participate in democratic politics. Caste has been able to perform this novel role by developing a new form for political activity, the caste association (*sabha* or *sangham*). Caste associations were already visible in the mid-nineteenth century. Over the last forty or fifty years, they have proliferated, their number and strength paralleling the growth of political literacy. After Independence, it became increasingly apparent that they would be a central feature of Indian politics for some time to come.

The political role and characteristics of the caste association resemble in many ways those of the voluntary association or interest-group familiar to European and American politics. On the other hand, the caste association is distinguishable in a number of important respects not only from the voluntary association but also from the natural association of caste out of which it has developed.

Membership in a caste is completely ascriptive: once born into a caste, a man has no way to change social identity insofar as the social structure and cultural norms recognize caste.[2] Caste norms prescribe the ritual, occupational, commensal, marital and social relationships of members, and caste organization and authority enforce these norms

---

[2]Alternative status systems which parallel that of caste are also visible in contemporary India. See for example S. C. Dube, *Indian Village*, London, 1956, pp. 161–6; see also our discussion of aspects of this problem in "Indian Political Studies and the Scope of Comparative Politics," *Far Eastern Survey* (XXVII) No. 9, September 1959, pp. 134–8, where articles by Sushil Dey, Baij Nath Singh, Evelyn Wood, John T. Hitchcock, Henry Orenstein, Alan Beal and Edward B. and Louise G. Harper are analyzed. These articles appear in Richard L. Park and Irene Tinker, eds., *Leadership and Political Institutions in India*, Princeton, 1959.

within the group and with other caste groups. Caste members are culturally and socially quite homogeneous since they share the same occupation, social status and ritual position.[3] This social homogeneity results in a sense of exclusiveness and identity which tends to subsume all social roles to that of caste membership. The unit of action and location of caste has been, until recently, the sub-caste in the village or group of villages. Traditionally, it has been concerned with settling problems at the village level, both internally and in relation to 'other castes. At most, its geographic spread took account of the reach of intra-caste (endogamous) marriages which often extended to other villages, but the village unit was crucial. Leaders were hereditary, generally the senior members of a specific lineage group. Social integration, the relationship of the caste to other castes, was governed by *dharma*, the sacred and traditional prescriptions of duty which permeate Hindu life. Finally, its organization was latent, embedded in habit and custom, rather than manifest and rationalized.

The emergence of caste associations seems to have been associated with the spread of communications and a market economy under British rule.[4] On the one hand, these forces undermined the hold of the traditional culture and society as it was organized in relatively autonomous local units; on the other hand, they created the conditions under which local sub-castes could be linked together in geographically extended associations. Caste associations, particularly those of lower castes, frequently undertook to upgrade the position of the caste in the social hierarchy. They pressed for the extension of privileges and rights to the caste either by turning to the state or by emulating the social or ritual behavior of higher castes. Thus, for example, in the South, where the caste culture has been conspicuously dominated by Brahmanical norms, the rising castes have emulated those norms by "sanskritizing" their caste practices; they have encouraged vegetarianism, abstention from liquor, the adoption of Brahman rituals, and the prevention of widow re-marriage.[5] Caste associations have often expedited and coordinated such emulative activities.[6]

---

[3]Occupational heterogeneity of castes is already well advanced, however, in towns and urban areas. The materials of the older caste ethnographers indicate that the breakdown of social and occupational homogeneity was apparent in the nineteenth century. Both Edgar Thurston, in his *Castes and Tribes of Southern India*, Madras, 1909, and William Crooke in his *The Tribes and Castes of the North West Provinces and Oudh*, Calcutta, 1896, bear this out.

[4]See M. N. Srinivas' articles bearing on the issues raised here: "A Note on Sanskritization and Westernization," *Far Eastern Quarterly* (XV), August 1956; "Caste in Modern India," *Journal of Asian Studies* (XVI), August 1957.

[5]It may be that "sanskritization," while also practiced in the North, may offer less compelling emulation patterns there than in the South because of the strength of *Kshatrya* norms in many areas.

[6]The caste association has not been alone in this type of activity. More parochial village caste groups have also pursued emulation as a vehicle for improving

When the caste associations turned to the state for furthering their purposes, their initial claims were aimed at raising caste status in terms of the values and structure of the caste order. But as liberal and democratic ideas penetrated to wider sections of the population, the aims of the caste association began to shift accordingly. Instead of demanding temple entry and prestigious caste names and histories in the Census, the associations began to press for places in the new administrative and educational institutions and for political representation. Independence and the realization of political democracy intensified these new concerns. Caste associations attempted to have their members nominated for elective office, working through existing parties or forming their own; to maximize caste representation and influence in state cabinets and lesser governing bodies; and to use ministerial, legislative and administrative channels to press for action on caste objectives in the welfare, educational and economic realms. Perhaps the most significant aspect of the caste association in the contemporary era, however, is its capacity to organize the politically illiterate mass electorate, thus making possible in some measure the realization of its aspirations and educating large sections of it in the methods and values of political democracy.

The caste association is no longer a natural association in the sense in which caste was and is. It is beginning to take on features of the voluntary association. Membership in caste associations is *not* purely ascriptive; birth in the caste is a necessary but not a sufficient condition for membership. One must also "join" the (*Rajput*) *Kshatrya Mahasabha* or the (*Jat*) *Kisan Sabha* through some conscious act involving various degrees of identification—ranging from attendance at caste association meetings or voting for candidates supported by caste association leaders, to paying membership dues. The caste association has generally both a potential and an actual membership; when it speaks, it often claims to speak for the potential represented in the full caste membership. While the purposes of caste are wide-ranging and diffuse, affecting every aspect of members' life paths, the caste association has come to specialize in politics. The traditional authority and functions

---

status, sometimes successfully. See for example the progress of the Boad Distillers, in F. G. Bailey, *Caste and the Economic Frontier*, Manchester, 1957. But McKim Marriott has pointed out that any caste group operating in an intimate local setting, where relative status positions are well understood and jealously protected, might have trouble advancing itself by emulation: "A mere brandishing of Brahmanical symbols by a well-known village group can scarcely hope to impress a village audience in its own parochial terms...." See his "Interactional and Attributional Theories of Caste Ranking," *Man in India* (39), April-June, 1959. Conversely, the caste association, operating in the wider, more impersonal setting of a district or a state, may encounter less resistance to its emulative claims because in the wider setting there is no clear standard for assessing its "true" position.

of the sub-caste are declining, but the caste association's concern with politics and its rewards serves to sustain caste loyalty and identification.[7] This loyalty and sense of identification tend to retain the exclusive quality of the natural association; the caste association seems to have a more complete and intense command of its members' commitments than is usually the case with voluntary associations.

Since modern means of transportation and communication have had the effect of broadening caste, binding together local sub-castes which had been relatively autonomous into geographically extended associations, caste associations today usually parallel administrative and political units—states, districts, sub-districts and towns—whose offices and powers of legislation or decision-making are the object of the caste associations' efforts.

Leadership in the caste association is no longer in the hands of those qualified by heredity—the senior or more able members of the lineage group which traditionally supplied village sub-caste leadership. The "availability" of association leaders is conditioned by their ability to articulate and represent the purposes of the caste association, and for this purpose they must be literate in the ways of the new democratic politics. Men whose educational and occupational backgrounds assure these skills have moved into the leadership positions. The new leaders stand in a more "accountable" and responsible relationship to their followers; their position depends to a great extent on their capacity to represent and make good the association's claims.

Finally, at the organizational level, the caste association is moving away from the latent structure of caste, towards the manifest structure characteristic of the voluntary association. It has offices, membership, incipient bureaucratization, publications, and a quasi-legislative process expressed through conferences, delegates and resolutions. On the other hand, the shared sense of culture, character, and status tends to create a solidarity of a much higher order than is usually found among voluntary associations where the multiplicity of social roles and the plurality of interests of its members tend to dilute the intensity of commitment and sense of identification.

The caste association brings political democracy to Indian villages through the familiar and accepted institution of caste. In the process, it is changing the meaning of caste. By creating conditions in which a caste's significance and power is beginning to depend on its numbers, rather than its ritual and social status, and by encouraging egalitarian

---

[7]For confirmation of these and other points, see also Selig Harrison, "Caste and the Andhra Communists," *American Political Science Review* (L), June 1956; M. L. P. Patterson, "Caste and Politics in Maharashtra," *Economic Weekly*, (VIII) 29, July 21, 1956.

aspirations among its members the caste association is exerting a liberating influence.

Liberties in the west have a dual paternity. They arose on the one hand from an assertion of political philosophy which placed the reason and interests of the individual in a central position. On the other hand, they were the end-product of a historical process in which the rights and liberties of a variety of corporate groups and orders in traditional feudal society were gradually extended to ever-widening sections of the population until many rights and liberties became available to all. In India, as formerly in 18th century Europe, one attack on tradition and the old order came from the modern middle classes who succeeded in writing into the new nation's constitution the values of 18th century liberalism.[8] But the modern middle classes' attack constituted only one aspect, and a formal and impersonal aspect at that, of the challenge to the old order.

The other challenge has come from the caste association; its successful assertions of privilege and rights are in many ways comparable to the extension of corporate feudal liberties which characterized the development of English liberalism. They are perhaps the more truly indigenous assertions of liberties than the liberalism of the modern Indian middle classes. Thus, for example, the *Shanans*, traditionally low caste southern tappers of palm-wine (toddy), asserted as early as 1858 that their women had a right to go about with an upper cloth, even though customary rules restricted such apparel to the higher castes. After a series of riots, the Maharaja of Travancore was persuaded to concede the claim: "We hereby proclaim that there is no objection to *Shanan* women either putting on a jacket like the Christian *Shanan* women, or to *Shanan* women of all creeds dressing in coarse cloth, and tying themselves round with it as the *Mukkavattigal* (Fisherwomen) do, or to covering their bosoms in any manner whatever, but not like women of higher castes."[9]

The caste's assertion, which could be multiplied many times with reference to other issues (such as extending the rights of temple entry to lower castes), exemplifies the caste association's liberating role. It also suggests that the corporate assertion of rights challenged the old order at points in which the "liberal" modern middle classes took rather little interest. Indian analyses of these developments have tended to attribute the entire credit for such victories to the state which concedes the right rather than to the group which agitates for it—a point of

---

[8]They also included the often conflicting values of popular sovereignty and political democracy and the "socialist" goals of economic and social justice.
[9]Edgar Thurston, *Castes and Tribes*, Vol. VI, p. 265.

view which gravely underestimates the role of liberating forces within the old society.

The very considerable extent to which caste associations are performing a liberating function has been obscured by the fact that the modern Indian middle classes tend to see caste (in any form) as a part of the old order which they hope to destroy. That a new social and political force clad in the institutions of the old order is to an extent collaborating in this activity, that caste is in a sense anti-caste, appears to them incomprehensible. Because the caste association presses home the interests of its followers, it is also seen as pursuing a form of group selfishness which is deplored in the name of social duty and discipline. Finally, the caste association is condemned along with other interest groups of both the natural and voluntary variety, by those economic planners, civil servants and political ideologues who deduce policy from theories of economic development, conceptions of the public good and utopian visions of a new society. Such persons see the goals and interests pressed by caste associations and other groups as self-interested, confusing and partial. That the public good should in some measure be worked out from the interaction and accommodations of many group purposes is seen as morally degrading, intellectually unsatisfactory or aesthetically displeasing. For them, the political community includes only the state on the one hand and the citizen on the other, with the state having an exclusive (or at least primary) role in the formulation and execution of the public good. They fail to see that associations, both voluntary and natural, have a vital role to play in the exercise of political freedom through group self-government which contributes to the process of finding an approximation of the public good, provides a means for furthering group purposes independent of, as well as supplementary to, the state, and helps to protect the liberties of both associations and individuals.

None of this is meant to imply, however, that the caste association is an unqualified asset in Indian politics. Its tendency to place group loyalties above merit and competence, and caste patriotism above the public interest, runs counter to both liberal and democratic values and jeopardizes the effectiveness of the government's vital functions. In the final analysis, the meaning of the caste association in politics is ambiguous. Up to the present its role has been seriously misunderstood and its positive contribution neglected.

The caste association's main impact on politics within the Indian federal systems is at the state level. Caste associations do not generally extend across state boundaries. Castes do not, as a rule, include persons of different linguistic-cultural backgrounds, and most Indian states today are organized on a linguistic-cultural basis.[10] The interest groups which seem to be most effective at the national level are voluntary associations (such as trade unions or chambers of commerce which have national constituencies) and natural associations like linguistic-cultural sub-nationalisms and religious communities.

At the state level, the strength of caste associations varies with the numbers that a particular association can attempt to mobilize, with the degree of self-consciousness and effectiveness of leadership, with the degree of internal cohesiveness, and with the power of countervailing interest-group forces. The balance of these factors has to be assessed separately in each state. Thus, in Rajasthan, a state which was formerly part of Princely India, the power of the *Jat* peasant caste, which constitutes 9 percent of the population of that state, may be explained by the particular constellation of all these factors. In part, the *Jats* profit from vigorous and effective leadership. The untouchable *Chamars* in the same state approach the *Jats* in numbers, but are relatively ineffectual politically because their level of self-consciousness and the quality of their leadership leave them for the moment merely a latent political force.[11] Among the organized castes, the *Rajputs* (a warrior caste) have served to check the power of the *Jats* by the lively activity of their association. The *Rajputs* are numerous, ranking fifth among castes in the state with 6 percent of population, very self-conscious politically, fairly well-led, and they still retain some of the authority of their traditional caste and class rank as *Kshatryas* (warrior rulers who constituted Rajasthan's monarchical-feudal order until 1947). But the *Rajput* caste association has not been able to exploit its full powers, in part because its internal cohesion suffered when *Rajputs* who were great feudal landholders and those who were petty landlords disagreed on the acceptability of the post-Independence land reforms.

The *Jats*, in addition to benefiting from these dissensions among the *Rajputs*, are also able to capitalize on the relative backwardness of the state. With very little industry or commerce and with a very high level of political illiteracy, neither voluntary associations nor other caste associations are particularly strong. In Bombay and Madras, which

---

[10]Bombay and Punjab are exceptions. Castes with approximately similar origins do exist in different states. *Jats* live in the Punjab, Uttar Pradesh and Rajasthan. But inter-state organization is weak both in caste structure and in the caste associations.

[11]The *Chamars* profit from the reservation of seats for untouchables in the Rajasthan legislative assembly; but even this crutch is not enough to make them influential in the absence of able leadership.

are more advanced economically and have higher levels of political literacy, the countervailing forces, both voluntary and natural, are considerably stronger. In addition then to the natural limitation to caste political power inherent in the fact that castes generally hold a minority status (at both the national and the state level) there are other possible checks—lack of cohesiveness, a low level of self-consciousness, ineffective leadership and the countervailing power of other caste associations or interest groups.[12]

The caste association differs from the other natural associations found in India—tribal, linguistic and religious—in its relationship to the political community, i.e., the nation-state. Tribal, religious and linguistic groups on the Indian scene represent *potential* political communities, which may claim (and often have claimed) a separate political identity, either in the form of a sovereign state or an autonomous unit in a federal system.[13] Caste, and its political expression, the caste association, have no such aspiration. Caste is a part of Hindu society; its meaning as a social institution is found in the values of Hindu culture. In this sense, all castes share a common culture, purpose and identity. The caste association is concerned with the distribution of values, status and rewards within a larger unit of action. It does not have a sense of nationality or aspire to separate political identity. It would be foolish, however, to suggest that such a development is out of the question. A caste like the Rajasthan *Jats*, with a tribal rather than an occupational caste origin, with a reasonably identifiable territorial base and a fairly recent (18th century) political history, might conceivably develop such aspirations. However, so far there is no evidence of such a development.

One of the key means in Indian democratic politics for "brokering" and integrating diverse social forces is the political party; at present, it is the parties, particularly the Congress Party, that link together the caste associations which tend to play so vital a role in state politics. The relationship of caste to party (i.e., to the institutional

---

[12]Of course India's constitutional structure, including the party system, also plays a crucial role. Space limitations prevent an exploration of this facet of the problem.

[13]Many religious groups (the Christians and the post-Independence Muslims) and many tribal groups (the Bhils for example) have not in fact posed such problems of integration. But others have, at various levels: the pre-Independence Muslims sought and found their political identity in the nation-state of Pakistan; the various Indian linguistic groups successfully pressed for a political identity and some measure of autonomy within the federal system; the Naga tribes rebelled in an effort to gain some form of political identity; and the Sikhs found a measure of political identity in the compromise achieved in the Punjab legislature whereby two intrastate Regional Committees with broad recommendatory powers were established for Sikh and Hindu legislators respectively. See Joan V. Bondurant, *Regionalism versus Provincialism*, Berkeley, 1958, pp. 114–124.

means of political integration) has been markedly different from the relationship of other natural associations to party. Party has subsumed caste, acting as a broker for caste association interests and accommodating in some measure its demands for representation on party tickets. In relation to other types of natural associations, however, the party has often been subsumed by them. The most outstanding example of this appeared in Bombay where the *Samyukta Maharashtra Samiti* and the *Maha Gujerat Parishad* (associations of the two linguistic groups of the state) subsumed the parties to their larger "national" drives for political identity.[14] So long as a religious, linguistic or tribal drive for political identity is in full swing, the party has been harnessed to it. The lesson of states reorganization in India, from the demand for Andhra state onward, was that the demand for linguistic-cultural autonomy through some form of separate political identity could not be compromised or accommodated, nor could the demand for religious-cultural autonomy and identity, as the case of the Muslims and Sikhs clearly indicates.

In their relationship to parties, caste associations play a role more akin to voluntary interest-groups than do the other natural associations. They have specific program and personnel demands which can be accommodated at the levels of policy formation, "ticket balancing" in constituencies and in the cabinet, and legislation.

The *Vanniyars,* or *Vanniya Kula Kshatryas,* illustrate the development of caste associations. They are primarily a caste of agricultural laborers, but also include substantial numbers of cultivating owners and petty landlords in Madras state. They make up slightly less than 10 percent of the population of Madras, but in the four northern districts of the state (North Arcot, South Arcot, Chingleput and Salem) where they are concentrated, the caste constitutes about a fourth of the population.[15] As early as 1833, the *Pallis,* as they were then called, had ceased to accept their status as a humble agricultural caste and tried to procure a decree in Pondicherry that they were not a low

---

[14]See Marshall Windmiller, "The Politics of State Reorganization in India: The Case of Bombay," *Far Eastern Survey* (XXV), No. 9, September 1956, pp. 129–143; and Phillips Talbot, "The Second General Elections: Voting in the States," American Universities Field Staff, New York, 1957 (India, PT-6-1957).

[15]These figures are necessarily tentative because they are based on the 1931 census, the last Indian census to enumerate caste. At that time, the *Vanniyars* numbered 2,944,014 and almost all of the *Vanniyars* were located in those parts of Madras which remained within the state after Andhra was detached in 1953. Presumably the *Vanniyar* population has increased substantially since then, at a rate not too different from the average population increase. In Chingleput, North Arcot, Salem and South Arcot there were 2,340,920 *Vanniyars* in 1931 in a total population for these districts of 8,810,583. See *Census of India,* 1931, Vol. XIV, Madras, Part II, Imperial and Provincial Tables.

caste.[15a] In anticipation of a census-taking in 1871, they petitioned to be classified as *Kshatryas* (high-caste warrior-rulers)—a claim which found support in their traditional caste histories if not in their then low occupational status. Twenty years later the community had established seven schools for its members, and an enterprising *Palli* who had risen to the status of a High Court *vakil* (lawyer) had produced a book on the caste, which he followed with another some years later, supporting the caste's claim to be *Kshatryas* and connecting *Pallis* by descent with the great Pallava dynasty.[16] Oral histories simultaneously were stressing descent from the traditional "fire races," which *Kshatryas* both north and south often claim as ancestors. This attempt to press history into the service of social mobility, to counter current ritual and occupational definition of caste status by a historically derived definition, has been a quite frequent practice among rising castes.

By 1901 the *Pallis* had not won any battles but everyone was aware of their efforts. The Madras Census Commissioner noted that "they claim for themselves a position higher than that which Hindu society is inclined to accord them," and added that they were attempting to achieve this status via "a widespread organization engineered from Madras."[17] The organization's sporadic seventy-year activities to make *Pallis* conscious of their dignified and glorious history was bearing fruit. Instead of giving the old name, *Palli*, many were beginning to refer to themselves as *Agnikula Kshatryas* or *Vannikula Kshatryas* (i.e. *Kshatryas* of the fire race). The associations of the caste were spreading and becoming increasingly effective in various districts, enforcing a higher "sanskritized" standard of social conduct:

> They have been closely bound together by an organization managed by one of their caste, who was a prominent person in these parts ... and their *esprit de corps* is now surprisingly strong. They are tending gradually to approach the Brahmanical standard of social conduct, discouraging adult marriage, meat-eating, and widow remarriage. ... In 1904 a document came before one of the courts which showed that, in the year previous, the representatives of the caste in 34 villages in this district had bound themselves in writing, under penalty of excommunication to refrain (except with the consent of all parties) from the practices formerly in existence of marrying two wives, and of allowing a woman to marry again during the lifetime of her first husband.[18]

[15a]On this and some of the material which follows, see Thurston, Vol. VI, pp. 1–28.

[16]T. Ayakannu Nayakar, *Vannikula Vilakkam: A Treatise on the Vanniya Caste*, 1891, and *Varuna Darpanam* (Mirror of Castes), 1901.

[17]*Census of India*, 1901, Madras, Part I, Report, p. 171.

[18]W. Francis in *Gazetteer of South Arcot District*. Cited in Thurston, Vol. VI, p. 12.

When these new caste associations turned to politics at the turn of the century, their main target was the census office, for its listing of caste and caste descriptions became more "real" than reality itself, carrying as it did the authority of official imprint. Mr. J. Chartres Moloney, of the Indian Civil Service, having survived the decennial onslaught of petitions from castes who wanted to be reclassified, remarked in the Census of 1911:

> The last few years, and especially the occasion of the present census, have witnessed an extraordinary revival of the caste spirit in certain aspects. For numerous caste *sabhas* have emerged, each keen to assert the dignity of the social group which it represents.[19]

The rising castes continued to persuade their members to give a new name to the census enumerators, and to persuade the census commissioners to list this new name when the old one bore some odium. They also urged the census officers either to revise the description of traditional caste occupations, where these were thought undignified, or to drop them altogether. The Madras Census dropped caste occupations in 1921 as a result of these pressures.[20] The effectiveness of the *Pallis* in influencing the official recorders on the one hand and their own members on the other was considerable. By 1931 the *Pallis* had disappeared altogether from the Census, and only the *Vanniya Kula Kshatryas* remained.

The explicit organization of the *Vanniya Kula Kshatryas* in an association called the *Vanniya Kula Kshatrya Sangham* dates back at least thirty years in some districts, although the 1901 census commissioner indicated that some organizational stirrings were visible then, and the efforts of 1833 indicate even earlier (probably sporadic) activity. The *Vanniya Kula Kshatrya Sangham* of North Arcot District held its 34th annual conference in 1953, and the South Arcot *Sangham* held its tenth in 1954.[21] For the *Vanniya Kula Kshatrya Sangham*, the district unit was initially more important than the larger, Madras-wide organization which developed somewhat later. In 1952, the *Vanniya Kula Kshatryas* published a volume,[22] the introduction of which gave

---

[19]*Census of India*, 1911, Madras, Part I, Report, p. 178.
[20]*Ibid.*, Vol. XIII. This successful agitation reflected the fact that some castes were abandoning the traditional occupations. They presumably felt that from a descriptive point of view this fact deserved recognition. Even where the caste still kept to its traditional tasks, the census description (i.e., "*Shanars*" are oil pressers") carried a normative appplication. From the point of view of mobile castes, the census looked like a new agency for sacred classification, an impression hardly alleviated by the fact that Brahmans, the traditional compilers of sacred classifications, tended to dominate the Indian cadres in the bureaucracy. In a society of flux, the problem of maintaining "objective" official social records becomes particularly difficult.
[21]*Hindu* (Madras), June 18, 1953; *Mail* (Madras), June 21, 1954.
[22]*Graduates and Diploma Holders among the Vanniya Kula Kshatrya*, Triplicane, Madras, 1952.

expression to the *sabha*'s attempt to build a sense of caste patriotism and solidarity which would make it a more effective force:

> The Vanniya Kula Kshatryas who till now were proverbially considered to be backward in education have made long strides in a short space of time and have come almost on a level with other communities ... the community has not realized its deserving status in society. ... A cursory view of the book will show every reader how many a desirable fruit of the community was veiled by the leaves ... (it) will stimulate the younger generation to greater deeds and will fill the hearts of the older with just pride in the achievements of the community. ....[23]

That the *Sangham* still had some work ahead may be inferred from the fact that it listed 298 names, or about .01 percent of the community, as holders of degrees or diplomas.[24]

After the war, when the electorate was expanding but had not yet reached the adult suffrage proportions which came with the 1952 general elections, the *Vanniya Kula Kshatrya Sangham* began to press the Congress Party state ministry with two demands: it wanted the appointments to the civil services (which are based on competitive examinations and merit) to reflect the *Vanniyars'* percentage in the population, and it wanted Congress itself, through party nominations, to assure the election of *Vanniyars* on a population basis to all elected bodies—municipal corporations, district boards, and the state legislature. The request was Jacksonian in its optimism concerning the universal distribution of the capacity to hold office. But it was not altogether unreasonable in view of the constitutional, statutory and administrative provisions both at the central and the state levels, which are designed to give special consideration to scheduled castes (untouchables) and backward classes (usually low castes) in the public services and educational institutions, and the Congress' known disposition to give some special consideration in candidate selection to "depressed" elements in the population. It assumed also that the authority of caste no longer depended on traditional rank but rather on numbers in the context of democratic authority. However, the Congress ministry of Madras did not respond favorably to the *Vanniyar* demand, nor did the nominating bodies of the Congress party. From that time, the *Vanniyars* decided that they could rely only on themselves, dropped the attempt to work through the Congress or any other party, and began to contest for public office as independents.

---

[23]*Graduates and Diploma Holders*, Introduction.

[24]A diploma holder is about the equivalent of an American high school graduate, while a graduate is one who has finished college. It is probably safe to assume that most of those listed were diploma holders rather than graduates.

Their first major electoral efforts were exerted in district board elections in the districts where their greatest strength lay. In fact, the district boards became one of their main targets, not only because they represented a convenient geographic unit within which caste influence could be maximized, but because the subjects falling under the competence of district boards, especially educational and medical facilities and road building, were of the greatest local and political interest. In 1949, the *Vanniyars* did well in the district elections, capturing, for example, 22 of the 52 seats in the South Arcot District Boards, and defeating many Congress Party candidates. They almost succeeded in electing the President of the board.[25]

In 1951, with the prospect of the 1952 elections before them, the *Vanniyars* convened a major conference of the *Vanniya Kula Kshatrya Sangham* on a state-wide basis. The conference resolved that the *Vanniyars* should contest the elections "in cooperation with the toiling masses," and formed a political party called the Tamilnad Toilers' Party. The leading spirits in the conference were men with modern and cosmopolitan qualifications rather than hereditary and traditional ones. Two of the most significant were Mr. W. A. Manikkavelu Naicker, a lawyer with experience in earlier state-wide party activities, notably the Swarajya Party, and Mr. S. S. Ramaswami Padayachi, a young man (33 in 1951), a high school graduate, Chairman of the Cuddalore Municipal Council, member of the South Arcot District Board and the man who was narrowly defeated for its presidency in 1949.[26] The names of Padayachi and Naicker, especially the former, provided an effective signal for caste solidarity in voting. Padayachi's youth is an interesting commentary on leadership patterns in castes coming to political self-consciousness; older members of lower castes generally do not command the necessary skills in communication and education for state-wide organization.

Organizationally, the conference represented a capstone in the expansion of the association, since it mobilized the *Vanniyars* on a state-wide basis. It sought at once to centralize control and to bring about a proliferation of operating sub-units, working toward a more rationalized campaign organization which could mobilize the potential membership. Mr. Padayachi was elected Chairman of the Central Election Committee, established to supervise *Vanniyar* candidate selections throughout the state, and District Election Committees were established for twelve districts.[27]

---

[25]See interview with S. S. Ramaswami Padayachi, a prominent *Vanniyar* leader, in *Mail*, April 27, 1954.
[26]*Mail*, April 13, 1954; *Indian Express* (Madras) April 14, 1954.
[27]*Mail*, October 13, 1951.

Subsequently, the unified state-wide effort represented by the conference broke down when the caste *sabhas* of North and South Arcot districts, which had always rested on local loyalties, failed to agree. The Tamilnad Toilers as a party remained strong in South Arcot and Salem under Mr. Padayachi's guidance, while the North Arcot and Chingleput *Vanniyars* rallied to a second caste party, the Commonweal Party, under Mr. Naicker.

At election time, the caste *sabhas*-cum-parties utilized the older village organization, mobilizing *Vanniyar* village leaders to assure solid caste voting for one or the other party. This mobilization device was effective because it defined the electoral issues in terms meaningful to an unsophisticated electorate: governmental services, especially roads and educational and medical services, could surely be more firmly secured for poor *Vanniyars* if men familiar with their plight (i.e., other *Vanniyars*) were elected to office. Watching Nehru speak to uncomprehending thousands, one might assume that there is an unbridgeable gap between the ordinary Indian voter and his government, but observers watching village election meetings, in which local caste headmen engage in running debate with aspiring or incumbent legislators, cannot come to the same conclusion. Common caste background is not essential to these exchanges but the fact that candidate and village headman often share a common caste culture provides a context in which discourse is natural and easy.

The Commonweal Party, representing the older caste *sabha* of North Arcot and Chingleput, which had no program to speak of (much less an ideology), won six seats in the state legislative assembly, while the Tamilnad Toilers, speaking for the younger South Arcot *sabha* and stressing a more leftist socialist platform, captured 19. This gave the *Vanniyars* 25 of the 190 seats in the legislature of post-1953 Madras, or 13 percent (though they numbered only 10 percent of the population).

In the same 1952 General Elections, the Congress Party failed to win a majority in the Madras state legislature, and in its search for enough legislative support to form a cabinet, persuaded the six Commonweal Party members to support a Congress ministry, but it could not persuade them to join the Congress. In return, Mr. Naicker, the Commonweal leader, was given a seat in the Cabinet, an event which delighted many *Vanniyars* but won him public catcalls from the Tamilnad Toilers, who decided to remain in opposition.[28] Shortly thereafter, the Tamilnad Toilers also opened "negotiations" with Congress, presumably to see what offices might be offered in return for support.[29] The nego-

---

[28]*Indian Express* and *The Hindu*, May 13, 1952.
[29]*Mail*, October 21, 1952.

tiations came to nothing until 1954 when Mr. C. Rajagopalachari, a Brahman statesman with a long and distinguished history in the nationalist movement, resigned as Chief Minister and was replaced by the shrewd and competent but less cosmopolitan and lower caste Kamraj Nadar. He had made his reputation as chief of the Madras Congress Party over more than a decade, and belonged to a large and prosperous peasant caste.[30]

The Tamilnad Toilers decided to support Mr. Kamraj's ministry, and Mr. Padayachi joined the cabinet, consisting of eight persons. Mr. Naicker too remained in the Cabinet, so that the *Vanniyars* could now call two of eight cabinet seats their own. Mr. Padayachi reported to the press that he was happy to see that the Ministry was so much more representative of the backward classes than any previous one. With two ministers in the Cabinet and cordial relations with Congress assured, the Commonweal and the Tamilnad Toiler parties were dissolved, their members joining the Congress.[31]

The procedure followed by the *Vanniyars* is not unusual. In Rajasthan, the (*Rajput*) *Kshatrya Mahasabha* pursued an almost identical tactic in 1952, campaigning successfully for the legislature, extracting not cabinet offices but concessions on land-reform from Congress, and then joining the party, which needed members to strengthen its very precarious majority. The *Jat* caste *sabhas* in Rajasthan very nearly did the same when many members in 1950 considered converting the Rajasthan branch of the *Krishikar Lok* Party into a *Jat* branch. But the *Jats*, with politically literate leaders and a self-conscious and effectively mobilized following, saw the expediency of infiltrating the weak Rajasthan Congress, gave up the idea of a separate party, and contested the elections for the most part under the Congress Party label.

Throughout this period, both before and after the dissolution of the two caste parties, the demands of the *Vanniya Kula Kshatrya Sangham* continued to find active expression. The *Sangham* had three primary objectives. The first was educational services. What was at stake were scholarships which might allow a village student to pay for room at the hostel of a distant secondary institution, fee concessions at institutions which still charged tuition, and reservation of seats for *Vanniyars* in institutions of higher learning. The second objective was

---

[30]The *Nadars* were formerly called *Shanans* and were once oil pressers. See Thurston, *op. cit.*, Vol. VI, pp. 363–378. Their caste *sabha* was influential in getting the old, odious name replaced (in 1921). They persuaded the census authorities to drop traditional caste descriptions, since many had moved out of oil-pressing, which had low status repute, into agricultural, commercial and financial pursuits. Mr. Nadar's strength is based on a combination of long service with the nationalist movement and on the faith which lower castes repose in him as "one of them."

[31]*Mail*, July 30, 1956. The parties were in fact dissolved before 1956. At that time, the election commission merely recognized their dissolution officially.

places in the civil service; these conferred status as well as a job. The third was winning Congress "tickets" (i.e., nominations) for seats in lower governing boards as well as in the legislature and places in the cabinet. The *Sangham* was also interested in various economic services affecting *Vanniyars.* That they could' hope for government help in several respects was clear from the fact that they had been officially classified as a Backward Class, that is, a caste above the Untouchable level but one whose status and condition was nevertheless so weak that it deserved special consideration under the policy of "progressive discrimination" which has been a central feature of Indian social policy.[32]

The way these demands were pursued and the responses of the two ministers to them is apparent from the proceedings of *Sangham* meetings and conferences. Shortly after his appointment in 1954, Mr. Padayachi explained to a *Sangham* conference why he had joined the Kamraj ministry when he had not joined the earlier one of Mr. Rajagopalachari. The *Vanniyars'* demands for educational facilities and representation in the civil services had not been met by the Rajagopalachari ministry, he said, and implied that he expected a more generous attitude from the Kamraj ministry.[33] At a North Arcot conference in 1955, he could report that the government had been doing its best to give school fee concessions, scholarships and employment preference to the *Vanniya Kula Kshatryas.*[34] At that time, 5 out of every 20 seats in the state civil service were reserved for "qualified candidates of the backward classes," in addition to the reservations for scheduled castes and tribes. These reservations were established by administrative order in cooperation with the Public Service Commission. (Unfortunately no figures are available on whether enough "qualified" candidates were found to fill these posts—formal reservation and actual seats filled by members of backward classes have by no means always coincided.)[35] In any case, Mr. Padayachi apparently kept an eye on the situation, and presumably his and Mr. Naicker's views on how this difficult problem might be handled were always available to the government. The frequency with which both men reported to *Vanniyar* meetings indicates that they considered themselves to some extent special agents of *Vanniyar* interests; drawing a line between this role and their role as cabinet members responsible for the formulation and administration of public policy is of course difficult.

---

[32]Progressive discrimination, especially in the services, was already a policy of the old Justice Party governments in pre-Independence Madras.
[33]*Indian Express*, April 28, 1954; *Mail*, May 30, 1954.
[34]*Mail*, January 5, 1955.
[35]See Government of India, *Report of the Backward Classes Commission* (3 Vols.), Delhi, 1955, especially Vol. I, p. 131.

The quality of the *Sangham's* economic demands is illustrated by another North Arcot conference, addressed by Mr. Naicker in 1953. The resolutions present a striking illustration of the fact that the *Vanniya Kula Kshatrya Sangham* operated as an economic interest group—one might expect similar resolutions from western farm groups in the U.S. They urged better irrigation in North Arcot district; electricity for agricultural areas; better roads; expansion of the Krishna Pennar multi-purpose water project; relief to tenants for rain failure; and (recalling the fact that many *Vanniyars* were tenants and laborers) making tillers owners of the soil.[36]

Negotiations with the Congress concerning the number of nominations which would be given to the *Vanniyars* in local board elections became very lively late in 1954, just before the District Board elections. One result of the negotiations concerning seats in North Arcot was the promise, given by the officers of the state Congress Party, that once the District Board was elected, it would choose a *Vanniyar* chairman. This promise came in response to *Vanniyar* pressure to extend to District Boards the principle of "community rotation" in the selection of officers, a principle which has long been recognized in the Madras Municipal Corporation Presidency. In this case, the promise caught the state party in a difficult situation: the non-*Vanniyar* Congress Party members of the North Arcot District Board, many of whom belonged to the higher caste of *Reddiars,* saw no reason why they should be bound at the district level by negotiations carried on by the state party with the *Vanniyars.* They accordingly decided not to vote for a *Vanniyar,* and elected a *Reddiar* president, in cooperation with non-Congress members of the board. The Madras Congress Party, knowing that they might not be able to count on *Vanniyar* support in the general elections in 1957 if they did not keep faith with the *Vanniyars,* took strict disciplinary action and suspended a number of the recalcitrant *Reddiar* members from the party. According to the newspaper report:

> Sri Karayalar (President of the state Congress organization) said that indiscipline in Congress ranks should not be tolerated as it would weaken the organization. . . . In the North Arcot case, Sri Karayalar said, the idea was that the Presidentship this time should go to a member of the Vanniyar community as in South Arcot. All along the Reddiars had been presidents there. The Vanniyar commmunity had supported the Congress in the Board elections and the understanding all along had been that the Congress nominee for the Presidentship should be a member of the Vanniyar community. . . .[37]

---

[36]*Hindu,* June 18, 1953.
[37]*Mail,* November 20, 1954.

Throughout this period, the *Sangham's* organizational structure was being elaborated and expanded. Local branches sprang up in many places, often at the level of smaller administrative units such as *taluks* (districts) and towns. Usually one of the ministers graced the occasion with his presence.[38] At all these sessions, the ministers and others sought to strengthen the *Sangham's* solidarity, to increase the sense of unity and of mission. Mr. Padayachi reminded a conference that his ministership was the result of the united efforts and sacrifices of the community over a long period, and the caste flag was ceremonially unfurled at the 34th annual conference of the *Sangham* at North Arcot.

It is clear that today the *Vanniya Kula Kshatrya Sangham* plays an important role in Madras politics. Village subcastes persist, but their relative role in the new democratic culture is gradually declining. It is the caste associations (*sabhas* or *sanghams*) which have given caste a new vitality, and it is political democracy which has transformed caste and enabled it to play its paradoxical role in India today. Rather than providing the basis for a reaction, caste has absorbed and synthesized some of the new democratic values. Ironically, it is the caste association which links the mass electorate to the new democratic political processes and makes them comprehensible in traditional terms to a population still largely politically illiterate. Caste has been able to play this curious political role as bearer of both India's *ancien régime* and its democratic political revolution by reconstituting itself into the *sabha*, with characteristics of both the natural and the voluntary association, of caste defined in terms of both *dharma* and democracy.

FOR FURTHER READING

PAUL R. BRASS, "Political Participation, Institutionalization, and Stability in India" (*Government and Opposition*, IV, 1, Winter 1969, 23–53)

JOSEPH R. GUSFIELD, "Political Community and Group Interests in Modern India" (*Pacific Affairs*, XXXVIII, 2, Summer 1965, 123–141)

SELIG S. HARRISON, *India: The Most Dangerous Decades* (Princeton: Princeton University Press, 1960)

KUSUM NAIR, *Blossoms in the Dust: The Human Element in Indian Development* (New York: Praeger, 1962)

N. PATNAIK, "Political Change and Economic Stagnation in a Tribal Block in Orissa" (*Behavioral Sciences and Community Development*, III, 1, March 1969, 13–22)

---

[38]Thus, the first conference of the North Madras *Vanniya Kula Kshatrya Sangham*, the conference of the Uttiramerur sub-*taluk Sangham*, the tenth annual meeting of the South Arcot *Sangham*, the second annual conference at Perambur, and a conference at Ayyumpet. See *Hindu*, May 23, 1955; *Mail*, June 21, 1954, and January 10, 1956; *Indian Express*, July 23, 1956.

K. RAGHAVENDRA RAO, "Caste, Secularism and Democracy in India" *(International Journal of Comparative Sociology*, VII, 1–2, March 1966, 197–208)

ARNOLD M. ROSE, "Hindu Values and Indian Social Problems" *(Sociological Quarterly*, VIII, 3, Summer 1967, 329–339)

LLOYD AND SUSANNE RUDOLPH, *The Modernity of Tradition: Political Development in India* (Chicago: University of Chicago Press, 1967)

M. N. SRINIVAS, *Caste in Modern India and Other Essays* (Bombay: Asia Publishing House, 1962)

MYRON WEINER, "India: Two Political Cultures," in Lucian W. Pye and Sidney Verba, eds., *Political Culture and Political Development* (Princeton: Princeton University Press, 1964), pp. 199–244

MYRON WEINER, *Party Building in a New Nation: The Indian National Congress* (Chicago: University of Chicago Press, 1967)

MYRON WEINER, *The Politics of Scarcity: Public Pressure and Political Response in India* (Chicago: University of Chicago Press, 1962)

THAILAND: THE POLITICS OF PASSIVITY

Donald Hindley

Although the Thais have gained political consciousness, their political system is not characterized by widespread political action. The reasons may be ascribed, in part, to the absence of either a colonial|ruler or the major dislocations of war. Traditional elements of the Thai world-view have not been profoundly disrupted, which has produced, Professor Hindley comments, political passivity. Such stability may be challenged by military disunity or social ferment in the neglected Northeast.

. . . One of the most remarkable phenomena of the Thai political system is the political passivity of the overwhelming majority of the people. They have watched royal dynasties rise and fall, foreign invasions roll in and out, and, since 1932, a series of military coups and military dictatorships. But they have not participated in these events as more than spectators or unwilling subjects. They have not demanded a part in either governmental decision-making or the selection of those who decide. In traditional peasant manner they may try to avoid the application of certain policies, or seek to acquire by contacts with persons of authority special treatment within a particular policy. The basic system, however, remains largely unchallenged.

Why is there little or no pressure from the non-elite groups of Thailand's political system for participation in governmental decision-making or in the selection of the rulers? An answer to this question is sought by following two approaches. The first examines to what extent Thailand has experienced those conditions that have impelled significant groups of the world's population into active opposition against an entrenched and resistant regime. The second identifies those characteristics of the Thai world-view and of the major Thai socioeconomic and ethnic groups which discourage political action of an oppositionist nature.

From *Pacific Affairs*, Vol. XLI, No. 3, pp. 355–71, by permission. Condensed by the editor.

Through the first approach, it is hoped to discover why most Thais have stopped short of political action in the politicization process. For present purposes, politicization refers to changing orientation towards the political system, and may be viewed as a rising line with three major stages. The start of the process is political nescience; that is, complete ignorance of or total disbelief in the ability of governmental power to alter one's environment (physical, social, economic, cultural), or one's position within that environment. The second major stage is political consciousness, in which an individual or group holds the belief that political power is an important tool for changing one's environment or one's place within it. The third stage is political action, action performed in the belief that it can effect changes in the environment or one's position within it. Political action may be, in terms of the existing political system, supportive (either status quo or reformist) or destructive.

Most people, including the Thais, have experienced government action that markedly affected or affect their lives, such as government irrigation projects, communication schemes, education, and the visible maintenance of public order; so that today, few are within the realm of complete nescience. The next stage, political consciousness, may be entered without fear of punishment because it entails no alteration in behavior. Many peasants as well as urban poor are aware of the instrumental nature of political power for effecting personal or environmental change; and many are remarkably well informed as to the operation and actors of the political system within which they live. But few believe that their own political action could possibly lead to an improvement in their lot.

How, then, can that belief be instilled? Under certain circumstances it may be gained through government-tolerated or government-fostered extension of political participation from the elite down through the lower strata of society. But in Thailand . . . there have been few honest elections and virtually none in which political competition reached into more than a small number of villages.[1] Even in the one or two less dishonest elections, few opposition candidates sought mass support for three simple reasons: first, it seemed a waste of limited funds and energy to deploy them among a passive and deferential population; second, most of Thailand's several constitutions gave the existing government the right to nominate one-half of parliament; and third, the politics of elite manipulation and intrigue were a well tested road to government office. Therefore, if the masses were wooed at all, it was generally in paternal and patronage terms.

---

[1]The only village-level study of a Thai general election known to the author is Herbert P. Phillips, "The Election Ritual in a Thai Village," *The Journal of Social Sciences*, Vol. 14, No. 4 (1958), pp. 36–50. I know of no study of the election process in the towns.

Since 1957, there have been no national elections in Thailand, and ...the electoral experience before that date was not a vehicle by which the Thai masses were introduced to political action of any kind. The prevailing and normal situation, whether under royal despotism or military dictatorship, has been governmental concern to retain an apolitical population by blocking the legal broadening of political participation. Both political reformists and radicals alike have been severely suppressed; thus there has been no ground where a non-elite Thai could become politically active without meeting the retaliatory might of the state apparatus.

It should not be surprising that the non-elite Thais have remained politically inactive under such circumstances. Political action against an entrenched and energetically self-defensive political regime is new and often inconceivable behavior for the bulk of the world's population. To take such action replaces the comfort and prestige of "I know about politics" with the danger and uncertainty of "I, by my actions, am able to change the system, and I am challenging the authorities." To make and believe this statement requires a major psychological breakthrough. The experience of the present century suggests that four conditions have provided the impulse for propelling significant groups of people into political opposition activities against resistant regimes: colonial rule, defeat in war, insecurity, and frustrated non-political aspirations.

Colonial rule often produces opposition, even mass opposition activities. The reasons for this are well-known and need not be elaborated here. In its direct form, colonial rule destroys or severely damages the indigenous authority and deference structures. It wittingly and unwittingly introduces new concepts, such as democracy, socialism, and Marxism-Leninism. It sets up invidious comparisons: between the wealth of the metropolitan country and the poverty of the colony, between the colonial masters and the native workers. It educates native people into new occupations and stimulates urbanization. And as a result, colonialism may create an alienated native educated class. This, the spearhead of the nationalist movement, is forced to advance the politicization of the masses in order to gain power either in an introduced electoral system or as a weapon to defeat the intransigent metropolitan power. Further, the native political elite is often forced to gain mass support through the inculcation of material and political aspirations that the colonizing country cannot or will not meet.

Thailand has escaped the dislocations of colonial rule. The ability and right of the political elite to govern has never been called into question either by alien overlordship or through educational or informational systems outside the control of the indigenous elite. The elite at no time has been compelled to arouse political and material aspirations among the masses as a weapon against a colonial master. And if "colonialism" has occurred, it has been used to strengthen the government vis-à-vis the people: Western advice, skills, technology and capital have been employed to increase the efficiency of the bureaucracy, national productivity, governmental influence over the formation of popular attitudes and opinions, and the fighting capacity of the armed forces.

Nor has Thailand for two centuries suffered defeat in war, with a concomitant discrediting of the existing authorities. Here are no Czars, no Kuomintang, no Hapsburgs. The Thai monarchs refused to wage war in the nineteenth century; the post-1932 leadership rolled with the Japanese punch and with equal skill avoided Allied retribution. More recent Thai participation in the Korean and Vietnamese Wars has brought rich dividends in Western aid, and the external communist "menace" has provided ample justification for large military expenditures and the repression of "leftists."

Insecurity can consist of an immediate threat to life (as in the case of banditry or starvation) or a threat to livelihood (as with inflation, job scarcity, or land hunger). Whether insecurity is a continuing situation or the result of either a deterioration in conditions or an increased expectation as to the level of security, it tends to raise doubts as to the right of rulers to rule because they are failing to provide a fundamental government service. In Thailand, however, insecurity is at a minimum. There has been no post-independence breakdown in administrative efficiency; currency inflation has been minor except in the years around the Second World War; national production has kept safely ahead of the population increase; and there is a relatively low ratio of men to land-resources, coupled with a relatively equal distribution of land ownership. The police force is fairly efficient, and expanding. And if small-scale banditry is present in many provinces, it always has existed and is being reduced. Further, government exactions and threats, affecting life, money or land, are not of an order to cause widespread insecurity and hostility.

The existence of frustrated non-political aspirations may also place the legitimacy of the political system in doubt. Two questions are important in this context: the nature and magnitude of the aspirations, and the degree to which the aspirations are frustrated. To produce significant political opposition within the environment of an efficient dictatorship, there must be either large numbers with important frustrations, or strategically located smaller groups with major frustrations, such as military officers or minorities. With the partial exception of the Chinese Thais, who will be discussed below, Thailand is fairly homogenous. Of the 1960 population of 30.6 million, for example, 93.6 per cent were Buddhist, while 97 per cent were able to speak Thai.[2] Thailand is a relatively open society in the sense that there are no insuperable barriers of race, religion, caste, region, class or language to prevent any person from climbing the socio-economic ladder. Equally significant are two other factors: first, the expectations of most Thais are not unrealistic; second, economic development is rapid enough to prevent the emergence of significant frustrations among most of the population. The Thai masses have not been subject to many influences that would produce unrealistic aspirations: they have not undergone anti-colonial nationalist agitation; the content and teachers of the education system are government-controlled; political competition below the elite level is stifled; agitational organizers are hunted down; and all mass media necessarily tread a circumspect line. And while aspirations cannot be held wholly in check as literacy and communications improve and the cities grow, the government's successful concern with educational and economic expansion permits at least minimal aspirations to be largely met, or presents the possibility that they can be.[3] In other words, a large part of the Thai population now has non-political aspirations, but is discouraged from oppositional political means for their fulfilment not only by Thai political experience but also by the relative modesty of expectations and the buoyancy of the economy.[4]

The Thai people have not undergone those experiences, traumatic or otherwise, that have produced widespread political action and opposition action in other countries. Moreover, in Thai culture and in the major Thai socio-economic and ethnic groupings, additional factors are found which help explain the lack of significant opposition to the dictatorship.

While it is clearly hazardous to generalize about an entire people's life-view, including attitudes to authority, the relative homogeneity of the Thai people makes such broad statements more applicable to a larger proportion of Thais than would be the case in more heterogeneous

---

[2]*Statistical Yearbook Thailand, Number 26, 1965* (Bangkok: National Statistical Office, 1966), p. 60. For an anthropologist's estimate that in fact 71 per cent of Thailand's population consists of minorities and tribals, see Peter Kunstadter (ed.): *Southeast Asian Tribes, Minorities, and Nations* (Princeton: Princeton University Press, 1967), Vol. I, p. 4.

[3]With a population growth of 3.2 per cent per annum, the GNP has risen over 7.0 per cent annually in recent years. Another indicator of widening opportunities is that in 1947, 53.7 per cent of the population over 10 years old was literate, in 1960, 70.8 per cent. The author is aware that these gross figures ignore important questions as to the distribution of the results of increased productivity, and the relationship of increased literacy and schooling to socio-economic mobility.

[4]For a politically perceptive survey of the Thai economy, see Robert J. Muscat: *Development Strategy in Thailand: A Study of Economic Growth* (New York: Praeger, 1966).

societies.[5] Three basic components of the Thai life-view have direct significance for political behavior. The first is a deference for and acceptance of authority, whether it be in the family, the school, the work situation, or the Buddhist church. At the apex of the authority-deference system stands the monarch, in whose name the government is careful to act. The second is an unquestioning acceptance of existing rules of conduct. This acceptance is related to the view of authority, and is instilled in most socialization experiences. Obviously many Thais attempt to circumvent or avoid rules, but outside the political elite very few could believe they had any right to alter them. The third is a belief that an individual's position in life is the result of good deeds (in the present or a past incarnation) and good luck. There is an expectation that those who achieve a "position" should reap its rewards, and there is little envy of the more fortunately placed.

These elements of the Thai life-view are traditional. Nothing has shaken the Thais enough for many to question them. Society and politics have been modernized to a degree, but without a profound disruption of the pre-existing value and deferential systems. Such conservatism is a normal human characteristic and is not unknown even among large pockets in the so-called modernized states.

Beneath the overarching Thai culture are several groups which, from the experience of other non-Western countries, might be expected to spawn an active opposition to the military dictatorship: the peasants, the urban working class, the urban middle class, the Buddhist clergy, the royalists, the students, and the armed forces. A closer examination of each concludes this exploration of the reasons why such an opposition has not materialized in Thailand.

In 1960, about 82 per cent of the economically active part of the Thai population were engaged in agriculture, forestry, hunting and fishing, of which the first took all but a few thousand. Their lot is by no means affluent, but few suffer bitter exploitation of landlords or money-lenders,[6]

---

[5]For a groundbreaking exploration of Thai personality, including attitudes towards authority, see Herbert P. Phillips: *Thai Peasant Personality: The Patterning of Interpersonal Behavior in the Village of Bang Chan* (Berkeley and Los Angeles: University of California Press, 1965). Extremely perceptive is Steven Piker, "The Relationship of Belief Systems to Behavior in Rural Thai Society," *Asian Survey*, viii (1968), 384–99. A classic study, written from secondary sources in 1943 and much debated, is Ruth Benedict: *Thai Culture and Behavior* (Ithaca: Cornell University Southeast Asia Program Data Paper, 1952).

[6]Of 3,214,405 landholdings in the year 1962-63, 2,632,960 were owner-operated, 130,968 were rented for cash or a share of the crops, and 450,477 came under other forms of land tenure; *Statistical Yearbook . . ., op. cit.*, p. 168. Several studies of peasant indebtedness show it to be insignificant except in some areas of the Central Plain, especially in the part close to Bangkok. In addition, the Thai ruling class attempts to focus any peasant resentment onto the middlemen, who are of Chinese extraction. There is a rapidly increasing body of published research on the Thai rural population. For a recent bibliography which includes this material, see Jacques Amyot and Suthep Soontornpasuch: *Provisional Paper on Changing Patterns of Social Structure in Thailand, 1851–1965; An Annotated Bibliography With Comments* (Delhi: UNESCO Research Centre, 1965). It is to be hoped that this excellent work will soon be made available to a wider public.

and the large majority face either an unchanged or an improving standard of living. The extension of communications, education and urbanization have opened non-farming opportunities for the more ambitious or intelligent young peasants. What is most notable about the peasantry in general, however, is how little its way of life has changed over the past century. Western clothes, watches, outboard motors, transistor radios, hair-styles and so on have been adopted, but the crops are the same and methods of cultivation change slowly. Taxes are mostly indirect, and if government assistance is rare, it is also as yet not widely expected to be considerable. Should floods or drought occur, the government descends with bounty, preferably in the shape of visits by the royal family. In general, then, peasant life, including inter-personal and intra-village relations, continues with only slight modification, each individual seeks his own salvation by merit-making, as was the custom of his ancestors; and the government remains a distant and awesome phenomenon, the source of paternal largesse and public order rather than a hated exploiter.

The urban working class is small in size and rent by major cleavages. Prior to the end of the Second World War, most workers were Chinese immigrants or the children of immigrants. They worked hard, saved, and aspired to open their own businesses. Most succeeded. Since about 1947 an increasing number of rural Thais have migrated to the cities, but unionization and politicization have been hampered by a number of factors. There is regional exclusiveness separating, for example, workers born in Bangkok-Thonburi from the Northeastern migrants. Many rural migrants view their stay in the towns as only temporary while they save to buy land or other commodities for use in their native villages. Most of the ethnic Thai working class are recent arrivals from the countryside. Wages in urban areas are far better, despite higher living costs, than in the villages. And the rural areas provide a large reservoir of potential urban labor. All of these.factors meant that the Thai government in the late 1940's could easily neutralize the few militant trade unions, and today the government experiences not the slightest trouble in controlling those minor labor organizations that exist.[7]

The urban middle class is probably unique in nature. In 1963, there were 3.9 million people living in Thailand's municipalities; the only large towns were Bangkok-Thonburi (2.1 millions), Chiengmai (73,000), and Korat (52,000). And yet there are approximately 3.5 million persons of Chinese or part-Chinese descent in Thailand, the great majority of them urban. Almost all the commercial middle class is of Chinese or part-Chinese origin, as well as a large but undefinable part of the bureaucracy, the students and the intelligentsia. An examination of Thai middle-class

---

[7]An out-of-date but interesting article on Thai trade unions is Ernest L. Fogg: "Labor Organization in Thailand," *Industrial and Labor Relations Review,* Vol. 6, No. 3 (April 1953), pp. 368–77.

political behavior therefore requires consideration of first the ethnic Thais, and then the biologically Chinese and part-Chinese. The ethnic Thais are found mostly in the bureaucracy, broadly defined to include the civil service, the teaching profession and the armed forces. As such they live within the Thai cultural world and the hierarchical-deferential patterning of life traditional to Thailand. Moreover, most enjoy a comfortable existence: salaries that permit a house and one or more servants, access to Western amenities and forms of entertainment, security of position, pensions at age 60, access for their children to the better educational institutions, and steady promotion that depends on obedience and deference to superiors. This is not the environment that produces revolutionaries, especially when obedience, nepotism or personal contacts may bring a trip abroad with resultant increased earnings and an automobile.

Those who are wholly or partly of Chinese descent are mainly in commerce, but as a result of easy assimilation and intermarriage with Thais they are to be found in all middle-class positions and even within the elite.[8] In several countries of Southeast Asia the ethnic Chinese constitute a constant source of opposition activists. Although most of the shadowy and diminutive Thai Communist Party is reportedly Chinese, and although the present government regularly unearths alleged communists of Chinese extraction, the overwhelming majority of Chinese Thais remain as politically inactive as the ethnic Thais. There are several special reasons for this inaction. First, the ethnic Chinese comprise only about 10 per cent of the total Thai population, a fact which makes specifically Chinese political action especially hazardous. Second, the Chinese are rapidly integrated into the larger Thai society. As Chinese immigrants arrived, they were faced with a Thai aristocracy and Thai political power. Social and economic advancements were safeguarded and accelerated by assimilation into the indigenous culture, which the Thai government did not oppose—a situation far different than that met by Chinese immigrants in Malaya or the Netherlands Indies. Furthermore, assimilation is relatively easy: Thais and Chinese alike are Buddhist, come from the same racial stock, speak tonal languages, and are attracted to similar elements of Western culture. A Chinese could and can adopt a

---

[8]To give just two examples: the Chakkri dynasty [1782–1932—ed.] contains a considerable element of Chinese blood, while many of the post-1932 military leaders, including Pibun and Prapat, are part-Chinese in ancestry or have married Chinese or part-Chinese wives. For major studies of the Chinese in Thailand, see Richard Coughlin: *Double Identity: The Chinese in Modern Thailand* (Hong Kong: Hong Kong University Press, 1960) and two books by George William Skinner: *Chinese Society in Thailand: An Analytical History* (Ithaca: Cornell University Press, 1957), and *Leadership and Power in the Chinese Community of Thailand* (Ithaca: Cornell University Press, 1958).

Thai name, learn the Thai language, follow Thai customs, and *be* Thai; or at least his children could and can be.

A third factor discouraging political action is the nature of Chinese material interests. The Chinese are predominantly traders, craftsmen and manufacturers, dependent upon a capitalist environment and freedom from government discrimination. In Thailand they have met a political elite that gladly offers political protection and bureaucratic partiality in return for participation in the profits of their industriousness. With the combination of well-remunerated governmental permissiveness and the expanding economy, today's Chinese youths in Thailand continue to find adequate outlets for their socio-economic ambitions. A fourth factor is that since before the Second World War the Chinese have been cut off from further immigration and are at the same time subject to government-controlled education and mass media. Lastly, the ethnic Chinese are afraid to act politically for fear of forceful retaliation. China and Communism are synonymous in government propaganda. Any ethnic Chinese who acts in opposition to the regime is subject to summary arrest, imprisonment, deportation or execution as "alien," "traitor" and "communist." Therefore, given the generally favorable condition of their existence in Thailand, Thais of Chinese descent forego political action unless it be of a purely supportive kind.

The Buddhist clergy remains apolitical. A clear and uncrossed line is drawn between the religious and secular aspects of life. Monks are used in many kinds of state functions, down to the inauguration of a new train service or a new building; a small number are currently being trained as missionaries for the Northeast and the northern hill tribes. Always the initiative is the state's which, through the person of the king, controls or supervises the selection of the highest echelon of the church hierarchy. The church is also subsidized by the state.

The supporters of the absolute monarchy understandably were unhappy with the 1932 revolution. The revolution, however, not only retained the monarchy and social deference towards the royal family; it left intact the wealth of the royal aristocracy, and with it the aristocracy's privileged access to the best education and to greater wealth through investment and the rising price of urban real estate. Also, as has been mentioned, the ouster of Field-Marshal Pibun in 1957 ushered in a new era in the symbiotic relationship between the monarchy and the military leaders. In short, the royalists have little to complain about, and a great deal to risk by opposition politics.

University students numbered 46,000 in 1964, but they have rarely taken political action, and none at all since the relatively mild protests over the rigged elections of February 1957. A basic explanation of the situation is to be found in the students' expectations of university education, and in the nature of the education they receive. University is a place to obtain a diploma and to make friends, both of which are expected to lead to civil service positions and steady promotion. Learning is by memorization; there is no expectation or stimulation of debate, enquiry, or discussion. Serious reading is at a minimum among both students and teachers, and any "agitational" literature is in English, a language few can read with even poor facility. In short, university inculcates a bureaucratic mentality and does not liberate the mind from old concepts and values. Furthermore, many students are of Chinese or part-Chinese ancestry, with the implications discussed above. And finally, to be fair to the more intelligent and perceptive students, they have sufficient political awareness to know important facts of Thai political life: that the secret police is omnipresent, that debate of the ongoing political system or its leaders brings severe punishment, that the great passive masses are no basis for genuine democracy or for overthrowing the military, that Thailand is materially in far better condition than other democratic or non-democratic countries of Asia, and that outward deference and obedience are rewarded by a secure middle-class existence. In these circumstances, the students cannot be blamed for leaving political agitation to their fellows in other states.

Lastly, it remains to consider the armed forces as possible sources of opposition to the political system. But this kind of opposition can hardly be expected to appear: the system is controlled by the military, the officer corps is a privileged club, the system brings social harmony and economic progress, there is no visible popular dissatisfaction with the system, and the communists are believed poised to exploit any signs of internal dissension. One may expect coups within the system, but Thailand in the foreseeable future is not likely to produce a Perón, an Arbenz, or a Supardjo.

Any discussion of the strength and stability of the Thai political system requires consideration of two final factors: the Northeast, and possible future situations that could significantly affect the present structure of power.

This is no place for a detailed study of the Northeast,[9] but some of the more important political considerations may be pointed out. One is that the Northeast has been a problem for many years. From 1932 until

---

[9]For an introduction to the Northeast, see the six brief articles in: "Symposium on Northeast Thailand," *Asian Survey*, Vol. 6, No. 7 (July 1966), pp. 349–80. The references quoted in these essays will lead the interested reader to more detailed studies of the subject. Another source of particular value is Charles F. Keyes, "Peasant and Nation: The Integration of a Thai-Lao Village into the Thai National System. (Cornell University: unpublished Ph.D. Thesis, 1966). It must be noted that very little is available to the non-governmental scholar pertaining to the political condition of the Northeast.

the Sarit coup of 1957, elected members of parliament from the region constituted the only persistent and self-styled socialist opposition to the several military governments; a separatist element was seemingly present by the early 1950's. Several of these courageous or foolhardy politicians were executed during the second Pibun regime (1948-1957); a few more were killed by Sarit. As far as is known to the author, no study has been made, or made public, of the extent and nature of popular support for these politicians, of the extent and level of political consciousness among the Northeasterners in general,[10] or of the connection between the earlier opposition and the communist rebellion that slowly gained momentum after 1961. There is no doubt that the communists have made the 10 million inhabitants of the region a target of subversion, and today there are armed rebels scattered through several Northeastern provinces.[11] But until we know the magnitude and basis of the support received by the former non-communist politicians, it is impossible to judge to what extent the long-standing causes of political dissatisfaction can be tapped by the present communist cadres.

Several communist recruitment themes have moved some people mightily in various parts of Asia: nationalism, the eradication of feudal exploitation, equality or autonomy for oppressed ethnic minorities, the elimination of government banditry, peace. According to the information available to the author, none of these themes is likely to move large numbers of Thai Northeasterners to political opposition of an active nature. The communists are evidently attempting to portray the Thai government as the lackey of American imperialism, but whether this can succeed depends on the answer to several questions; for example, to what extent are the Northeasterners nationalists, parochials, secessionists, or regionalists? How deep is their loyalty to the king? Do they view the American presence as alien benevolence, foreign occupation, a source of well-paid employment, or what? Throughout almost the entire Northeast, peasant indebtedness is minimal and landlords unknown. If the Northeasterners consider them-

---

[10]An indication of an unusually high level of political consciousness in the Northeast is to be found in Robert J. Textor: *From Peasant to Pedicab Driver: A Social Study of Northeastern Thai Farmers Who Periodically Migrated to Bangkok and Became Pedicab Drivers* (New Haven: Yale University Southeast Asian Studies, 1961), pp. 43-4. Textor noted that the Northeastern temporary migrants seemed "considerably more interested in politics and government-administration affairs" than people from other regions. "The main reason for this is doubtless the extreme poverty of the Northeast and a feeling that only the political-and-administrative mechanism is powerful enough to bring economic improvement."

[11]Estimates of guerrilla forces differ widely. One source states that there are 600 to 1,000 hard-core "terrorists" *(The Economist,* 1 April 1967, p. 25). Another states that there are 3,000 to 5,000 active members of the communist underground organizations in the Northeast, including at least 1,000 armed guerrillas (Harald Munthe-Kaas, "Far From Bangkok," *Far Eastern Economic Review,* 19 May 1966, p. 326). Deputy Defense Minister Air Chief Marshal Dawee Chulasap has opted for the figure of somewhat fewer than 5,000 "terrorists" in the Northeast, divided into five groups of less than 1,000 men each *(Bangkok World,* 17 November 1966).

selves Thais, they cannot believe they are an oppressed ethnic minority, though they can feel strongly that theirs is a neglected region. Far from there being extensive government brutality, very little government presence is felt below the district level in many rural areas of the region. And rebellion disturbs existing order.

There is, however, a long history of government neglect of the Northeast, a pressing land-hunger in several provinces, a lower average standard of living than in the Central Plain, due in part to the poorer natural resources, and an unequal distribution of the available wealth, in addition to a higher level of political consciousness than is usual elsewhere in Thailand. Most of these conditions are traditional, in the sense that they have existed from time immemorial, and even combined they do not appear the sort of factors that produce instant and widespread oppositional political action at the first whisper of communist propaganda. Time may be on the side of the communists, especially in view of the long and porous boundary with Laos and Cambodia, but this is by no means certain. The government, partly at the prodding of foreign advisers, is cognizant of "the Northeast problem" and is moving to do something about it. The idea of the king as the national symbol is being constantly stressed through powerful new radio transmitters, newspapers and the expanding education system; the communists are labelled as foreigners or as traitors working as the agents of foreign enemies against Thailand and the Thai nation.[12] Local officials, village heads and youths are brought to Bangkok for special training or for sight-seeing trips as rewards for loyalty. A rural development program is accelerating the provision of all-weather roads, schools, health centers, water supplies, new and improved crops, and technological advice. Even Buddhist monks are being trained in Bangkok for missionary work in the Northeast. And the instruments of repression and protection are being hastily refined and expanded in the form of special border police, helicopters, new airfields, more police stations, and troops trained in counter-insurgency operations. Whether or not the government's efforts will avert the communist revolution depends upon many variables and cannot be determined with any certainty. What is certain is that the politically conscious inhabitants of Bangkok do not view the situation with alarm. Maybe they are latter-day Diems, but there is insufficient evidence as yet to condemn them as such.

Mildly benevolent despotism has survived in Thailand for at least 150 years. It need not, of course, last forever, and a number of future situations could arise to shake the foundations of the system.

---

[12]See, for example, the April 1967 statement of Thailand's strongman, General Prapat, that most of the communist "terrorists" arrested recently were foreigners sent from without, including Laotians, Viet Minh and Chinese nationals (*Bangkok Post*, 6 April 1967).

The first could be a greatly intensified communist drive, based on the Northeast. This would probably have to come from Chinese or Vietnamese initiative because the indigenous communists are seemingly as weak as the Pathet Lao in native resources and energy. And the desire of the Chinese or Vietnamese to push a major rebellion in Thailand depends upon so many factors, ranging from domestic Chinese and Vietnamese developments to the course of the Vietnamese war, that prediction is impossible.

A second could be a slackening of economic development, always remembering the high birthrate, or imbalances in that development. As long as internal stability is maintained, and barring a world depression, the prospects are bright for continued rapid economic growth, given Thailand's resources, the abundance of foreign aid, and government policies. But two major imbalances are possible. One is the concentration of development in the Bangkok area, which could produce resentment in the provinces and declining per capita availability of basic foodstuffs. The second stems from the government's announced intention greatly to expand higher education, including a doubling of the number of university students over the next few years. Graduates are already experiencing some difficulty in obtaining positions they deem commensurate with their diplomas. A doubling of the number of graduates could produce considerable dissatisfaction among the enlarged student population, with intensifying and spreading effects seen in other countries.

A third possible threat to the present system could arise from the introduction of an electoral democracy. There is not much likelihood of this occurring. A government-appointed constituent assembly has been meeting for more than six years to prepare a replacement for the constitution discarded in 1958. Whenever the assembly completes whatever it is writing, there is no expectation that genuine political competition will be tolerated. Perhaps civilians will be permitted controlled competition among circumscribed sectors of the population. No one expects the replacement of the military as the arbiters of Thai politics.

The chances, then, are that none of these possibilities will occur, although if one or more of them did, it could then lead to policy disputes and ideological conflict within the armed forces. The most that can be foreseen is a temporary shattering of army unity as one group of officers seeks the support of civilians or other armed forces in order to defeat a competing army faction. But after a period of coalition, the overwhelming might of the purged and re-united army would probably ensure a return to the present unequal triumvirate system that combines the army leadership, the Monarchy, and civilians of useful expertise. Only a major catastrophe, in civil or foreign war or economic chaos, could create within the army a significant element that desired a different system.

The near future is unlikely to bring any major change in the Thai political system, always excluding the little-known potential of the Northeast. Probably there will be some form of controlled parliament in which especially the middle class is granted increased expression of interests, a larger number of civilians are coopted into the spoils system, and the age-long political passivity of the masses is left as little disturbed as possible. In short, the basic pattern will persist with expedient and slight modification.

The politically conscious middle class, the usual motor of political action in other states, just does not believe in democracy. It views the lower orders from an elevated, educated and urban position as people who are fundamentally passive and incapable of making sound choices on such serious matters as national policies and national leadership. In this respect the middle class has no ideological conflict with benevolent dictatorship; what it wants is a part in the dictatorship, or to use the electoral system as a spring-board for its own form of elite control. But the middle class is also aware of the power of the mailed fist. While it grumbles privately about corruption and military domination, it is at the same time cognizant of the rewards of obedience, is trained to obey, and sees any dream of civilian rule shattered on the believed passivity of the masses. To borrow from a traditional Thai saying, the middle class prefers the tiger it knows to the crocodile it does not. In short, and in refutation of William Ralphe Inge, the Thai army has learned not only how to build a throne of bayonets, but also how to sit on it.

FOR FURTHER READING

PETER F. BELL, "Thailand's Northeast: Regional Underdevelopment, 'Insurgency,' and Official Response" *(Pacific Affairs*, XLII, 1, Spring 1969, 47–54)

HANS-DIETER EVERS, "The Formation of a Social Class Structure: Urbanization, Bureaucratization, and Social Mobility in Thailand" *(American Sociological Review*, XXXI, 4, August 1966, 480–488)

INTERNATIONAL BANK FOR RECONSTRUCTION AND DEVELOPMENT, *A Public Development Program for Thailand* (Baltimore: Johns Hopkins Press, 1959)

STEVEN PIKER, "Sources of Stability and Instability in Rural Thai Society" *(Journal of Asian Studies*, XXVII, 4, August 1968, 777–790)

FRED W. RIGGS, *Thailand: The Modernization of a Bureaucratic Polity* (Honolulu: East-West Center Press, 1966)

WALTER F. VELLA, *The Impact of the West on Government in Thailand* (Berkeley and Los Angeles: University of California Press, 1955)

DAVID A. WILSON, *Politics in Thailand* (Ithaca: Cornell University Press, 1962)

STEPHEN B. YOUNG, "The Northeastern Thai Village: A Non-Participatory Democracy" *(Asian Survey*, VIII, 11, November 1968, 873–886)

3

MODELS AND MEASURES OF
MODERNIZATION

Are there distinctive stages or patterns of modernization? Thus far, three models of societies have been suggested: a "traditional" society, usually small scale in its setting and constricting its members' views; a "transitional" society, torn from the bondage of time-honored ways by forces of change; and a "modern" society, moving confidently toward a future expected to be different and better. Political modernization is linked with social change. Our analysis has suggested three significant aspects of political modernization: increased centralization of power in the state; increased differentiation and specialization of political institutions; and greater political participation and popular identification with the state. This section seeks historical parallels to the shifts now occurring in the modernizing states and more precise measures of these shifts.

Scholars have yet to agree on the stages of political modernization. C. E. Black, noted historian of Russia, distinguishes seven patterns.[1] He

---

[1]C. E. Black, *The Dynamics of Modernization: A Study in Comparative History* (New York: Harper & Row, 1966).

classifies 175 states in accordance with five variables: (1) the timing of the transfer of political power from traditional to modernizing leaders; (2) the external or internal source of the modernizing challenge; (3) the relative stability of territory and population during change; (4) the presence or absence of colonial rule; and (5) the presence or absence of institutions that can be adapted to meet new challenges. In *The Stages of Political Development*, A. F. K. Organski offers a sequence of modernization. He suggests four stages in the march "toward industrial efficiency and national political organization":[2] (1) primitive unification, devoted to the development of links among peoples with relatively few ties; (2) industrialization, subdivided into bourgeois, Stalinist, and "syncratic" patterns; (3) national welfare, marked by prime concern for the economic and social welfare of ordinary citizens; and (4) abundance, a stage that may bring an end to the nation-state.

The first three readings in this section analyze three widely separated states—Japan, Turkey, and Uganda—with typical problems of political modernization. As Professor Ward suggests, Japan embarked on rapid change with a homogeneous, geographically concentrated population. Turkey, by contrast, had to be reduced to its Anatolian heartland before Kemal Atatürk could undertake his brilliant efforts at modernization. When Uganda achieved independence from British administration, the Kingdom of Buganda was a greater focus for "national" unity than the surrounding state. Only a brief civil war in 1966 and the flight of the Kabaka (the traditional ruler of the kingdom) enabled the government to achieve greater centralization.

Measurement of political change—or, more precisely, the effort to define quantifiable variables—has encountered many obstacles. Basic demographic data, such as census statistics, often are lacking. Public opinion polls remain in their infancy. Most significant, the absence of a widely accepted empirical foundation for the assessment of political modernization complicates the tasks of the measurement-minded social scientist. One of the earliest and most brilliant efforts at empirical analysis, Karl Deutsch's "Social Mobilization and Political Development," concludes this section. Deutsch lists seven variables that indicate how individuals break away from long-standing social, economic, and psychological commitments. This social mobilization includes the erosion of traditional sources of authority, which may be followed by the inculcation of loyalty to the national political system. In states that have different ethnic and linguistic groups, social mobilization may increase fragmentation. Conflicting na-

---

[2]A. F. K. Organski, *The Stages of Political Development* (New York: Knopf, 1965), p. 4.

tionalisms thus spring up with social change, complicating the problems of integration and institution building, to which Sections 4 and 5 are devoted.

POLITICAL MODERNIZATION
AND POLITICAL CULTURE
IN JAPAN

Robert E. Ward

As the outstanding example of speedy modernization outside the Western world, Japan merits close attention. Professor Ward notes that Japan benefited from a long period of preparation for change before 1868, the date usually given for the start of the revolution of modernization in that country. The manipulation of tradition, a homogeneous population, and an enlightened authoritarian government help account for the rapid pace of alteration.

I

The concept of "political modernization" assumes and is intelligible only in terms of the existence of a "modern" society as the essential environment for a modern political system. A modern society is here viewed as a massive and new type of social development which has come upon the scene in mature form only in the course of the last century. It is characterized by its far-reaching ability to control or influence the physical and social circumstances of its environment, and by a value system which is fundamentally optimistic about the desirability and consequences of this ability. More specifically, in its non-political sectors it is also characterized by low birth, death, and morbidity rates and by high ratios, degrees, or levels of: (1) inanimate to animate sources of energy; (2) tool technology, mechanization, and industrialization; (3) specialization and professionalization of labor: (4) gross and per capita national product of goods and services; (5) urbanization; (6) differentiation, achievement orientation, and mobility in social organization; and (7) literacy, mass education, and mass media circulation.

No society, of course, possesses all of these qualities in a complete

From *World Politics*, Vol. XV, No. 4 (1963), pp. 569–596, by permission. Text and footnotes abridged by the editor.

or polar sense. Even the most "modern" society contains substantial admixtures of what might be described as pre-modern or traditional elements and is, in this sense, mixed or dualistic in character. Despite the measure of commonality which this fact ensures to all societies, there obviously exist profound differences in the proportion and pattern in which modern and pre-modern elements are distributed or "mixed" in various societies. In some cases, the "mix" is such as to yield almost purely traditional types such as Yemen or Afghanistan; in others, it produces something as innovational, as "modern" as the United States or the USSR. In this sense judgments of modernity are more concerned with the central tendency or thrust of societies than with any undiluted conception of uniformly modern or traditional social characteristics.

A "modern" polity is a subsystem of a "modern" society. As such it has separable characteristics, the most important of which are a high degree of both functional differentiation and integration of political structure and political roles; a rational, secular, and scientific system of political decision-making; and the volume, range, authority, and efficacy of its output of political decisions and administrative actions. More specifically, it is also characterized by: (1) a reasonably general and effective sense of popular identification with the history, territory, myths, and national identity of the state concerned; (2) widespread popular interest and involvement in the political system, though not necessarily in the decision-making aspects thereof; (3) an allocation of political roles in accordance with standards of achievement rather than ascription; and (4) judicial and regulatory techniques based upon a predominantly secular and impersonal system of law. . . .

II

As one looks back upon the history of political modernization in Japan, one might well be impressed first by the neatness of the manner in which it is usually periodized. In gross terms, for example, one is accustomed to distinguishing periods called Tokugawa (1603-1868) and post-Restoration (1868-) in Japanese political history. For somewhat more specific purposes, many distinguish an overlapping Restoration Period (ca. 1850-1890) when considering the beginnings of modern Japanese political development. Over the years these convenient denominators for the categorization of historical data have assumed an authority and potential for distortion which were never intended.

The series of events attendant upon the so-called Restoration in 1868 of the Emperor Meiji to the position of temporal authority putatively enjoyed by his distant forebears undoubtedly constitutes the major single turning point in the political modernization of Japan. It marked the initial and critical success of the political forces which underlay and made possible the specific modernizing developments that followed. Despite this, the extent to which this year, or even the Restoration Period as a whole, marked a time of new beginnings in an across-the-board political and social sense has, until very recently, been seriously exaggerated by both Japanese and foreign scholarship. . . .

As a consequence, the real beginnings of modernization in Japan have frequently been overlooked or attributed to much later periods than was actually the case.

The degree of literacy and of formal institutionalized education in pre-Restoration Japan provides a case in point. The educational preparation of at least sizable segments of a population is a basic factor in both the general and the political modernization process. Until recently it has been widely assumed that any really critical advances in this sphere waited upon the introduction of compulsory mass education in the 1870's. In fact, this was far from true. Consider, for example, the following statement by Professor R. P. Dore in this connection:

> The first thing to be stressed [with respect to education during the Tokugawa Period] is not simply the kind, but the sheer *amount* of formal education that went on. If the Tokugawa Period was a time of stagnation in some respects and of cyclical fluctuation in others, at least in the field of education there was a steady trend of growth. In Ieyasu's* time a samurai who could express himself cogently on paper was a rarity, and total illiteracy was common. But gradually peace "civilized." Saikaku, by the end of the seventeenth century, already speaks of an illiterate samurai as sadly behind the times, and by the middle of the nineteenth century the situation was vastly different. Nearly every fief had its fief-endowed school and there were hundreds of private schools for samurai. Not only was every samurai capable of reading and writing his own language; most of them had undergone a sufficiently prolonged and disciplined intellectual training to be able to read some Chinese as well.
>
> If public provision for formal education was limited to the samurai class, the lower orders were already managing to provide very well for themselves. In the towns a good proportion of the population could read and write Japanese. Parents bought such education for their children, voluntarily and with hard cash, from teachers who derived their total income from fees. In country districts paternally disposed richer villagers did a great deal to supplement the operations of an otherwise private enterprise system. At a very rough estimate it would seem that by the time of the Restoration forty to fifty per cent of all Japanese boys, and perhaps fifteen per cent of girls, were getting some formal schooling outside their homes.

---

*[Tokugawa Ieyasu was appointed shogun in 1603, died in 1616.—Ed.]

This suggests a spread of literacy greater than in most modern under-developed countries, and greater than in any European country at a comparable stage of economic development, with the possible exceptions of Prussia and Holland. It even compares favorably with some mid-nineteenth century European countries. As late as 1837 a British Select Committee found that in the major industrial towns only one child in four or five was ever getting to school, and it may have been more than a desire to jolt his fellow-countrymen which prompted one Frenchman to write in 1877 that "primary education in Japan has achieved a level which should make us blush.... There is no village without its school, hardly a person who cannot read."[1]

Dore concludes that, despite the Confucian orientation of most of this pre-Restoration education, "the attitudes to popular education, the sense of the contingency of social institutions on the human will, the training in abstract analysis and the application of evaluating principles to policy, the development of a respect for merit rather than status, the stimulation of personal ambition and the strengthening of a collectivist ideology ..."[2] represented important contributions to the modernizing process in Japan, and that all of these had undergone very considerable development long before the Restoration.

In a more specifically political sense, the same could be said of the origins and development of another major element in the modernizing process—the emergence of a professionally trained, rationally structured, and achievement oriented bureaucracy....

In the light of insights such as these into what was actually taking place throughout the Tokugawa Period in Japan, one begins to appreciate the long, gradual process of institutional and attitudinal preparation for modernization which was well under way at least a century before the Restoration. Comparable "preparations" may readily be identified at the village level or in the economic sphere;[3] there is nothing unduly selective about these examples. Japanese society during the Tokugawa Period may still be appropriately described by such terms as "centralized or nationalized feudalism" but, if so, it was feudalism with an important difference. Japan had come a long way from the hierarchic, personal, loyalty-focused relationships and the intricate structure of fiefs and practically enserfed villagers which had characterized the polity in the sixteenth and early seventeenth centuries. On balance the "feudal" attributes of the society perhaps still predom-

---

[1]Ronald P. Dore, "The Legacy of Tokugawa Education" (unpublished paper prepared for the first seminar of the Conference on Modern Japan, January 1962), 1–2.
    [2]Dore, 2.
    [3]See, e.g., Thomas C. Smith, *The Agrarian Foundations of Modern Japan* (Stanford, 1959).

inated. But mingled with and gradually subverting these were a number of the most salient and potent elements of "modern" society.

When evaluating the modernization of Japan, it is useful to keep in mind this long, complex history of covert preparation from which the society benefited. This still stands as a unique accomplishment in Asia, but its main roots are buried at least two hundred years deep in the country's social and political history. The florescence of national leadership during the early Meiji Period, combined with the international circumstances and opportunities of the times, had a great deal to do with the amazing speed at which Japan modernized, but in a more fundamental sense Japanese society seems to have been prepared for the experience to a degree still unmatched in some important respects among many contemporary Asian societies. In this context the Japanese preparations for more modern forms of social, economic, and political organization may not be so completely different from their Western analogues as the apparent persistence of a "feudal" period until 1868 makes it seem.

III

This extension in historical depth of the development of a modern society and polity in Japan also calls attention to what Professor Almond has termed the "dualism" of political institutions.[4] All modern polities contain substantial admixtures of traditional elements, and these are frequently not confined to isolated or backwater areas but may play a prominent and functionally important role in the modernization process.

In the Japanese case, this is well illustrated by our earlier account of the historical development of a professionally trained, rationally structured, and achievement-oriented bureaucracy in Japan. In this instance it was pointed out that what seemed to be a purely feudal institution performing functions of major importance in a predominantly feudal society was at the same time gradually acquiring more and more of the basic characteristics of a modern professional bureaucracy. In a historical sense, therefore, the late Tokugawa bureaucracy played a Janus-like role. It faced both backward toward the truly feudal institutions and times of the sixteenth century and forward toward the emergent modern society of the twentieth. It also served in gradually shifting proportions the purposes of both waning and emergent societies, and it continued to do this for upward of one hundred and fifty years.

---

[4]Gabriel A. Almond and James S. Coleman, eds., *The Politics of the Developing Areas* (Princeton 1960), 20–25.

In other words, the capacity for peaceful coexistence—and even mutual supportiveness—of "feudal" or traditional with modern elements within a given institution, as well as within a society, is well demonstrated by the Japanese experience....

The history of the modernization of Japan ... demonstrates in many ways not only the ability of "modern" institutions and practices to coexist with "traditional" ones for very substantial periods of time, but also the manner in which "traditional" attitudes and practices can be of great positive value to the modernization process.

The modernizing experience is a strenuous one for any traditionally organized society. If successful, it demands sacrifice, discipline, initiative, and perseverance in quantities and for periods of time which are certain to place the people concerned under very severe strains. One of the greatest problems of leadership under these circumstances is to devise conditions and motivations which will both liberate and focus an appropriate amount of popular energy, initiative, and resources and at the same time minimize dysfunctional behavior on the part of all significant elements in the population. Consider briefly some of the techniques used in Japan to achieve these goals and note the role played therein by traditional elements.

Most obvious of all, perhaps, was the use made of the emperor. This is not to say that there was not some measure of sincerity and philosophic or ethical commitment in the movement to restore the emperor to at least the semblance of temporal power. But the subsequent revival and institutionalization of Shinto* and the cultivation of mass loyalty, obedience, and reverence for the emperor were too systematic and innovational to be anything but a deliberate and very clever attempt by the Meiji leadership to channel popular attitudes and conduct along lines which they considered constructive. In this instance the appeal was to an institutional complex that not only was traditional in terms of the circumstances of the 1870's, but would have been equally so in terms of those of 1603. The tradition of imperial rule, with very few exceptions, had possessed little validity since approximately the ninth century, while Imperial Shinto as a national cult had been moribund for at least as long, if indeed it had ever before existed in comparable form.

Again, one of the real keystones to the successful modernization of Japan was the device of holding constant, i.e. traditional, the circumstances of life in rural and agricultural Japan while at the same time

---

*[Shinto developed originally from folk beliefs and rituals. The Meiji leadership instituted a "state" Shinto that stressed patriotism and fealty to the emperor and was practiced alongside religious Shinto.—Ed.]

using and exploiting the countryside as a means of building and rapidly developing the urban, commercial, industrial, and military sectors of the society. Modernization is an expensive undertaking and the costs must be borne by some segment of the population. In Japan in the early and critical years, it was the peasantry who, through the land tax, bore the bulk of this burden. A docile and productive agrarian labor force was, therefore, an element of crucial importance to the leaders of a modernizing Japan. In a social engineering sense, they strove to ensure this result by altering the actual socio-political circumstances of the pre-Restoration countryside as little as possible. Land reform was assiduously avoided; the existing political, social, and economic elites of the villages were insofar as possible confirmed in their status and authority; the traditional community and family systems were not only maintained but in a number of ways were reinforced and given new legal status and sanctions.

A systematic endeavor was made to ensure the tranquility, obedience, and loyalty of the countryside, and the control devices utilized were almost without exception traditional. This not only assured the government of a maximal flow of food, revenue, recruits, and urban-bound emigrants from the countryside, but also left them free to concentrate their attention and resources on the building of the more critical urban aspects of the national economy and defense establishment. This was a strategy of enormous importance to the rapid development of Japan, and its success rested ultimately on the effective enlistment of traditional institutions and appeals in the service of the modernizing process.

If one looks to the contemporary rather than the historical scene in Japan, many examples of this type of "reinforcing dualism" may still be discerned. The most reliable and important element in the long political dominance of the Liberal-Democratic Party in the postwar period has been its control of the rural vote. Below the surface of this phenomenon, one will find a political support system compounded of largely personalized allegiance and loyalties reaching downward through the prefectures to roots in every farm hamlet in Japan. The ultimate approach of this apparatus to the voter is based upon a very shrewd admixture of appeals to personal and local advantage phrased in terms of traditional values and relationships. Again, the primacy of personal and hierarchical relations and loyalties in Japanese politics is obvious and well-known. The persistence of *oyabun-kobun* and similar forms of traditional fictive family relationships is but an extreme form of this trait. It would probably also be proper to regard the national predilection for consensual rather than adversary forms of decision-making and the dualistic nature of the national economy as other examples of the continued vitality and real functional importance of traditional attitudes and practices in the Japan of 1963.

In short, post-Restoration Japan has continuously represented a very complex amalgam of traditional and modern elements, a sort of mutually supportive or "reinforcing dualism" in which the relationship between the two sectors has often been symbiotic rather than antagonistic. This has been true to such an extent that it is probably accurate to claim that Japan could not have been successful in modernizing so rapidly and effectively had it not been for the many planned and unplanned ways in which traditional values and behavior positively contributed to and supported the process. Furthermore, there is a good deal of evidence indicative of the continued vitality of some segments of the traditional sector. It is still too early to predict even their gradual displacement by what we regard logically as more modern traits.

IV

Any characterization of modern political culture in Japan must take into account at least two sets of factors: those making for unity and stability, and those making for diversity, tension, and change. Although the former are not at present of major concern, they do condition and set limits to the operations of the factors making for tension and change, and should thus be noted as an essential part of this picture. For present purposes they may be described briefly.

Japan's combination of insularity and racial and linguistic homogeneity makes under modern circumstances for a high degree of ingroup feeling and national unity vis-à-vis the non-Japanese world. Particularly since the loss of her empire, the country has had natural frontiers sharply demarcated from foreign territory—in all but the Russian case—by sizable bodies of water. Historically, these have given to the Japanese people a degree of national security unprecedented among major states. They have also, until recently, sharply limited any opportunity for massive contact or interaction with foreign peoples, enhanced and supported the popular sense of the uniqueness of being Japanese, and encouraged a sort of narcissistic absorption in Japan's own culture, problems, and viewpoints. This last attribute has persisted throughout all of the country's recent periods of intense acculturative experience and has invariably reasserted itself. These centripetal tendencies are reinforced by practically complete linguistic uniformity, qualified only by a few dialect problems, and by a degree of racial homogeneity unmatched among major states. Japan is 99.3 per cent pure in terms of racial composition, having fewer than 700,000 identifiable aliens among her populace. Immigration by non-Japanese peoples has never been a problem of serious proportion in the past two thousand years.

The contemporary Japanese also inherit a myth of national unity at least twelve hundred years old. Despite the fact that much of the history of this period was marked by localism, civil strife, and the emergence of powerful clans and nobles with high degrees of independence within their own territories, the tradition and forms of national unity and of a Japanese state have always been maintained. The symbol—some would claim the embodiment—of this tradition has been the imperial institution which, although its fortunes and authority have varied widely, has existed continuously and has continuously asserted both its own legitimacy and the essential unity of the state. Although today the efficacy of the imperial institution as a legitimizing and unifying force has doubtless diminished—especially where important sectors of the youth of Japan are concerned—it would be a mistake to overestimate the degree of either its obsolescence or its impotence as a symbol of the nation's unity. The very absence of acceptable alternatives lends it a strength and resilience which may not be immediately apparent.

A still more important factor making for national unity and stability is the spectacular success of the Japanese state as an instrument for the achievement and sharing of values. This has historical dimensions to it which evoke past greatness and satisfactions, somewhat flawed by the disastrous defeat of 1945. But, for the present, this is overmatched by the sense of shared suffering and accomplishment in postwar times. The Japanese economy has expanded at a startling rate and the resulting prosperity has been more widely shared than ever before in the national history. It is hard to establish the extent to which the Japanese political system is entitled to credit for this accomplishment, but in practice it gets a great deal. It has worked and, after a painful wartime lapse, is working again. The people are prospering and—party politics aside—they tend to have few basic or bitter criticisms of the system. This element of practical success is a very important aspect of the factors making for unity and stability in present Japanese political culture. Indeed, it is possible to feel considerable concern as to whether it may not be the crucial factor. The resiliency and strength of the postwar Japanese political system have yet to be tested under conditions of real economic adversity or political stress, and it is difficult to predict what the reaction to such circumstances would be. . . .

The issues involved in political modernization are simply not that much in contest in present-day Japan. The mode or central tendency of the political system is predominantly, if not exclusively, modern. There does not exist any significant political party or group with an across-the-board or major commitment to traditional as opposed to modern political institutions, values, or behavior. . . .

Japan has thus achieved the "modern state"; in Rostow's terms, she has passed her stage of "take-off" and entered upon a stage of "self-sustaining development." As a consequence, tensions, competition, and decisions in the Japanese political system tend to relate only tangentially or instrumentally to the traditional-modern dimension within Japanese political culture. Certain aspects of traditional culture offer tactical advantages to certain participants in the political struggle. They, therefore, try to preserve these aspects as long as possible, but usually with some recognition of the fact that their returns are diminishing and that other tactics will eventually have to be devised to replace the traditionally based ones. The commitments involved tend in this sense to be limited and instrumental rather than ultimate and principled. Increasingly, the terms and goals of political competition in Japan tend to focus on the quest for specific sorts of economic or political advantage for functionally defined groups or interests along lines already familiar in the West. Japan has now largely outgrown political competition based upon the desirability of the constituent elements of a modern polity. These exist and are generally accepted in Japan as in other modern states.

V

The course of political modernization in Japan raises some interesting questions with respect to the form and organization of authority in modernizing societies. It was pointed out earlier that states which have achieved modernity may have democratic, totalitarian, or some intermediate type of political organization. The form of government does not seem to be a defining factor in mature cases of political modernization. The experience of Japan, however, makes one wonder if the same judgment applies with respect to forms of political organization in all earlier stages of the political modernization process. Is the process neutral in this respect throughout, or can one identify stages which demand authoritarian forms of government and which are antipathetic on grounds of developmental efficiency and potentiality to the introduction of democratic institutions on more than a very restricted basis? The question is of great importance from the standpoint of those who would prefer to see "backward" political systems develop along lines which are both modern and democratic. These are compatible but not necessary consequences of the developmental process. This poses the problem of how one can maximize the probability that developing polities will become both modern and democratic.

The experience of Japan alone certainly cannot provide definitive answers to either of the above questions. But neither is it irrelevant, and in circumstances where it represents the sole mature non-Western exemplar of the modernization process in all of Asia, it should be examined with unusual care and attention. The Japanese experience seems to suggest: (1) that authoritarian forms of political organization can be extraordinarily effective in the early stages of the modernization process; (2) that they need not debar the gradual emergence of more democratic forms of political organization; and (3) that some such process of gradual transition from authoritarian to democratic forms may be essential to the emergence of politics that are both modern and durably democratic. It should be emphasized again that these are no more than highly tentative hypotheses based upon the experience of Japan, but they do possess at least this much historical sanction and support. Let us then consider in a general way selected aspects of Japan's experience with the political modernization process which relate to the above three propositions.

First, authoritarian forms of political organization can be extraordinarily effective in the early stages of the modernization process. It is implied—though not demonstrable on the basis of the Japanese experience—that democratic forms are significantly less effective and that their early introduction may in fact result in conditions that will seriously inhibit the prospects of long-term democratic development.

This contention rests primarily on observations with respect to the relationship between the political modernization process and the process of social modernization in a general or total sense. The former is not autonomous, not a goal in itself. It is instrumentally related to the larger process and goal and should serve and expedite its purposes. This larger process of modernization entails for the society concerned, especially in the critical early or "take-off" stages, a series of shocks and strains of major proportions. It equally creates emancipations and new opportunities for some, but for major segments of the population this is apt to be a lengthy period of adjustment to new economic, social, and political situations and demands. Large-scale material and psychological stresses are invariably involved. One of the routine consequences of such a situation—at least in the non-Western world of the late nineteenth and the twentieth centuries—seems to be a greatly expanded role for government. A certain and perhaps very important amount of the modernization process may still take place under private auspices, but in recent times the needs and expectations which set the standards of modernization have been so urgent and expensive that national governments have had to assume a leading and dominant role. Only power organized at this level seemed capable of massing the resources and taking and enforcing the wide-ranging and difficult decisions involved.

This primacy of government in the modernizing process is more or less taken for granted throughout the underdeveloped world today. The situation was doubtless historically different in the case of the modernization of certain Western European societies and their offshoots, but in present-day underdeveloped societies there simply are no plausible and politically viable alternatives to the primacy of government as an agent of modernization. This was also true in the Japanese case at the time of the Restoration.

The overriding problems and goals of the 1870's and 1880's in Japan were well expressed by the popular political slogans of the day— *fukoku kyōhei* (a strong and wealthy nation). This captures the essence of the complex of forces and aspirations which underlay the Restoration movement and motivated its leaders in the difficult days that followed the initial successes of 1868. The greatest and most urgent needs were for national unity and the creation of armed strength sufficient to guarantee the national security against both real and fancied dangers of foreign imperialist aggression and economic exploitation. Instrumental thereto, of course, was the creation of a strong and stable government to lead the nation along suitable paths. Fortunately for Japan, her leaders were wise enough to define these goals in broad and constructive terms. Military strength meant to them far more than a large army and navy well-equipped with Western armaments; it also meant the industrial plant to sustain and expand such a military establishment and appropriate training for the men who must staff it. National wealth came to mean a radical diversification of the predominantly agrarian economy, urbanization, systematic mass and higher education, planned industrialization, new commercial and financial institutions, and a variety of other commitments which were perceived as essential to survival and effective competitive status in a Western-dominated world. Not all of these commitments were either generally perceived or welcomed at the outset by the leadership group, but in their search for national unity, strength, and security they found themselves embarked upon a species of "modernization spiral" similar in some respects to the "inflationary spiral" of the economists. The most intelligent and able of them adapted to the general course set by the imperatives which these goals entailed; the others were eliminated from leadership circles.

The realization of national goals of this sort did not come easily to a society such as Japan's, even given the forms of covert preparation for modernization which had characterized the later Tokugawa Period. The really critical years between 1868 and 1890 must sometimes have seemed an unending series of crises. Civil war, the threat of international war and the fact of foreign economic exploitation, a series of economic crises, inflation and deflation, the recurrent threat of samurai conspiracies against the government, the embitterment of the peasantry at the failure of the government to improve their lot, the dearth of desperately needed technical knowledge and personnel, and all of the widespread fears and tensions which attend a time of new beginnings —these were merely some of the problems which constantly confronted the new political leadership. Yet, by 1890, policies capable of dealing with all of these problems had been developed and the country was firmly embarked on the path to modernization. The foreign threats had been faced and Japan's international position was secure; the menace of civil war had been permanently liquidated; the structural vestiges of feudalism had been eliminated and the country effectively unified; the position and authority of the government had been confirmed and regularized by constitutional arrangements; the economy had been stabilized and a promising start made upon its diversification and industrialization; a system of mass compulsory education had been inaugurated and mass media of communication established; in every critical category the strength of Japan showed remarkable and promising improvements.

Under such circumstances it may be that some measure of democratic participation could successfully have been introduced into the political system. There were those who advocated such changes. The *Jiyuminken Undō* (Freedom and Popular Rights Movement), for example, called for the establishment of a national parliament, a limited suffrage, and some dispersion of political authority. Had this been attempted during these years, the results need not have been fatal to the modernization of Japan. But under conditions of more or less constant political or economic crisis, widespread popular disaffection and lack of understanding of the necessity for the sacrifices entailed by many government programs, the unpredictable qualities and perils of the country's foreign relations, and what we have learned in general of the limitations of fledgling democratic institutions in largely unprepared contexts, it is difficult to envisage the feasibility or practicality of any very significant democratic innovations at this time.

These years from 1868 to 1890, or some similar period, would seem to be a time in Japan's modernization when an authoritarian form of political organization offered distinct advantages where rapidity of response, flexibility, planning, and effective action were concerned. This is said with full appreciation of the fumbling and shortcomings of authoritarian leadership groups and irresponsible bureaucracies—including the Japanese of this period—in all of these departments. It thus assumes the availability of some at least minimally competent and unified political leadership. If this is not available—and there are obviously cases where it is not—political modernization is not a practicable proposition for the countries concerned.

In the Japanese case, however, it seems on balance highly improbable that (1) the addition of any significant or effective democratic institutions to the decision-making apparatus at such a stage of national development could have had other than deleterious effects upon the speed and decisiveness with which urgent problems were handled; and that (2) this stage of the modernization process, beset as it inevitably was by so many and such desperate problems, would have been an appropriate time to launch so delicate an experiment as democratization.

Our second hypothesis was that the dominance of authoritarian forms of political organization in the initial stages of the political modernization process need not debar the gradual emergence of democratic forms of organization. This is not intended to imply any quality of inevitability in such a development, although in a secular sense some such tendency may exist.

In the Japanese case, no significant measures of democratization were introduced into the political system until the enactment of the Meiji Constitution in 1890, twenty-two years after the Restoration. Even then it is very doubtful if any of the authors of this document thought of their handiwork as an act of democratic innovation. It is certain that their so-called "liberal" opposition did not. Rather does it seem that the Meiji leadership group conceived of this constitution primarily as a means of regularizing the structure and operations of political authority—the absence of any rationalized or stable structure and the continual innovation and experimentation of the intervening years must have been very trying—and of further unifying and solidifying both the country and their own authority. As a consequence of this and a variety of later developments, there has been a tendency to undervalue both the degree of political change which the Meiji Constitution brought to Japan and the measure of democratic development which took place under it. . . .

There are two things about this gradual emergence of democratic politics from the authoritarian system of pre-1890 Japan which might have more general validity and interest. The first is that even the concession of a very carefully restricted and seemingly impotent governmental role to a popularly elected body can, over a period of time, have consequences well nigh fatal to sustained authoritarian rule. It would be hard to be optimistic about the influence or authority of the Japanese House of Representatives in terms of the provisions of the Meiji Constitution or the relevant basic laws. These faithfully reflect and implement the desire of the founders to make of the House an appealing but powerless sop to the demands of the opposition and public opinion. But the lessons to be learned from the subsequent history of the lower house are: (1) that it provides a means of institutionalizing and enlarging the role of political parties; (2) that, in modernizing circumstances, even vested powers of obstructing the smooth and effective flow of governmental decisions and actions can be critical—positive powers of initiation and control are not necessary; and (3) that in circumstances where a popularly chosen body can thus blackmail an authoritarian leadership, there is a fair possibility of forcing the latter into piecemeal but cumulative accommodations which are democratic in tendency.

The second generalization suggested by the history of democratic development in Japan relates to the conditions necessary to support an effectively authoritarian system of government. Japanese experience suggests the existence of a close relationship between effective authoritarian rule and the unity and solidarity of the oligarchy involved. The limits involved cannot be described with much precision, but authoritarian government in Japan began to disintegrate as the heretofore fairly solidary oligarchy began to split into competing cliques and factions. The probability of such rifts seems to be very high in modernizing societies. The development of role specialization and professionalization even at high levels is an essential part of the process of modernization, and this makes it hard for an oligarchy to maintain the degree of unity and cohesion feasible in revolutionary or in simpler times. Pluralism in this sense seems to be built into the process. And as an oligarchy breaks down into competing factions in this fashion, the terms of political competition in that society undergo an important change. Extra-oligarchic groups such as emergent political parties acquire new room for maneuver and new political leverages, and the ex-oligarchic cliques themselves acquire new incentives for broadening the basis of their support. Out of these altered political circumstances are apt to come new political alliances involving elements of the former oligarchy with elements of more popularly based bodies—in particular, with political parties. The total process is dilutive from the standpoint of authoritarian government and supportive of the gradual emergence of greater degrees of pluralism and democracy.

It is not intended to depict either of the foregoing generalizations on the basis of Japanese experience as controlling or inevitable. But they did occur within a fairly authoritarian context in Japan's case and there seem to be some reasons for regarding them as of more general validity. The conclusion would seem to be that an initial or early stage of authoritarian government on the path to modernization (1) does not commit a polity to long-term adherence to authoritarian forms; (2) does not necessarily make an authoritarian course of development probable; and (3) may even contain built-in elements calculated with time and development to break down and liberalize such authoritarian forms.

Our third hypothesis is even more tentatively stated and adds up to a feeling that some such process of gradual transition from authoritarian to democratic forms may be essential to the emergence of a political system which is both modern and durably democratic. In this connection Japan's experience suggests several notions of possible interest.

First, our commonly employed systems of periodization may involve serious distortions where the history of political modernization is concerned. Thus, in Japan's case, while the feudal-modern or Tokugawa-Restoration frameworks have a plausible amount of relevance to the emergence of a modern Japanese political system, they also serve to obscure important aspects of the process. They are calculated, as is the prewar-postwar framework, to produce an overemphasis on the significance of certain dramatic and allegedly "revolutionary" events in a country's history—in this case, the Restoration or the 1945 defeat plus the Occupation. This is conducive to a dichotomous view of the political development process which seriously overstates the enduring importance of alleged discontinuities in a national history at the expense of the less dramatic but fundamentally more important continuities.

Second, if the history of the development of democracy in Japan is weighted for this distorting effect of the commonly employed categories and system of periodization, the differences in preparation, timing, and depth of democratic experience which are often held to distinguish a democratic political system in Japan from its Western analogues would perhaps seem appreciably less valid and important than is usually assumed. The two patterns of development probably have more in common than is generally recognized.

Third, if the foregoing assumptions are valid, one is tempted to conclude that all practicing and at least ostensibly solid and durable democracies today are the products of lengthy and multifaceted evolutionary processes. In the Japanese case, if one looks only to the direct antecedents, seventy-three years intervene between the Meiji Constitution and the present. But far longer periods of preparation are involved if one looks to the less direct consequences of the introduction of mass literacy or a rationalized bureaucratic structure. In this sense it is questionable whether history provides any very encouraging examples of short-cuts to the achievement of a democratic political system.

Finally, such a train of argument suggests the importance of the relationship existing between a "modern" political system and a "democratic" political system. One hesitates to claim that all or a specific proportion of the attributes of a modern polity must be achieved before a society becomes capable of durably democratic performance or achievement, but Japan's experience at least suggests an important correlation between the two. It is hard to specify the proportions involved, but, in a rough and approximate way, one might say that perhaps only modern societies with modern political cultures of the sort defined in Section I are practical candidates for democratization.

FOR FURTHER READING

ARDATH W. BURKS, "The City, Political Change, and Modernization in Japan" *(International Journal of Comparative Sociology,* VII, 1–2, March 1966, 29–51)

ALLEN B. COLE, "Factors Explaining the Disparate Rate of Modernization in China and Japan" *(Asian Studies,* IV, 1, April 1966, 1–15)

MARIUS B. JANSEN, ed., *Changing Japanese Attitudes Toward Modernization* (Princeton: Princeton University Press, 1965)

MARION J. LEVY, JR., "Contrasting Factors in the Modernization of China and Japan," in Simon Kuznets, Wilbert E. Moore, and Joseph J. Spengler, eds., *Economic Growth: Brazil, India, Japan* (Durham: Duke University Press, 1955), pp. 496–536

MARION J. LEVY, JR., "Some Aspects of 'Individualism' and the Problem of Modernization in China and Japan" *(Economic Development and Cultural Change,* X, 3, April 1962, 225–240)

WILLIAM W. LOCKWOOD, "Japan's Response to the West: The Contrast With China" *(World Politics,* IX, 1, October 1956, 37–54)

THEODORE MCNELLY, "The Role of Monarchy in the Political Modernization of Japan" *(Comparative Politics,* I, 3, April 1969, 366–381)

HERBERT PASSIN, "Japan," in James S. Coleman, ed., *Education and Political Development* (Princeton: Princeton University Press, 1965), pp. 272–312

E. HERBERT NORMAN, *Japan's Emergence as a Modern State* (New York: Institute of Pacific Relations, 1940)

ROBERT A. SCALAPINO, "Ideology and Modernization: The Japanese Case," in David E. Apter, ed., *Ideology and Discontent* (New York: Free Press of Glencoe, 1964), pp. 93–127

THOMAS C. SMITH, "Japan's Aristocratic Revolution" (*The Yale Review*, L, 3, Spring 1961, 370–383)

ROBERT E. WARD, "Japan: The Continuity of Modernization," in Lucian W. Pye and Sidney Verba, eds., *Political Culture and Political Development* (Princeton: Princeton University Press, 1965), pp. 27–82

ROBERT E. WARD AND DANKWART A. RUSTOW, eds., *Political Modernization in Japan and Turkey* (Princeton: Princeton University Press, 1964)

CLAUDE E. WELCH, JR., "The Challenge of a Change: Japan and Africa," in Herbert J. Spiro, ed., *Patterns of African Development* (Englewood Cliffs, N. J.: Prentice-Hall, 1967)

POLITICAL PARTICIPATION AND MODERNIZATION IN TURKEY

Joseph S. Szyliowicz

The societies of new states are characteristically rural rather than urban. Modernization, however, occurs more rapidly in cities than in the more isolated villages. Do aspects of modernization readily spread from the urban centers to the countryside? Professor Szyliowicz suggests that the disparities between city and village may increase, not decrease, thereby exacerbating political and social tensions.

The transition in Turkey from a one-party system to a multi-party system in 1950 was universally hailed as a great achievement. To many observers it appeared as evidence that a modernizing oligarchy could provide the necessary underpinnings for the creation of a democratic society and that democracy could evolve from dictatorship.

These high expectations were rudely dashed by the army coup of May 1960 and indeed to some extent by the policies of the government in the years preceding the revolution. Turkey, which had appeared as a model for development within a non-totalitarian framework, now seemed to have lost its initial drive and momentum, apparently to be diverted from its course of economic development and modernization.

The example of Turkey is particularly instructive because the past few years have witnessed an outstanding phenomenon, the proliferation of new states throughout the world. All of them are attempting to create viable polities and to modernize their societies as rapidly as possible, and they face many of the same problems that previously confronted the elites of the Ottoman Empire, and later, of the Turkish Republic.

One of the most critical problems is the rate and manner in which certain groups, especially the peasantry, are politicized and inducted into the national political system. The creation of a modern society entails a closing of the gap which exists between the modern and the traditional

From *Western Political Quarterly*, Vol. XIX, No. 2 (1966), pp. 266–284.
Reprinted by permission of the University of Utah, copyright owners.

sectors—a complicated task involving the disruption of the peasantry's traditional way of life, and thus one which would probably engender considerable opposition to the policies of the modernizing elite.

Accordingly, the regime may temporarily ignore the rural mass and concentrate its energies and resources upon mobilizing the urban elements in order to gain time and to obtain new sources of support. Such a policy will lead to the establishment of an enclave of modernity within the society and may be camouflaged by expressions of concern for the villager's welfare and by the introduction of various programs which are either not applied or to which sufficient resources are not allocated. But at best, such a policy merely postpones the problem of modernization and integrating the peasantry and may, in fact, aggravate it by increasing the disparity between the rural and urban sectors.

This was essentially the result of the policy followed by the Turkish elite led by Mustapha Kemal Ataturk. Political modernization in Turkey, as elsewhere, is reflected in the continual and progressive enlargement of the number of groups and social strata which were gradually mobilized and inducted into the mainstream of the national life. One group, however, the peasantry, was left relatively isolated and did not play a significant role in the nation's affairs until after World War II when the establishment of a multi-party system meant that the competing political parties would be forced to appeal for rural support.

Consequently, the success of Ataturk in politicizing the urban elements while neglecting the rural mass meant that a conflict between tradition and modernity, between urban and rural groups, would result unless the governing elite possessed such qualities as self-restraint, a reasonable degree of competence, and a high degree of probity. Unfortunately, the Menderes regime (1950-60) could not live up to these qualifications. The modern sectors of the society were alienated, the legitimacy of the regime was undermined, and the new democratic framework was strained to the breaking-point.

To place this development in its proper perspective, it is necessary to examine Turkish modernization from the point of view of political participation and political socialization, first within the Ottoman Empire, secondly during the Ataturk-Inönü era, and lastly during the multi-party system following World War II. At each stage the focus will be upon the agencies of politicization, the groups and social strata affected, and the influence of these groups upon the national political system.

I

The Ottoman Empire was a vast multi-national and polyglot state with a sharp division between the ruling elite and the mass of the population, which had but little knowledge of national affairs and which played almost no part in the government of the Empire. Decision-making was concentrated in the hands of a small group known as the Ruling Institution, at the center of which stood the Sultan. His power, although theoretically absolute, was limited by the existence of three major power structures, the *Ulema* (religious), the military, and the bureaucracy.

Following centuries of the declining power marked by numerous military disasters and loss of territory, some of the Ottoman leaders became aware of the need for change. At first they were concerned only with military matters and felt that borrowing European army techniques and weapons would suffice to halt the decline and lead to a resurgence of the Empire. However, it rapidly became evident that innovations could not be limited to military technology and that drastic reforms in all phases of Ottoman life were necessary. Furthermore, the increased contacts with Western Europe in the eighteenth century led to the development of a new class within the Ottoman Empire. This group, part of the bureaucracy, rapidly emerged as a new elite, owing to its monopoly of contacts with Europe and its mastery of European languages.

Above these bureaucrats were the high civil servants, the ministers of the Empire who came from the same prominent families which had successfully maintained their position for centuries. The Young Ottomans, the westernized intellectuals, occupied the middle and lower rungs of the bureaucracy. It was they, whose chances of advancement were frustrated by a lack of family connections, who were to play such an important role in the political modernization of the Ottoman Empire.[1]

These Young Ottomans found ready support within the new military organization. Since the destruction of the Janissaries in 1826, the army had consisted increasingly of individuals who were concerned with the question of reform and modernization, who were not a part of the traditional ruling class, and who also had limited prestige.[2]

Modernity in the bureaucracy and in the military was further spurred by the educational reforms of the nineteenth century. New military and administrative schools were opened which proved to be important

---

[1]Serif Mardin, *The Genesis of Young Ottoman Thought* (Princeton: Princeton U. Press, 1962). Chapter 4 *passim;* cf. Halil Inalcik, "The Nature of Traditional Society: Turkey," in Robert E. Ward and Dankwart A. Rustow (eds.), *Political Modernization in Japan and Turkey* (Princeton: Princeton U. Press, 1964), pp. 53ff. The role of the bureaucracy in modernization is discussed by Richard L. Chambers, "The Civil Bureaucracy: Turkey," in Ward and Rustow, *op. cit.,* pp. 301–27.

[2]Mardin, *op. cit.,* p. 130. On occasion the Young Ottomans were also able to ally themselves with the lower members of the *Ulema* who were losing prestige as a result of the secularization of the administrative, judicial, and educational institutions of the Ottoman Empire, carried out during the Tanzimat, the nineteenth-century reform movement. *Ibid.,* p. 142.

channels for the transmission of Western ideas and concepts.[3] The graduates of the *Mülkiye*, founded in 1859, became civil servants. The efforts of the Young Ottomans and their allies were crowned by the proclamation of the Constitution in 1876 and the convening of the first genuine parliament in Ottoman history.[4] Although elections were held for the lower house (the Senate being appointed by the government), little interest was aroused within the Empire. This was due not only to the nature of the Electoral Law,[5] which enfranchised only a minute percentage of the population, but more importantly, to the low level of political consciousness within the Empire. Only in Istanbul did a public opinion exist and even here it was neither articulate nor aroused.

Two parliaments were actually convened, the first in March 1877, the second in December of that year. Somewhat surprisingly the deputies, despite a lack of experience, maintained a high level of debate and did not hesitate to criticize the government. The maturity and independence displayed by these men led directly to the failure of the Assembly— Sultan Abdul Hamid paid them a high compliment by suspending the Constitution in 1878.[6] A long period of political reaction followed, which ended in the summer of 1908 when a revolution forced the Sultan to restore the Constitution.[7]

The downfall of the Hamidian tyranny was greeted with an enthusiastic outburst of hope for representative government and democracy. Although the high expectations were soon dispelled, the revolution

---

[3]Their influence is assessed by Roderic H. Davison, "Environmental and Foreign Contributions: Turkey," in Ward and Rustow, *op. cit.*, pp. 114–15. See also Roderic H. Davison, "Westernized Education in Turkey," *Middle East Journal*, 15 (Summer 1961) 294ff.

[4]The first assembly in the Ottoman Empire met in 1845. One prominent historian has dismissed it as a "farce," stating: "But of course the election of its representatives could not be left to the entirely unprepared populace; they were, rather, culled out by the government. These representatives responded to the Sultan's speech from the throne, introduced after the British example, by an address of thanks, and were then graciously dismissed." Carl Brockelman, *History of the Islamic Peoples* (London: Routledge and Kegan Paul, 1956), p. 361. This point of view is supported by Recai G. Okandan, *Umumi amme hukukumuzun ana hatları, birinci kitap* (Istanbul: Ismail Akgün Matbaası, 1948), pp. 73, 119. For a more sympathetic assessment see Bernard Lewis, *The Emergence of Modern Turkey* (London: Oxford U. Press, 1961), pp. 110–11 and Roderic H. Davison, *Reform in the Ottoman Empire 1856–1876* (Princeton: Princeton U. Press, 1963), pp. 46–47.

[5]I am grateful to Mr. Donald Sherinian for providing me with his translations of several electoral laws. A French version of this law may be found in Aristarchi Bey (Gregoire), *Legislation Ottomane* Quatriéme Partie (Constantinople: Bureau de Journal Thraky, 1874), pp. 306ff. The Ottoman text may be found in Sarkis Karakoc, *Intihabi-i Mebusan Kanunu* (Istanbul: Kütüphanesi Cihan, 1923), pp. 24ff. The law is discussed by Robert Devereux, *The First Ottoman Constitutional Period* (Baltimore: Johns Hopkins Press, 1963), pp. 124–26 and by Davison, *Reform . . .* , pp. 374ff.

[6]Devereux, *op. cit.*, pp. 255–56; summaries of the chamber's debates were published by Hakkı Tarik Us (ed.), *Meclis-i Mebusan 1293: 1877 Zabit Ceridesi* (2 vols.; Istanbul: Vakit Matbaası, 1940, 1954). Contemporary newspaper accounts were compiled by Hakkı Azimzade, *Türkiyede Meclis-i Mebusan* (Cairo: Matbaa-i Ietihat, 1907).

[7]The background to the revolution and the role of the CUP is discussed by E. E. Ramsaur, Jr., *The Young Turks* (Princeton: Princeton U. Press, 1959).

demonstrated the extent to which previous reforms (which ironically in some fields, notably education, had been greatly expanded by Abdul Hamid II), had succeeded in increasing the number and strength of the modernizers.

Elections for a new Ottoman Parliament were held in 1908,[8] a few months after the revolution and took place in an atmosphere of intense emotion. According to an eyewitness: "Masses of people followed the election urns, decked in flowers and flags. In carriages sat the Moslem and Christian priests, hand in hand. Christian and Moslem maidens, dressed in white, locked in childish embrace, passed on, while the crowd that followed sang enthusiastically, 'O, Country, O Mother, Be Thou Joyful and Happy Today.' "[9]

However, the high hopes symbolized by such demonstrations soon proved illusory. Although the revolutionists had been concerned with the restoration of representative institutions, more fundamentally they had envisaged the revival of the Empire and its transformation into a powerful modern state. Whether they had any chance of success is doubtful: the attempt to weld together a strong multi-national state ran counter to the feelings of nationalism so widely accepted by the minorities of the Empire; the new leaders were inexperienced; reactionary forces posed the threat of counterrevolution; and finally the threat of external aggression remained ever-present. It is therefore not surprising that the attempt to revive democratic processes failed and that the Committee of Union and Progress (CUP) which had emerged as the dominant political organization established a one-party rule within a few years.

Nevertheless, the CUP period was an important stage in the political development of the society. The CUP itself was a powerful agent of political socialization. Its organization extended from national congresses to party locals in small towns. Everywhere the party's branches were centers of political, social, and educational activity. Courses in such subjects as writing, foreign languages, and social welfare were offered.[10] The discussions and meeting doubtless served to promote increased interest and participation in national affairs among groups heretofore isolated from the political scene.

---

[8]The elections were held according to the "Law for the Election of Deputies" (Intihabi-i Mebusan Kanunu), which had been debated and approved in the first session of the Chamber of Deputies in 1877. The law enfranchised almost all male Ottomans over twenty-five, albeit only in an indirect way, since a system of electoral colleges was established. The Ottoman text may be found in *Düstur*, 2nd series, I, 18; an English translation was made by the British Occupation Forces in Iraq and published by the Ministry of Justice, Baghdad, 1920, under the title *Law for the Election of Deputies*; a French version may be found in A. Biliotti and Ahmed Sedad, *Legislation Ottomane Depuis le Rétablissement de la Constitution* (Paris: Jouvet, 1912), I, 10.

[9]Halide Edib, *Memoirs of Halide Edib* (New York: Century, 1926), pp. 271–72.

[10]Tarik Tunaya, *Turkiyenin Siyasî Hayatında Batılılasma Hareketleri* (Istanbul: Yedigün Matbaası, 1960), pp. 49–50.

The national congresses of CUP were important meetings where the politically conscious elements had an opportunity to gather, debate, and help shape party policy.[11] They focused attention upon the problems of the Empire, and their debates and speeches were widely reported in the press. Out of these debates came the adoption of significant reforms including a new Family Law giving women greater rights, a judicial system under secular control, the overhauling of municipal and provincial administration, a great expansion in educational opportunities for girls, and the establishment of the *Türk Ocagı*, designed to disseminate the nationalist ideology of the CUP in many towns and cities.[12]

Although the CUP was the dominant party, numerous other political organizations had been established, each with its own program and personalities. Most of these programs were short-lived, but they stirred excitement and discussion of contemporary problems. As a result, newspaper circulation increased sharply, numerous new magazines and books were published, and political rallies and demonstrations became common occurrences in all the important cities.[13]

Owing to all this activity, political leaders were no longer recruited mainly from the army or the bureaucracy; now they began to emerge from other social strata. However, only a small percentage of the population was affected, and this minority was still concentrated in the large urban centers. National affairs continued to be of little importance to many townspeople and the rural inhabitants remained almost completely isolated from the national political system. Nevertheless, the number of active political participants had grown sharply.

Most important was the fact that the basic problems facing the Ottoman Empire could not be resolved by the Young Turks because there was no consensus among the intellectuals as to the structure of the state. Debate raged over whether it should remain a multi-racial, multi-national empire (Ottomanism), whether it should consist of Muslims only (Pan Islam), or whether all Turks, including those in Central Asia, should be included (Pan Turkism). Nor did agreement exist as to how the problems of the state should be resolved, whether through democratic or authoritarian means, whether through a radical reform program or a slower evolutionary policy. Out of the continuing debate over these questions, a realization among the intellectual elite gradually evolved that a new solution to the questions they were raising was necessary. Mustapha Kemal was to supply it.

---

[11]For a description of these Congresses, see Tarik Tunaya, *Turkiyede Siyasi Partiler 1859–1952* (Istanbul: Dogan Kardes Yayınları A. S. Basımevi, 1952), pp. 161ff.
[12]Tarik Tunaya, *Hürriyetin Ilanı* (Istanbul: Baha Matbaası, 1959), pp. 50–51.
[13]Dankwart A. Rustow, "The Army and the Founding of the Turkish Republic," *World Politics*, July 1959, p. 541. For a discussion of the press in this period, see Kemal H. Karpat, "The Mass Media: Turkey," in Ward and Rustow, *op. cit.*, pp. 268–70.

II

The victory of the Allies in World War I marked the end of the Ottoman Empire and the birth of a Turkish nation. The events of 1919 and 1920 vividly demonstrated the strength of the nationalist tide sweeping through Anatolia—all that remained of a once great Empire. The Sultan's government, even though supported by the Allies, proved unable to withstand the nationalists under the leadership of Mustapha Kemal. In 1920 he was elected President of the Assembly, and by the end of 1922 he had defeated the Greek invaders and expelled the Allies.

The destruction of the Ottoman Empire, the policy of the Allies, and the War of Independence were all important socializing events for the new homogeneous state, for out of the hardships and common experiences of the populace was forged a deep sense of nationalism. Moreover, as a result of his inspired leadership Mustapha Kemal was endowed with a charisma which he utilized to elicit allegiance and to organize consent for the fulfillment of his vision of a powerful modern nation.

To do so was no easy task. To begin with, the number of western-oriented individuals committed to the radical changes that Mustapha Kemal envisaged was small. His support came from the same elements that had been the course of Young Turk support—the bureaucracy, the military, and the professions—but they comprised only a small part of the society. Furthermore, even among Mustapha Kemal's supporters, there were many individuals who opposed him on various matters.

Only the largest towns had been politicized, and although most urban dwellers had been exposed for some time to western values and technology, they could at most be classified as "transitionals."[14] Even within the elite, a majority was still not certain of the desirability of the radical transformation of the society, having in fact accepted the previous reforms and changes with scant fervor. As a result, Mustapha Kemal concentrated his efforts upon an increase in the size of the elite and its transformation into a cohesive group united in the belief that complete modernization was the only road for the new state to follow.[15]

In addition, he had also to strengthen the feelings of loyalty to the new nation among the uneducated mass of the people and to inculcate in them an acceptance of modernity. Accordingly, he embarked upon a policy of transforming the very nature of the polity and of adopting

---

[14]According to Davison, "Westernized Education," p. 301, one of the results of westernized education was to increase the gap between various social strata. The elite consisted of three distinct groups: individuals who had received a modern education, those who had attended the traditional schools, and those who had obtained a partly westernized primary education.

[15]Lewis V. Thomas and R. N. Frye, *The United States and Turkey and Iran* (Cambridge: Harvard U. Press, 1952), pp. 71–72.

reforms that would change not only the outward appearance, but hopefully the mentality and behavior of the people as well.

The next few years witnessed the rapid succession of well-known reforms which reflected the basic goal of the government, the creation of a modern secular nation with a republican form of government based on the popular will. In 1931 Atatürk defined the principles of his program as Republicanism, Nationalism, Populism, Étatism, Secularism, and Revolutionism (Reformism). These six principles were incorporated into the constitution in 1937.

A continuous effort was made to disseminate this ideology and the values reflected therein among the people, and many institutions including the schools, the party, the mass media, and the electoral system played an important role in this attempt. Throughout, stress was laid upon such symbols of nationhood as flags, anthems, national holidays, monuments, and parades, and partly to compensate for the destruction of the Ottoman past as well as to strengthen Turkish pride, it was shown that all languages of mankind are derived from Turkish (Sun Language Theory), and that Turks have played a central role in world history since antiquity (National Historical Thesis).

The relationship between education and modernization was fully understood by Mustapha Kemal[16] who enacted several reforms to speed educational development and to cut off the people from the Ottoman past, notably the introduction of the Latin alphabet and the subsequent language reform. Great efforts were also made to enlarge educational opportunities, and the number of educational institutions rapidly increased. The number of primary schools and students rose from 4,898 and 343,498, respectively, in 1923–24 to 14,010 and 1,357,760 in 1945–46; the number of secondary schools and students from 72 and 5,905 to 252 and 65,608; and the number of *lycées* and students from 23 and 1,241 to 83 and 25,515.[17]

Special attention was paid to higher education and large numbers of foreign experts were brought to Turkey to aid in the expansion and modernization of universities and professional schools. A scholarship system which gave students free education in return for future government service served to integrate the society by enabling persons from all parts of the nation to become agents of modernity by acquiring a university education.

---

[16]It is significant, for example, that the book, *The Aims of the Primary Schools*, published in 1936, contains a long introductory statement which discusses the methods to be used in applying the ideology of the CHP. Donald E. Webster, *The Turkey of Atatürk* (Philadelphia: American Academy of Political and Social Science, 1939), p. 228.
[17]These statistics are drawn from *Istatistik Yıllığı, 1941–2* (Ankara: Istatistik Umum Müdürlügü, 1943), Vol. 13 and *Istatistik Yıllığı* (1949) (Ankara: Basbakanlık Istatistik Genel Müdürlügü, 1949), Vol. 17.

Two other institutions which proved of importance in disseminating the values of the elite were the Village Institutes *(Köy Enstitüleri)* and the People's Houses *(Halkevleri)*. The former were teacher-training institutes for village youths who, upon graduation, would return to become rural teachers. Despite certain shortcomings, about 25,000 persons were graduated, and a new group of intellectuals was created, drawn from elements which had heretofore been isolated from modern ideas and attitudes.

The People's Houses were designed to serve as agencies for political communication and socialization. They replaced the *Türk Ocagı* and were officially opened in 1932 in fourteen provinces; in 1940 the idea was extended to the rural areas through the People's Rooms *(Halk Odaları)*, and by 1945 there were over 400 People's Houses and 2,338 People's Rooms.[19] The constant emphasis was upon modernization, laicism, and nationalism, and they served to create a favorable climate for the values of the modernizing elite.[20]

The People's Houses were owned and operated by the *Cumhuriyet Halk Partisi* (CHP), which played a central role not only in the dissemination of political ideology, but indeed in every aspect of Turkish society. The CHP, which Mustapha Kemal created out of the existing nationalist organizations, was the only political party in Turkey until 1946 except for two brief periods in 1924 and 1930.

Power in the party was concentrated in the hands of the elite headed by Mustapha Kemal, the Permanent President General, and their decisions were to be "obeyed by party members without reserve or condition."[21]

The party's organization, which consisted of national, provincial, district, and local branches, stretched throughout Turkey. At all levels the party's branches were centers of political activity, serving as important channels for political communication and recruitment. It has been estimated that one million persons were members in 1935 out of a total population of sixteen million.[22] The bulk of the membership was

[18]Kemal H. Karpat, Turkey's Politics: *The Transition to a Multi-Party System* (Princeton: Princeton U. Press, 1959), p. 128. For a detailed examination of the Village Institutes see Fay Kirby Berkes, "The Village Institute Movement of Turkey: An Educational Mobilization for Social Change" (Ph.D. dissertation, Teacher's College, Columbia University, 1960). A vivid account of the experiences of one graduate may be found in Mahmut Makal, *A Village in Anatolia* (London: Valentine Mitchell, 1954), Sir Wyndham Deedes trans.
[19]Kemal H. Karpat, "The People's Houses in Turkey, Establishment and Growth," *Middle East Journal*, 17 (Winter, Spring 1963), 61, 63.
[20]Originally they appeared to have been greeted with public indifference and in some instances, never managed to fulfill their objectives. *Ibid.*, pp. 65–66.
[21]These regulations which were adopted by the Fourth General Congress (1935) of the CHP are discussed by Webster, *op. cit.*, pp. 173–77.
[22]Webster, *op. cit.*, p. 177. The population figures are drawn from *Istatistik*

drawn from the politicized groups—intellectuals, bureaucrats, professionals, ex-military men, businessmen, and landlords. There were, undoubtedly, many who joined for opportunistic reasons or as a result of pressure.[23]

Membership in the party was a privilege and an achievement. Candidates were required to meet certain qualifications, and once inducted, were expected not only to obey party policy but to "know, propagate, and defend the program and the principles of the party" (Art. 4) as well as to "unremittingly carry on propaganda for and explanations of Party principles among all fellow citizens" (Art. 5).

The party's congresses served to promote the goals of education, mobilization, and integration. These were held at all levels of the party's organization, but most important were the national congresses held every four years.[24] The party's leaders, deputies, and representatives from the entire country gathered here. Theoretically the congress adopted the party's program, appointed various commissions, and listened to "state of the nation" messages—Atatürk's famous seven-day speech delivered in 1927 was one of these—but in practice the congresses served to confirm decisions made by the party elite, and thus legitimized party and government policy. Another function was to generate enthusiasm and to activate party members. Hopefully they would return home stimulated and well informed of party activities and policies.

Despite one-party rule, the forms of representative government were preserved and indeed deliberately utilized by Mustapha Kemal to legitimize his rule and to further his goals of modernization and eventual democratization.[25] Elections were held regularly from 1923 onwards, and in 1934 women were allowed to vote in national elections. The *New York Times* commented that the opportunity to vote for a woman instead of a man would lend "a certain color which has previously been lacking at the polls,"[26] but following the election of seventeen female deputies, it noted that there were nearly three times as many women in the Grand National Assembly as in the U.S. Congress.[27]

Yıllığı, 1941–42.

[23] Arif T. Payaslioglu, "Political Leadership and Political Parties: Turkey," in Ward and Rustow, *op. cit.*, pp. 420–21.

[24] For an account of these meetings, see Tunaya, *Siyasi Partiler*, pp. 568ff.

[25] It is worth emphasizing, as Maurice Duverger, *Political Parties* (New York: Wiley, 1963), pp. 276–78, points out, that the CHP cannot be classified as a totalitarian party. On the contrary, it lay claim to democratic ideals and based its right to govern on its electoral success. Nor was the organization of the party totalitarian. In fact, there apparently was a democratic spirit within the party which allowed factions to develop without purges or expulsions. See also Turhan Feyzioglu, "Les Partis Politiques en Turquie," *Revue Francaise de Science Politique*, 1954, pp. 137–39.

[26] *New York Times*, December 16, 1934.

[27] *New York Times*, February 8, 1935.

These changes reflected the ideological commitment of Mustapha Kemal to politicization, but since for many years the CHP candidate was the only name on the ballot, the elections were routine affairs and the voters reacted generally with disinterest. In the 1930's, however, following the ill-fated attempt of Mustapha Kemal to establish a "loyal opposition," various attempts were made to arouse the electorate. Although all the candidates were still approved by the CHP, there appears to have been real competition for some offices, and several independent deputies were elected.[28]

By Atatürk's death in 1938, all the indices showed that some progress had been made in economic development. Since 1923 the road network and the railroad net had almost doubled to 40,871 kilometers and 7,148 kilometers respectively.[29] Through strenuous efforts a limited amount of industrialization had taken place; an iron and steel industry, and cement, chemical, textile, paper, and food processing plants had been built. Per capita income rose from 73 TL in 1927 to 92 TL in 1938.[30]

As a result of these developments, new social classes emerged in the towns and cities—entrepreneurs, workers, professionals, businessmen —but the rural areas remained relatively unchanged, for the limited development of transportation, communication, and industry thus far achieved had not yet affected the villager. He remained outside the market economy, isolated from the mainstream of the nation.

It has been argued that the scant attention paid by the government to agricultural development was inevitable because the lack of literate and technologically knowledgeable farmers would have rendered investment in agriculture unproductive.[31] But it has also been pointed out that "the neglect of agricultural development might be deemed the original sin of the whole system of planning. Consequently . . . agricultural production did not increase, and only a limited labor force was released for urban industries. The large mass of peasants remained quite detached from the development trends of the new regime."[32]

Regardless of policy motivations, the Atatürk reforms—even those few which were specifically aimed at rural conditions—did not lead to any substantial change in peasant life. The Village Law of 1924, for

[28] See Walter F. Weiker, *The Turkish Revolution 1960–61* (Washington: Brookings, 1963), pp. 5–6. See also Eleanor Bisbee, "Test of Democracy in Turkey," *Middle East Journal*, 4 (1950), 175–76.

[29] These statistics are derived from the *Istatistik Yıllığı* cited above. It should be mentioned that a large part of the road network consisted of dirt roads of varying condition.

[30] Z. Y. Hershlag, *Turkey: An Economy in Transition* (The Hague: Uitgeverij Van Keulen N.V., 1958), p. 164.

[31] Richard D. Robinson, *The First Turkish Republic* (Cambridge: Harvard U. Press, 1963), p. 121.

[32] Hershlag, *op. cit.*, p. 169.

example, one of the first major laws enacted by the government, was designed to promote rural self-help. Unfortunately, it was largely irrelevant to the basic conditions in the villages and reflected elite ignorance of rural life. Nor did the other reforms affect village life. The peasants remained largely unaware of the significance of the new law codes. Even in those rare cases where an individual had learned of their contents they were ignored since, for example, the new position granted to women conflicted sharply with existing social customs and values. The attempt to induce change through education as reflected by the Village Institutes and the People's Houses also did not produce appreciable results. The literacy rates remained low and most villagers were untouched by any vestige of modernity. They were isolated from the national political arena except for occasional visits from the gendarmerie and the tax collector, whom they feared and hated.[33]

The gap which existed between town and village can perhaps best be highlighted by the comments of a student from Istanbul who visited a village school teacher several years after the death of Mustapha Kemal: "Mahmut—my dear fellow," he said, "the squalor, the primitive conditions in this village—they're indescribable! What do people mean by having houses and stables in these conditions? It might be the Stone Age, which one only reads about in history books!"[34]

III

Atatürk's success in politicizing the urban elements was vividly demonstrated following World War II when many people began to demand the establishment of democratic processes. For various reasons including domestic realities—growing opposition within the country and within the party—the desirability of gaining western support, and the acceptance of Atatürk's ideal of permitting an active opposition, Ismet Inönü, on November 1, 1945, declared that the country had achieved political maturity and expressed the hope that an opposition party would be founded.[35]

The organization of a minor party proved the good faith of Inönü, and the Democratic party was formally established in January 1946 by four members of the CHP.

Elections were held on July 26 (earlier than anticipated) in "an atmosphere reminiscent of the Second Constitutional Period,"[36] but the

---

[33] The impact of the Ataturk Reforms and of subsequent developments upon village life is discussed in detail by the author in *Political Change in Rural Turkey; Erdemli* (The Hague: Mouton & Co. for the Near and Middle East Institute of Columbia University, 1966).
[34] Makal, *op. cit.*, p. 162.
[35] Gotthard Jäschke, *Die Türkei in den Jahren 1942–1951* (Wiesbaden: Otto Harrassowitz, 1955), p. 53.
[36] Tunaya, *Siyasi Partiler*, p. 657.

Democrats elected only sixty-one deputies. This announcement caused an uproar within the country and charges of fraud were leveled at the government. There seems little doubt that the results were falsified.

The DP promptly began to call for reforms to prevent a repetition of these occurrences. It charged that a new electoral law was basic to fair and honest elections. Following much discussion and maneuvering by the parties, the law was amended prior to the by-elections of 1948, and a new electoral law embodying the principle of "secret ballot—open count" was adopted in 1950.[37]

The basic electoral unit was the vilayet. One deputy was allotted for every 40,000 voters, and the party slate which won a plurality of the total vote cast within the province was elected.

Such a system tends to inflate majorities and means that the parties are not represented in the Assembly in proportion to their popular vote. The CHP, for example, received 35 per cent of the popular vote in 1950 and 1954, and 41 per cent in 1957, but its deputies comprised only 13 per cent of the total in 1950, 6 per cent in 1954, and 28 per cent in 1957.[38]

In 1950 the Democratic party won an overwhelming victory. Eighty-nine per cent of the eligible voters went to the polls, and the DP won 54 per cent of the vote, electing 416 deputies out of a total of 487 as compared to 35 per cent of the vote and 67 seats for the CHP. What had happened was that the first free elections in Turkish history had allowed all segments of society to voice their dissatisfaction with the CHP which had been in power for twenty-seven long years. Intellectuals wanted democracy, businessmen resented the étatist economic policy, landowners were disturbed by the attempts—however unsuccessful—to induce change in rural areas, and the peasantry felt neglected and abused by a tyrannical administration.

Secure in its mandate, the DP attempted to carry out its campaign promises, launching an ambitious program of economic development, financed in large part by U.S. aid, and liberalizing various re-

---

[37]For an English translation, see Leslie L. Beeler, "Election of National Deputies Act," *Constitutions, Electoral Laws, Treaties of States in the Near and Middle East*, ed. Helen M. Davis (Durham: Duke U. Press, 1953), pp. 467ff. For the Assembly debates, see BMMTD, D. 8, C. 24, pp. 149–405; pp. 667–714. All the documents pertaining to this law were published by İhsan Olgun and Sait Koksal, *Yeni Milletvekilleri Secimi Kanunu* (Ankara: Yeni Matbaa, 1950). The attitude of the parties towards electoral reform is discussed by Haluk Ülman, "Secim Sistemimiz ve Başlıca Siyasî Partilerimiz," *Siyasal Bilgiler Fakültesi Dergisi*, 12, No. 2 (June 1957), 44–75.

[38]Not surprisingly, the CHP began to agitate for a system of proportional representation, although it had previously rejected the idea. Ülman, *op. cit.*, p. 71. The author concludes that "since 1946 . . . the opposition parties always found the electoral system to be inadequate, but the party in power always defended it as being the best system." Unless otherwise noted, election statistics are drawn from *Secim Neticeleri Üzerinde Bir Inceleme* (Ankara: CHP Arastirma Bürosu, 1959).

strictive laws.[39] Furthermore, the DP was aware of the importance of rural support and did its utmost to maintain the favor of the villagers by a partial relaxation of religious restrictions: the call to prayer could once again be chanted in Arabic and religious instruction became a regular school subject unless the parents requested that their children be excused.[40]

Its economic development program led to the growing integration of the villager into the national economy. The rural areas became increasingly market-oriented and the inhabitants' way of life began to change from self-sufficiency to one of greater dependence upon the market. The highway construction program and the availability of transportation[41] meant that the peasant could easily migrate to the cities and make frequent visits to market towns where he was exposed to new ideas, attitudes, and values—but since these towns are noted for their conservatism, such contacts may in fact have led to a rise in rural conservatism.

Even the peasant who was disinclined to travel was exposed to new concepts via radios which were to be found in every coffee house or party local.[42] In these places groups of villagers would gather to pass the time of day and discuss local problems or, occasionally, political issues. The army, reorganized with American support, proved to be an important means of reinforcing the changes taking place in rural areas. The peasant draftees became part of a new social environment where they were given technical training and exposed to modernism.[43]

The parties themselves were a major force in rural politicization through their organization, campaigning, and attempts to mobilize the electorate. Within a short time after the establishment of a multi-party system, all the parties had branches in almost every part of the country. At first the traditional local elites assumed the primary role in these formal structures, but increasingly, efficiency and skill became criteria

---

[39]These included the Military Service Law, the Amnesty Law, the Passport Law, the Law on Travel and Residence of Foreigners in Turkey. A new Press Law was also adopted. Karpat, *Turkey's Politics*, p. 419.

[40]In an effort to avert defeat at the polls, the CHP between 1946 and 1950 had enacted several religious reforms, including the provision of funds for the pilgrimage to Mecca, the permitting of religious instruction in primary schools, and the establishment of a theological faculty in Ankara. Dankwart A. Rustow, "Politics and Islam in Turkey 1920–1955," in Richard N. Frye (ed.), *Islam and the West* (The Hague: Mouton & Co., 1957), p. 94.

[41]By 1960, for example, the number of autos, trucks, and busses amounted to 94,591, and the number of railroad passenger/kilometers had climbed from 98,793 in 1938 to 366,327 in 1960. These figures are drawn from the *Aylık İstatistik Bülteni*, No. 79 (September 1960), 132, and No. 88 (June 1961), 12.

[42]There were 1,341,272 radios in 1959 as compared to 46,230 in 1938 and 362,466 in 1950. *Ibid.*, No. 61 (March 1959), 14.

[43]See Daniel Lerner and Richard Robinson, "Swords and Ploughshares, The Turkish Army as a Modernizing Force," *World Politics*, 1959, pp. 19–44.

for recruitment, and new leaders began to emerge who could manipulate the organizations effectively. Within a short period, the DP administration was subject to local pressures and the party structure began to serve as an effective intermediary between the villager and the government.

In their efforts to gain the support of the electorate, the parties emphasized personal contacts by party leaders with villagers through frequent meetings at all levels and by vigorous campaigning at election time. In this the DP was more successful than its opponent, which was handicapped by its past record and a rigid organization which prevented it from adjusting to the new competitive environment.

All these factors led to the emergence of the peasantry as an important factor in the political arena.[44] Although unorganized and unable to articulate its demands consistently, this class became politically conscious and aware of its potential power. Increasingly it began to apply pressure upon the existing administrative organization with the result that the traditional negative notions of government, the master-servant relationship between the administration and the peasantry, were transformed and the villager began to view the bureaucracy and the government as institutions which he could manipulate for his own benefit.

Not surprisingly, the DP was overwhelmingly re-elected in 1954. Almost the same high percentage of the electorate voted in 1950, about 89 per cent, but the DP increased its percentage of the vote to 56.6 and won 503 seats in the Assembly out of a total of 541. The CHP won 35 per cent of the vote, and only 31 seats.

Encouraged by this evidence of popular support, the Menderes government embarked upon an ambitious program of economic development which it proved unable to complete owing to haphazard planning, adverse terms of trade, large defense expenditures, and a shortage of capital. The result was a drastic inflation[45] and a scarcity of consumer items. Affected most by this economic crisis were the urban elements, especially the salaried classes, who began to criticize the administration more and more frequently.

The government proved to be highly sensitive to opposition, and many restrictive measures were adopted which limited the rights of free speech, assembly, campaigning, and the autonomy of the universities. The electoral law was also amended to make coalitions difficult, and as the elections approached, the DP amended the electoral law once again to prevent the formation of a united opposition.

---

[44]For an examination of rural political behavior, see the author's "Political Dynamics of Rural Turkey," *Middle East Journal*, 16 (Autumn 1962), 430–42.
[45]The price index for Ankara rose from 100 in 1938 to 321 in 1946, to 340 in 1950, to 403 in 1954, to 567 in 1957, to 861 in 1960. *Aylık İstatistik Bülteni*, No. 61, March 1959, p. 27.

As a result, although fewer people went to the polls and only 77 per cent of the electorate participated, the DP was again victorious. Despite its diminished support (48 per cent of the vote), it elected 424 deputies out of a total of 610, as compared to 41 per cent and 178 seats for the CHP.[46]

These results served to increase ill will between the various segments of the society, many opposition leaders charging that the DP's victory was due to its manipulation of the electoral system. The growing bitterness between the two major parties was aggravated by the changes in the country's socio-economic structure which had been occurring since 1946. Groups which had traditionally enjoyed high social status and a near-monopoly of political power, such as the intellectuals and the bureaucracy, saw their position seriously threatened by a new social stratum (including, for example, landowners and businessmen) which had assumed leadership positions in the DP and had successfully mobilized the peasant electorate.

Nor did the traditional elite approve of the economic and fiscal policies of the Menderes government. The peasantry's exemption from direct taxation placed a heavy burden upon the salaried classes while their living standard was lowered due to the inflation caused by the government's development program. And, as social status became more closely correlated with economic power, the prestige of the bureaucrats, the intellectuals, and above all, the military, began to drop.[47]

In addition to its deteriorating financial position and lowered prestige, the military was also influenced by the same factors which alienated the other "modern" segments of the society from the DP, namely the growing authoritarianism and the supposed slowdown in modernization. But it apparently remained faithful to the tradition of army neutrality and was unwilling to intervene.[48]

Nevertheless, by the middle of 1960 the military, for reasons which are still not clear despite subsequent attempts to justify its decision, abandoned its posture of political neutrality and overthrew the Menderes government.[49]

There is little doubt that from 1959 the political situation degenerated rapidly. The debate between the DP and the CHP had assumed

---

[46]For a detailed description of this election, see Kemal H. Karpat, "The Turkish Election of 1957," *Western Political Quarterly*, 14 (June 1961), 436–59.
    [47]Kemal H. Karpat, "Recent Political Developments in Turkey and their Social Background," *International Affairs*, July 1962, p. 312.
    [48]Frederick W. Frey, "Arms and the Man in Turkish Politics," *Land Reborn*, 1961, p. 10.
    [49]See Robinson, *op. cit.*, pp. 254ff. for a skeptical analysis of the stated reasons for the coup.

an increasingly inflammatory tone, and Prime Minister Menderes and President Bayar apparently decided to eliminate all opposition. Most explanations of this startling decision concentrate upon purely personal factors such as Bayar's hatred of Inönü and Menderes' sensitivity to criticism, since it is generally recognized that the DP was likely to win the next election.

In addition to psychological analyses, however, the attitude of the opponents of the Menderes administration deserves examination. It is possible to argue that their hopes of overthrowing the DP by peaceful means had been frustrated in 1957 by the government's manipulation of the electoral system and by restrictions on free speech and campaigning which had limited the opposition's opportunities of gaining public support. Now their expectations that the continuing inflation and shortages of consumer goods would lead to the electoral defeat of the government were dashed by the decision of the U.S. and the Western European countries to come to the economic rescue of the Menderes administration. Viewing the future with despair the military, the bureaucracy, and the intellectuals saw only the continuing rule of the DP and a further decline in their own position. Under these circumstances, it is plausible that personal advantage and national interest merged in the conclusion that since no other alternatives existed, direct action was necessary. An astute observer of Turkish politics appears to favor this argument, stating, "there was also reason to believe that there was afoot a deliberate move to destroy the Menderes administration by ways other than by defeating it at the polls."[50]

IV

In any event, the revolution, which took place on May 27, 1960, was greeted with passivity and resentment in the rural areas, and it was apparent that the military's support was derived solely from urban elements. Once in power the military found itself confronting serious problems including the basic question of how to reintroduce democratic processes without jeopardizing the legitimacy of the revolution. How difficult this proved to be can be seen from the fact that although the Junta had hoped to hand the government back to civilians within three months, it could not do so for nearly one and one-half years.[51]

Not only did dissension between the Junta and the armed forces develop rapidly, but within the Junta itself there was acute disagreement

---

[50]*Ibid.*, p. 264.

[51]For a discussion of the policies of the military goverment and of political developments since 1960, see the works cited by Frey, Weiker, and Karpat. See also Dankwart A. Rustow, "Turkey's Second Try at Democracy," *Yale Review*, 1963.

on basic issues such as the fate of the DP leaders and the framework of the new constitution. This struggle was resolved by the expulsion from the Junta of fourteen "radicals" who seemed more concerned with the need for basic changes in Turkish society than with the restoration of democratic processes.

The most difficult problem confronting the new regime was the fate of the arrested DP leaders, and the decision to try them was based on various considerations, including the need to legitimize the revolution and to undermine the bipolarization of the political system which had taken place during the preceding decade. Accordingly, every effort was made to tarnish the image of the DP regime by accusing Menderes of having conspired to kill his illegitimate child and Bayar of having sold a dog given to him by the King of Afghanistan. However, the attempt revealed a lack of understanding of rural political behavior and such charges did little to win the peasant away from the memory of the DP as an active, dynamic organization genuinely interested in his welfare.

The trial ended with 15 prisoners sentenced to death, 31 to life imprisonment, and 402 to prison terms of from two to twenty years. Only Menderes and two ministers were executed, Bayar's death sentence being commuted to life imprisonment on account of his age.

The new constitution and the Electoral Law which were drawn up by the Constituent Assembly convened in January 1961, were also designed to help overcome the division within the country. Among the many innovations are the bicameral legislature—one of several checks to prevent the concentration of power in the hands of the majority, a long list of fundamental rights and duties designed to prevent the abuses of the Menderes regime in such fields as freedom of speech, press, assembly, and personal liberty, and detailed economic and social provisions which include the right to strike, the right of property, freedom of work and contract, and the right to nationalize with compensation.[52]

The new electoral law was also written so as to prevent a repetition of past abuses. Every precaution was taken to ensure that elections be fair and honest; and to prevent one party from winning control of both houses, the senators were to be elected by majority vote (except for the Junta members who were appointed to the Senate following their resignation from the military), the deputies by proportional representation. Furthermore, each house is elected for a different term—four years for the Assembly, six for the Senate.[53]

---

[52]For the background of the new constitution, see Ismet Giritli, "Some Aspects of the New Turkish Constitution," *Middle East Journal,* 16 (Winter 1962); its text was published in *ibid.,* 16 (Spring 1962); it is discussed by the author in "The 1961 Turkish Constitution, an Analysis," *Islamic Studies,* September 1963.

[53]For the Constituent Assembly debates over the new electoral law, see *Temsilciler Meclisi Tutanak Dergisi,* C. 1, 1961, pp. 500ff. and C. 2 *passim.*

The fact that problems of consensus cannot be resolved by legal arrangements was vividly demonstrated by the referendum of July 9, 1961, when over 38 per cent of the voters rejected the constitution—a vote that was widely interpreted as showing dissatisfaction with the National Unity Committee (NUC) and its policies. The continuing strength of the DP was also demonstrated by the active competition between several parties to capture the support of the DP rank and file which had been deprived of its leadership by the Yassiada trials.

Of the four major parties which contested the general election in October 1961, three attempted to gain the allegiance of the former DP electorate. Two of these, the *Adalet Partisi* or Justice party (AP) and the *Yeni Turkiye Partisi* or New Turkey party (YTP) were new parties formed after the coup; the other was the existing *Cumhuriyet Millet Partisi* or Republican Nation party (CMP). The election results confirmed the success of the constitution makers; at the same time it reaffirmed the deep division which existed within the country.

The CHP actually polled a smaller percentage of the vote (37 per cent) than in 1957 although it emerged as the largest party in the Assembly with 173 seats (38 per cent) out of 450. The AP polled 35 per cent of the vote and emerged as the chief successor to the DP. It won 158 seats in the Assembly (35 per cent) and 70 seats in the Senate (46.7 per cent) out of 150 as compared to 36 seats (24 per cent) for the CHP. The CMP and YTP each polled about 14 per cent of the popular vote and won roughly that percentage of the seats in the Assembly and a slightly higher figure in the Senate.[54]

It was thus clear that a coalition government was necessary but only after the intervention of General Gürsel, who was elected President, could a government composed of the CHP and the AP be formed under the premiership of Ismet Inönü. From the outset there was widespread disagreement over policy, especially over the question of an amnesty for the ex-DP leaders—an issue which was naturally strongly stressed by the AP. The coalition broke up over this issue within seven months, and it took a month of considerable pressure by the military and agreement on the amnesty problem before Ismet Inönü was able to form a new government without the AP.

Shortly thereafter most of the political prisoners were freed and eventually the remainder were released as well. Despite the settlement of this question, Ismet Inönü was unable to provide the country with strong leadership and there was widespread dissatisfaction with the weakness of the coalition government which broke up in November 1963 following the

[54]Weiker, *op. cit.*, p. 110.

victory of the AP in local elections. Although Inönü succeeded in forming a third coalition, this one, too, was characterized by a lack of cohesion and strong leadership. Furthermore, the economic scene remained stagnant. The five-year plan inaugurated in 1963 failed to achieve the planned growth rate of 7 per cent a year[55] and Turkey continued to face serious socio-economic problems which were aggravated by its rapidly growing population. As a result the country was in a state of intellectual ferment. Ideologies of all types were discussed, conservative and even reactionary ideas were prevalent, "socialism" was attracting the attention of a growing number of persons, and many intellectuals were again considering the desirability of military rule.

However, the military remained unsure of its posture. Although two attempts at a coup, one in 1962 and the other in 1963, failed as senior officers, remembering the weaknesses and shortcomings of the previous period of military government remained aloof,[56] the military continued to be vitally concerned with political developments. In November, for example, General Cevdet Sunay, the Army Chief of Staff, warned against the actions of political parties who were allegedly dividing the nation into two camps and turning the people against the army.[57] The statement was obviously directed at the AP which was scheduled to hold its national congress shortly thereafter to elect a new leader following the death of its founder, Ragip Gümüspala. The election of Süleyman Demirel was widely hailed as a victory for the moderates.

Demirel rapidly demonstrated his political acumen, consolidating his position within the party and engineering the defeat of the Inönü coalition in February 1965 during the budget debate. This defeat, and the subsequent formation of a four-party coalition headed by a political neutral, Senator Suat Hayrı Urgüplü with Demirel as Vice Premier, were measures carefully designed to prove to the Turkish people that the army would not prevent the AP from coming to power unless it were forced to intervene because of extremist policies.

This government remained in office until the elections of October 1965, in which the AP won an overwhelming victory, polling 55 per cent of the vote and winning 240 out of 450 seats in the GNA despite an electoral system designed to strengthen the minor parties at its expense.

---

[55]The details of the plan are contained in Republic of Turkey, Prime Ministry State Planning Organization, *First Five Year Development Plan, 1963–1967* (Ankara, 1963). According to *A Summary of the Progress Report of the Implementation of the 1963 Annual Program* (Ankara, 1964), p. 36, the targets for industry, construction, and transportation were not met. In fact, the rate of increase in industry was only slightly more than half of the 12-12½ per cent target.
[56]For a discussion of the 1963 coup, see Walter F. Weiker, "The Aydemir Case and Turkey's Political Dilemma," *Middle Eastern Affairs*, 14 (November 1963), 258–70.
[57]For the text see *Yeni Gazete*, November 19, 1964.

The CHP proved once again that its appeal was limited to a minority of the electorate. Its attempt to obtain new sources of support by presenting itself as a "left of center" party not only failed but probably alienated some of its old public. It polled only 30 per cent of the vote and elected but 134 deputies. Of the minor parties, the one which attracted the most attention was TIP *(Türkiye Isci Partisi)*, a Marxist party whose strength (3 per cent of the vote) came not from the peasantry and workers it had so assiduously wooed during the campaign, but from intellectuals who had previously supported the CHP.

CONCLUSION

The story of the political development of Turkey can be viewed as essentially a case study of the basic problem confronting the under-developed world: can a country modernize rapidly within a democratic framework? From the Turkish experience it would appear at first that the answer is a qualified no—at least if democracy is equated with a universal franchise and a meaningful choice between policies and parties.

This is because the induction of the peasantry into the political arena means that a class which comprises an overwhelming majority of the population and which has usually played a negligible role in the national life is suddenly transformed into an active participant. The influx of new voters leads to the emergence of new cleavages as members of the existing elite who are probably competing among themselves for power seize the opportunity to obtain new sources of support. Thus, new alignments inevitably arise to reflect the concerns and interests of the new participants who, once given the opportunity, will quickly learn to manipulate the system for their own advantage.

But a wide gap exists between the aspirations of the rural popu-lation in the underdeveloped world and those of an elite determined to create a modern state. Upon coming to power, the party based on the peasant vote naturally adopts policies which are popular in rural areas but which the modernizers view as regression and deviation from the course of development. Therefore, unless the leaders of the society possess exceptional moral and mental qualities, it is likely that a polarization will take place and that passions and bitterness will be aroused as the division between the traditional and the modern segments of the society deepens.

This, certainly, was the experience of Turkey. Only during the reign of Atatürk were the types of reforms so basic to the creation of a modern nation state carried out. And today, although further reforms are needed if Turkey is to continue on the path of development, many of these threaten the fundamental values of the rural population which is still largely tradition-oriented, conservative in religion, and averse to the types of controls which economic planning would entail.

However it would be a mistake to consider developments only from this perspective for such an analysis overlooks one crucial factor in modernization—the wisdom and ability of the national elite. Unless enlightened leadership is forthcoming, "tutelary democracy" may achieve neither development nor democratization of the polity, and single party systems may become ossified. On the other hand, if a consensus exists among the elite rapid economic and social change can be accomplished within a democratic framework.

Furthermore, although it may be true that during the first stages of modernization, authoritarian means facilitate the introduction of the infrastructure of modernity, the very success of the reforms inaugurated in this manner may bring the society to a new stage of development where democratic processes can play a vital role. It is at this point that a new relationship between the elite and the mass has to be established, for not only does modernization entail the creation of a participant society, but if the energies of the populace are to be harnessed successfully to the difficult task of nation-building, a political society must be inaugurated wherein the peasantry is allowed to articulate its opinions and demands into a responsive political system. Clearly this is a delicate task as the example of Turkey has demonstrated, albeit a vital one for modernization. There, the DP could not provide the quality of leadership so vitally needed and a split developed between the leaders of that party and the rest of the national elite, which led ultimately to the revolution of 1960. One may ask, therefore, whether the crucial variable affecting the successful integration of the peasantry into the national political arena is not the existence and maintenance of a consensus on goals and methods among the elite.

In any event, politicization like modernization is a process which cannot be reversed and today there not only exists a deep-rooted commitment among all sectors of the populace to democratic processes but new leaders have emerged who hopefully will profit from the mistakes of the past. Accordingly, one may hope that the 1965 election will represent as great a turning point in Turkey's history as the one in 1950 and that out of the ferment of the past few years there will emerge a sense of coherence, purpose, and unity, which will enable the second Turkish republic to endure, and genuine development to take place.

FOR FURTHER READING

DOUGLAS E. ASHFORD, "Contradictions of Nationalism and Nation-Building in the Muslim World" (*Middle East Journal*, XVIII, 4, Autumn 1964, 421–430)

FREDERICK W. FREY, "Socialization to National Identification among Turkish Peasants" (Journal of Politics, XXX, 4, November 1968, 934–965)

FREDERICK W. FREY, The Turkish Political Elite (Cambridge: M.I.T. Press, 1965)

MANFRED HALPERN, The Politics of Social Change in the Middle East and North Africa (Princeton: Princeton University Press, 1963)

GEORGE S. HARRIS, "The Role of the Military in Turkish Politics" (Middle East Journal, XIX, 1, Winter 1965, 54–66; XIX, 2, Spring 1965, 153–168)

KEMAL H. KARPAT, Turkey's Politics: The Transition to a Multi-Party System (Princeton: Princeton University Press, 1959)

DANIEL LERNER, The Passing of Traditional Society: Modernizing the Middle East (New York: Free Press, 1958)

BENJAMIN RIVLIN AND JOSEPH S. SZYLIOWICZ, eds., The Contemporary Middle East: Tradition and Innovation (New York: Random House, 1965)

LESLIE L. ROOS, JR., "Attitude Change and Turkish Modernization," (Behavioral Science, XIII, 6, November 1968, 433–444)

A. HALUK ULMAN AND FRANK TACHAU, "Turkish Politics: The Attempt to Reconcile Rapid Modernization with Democracy" (Middle East Journal, XIX, 2, Spring 1965, 153–168)

ROBERT E. WARD AND DANKWART RUSTOW, eds., Political Modernization in Japan and Turkey (Princeton: Princeton University Press, 1964)

IDEOLOGY AND CULTURE
IN UGANDA NATIONALISM

Lloyd A. Fallers

"Nationalism" is a slippery concept in states whose population has been united through a colonial administration. What constitutes "the nation"? Is it the collection of different peoples united by the accidents of history—or is it a smaller group (such as a tribe) whose members share a common language, land, history, and myth of unity? Professor Fallers analyzes the difficulty Uganda confronts in choosing between conflicting ideologies of nationalism: between the ethnic solidarity of the Baganda tribe and the imposed unity of the diverse groups that live within the country's frontiers.

I

Nationalism is an ideological commitment to the pursuit of the unity, independence, and interests of a people who conceive of themselves as forming a community. It may aim at uniting a community divided by political boundaries, or it may pursue the independence of a community which is incorporated within some larger political entity. In most parts of Africa, nationalism and nationalists have faced a difficult dilemma: What is the unit to which nationalist ideology should be directed? On the one hand, the colonial territories into which the continent was divided during the 19th century usually have little community of language or culture. Although these territories form the organizational matrix for the formation of political movements aimed at independence—and must necessarily do so because they are the organizational base of the power which nationalists hope to displace—still, these territories as such hold little permanent inspiration for Africans beyond opposition to the colonial powers which created them. There is

From *American Anthropologist*, Vol. LXIII, No. 4 (1961), pp. 677–686, by permission.

little that could make up the ingredients of a Nigerian or Congolese or Tanganyikan "personality." On the other hand, the indigenous communities of Africa—the tribes—are obviously unsatisfactory bases for modern nationhood. They are usually too small and their institutions are too inadequate to the tasks of a modern state—in fact are often incompatible with these tasks. African leaders, however, want both community and viable political units; they want both the loyalty and consensus which will induce their people to support, or at least acquiesce in, the difficult tasks which lie ahead, but they also want states large enough and homogeneous enough to be capable of responding to these tasks. These problems, of course, exist in Asia as well, but the greater indigenous heterogeneity of Africa makes them particularly difficult there.

Now, in one of its aspects, this is a cultural problem. There are also, of course, organizational problems in the emergence of new nations in Africa—problems concerning the arrangement of persons and groups—but we should like to draw attention here to the cultural aspect of the process—the aspect which is concerned with the emergence of new patterns of value and belief. The new nations, in order to achieve a degree of unity of purpose, need cultures which, first, will provide a measure of consensus among their diverse peoples and, second, will be capable of the constant innovation which existence in the modern world requires. It is perhaps not an abuse of words to speak of this as a problem in "cultural management" and to use the term "ideology" to refer to that part of culture which is actively and explicitly concerned with the establishment and defense of patterns of value and belief. Ideology is thus the apologetic part of culture. If we look at it this way, those whose task it is to create cultures for the new nations—the ideologists of nationalism—have two major sources to draw upon: on the one hand, traditional African cultures and, on the other, the many and diverse elements of value and belief which may be imported from modern Europe, Asia, and America. The task is a difficult one and fraught with dilemmas: how to create in Africans a sense of self-esteem without encouraging tribalism; how to be "modern" without being "Western"; how to change rapidly without losing a sense of continuity and cultural "wholeness."

In Uganda, the territory which we shall discuss, these dilemmas are very apparent. Uganda is a British protectorate, the core of which is formed by the Kingdom of Buganda.* Buganda is the core in the

---

*[The reader should note that the language of Buganda indicates changes by prefixes, not suffixes as in Western languages. The *Baganda* are the inhabitants of the territory of *Buganda*, which is part of the East African Republic of *Uganda*. An individual member of the ethnic group is a *Muganda*; he speaks *Luganda*; the adjectival form is *Kiganda*.—Ed.]

sense that the political arrangements upon which the Protectorate rests were originally entered into in the 1880's and '90's by the British and the Baganda and, only later, and in most cases with considerably less consent, were extended to the penumbra of tribes which now make up the Eastern, Western, and Northern Provinces. A good deal of this added territory was, in fact, conquered jointly by the British and the Baganda. Buganda is also the core of the country in another, and more contemporary, sense. Buganda has contained both the capital and the commercial center of the Protectorate and consequently the new political and economic institutions which have grown up during the association with Great Britain have their locus in Buganda.

Now in Buganda, which because of its central position in the country greatly influences the quality of its politics, there has developed a peculiar combination of receptivity to innovation—a receptivity which in itself is a great asset to a nation attempting to modernize—together with a very profound commitment to certain traditional institutions and to the independent identity of Buganda—a commitment which militates against the development of a Uganda-wide unity. The Baganda have enthusiastically embraced Western education, Christianity, and a whole range of modern techniques and skills. They have, in fact, developed a deep ideological commitment to modernity—to progress—have made these things part of their culture to such an extent that Western observers ever since the turn of the century have called them "the most progressive people in eastern Africa," "the Japanese of Africa," etc. At the same time, they have retained such a deep sense of cultural identity and integrity that they are the despair of both colonial administrators and non-Baganda political leaders, each in their own way interested in territory-wide unity. Thus, they also appear to be the least assimilable people in eastern Africa. The Baganda have replaced huge chunks of their traditional culture with Western elements and yet are able to feel that their present culture has unity and is essentially theirs.

It is this paradox of profound change combined with profound separatism and conservatism (of a sort) which is at the heart of the Uganda version of the African nationalist's dilemma and which we want to try to explain. The problem may be stated thus: How has it happened that in Uganda the people who are ecologically at the center of modern economic and political development and who are ideologically most committed to modernization are at the same time the least prepared to subordinate their identity to a wider Uganda nationhood? First, we may survey briefly what we may call the acculturation situation in Uganda—try to indicate how much of Kiganda culture has changed as compared with the cultures of neighboring peoples. Then we must try to say something about the Kiganda ideology of culture change—the way the Baganda think about and justify their new culture. In doing this we shall have to say something about the historical context in which this ideology developed.

II

We may look first at the traditional state and the changes which it has undergone. Traditional Buganda was a despotism—a polity in which the independent legitimate authority of the monarch, the *Kabaka*, was maximized. At some time in the past, according to legend, the most important political offices were held by the heads of, and on behalf of, patrilineal clans and lineages. In more recent times, unilineal descent groups continued, as they still do today, to govern inheritance and succession in the domestic sphere, but more and more the government had passed out of their hands and into the hands of chiefs who were appointed by a Kabaka and loyal to him alone—a kind of proto-bureaucracy. We know something of how this happened, for the process was still going on in the late 19th century, a period for which we have documentation. However, it is sufficient to say that by the late 19th century, the kingdom was ruled by a corps of chiefs who owed their positions to the personal grace of the Kabaka, who might appoint, dismiss, transfer, and even execute them at will. Every able young man aspired to a career in the service of the Kabaka, around whom was woven a cultural tissue of arbitrary fierceness and power. The Kabaka was "the lion," "the queen ant who feeds upon her subjects," the "charcoal fire in which the nation is forged." A chief might one day be at the pinnacle of wealth and influence—the ruler of a large district and the recipient of lavish tribute from his people and estates from the Kabaka; next day, having incurred the monarch's disfavor, he might be stripped of property and office, lying in stocks, the object of scorn and physical tortures of a most imaginative kind. As we know, absolute power does not exist; there were checks in the form of advice from friends and kinsmen, but these were minimal. Consent was secured, not so much by constraint upon the Kabaka as by a nation-wide psychic and material pay-off in the shape of the spoils of war. The whole kingdom in the 19th century had become organized for expansion and plunder at the expense of neighboring peoples.

Today there is still a Kabaka's Government, recognized by the British Protectorate Government and granted a wide measure of autonomous authority. The material manifestations of this government and the activities of its members have been transformed. It occupies a large and magnificent new building at one end of a wide, tree-lined boulevard, at the other end of which is the Kabaka's modern palace. Inside the building are the most modern offices, with typewriters, filing cabinets, and telephones, occupied by the Ministries of the Treasury, Justice, Education, Health, and National Resources. In another part of the building is a legislative hall in which sits the modern Buganda parliament, a largely elected body. In the districts outside the capital there are, again, offices manned by functionaries employed on civil service terms and engaged in the tasks associated with modern government. The Kabaka himself is an elegantly-tailored, Cambridge-educated young gentleman who speaks flawless English. Along with all this change, there is also continuity: The government building is called the *Bulange* after the traditional audience-hall of the Kabaka; the parliament is called the *Lukiiko* after the traditional gathering of the chiefs to pay homage; the administrator in charge of the District of Buruli carries the title of the *Kimbugwe*, the traditional Keeper of the King's Umbilicus, which has great ritual significance. A man appointed, say, senior assistant to the Minister of Health, appears before the Kabaka, in a well-tailored business suit, and performs a war-dance, holding an imaginary spear, and recites, as did his ancestors: "I am a Muganda, a man of the Kabaka; my totem is the lung-fish and my great-great-grandfather was Serukenya of the lineage of Nalimanga, who sired Makino, who sired Sebbanja, who was my father." He then throws himself to the floor, new suit and all, and begs the Kabaka to accept his thanks. Perhaps most important of all, the doings of the government are reported and discussed in some half-dozen substantial newspapers printed in Luganda—certainly one of the very few really vigorous native-language presses in Africa.

In the field of religion, too, there has been tremendous change, with overtones of continuity. Traditional religion centered upon the cults of gods, ancestors, and nature spirits. Communication through spirit possession with these beings, all of whom were capable of influencing man's life on earth, was the principal form of religious activity. Ordinary persons sought communication with the spirits in order to cure a disorder, to secure children, or to further their political careers. The Kabaka sought it on behalf of the nation, particularly to secure supernatural support in war.

Today most of this has passed away and the vast majority of Baganda are Anglican or Roman Catholic Christians, with a strong minority of Sunni Muslims. The Christian churches are all but legally established. The Kabaka is crowned in the Anglican cathedral and there is an agreement whereby major posts in the government are shared out among the three religious groups. Both Anglican and Roman Catholic churches have largely Baganda clergies, including bishops. There is no doubt at all that the churches have entered deeply in Baganda life—have become Kiganda churches. Most importantly, perhaps, the leading members of society, in a traditional sense, are pillars of the church. Chiefs and wealthy landowners often have reserved for them special pews in little country churches which they have built. There are, of course, thousands of merely "nominal" Christians, just as there are in Europe and America, and there is a similar secularizing tendency, but an objective observer would probably say that, while Baganda are typically tempted, and sin—in rather different directions from Westerners because they live in a different milieu—probably, on the whole, they sin no more frequently. For example, there are important remnants of the past in the shape of a social system which encourages polygamy and a tradition of "pagan" magic, and Baganda often yield to both. This, however, only makes the Baganda more exotic sinners than Westerners, not more frequent or more profound sinners, for they remain Christians in a real sense all the while.

Closely associated with religion in the field of cultural change is education, for the missions which brought Christianity also founded Western-type schools. The response to Western education—and to technical training of all kinds—has been enthusiastic from the very beginning. The problem for the missions and for the government has always been to provide sufficient schools to satisfy the demand. Again, the leading members of society—the Kabaka and his leading officials—are moderately-to-well educated and they make great efforts to see that their children are even better educated. Furthermore, a good many of the elite have for half a century been educated in the very type of institution best calculated to produce the maximum socialization impact—the English "public school" type of boarding school, after which the Baganda schools were modeled. The leading Buganda government officials and the leaders of the most important political parties are overwhelmingly "old boys" of the two elite boarding schools—one Anglican and the other Roman Catholic.

Finally, there has been a radical transformation of the economy. In traditional Buganda, the average family was engaged in subsistence agriculture, growing plantains for its staple food and perhaps producing a specialized handicraft product—pottery or barkcloth or iron hoes—for exchange with its neighbors at the weekly market. Most circulation of goods and services was incidental to the exercise of political authority; that is to say, jurisdiction over land and people were one and the political hierarchy was supported by taxes and tribute in goods and services levied upon the ordinary people.

Today the average Muganda is a cash-crop farmer growing cotton or coffee for money with which to buy an ever-expanding range of imported goods. Often he holds freehold title to his land and he very frequently hires migrant foreign workers from Belgian Ruanda-Urundi by the day to supplement the family labor force during the busy season. He responds to the market in much the same way as a midwestern American farmer and tends to be coldly instrumental in his approach to agricultural technique. For example, during the political crisis of 1953-55, when the Kabaka had been exiled by the Protectorate government and when relations between the Baganda and British political officers were extremely bad, British officers of the Agriculture Department reported practically no disruption of their normally good relations with farmers. Agriculture, the Baganda felt, was a matter which should not be confused with politics.

There are more subtle levels of cultural change at which it is possible here only to hint. One of the striking characteristics of Baganda is their ability to wear Western clothing with a real feeling for style. Over much of Africa, Western clothing is worn like an uncomfortable, ill-fitting uniform, but Baganda men and women have penetrated sufficiently into the inner recesses of Western style that many of them can wear Western clothes with real taste.

III

So: Baganda are, in many ways, extremely "acculturated" and the leading members of society are the most acculturated of all. There are here no culturally conservative, traditional chiefs pitted against a group of young, Western-educated, commoner politicians. Baganda do not see, or practice, politics in these terms, as so many African peoples do. Rather, Kiganda society has acculturated, as it were, from the top down and hence the new culture tends to have universal legitimacy. Indeed, from the point of view of the Baganda, this new culture, which includes many Western ideas of government, Western education, Anglican and Roman Catholic Christianity, the motivations appropriate to a money economy—all this has become *their* culture in a fundamental way. They have, so to speak, "naturalized" the foreign elements and thus kept a sense of cultural integrity and "wholeness" through a period of radical change. They have, furthermore, developed an ideology to account for all this—an ideology which allows them to absorb foreign elements wholesale without loss of self-esteem, without loss of their deep feeling of "Ganda-ness."

This ideology is expressed in the remarkable body of Luganda literature which the Baganda have produced since they became literate at the end of the last century, a literature which includes histories, memoirs, biographies, novels, and political pamphlets. Brief quotations from a few representative works will illustrate the ideology to which we wish to draw attention.

First, an Anglican clergyman, who introduces his history of Buganda with an allegorical summary comparing the history of the kingdom with the life of an individual. Buganda, he says, was born under Kabaka Kintu, the legendary first king; went to school under Kabaka Mutesa, who was king when the first Europeans arrived in the 1860's; and came to maturity under Mutesa's son, Mwanga:

> It was Mutesa who taught the child Buganda its future.... He called the Europeans to come and teach his people ... the higher school in which he taught them was summoning the Christian missions to come to Uganda and ordering his people to become Christians (Zimbe 1939).

Then we may turn to a politician and newspaper editor, who has written two successful novels (Mulira n.d; 1951). Both are "young man makes good" stories and in both cases "making good" consists in being "progressive" in the sense of learning things Western. The novelist clearly distinguishes between Western people and Western culture. In *Aligaweesa* (the title is the name of the hero), the career of the young man is blocked by racial discrimination but he continues to pursue "progressivism" anyhow.

Lest it be thought that the ideology we refer to is confined to a group of "Uncle Toms" subservient to Europeans, let us cite a passage from a political pamphlet which was banned as seditious and which British officials regard as the most bitterly anti-European piece of writing ever published in Uganda. In a pamphlet entitled *Buganda Our Mother*, which carries roughly the chauvinistic emotional overtones of Hitler's phrase "blood and soil," the author accuses Europeans of trying to steal the land of Buganda and enslave its people. Nevertheless, he, too, is concerned to begin his work with the assurance that he regards the acceptance of elements of European culture as a good and necessary thing. The first British governor, he says, introduced the freehold land system:

> ... intending to preserve the ties of great friendship entered into by *Kabaka* Mutesa with Her Majesty the Queen of the great Kingdom of England.... We were greatly helped by the European missionaries who had been invited by *Kabaka* Mutesa to come and preach the Gospel of the Light of Truth (Mukubira n.d.).

The theme is made most explicit in the work of the greatest Muganda ideologist of them all, the late Kabaka Daudi Cwa, the father of the present Kabaka, who wrote a number of pamphlets for the guidance of his people. In a most interesting one entitled *Education, Civilization and Foreignization in Buganda,* he says:

> ... I have considered it my duty to warn very strongly all members of this young generation of Baganda that while they are legitimately entitled to strive to acquire education and civilization, they should also take very great care that acquisition of Western education and civilization do not destroy their best native traditions and customs, which in my opinion are quite as good as those found among Western civilized countries but which only require developing and remodeling where necessary ... (Daudi Cwa 1947).

If we were to synthesize what these people are saying, it would go something like this: Traditional Buganda was a progressive and vigorous country which, unfortunately, had not had the opportunity of becoming Christian and modern but which was ready to respond to these things when they were offered. Kabaka Mutesa recognized this and invited the Europeans to come and teach the Baganda. The "deal" was thus entirely voluntary on Buganda's part. When the Europeans have finished teaching what they know, they should leave. There is nothing basically incompatible between Kiganda culture and the "useful" parts of European culture; on the contrary, these European elements should be absorbed into what remains a basically Kiganda way of life.

This is the ideology by which the Baganda have lived and by which they have tried to regulate their dealings with Europeans. It has allowed them to be both intensely chauvinistic and remarkably progressive. The combination is a somewhat unusual one, and in order to explain how it was achieved we must refer to the structure of traditional Kiganda society and the way it reacted to Western intrusion. This is necessary because, as Max Weber has taught us, ideology does not work by itself; ideologies only develop and become dominant when there are groups within society capable of, and interested in, promoting them.

IV

The creators and carriers of the new ideology in Buganda were the young chiefs who achieved high office under the Kabaka in the 1880's and '90's. We may recall that in traditional Buganda, at any rate by the 19th century, most of the important political offices had ceased to be hereditary. Most were appointed by the Kabaka and the most important recruiting-ground for chiefs was the corps of pages—young boys who were sent to the palace to serve the Kabaka. A quick-witted boy would catch his master's eye and be given a subordinate post—the first step toward the higher reaches of power if he continued to serve loyally and intelligently. Now, in comparative perspective, this was, for Africa, an unusually mobile and open type of political hierarchy. It is much more common in African kingdoms for there to be an important hereditary element in political recruitment. The difference in Buganda is important for our purposes, for it meant that *within the traditional system* there was room for the wholesale replacement of personnel. An entirely new group of men could take power without violating the system, and this is what happened.

First the Arab traders and then the Christian missionaries established themselves at court and began to proselytize among the pages. Why traditional Kiganda religion did not oppose this with greater vigor is a question which we need not pursue; we may say simply that the Kabaka regarded all religion in an essentially instrumental way and hence encouraged competition among Christianity, Islam, and the traditional cults in the hope of deriving maximum benefit from all of them without committing himself to any. The result was a struggle among factions of young chiefs, aided by the Arabs in the case of the Muslims and the Europeans in the case of the Christians. The Christians won.

Thus it happened that a new set of chiefs, committed to Christianity and progress, came to power at a time when the fundamentals of the relationship between the British and the Baganda were being worked out. Because they had been recruited from traditional sources and because the traditional system provided for recruitment through achievement, they did not look upon themselves as revolutionaries in the sense of basically altering political arrangements; rather they were Christianizing and improving a king and kingdom to which they remained intensely loyal. (We know something about how they saw these events because several of them wrote memoirs.) Although they were at times made aware of British power in a way which indicated quite clearly that the protectorate was not really an arrangement arrived at between equals, still they could believe that they had secured the benefits of association with Britain with a minimum of political interference. There was much rancor in later years between the two parties over the interpretation of the Agreement which set the terms of relationship, but the Baganda have always held, with substantial success, to their version, elaborated in the ideology which has been described.

Thus it happens that the Baganda, the pivotal tribe in Uganda, have contributed to the country a powerful impulse toward modernization but have also remained intensely chauvinistic and reluctant to merge themselves into a wider Uganda nationalism. The other peoples of Uganda tend to regard the Baganda with a mixture of admiration and resentment. Among their Bantu-speaking cousins in southern Uganda, admiration tends to predominate, while among the Nilotic—and so-called "Nilo-Hamitic"—speaking peoples of the north, resentment is perhaps the stronger element. Everywhere, however, there is reluctance to solve the problem by accepting Baganda domination, for the Baganda, in their peculiar form of "progressive isolationism," have been emulated by the other tribes during most of the past fifty years with the active encouragement of the British Protectorate Government. The Baganda, it would seem, must either seek their political future alone or else be prepared to give up the unique ideological advantages of their isolation.

V

The situation which we have described is an unusual one in Africa. In most parts of the continent there has been less continuity between traditional and modern culture, either because colonial regimes have actively promoted discontinuity, as in the French territories, or because traditional societies have been too inflexible to permit the rise to positions of influence within traditional society of the bearers of the new cultural syntheses—a situation common in British areas even where continuity has been favored. But if this case is unusual, the broader problem of "cultural management" is not. Everywhere there is the need to create cultural community where in the past little existed. African ideologists lack the cultural resources which their Asian counterparts find in the religious "high cultures" of Hinduism, Buddhism, and Islam. (Many Africans, of course, are Muslims, but few new African nations are even largely Muslim.) The more general, underlying cultural unities of traditional Africa, or even of those regions which form the new national states, though undoubtedly real on some level, are as yet too vaguely understood to make good ideological material. (By contributing to an understanding of these unities anthropologists may, indeed, contribute in an important way to nation-building!) Neither do the cultures of the metropoles—France, Britain, Belgium, and Portugal—provide satisfactory sources for new national cultures (though of course they contribute to them), if for no other reason than that these have for too long been identified with negrophobia. The French African intellectuals who have so whole-heartedly identified themselves with French culture can find in it a real source of self-esteem only by reversing its judgment of themselves. Their slogan, "negritude," tends to be little more than a call for equality, or dominance, for dark-skinned Frenchmen—a thin, and even dangerous, basis for a national culture.

Our purpose, however, is not so much to relate the difficulties faced by modern Africa's ideologists; rather we wish to draw atten-

tion to the burst of cultural creativity which these difficulties will undoubtedly call forth. Far from robbing anthropologists of their material, the "winds of change" in Africa may provide them with an unprecedented opportunity to study culture in the making.*

---

*References Cited:
DAUDI CWA, KABAKA, 1947, Obuyigirize, Obulabufu n'Okwezaya mu Buganda,
In Kabaka Daudi Cwa, Obulamu, Omulembe n'Ebirowoozo Bye, M. Kaizi, ed. Kampala,
Baganda C. S. Press.
FALLERS, MARGARET C., 1960, The Eastern Lacustrine Bantu. Ethnographic
Survey of Africa, East Central Africa Part XI, London, International African Institute.
MUKUBIRA, D., n.d., Buganda Nyaffe, Kampala, Baganda, C. S. Press.
MULIRA, E. M. K., n.d., Aligaweesa. Publisher unknown; and, 1951, Teefe,
Kampala, Uganda Bookshop.
ZIMBE, B. M., 1939, Buganda ne Kabaka. Kampala, Gambuze Press.

FOR FURTHER READING

DAVID E. APTER, *The Political Kingdom in Uganda: A Study of Bureaucratic
Nationalism* (Princeton: Princeton University Press, 1961)
DAVID E. APTER, "The Role of Traditionalism in the Political Modernization of
Ghana and Uganda" *(World Politics, XII, 1, October 1960, 45–68)*
FRED G. BURKE, *Local Government and Politics in Uganda* (Syracuse: Syracuse
University Press, 1964)
KENNETH INGHAM, *The Making of Modern Uganda* (London: Allen and Unwin,
1958)
INTERNATIONAL BANK FOR RECONSTRUCTION AND DEVELOPMENT, *The Economic
Development of Uganda* (Baltimore: Johns Hopkins Press, 1962)
D. A. LOW, *Political Parties in Uganda 1949–1962* (London: Athlone Press, 1962)
D. A. LOW AND R. C. PRATT, *Buganda and British Overrule 1900–1955* (New York:
Oxford University Press, 1960)
JOSEPH S. NYE, JR., *Pan-Africanism and East African Integration* (Cambridge:
Harvard University Press, 1965)
DONALD ROTHCHILD AND MICHAEL ROGIN, "Uganda," in Gwendolen M. Carter, ed.,
National Unity and Regionalism in Eight African States (Ithaca: Cor-
nell University Press, 1965), 337–440
SPECIAL CORRESPONDENT, "The Uganda Army: Nexus of Power" *(Africa Report,
XI, 9, December 1966, 37-39)*
M. CRAWFORD YOUNG, "The Obote Revolution" *(Africa Report, XI, 6, June 1966,
8–14)*

SOCIAL MOBILIZATION AND POLITICAL DEVELOPMENT

Karl W. Deutsch

How does social change affect politics? Professor Deutsch illustrates how social mobilization influences popular demands for government services, for political and administrative reform, for broadening of the political elite, and for greater participation. In states divided by language or culture, social mobilization may exacerbate problems of national unity.

Social mobilization is a name given to an over-all process of change, which happens to substantial parts of the population in countries which are moving from traditional to modern ways of life. It denotes a concept which brackets together a number of more specific processes of change, such as changes of residence, of occupation, of social setting, of face-to-face associates, of institutions, roles, and ways of acting, of experiences and expectations, and finally of personal memories, habits and needs, including the need for new patterns of group affiliation and new images of personal identity. Singly, and even more in their cumulative impact, these changes tend to influence and sometimes to transform political behavior.

The concept of social mobilization is not merely a short way of referring to the collection of changes just listed, including any extensions of this list. It implies that these processes tend to go together in certain historical situations and stages of economic development; that these situations are identifiable and recurrent, in their essentials, from one country to another; and that they are relevant for politics. Each of these points will be taken up in the course of this paper.

Reprinted from *The American Political Science Review*, Vol. LV, No. 3 (September, 1961), pp. 493–514, by permission of The American Political Science Association.

A draft version of this paper was presented at the meeting of the Committee on Comparative Politics, of the Social Science Research Council, Gould House, Dobbs Ferry, N.Y., June 10, 1959. An earlier version of this text is appearing in *Zeitschrift für Politik* (Köln, Germany).

Further work on this paper was supported in part by the Carnegie Corporation, and I am indebted for assistance in statistical application to Charles L. Taylor and Alex Weilenmann.

Social mobilization, let us repeat, is something that happens to large numbers of people in areas which undergo modernization, *i.e.*, where advanced, non-traditional practices in culture, technology, and economic life are introduced and accepted on a considerable scale. It is not identical, therefore, with this process of modernization as a whole,[1] but it deals with one of its major aspects, or better, with a recurrent cluster among its consequences. These consequences, once they occur on a substantial scale, influence in turn the further process of modernization. Thus, what can be treated for a short time span as a consequence of the modernization process, appears over a longer period as one of its continuing aspects and as a significant cause, in the well-known pattern of feedback or circular causation.

Viewed over a longer time perspective, such as several decades, the concept of social mobilization suggests that several of the changes subsumed under it will tend to go together in terms of recurrent association, well above anything to be expected from mere chance. Thus, any one of the forms of social mobilization, such as the entry into market relations and a money economy (and hence away from subsistence farming and barter) should be expected to be accompanied or followed by a significant rise in the frequency of impersonal contacts, or in exposure to mass media of communication, or in changes of residence, or in political or quasi-political participation. The implication of the concept is thus to assert an empirical fact—that of significantly frequent association—and this assertion can be empirically tested.

This notion of social mobilization was perceived early in intuitive terms, as a historical recollection or a poetic image. It was based on the historical experiences of the French *levée en masse* in 1793 and of the German "total mobilization" of 1914-18, described dramatically in terms of its social and emotional impact by many German writers, including notably Ernst Jünger. A somewhat related image was that of the long-term and world-wide process of "fundamental democratization," discussed

---

[1]For broader discussions of the modernization process, see Rupert Emerson, *From Empire to Nation* (Cambridge, Harvard University Press, 1960); Harold D. Lasswell, *The World Revolution of Our Time* (Stanford University Press, 1951); and Gabriel A. Almond and James S. Coleman, eds., *The Politics of the Developing Areas* (Princeton, Princeton University Press, 1960). *Cf.* also Daniel Lerner, *The Passing of Traditional Society* (New York, Free Press, 1958), and Lerner, "Communication Systems and Social Systems: A Statistical Exploration in History and Policy," *Behavioral Science*, Vol. 2 (October, 1957), pp. 266–275; Fred Riggs, "Bureaucracy in Traditional Societies: Politics, Economic Development and Administration," American Political Science Association Annual Meeting, September, 1959, multigraphed; Dankwart Rustow, *Politics and Westernization in the Near East* (Center of International Studies, Princeton University, 1956); and Lyle Shannon, "Is Level of Development Related to Capacity for Self-Government?" *American Journal of Economics and Sociology*, Vol. 17 (July, 1958), pp. 367–381, and Shannon, "Socio-Economic Development and Political Status," *Social Problems*, Vol. 7 (Fall, 1959), pp. 157–169.

in some of the writings of Karl Mannheim.[2] All these images suggest a breaking away from old commitments to traditional ways of living, and a moving into new situations, where new patterns of behavior are relevant and needed, and where new commitments may have to be made.

Social mobilization can be defined, therefore, as the process in which major clusters of old social, economic and psychological commitments are eroded or broken and people become available for new patterns of socialization and behavior. As Edward Shils has rightly pointed out,[3] the original images of "mobilization" and of Mannheim's "fundamental democratization" imply two distinct stages of the process: (1) the stage of uprooting or breaking away from old settings, habits and commitments; and (2) the induction of the mobilized persons into some relatively stable new patterns of group membership, organization and commitment. In this fashion, soldiers are mobilized *from* their homes and families and mobilized *into* the army in which they then serve. Similarly, Mannheim suggests an image of large numbers of people moving away *from* a life of local isolation, traditionalism and political apathy, and moving *into* a different life of broader and deeper involvement in the vast complexities of modern life, including potential and actual involvement in mass politics.

It is a task of political theory to make this image more specific; to bring it into a form in which it can be verified by evidence; and to develop the problem to a point where the question "how?" can be supplemented usefully by the question "how much?" In its intuitive form, the concept of social mobilization already carried with it some images of growing numbers and rising curves. In so far as the constituent processes of social mobilization can be measured and described quantitatively in terms of such curves, it may be interesting to learn how fast the curves rise, whether they show any turning points, or whether they cross any thresholds beyond which the processes they depict have different side effects from those that went before. Notable among these side effects are any that bear on the performance of political systems and upon the stability and capabilities of governments.[4]

I. AN ANALYTICAL FORMULATION

Let M stand for the generalized process of social mobilization, and let us think of it as representing the general propensity or availability of persons for recommitment. In this sense, M could be measured by the

---

[2]Karl Mannheim, *Man and Society in an Age of Reconstruction* (New York, 1940).

[3]Edward Shils, at the Social Science Research Council Conference on Comparative Politics.

[4]For a broader discussion of quantitative indicators, bearing on problems of this kind, see Karl W. Deutsch, "Toward an Inventory of Basic Trends and Patterns in Comparative and International Politics," *American Political Science Review*, Vol. 54 (March, 1960), p. 34.

average probability that any person, say between fifteen and sixty-five years old, would have undergone, or could be expected to undergo during his lifetime, a substantial change from old ways of living to new ones. In order to define this change more precisely, it is necessary to make three assumptions: (1) there are different forms of social recommitment relevant for politics; (2) these forms tend to be associated with each other; and (3) these forms tend to reinforce each other in their effects. Two further points may be noted for investigation: (4) each of these forms may have a threshold at which some of its effects may change substantially; and (5) some or all of these thresholds, though not identical in quantitative terms, may be significantly related to each other.

For these constituent processes of social mobilization we may then choose the symbols m_1, m_2, m_3 . . . , mn. Thus we may call m_1 the exposure to aspects of modern life through demonstrations of machinery, buildings, installations, consumer goods, show windows, rumor, governmental, medical or military practices, as well as through mass media of communication. Then m_2 may stand for a narrower concept, exposure to these mass media alone. And m_3 may stand for change of residence; m_4 for urbanization; m_5 for change from agricultural occupations; m_6 for literacy; m_7 for per capita income; and so on.

Our m_1 could then stand for the percentage of the population that had been exposed in any substantial way to significant aspects of modern life; m_2 for the percentage of those exposed to mass media, *i.e.,* the mass media audience; m_3 for the percentage of the inhabitants who have changed their locality of residence (or their district, province or state); m_4 for the percentage of the total population living in towns; m_5 for the percentage of those in non-agricultural occupations among the total of those gainfully occupied; m_6 for the percentage of literates; m_7 could be measured simply by net national product, or alternatively by gross national product in dollars per capita. At this stage in the compilation of evidence the exact choice of indicators and definitions must be considerably influenced by the availability of statistical data. In many cases it may be most satisfactory to use the data and definitions published by the United Nations, in such volumes as the *United Nations Demographic Year Book*, the *United Nations World Social Survey*, the *United Nations Statistical Year Book*, and a host of more specialized UN publications.[5]

[5]*Cf.* the pamphlets issued by the Statistical Office of the United Nations, Statistical Papers, Series K, No. 1, "Survey of Social Statistics," (Sales No.: 1954. XVII. 8), New York, 1954, and Statistical Papers, Series M, No. 11, Rev. 1, "List of Statistical Series Collected by International Organizations," (Sales No.: 1955. XVII. 6), New York, 1955. For somewhat earlier data, see also W. S. Woytinsky and E. S. Woytinsky, *World Commerce and Governments: Trends and Outlook* (New York, The Twentieth Century Fund, 1955), and *World Population and Production: Trends and Outlook* (New York, The Twentieth Century Fund, 1953).

In a modern, highly developed and fully mobilized country m_7 should be above $600 gross national product per capita: m_1, m_2, and m_6 should all be well above 90 per cent; m_4 and m_5 should be above 50 per cent, even in countries producing large agricultural surpluses beyond their domestic consumption; and even m_3, the change of residence, seems to be higher than 50 per cent in such a country as the United States. In an extremely underdeveloped country, such as Ethiopia, m_7 is well below $100 and the remaining indicators may be near 5 per cent or even lower.

In the course of economic development, as countries are becoming somewhat less like Ethiopia and somewhat more like the United States, all these indicators tend to change in the same direction, even though they do not change at the same rate. They exhibit therefore to some extent a characteristic which Paul Lazarsfeld has termed the "interchangeability of indicators"; if one (or even several) of these indicators should be missing it could be replaced in many cases by the remaining ones, or by other indicators similarly chosen, and the general level and direction of the underlying social process would still remain clear.[6] This characteristic holds, however, only as a first approximation. The lags and discrepancies between the different indicators can reveal much of interest to the student of politics, and some of these discrepancies will be discussed below.

The first and main thing about social mobilization is, however, that it does assume a single underlying process of which particular indicators represent only particular aspects; that these indicators are correlated and to a limited extent interchangeable; and that this complex of processes of social change is significantly correlated with major changes in politics.

The overall index of social mobilization, M, is a second order index; it measures the correlation between the first order indices m_1 ... m_n. It should express furthermore, the probability that the $(n + 1)$th index will be similarly correlated with its predecessors, regardless of how large a number n might be, provided only that the index itself was appropriately chosen. Differently put, to assert that social mobilization is a "real" process, at certain times and in certain countries, is to assert that there exists for these cases a large and potentially unlimited number of possible measurements and indicators, all correlated with each other and testifying by their number and by the strength of their correlation to the reality of the underlying phenomenon.

---

[6] See Hortense Horwitz and Elias Smith, "The Interchangeability of Socio-Economic Indices," in Paul F. Lazarsfeld and Morris Rosenberg, *The Language of Social Research* (New York, Free Press, 1955), pp. 73–77.

In practice, of course, the range of available measurements and indicators is likely to be limited, and ordinarily there should be no need to compile for any particular time and country even all those data that could be found. On the contrary, one's usual aim will be economy: to get the greatest amount of useful information from the smallest body of data. The seven indicators of social mobilization listed above as m_1 to m_7 should quite suffice, in most cases, to give a fairly good first picture of the situation. They were chosen in part on grounds of availability and convenience, but also because they are less closely correlated, and hence less completely interchangeable, than some other indices might be.

Each of the seven processes chosen could itself be measured by several different indicators, but in each case these subindicators are apt to be very closely correlated and almost completely interchangeable. Literacy, for instance, can be measured as a percentage of the population above fifteen or above ten, or above seven years of age; it could be defined as the ability to recognize a few words, or to read consecutively, or to write. Each of these particular definitions would yield a different numerical answer, but so long as the same definition was used for each country, or for each period within the same country, each of these yardsticks would reveal much the same state of affairs. If applied to Morocco between 1920 and 1950, *e.g.*, each of these tests would have shown how the number of literate Moroccans began to outgrow the number of literate Frenchmen in that country, with obvious implications for its political future.

Similarly, urbanization could be measured in terms of the population of all localities of more than 2,000 or more than 5,000, or more than 20,000, or 50,000 inhabitants; or it could be measured, less satisfactorily, in terms of the population of all those localities that had a charter or a city form of government. Each of these criteria of measurement would have revealed the same process of large-scale urban growth in Finland between 1870 and 1920, for instance, or in India between 1900 and 1940, which had such far-reaching effects on political life in these countries. A recent unpublished study by Frederick E. Tibbetts 3d suggests once again the close interchangeability of different indicators of urban growth in Canada, as they bear upon the problems of assimilation and differentiation among the French-speaking and English-speaking population of that country. Urbanization, Tibbetts finds, has outstripped in recent decades the learning of English among French-Canadians; he finds among urban residents, and generally in non-agricultural occupations, a growing number of persons who speak no other language but French. The political significance of this development, which was largely concentrated in the province of Quebec, is highlighted by his observation that in 1951 Quebec (omitting Montreal), with 21 per cent of the total population of Canada, had only 4 and 7 per cent, respectively, of the veterans of World Wars I and II.[7]

Among the seven major indicators of social mobilization proposed in this paper, the correlations between economic development and literacy are less complete and the discrepancies more revealing. Ethiopia and Burma both have per capita gross national products of about $50, but Ethiopia has less than 5 per cent literates and is politically stable; Burma reports over 45 per cent literates and is not.[8] Of the states of India, Kerala, with one of the highest rates of literacy, elected a Communist government in the late 1950s.

It may thus be useful to seek answers to two kinds of questions: (1) how good is the correlation between the seven main indicators and (2) how interesting are the variant cases? As regards the first question, it has already been pointed out that the numerical values of the seven main indicators will not be identical. However if we think of each of these indicators as forming a separate scale, on which each country could rank anywhere from, say, the top fifth to the bottom fifth, then we could measure the extent to which the ranking of a country on each of these indicator scales is correlated. From general impressions of the data, I should surmise that these rank order correlations should have coefficients of correlation of about 0.6 to 0.8, accounting on the average for perhaps one-half of the observed variation. As regards the second question, each of the cases showing substantial discrepancies between some of the main indicators will have to be studied separately, but the examples of Burma and Kerala, just mentioned, suggest that such cases may well repay investigation, and that the comparison of indicators may serve political scientists as a crude but perhaps useful research device.

For a somewhat more refined study the notion of two thresholds may be introduced. The first of these is the threshold of significance, S, that is, the numerical value below which no significant departure from the customary workings of a traditional society can be detected and no significant disturbance appears to be created in its unchanged functioning. For each of the particular indicators, m_1 through m_7, we should expect to find a corresponding particular threshold of significance, s_1 through s_7; and our concept of social mobilization should imply that, once several major indicators move to or beyond this threshold of significance, the

---

[7]Frederick E. Tibbetts, 3d, "The Cycles of Canadian Nationalism," Yale University, typescript, 1959, pp. 24, 26–31. For details of the Finnish and Indian cases referred to above, see K. W. Deutsch, *Nationalism and Social Communication* (New York, 1953), pp. 102–110, 170–182, 197–204.

[8]Note, however, the comment on Burmese literacy, in the Appendix to this article. [Ed. note: This appendix has been omitted.]

remaining indicators should also be at or above their respective levels of significance. The probability that this will be in fact the case should indicate once again what degree of reality, if any, may be inherent in the concept of social mobilization as an overall process.

The second threshold would be that of criticality for significant changes in the side effects, actual or apparent, of the process of social mobilization. At what level of each of the indicators we listed above do such changes in social or political side effects appear?

The indicator of literacy may serve as an example. It has often been remarked that even a considerable advance in literacy, say from 10 per cent to 60 per cent of the population above fifteen years of age, does not seem to be correlated with any significant change in the birthrate, if one compares literacy and birthrate levels of a large number of countries in the 1950s. At the level of 80 per cent literacy, however, there appears a conspicuous change: for the same collection of countries, not one with a literacy rate above 80 per cent has a birthrate above 3 per cent a year.[9] As a provisional hypothesis for further testing, one might conjecture that a literacy rate of more than 80 per cent might indicate such an advanced and thoroughgoing stage of social mobilization and modernization as to influence even those intimate patterns of family life that find their expression in the birthrate of a country. Obviously such a hypothesis would require other evidence for confirmation, but even in its quite tentative stage it may illustrate our point. If it were true, then the 80 per cent level would be a threshold of criticality on the particular scale of literacy as an indicator of social mobilization.

Since we called the indicator of literacy m_6, we might write c_6 for the particular threshold of criticality on that scale and put it as equal to 80 per cent. It would then be a matter for further investigation to find out whether other critical changes also occur near the passing of the 80 per cent literacy level. If so, c_6 might turn out to be the main threshold of criticality for this indicator. If important side effects should show critical changes at different literacy levels, we might have to assume several thresholds of criticality, which we might write c_6', c_6'', and so on.

Other indicators might well have their own thresholds of criticality at other percentage points on their particular scales. It might turn out, for instance, that most of the countries with more than 80 per cent literacy were also more than, say, 40 per cent urban, and that the apparent side effects observable above the 80 per cent literacy mark were also observable above the 40 per cent level on the urbanization scale. If such

---

[9]Rosemary Klineberg, "Correlation of Literacy Rates with 1956 Birth Rates," Fletcher School of Law and Diplomacy, 1959, unpublished.

different but correlated thresholds of criticality could be found for all of our seven indicators, then the concept of social mobilization could be expressed as a probability that, if for some country n different indicators should show values equal to or greater than their respective critical levels, then any relevant $(n + 1)$th indicator also would turn out to be at or above its own critical threshold.

Much of what has been said thus far may be summarized in concise notation. If we write P as the conventional symbol for probability, M_S as the symbol for the overall process of social mobilization in regard to the thresholds of significance, and M_C as the symbol for the same process in regard to the thresholds of criticality, then we may write the general concept of social mobilization briefly as follows:

(1) $M_S = P$ (if $m_n \leqq s_n$, then $m_{n+1} \leqq s_{n+1}$)
or briefly,

(1a) $M_S = P \ (m_n \leqq s_n)$
and

(2) $M_C = P$ (if $m_n \leqq c_n$, then $m_{n+1} \leqq c_{n+1}$)
or briefly,

(2a) $M_C = (m_n \leqq c_n)$
and perhaps also

(3) $M = P \ (M_S = M_C)$

None of these shorthand formulas should require further comment here. They merely summarize what has been said at greater length in the preceding pages. Readers who find such formulations uncongenial may skip them, therefore, without loss, so long as they have followed the verbal argument.

II. SOME IMPLICATIONS FOR THE POLITICS OF DEVELOPMENT

In whatever country it occurs, social mobilization brings with it an expansion of the politically relevant strata of the population. These politically relevant strata are a broader group than the elite: they include all those persons who must be taken into account in politics. Dock workers and trade union members in Ghana, Nigeria, or the United States, for instance, are not necessarily members of the elites of these countries, but they are quite likely to count for something in their political life. In the developing countries of Asia, Africa and parts of Latin America, the political process usually does not include the mass of isolated, subsistence-farming, tradition-bound, and politically apathetic villagers, but it does include increasingly the growing numbers of city dwellers, market farmers, users of money, wage earners, radio listeners and literates in town and country. The growth in the numbers of these people produces mounting pressures for the transformation of political practices and institutions; and since this future growth can be estimated at least to some extent on the basis of trends and data from the recent past, some of the expectable growth in political pressures—we may call it the potential level of political tensions—can likewise be estimated.

Social mobilization also brings about a change in the quality of politics, by changing the range of human needs that impinge upon the political process. As people are uprooted from their physical and intellectual isolation in their immediate localities, from their old habits and traditions, and often from their old patterns of occupation and places of residence, they experience drastic changes in their needs. They may now come to need provisions for housing and employment, for social security against illness and old age, for medical care against the health hazards of their crowded new dwellings and places of work and the risk of accidents with unfamiliar machinery. They may need succor against the risks of cyclical or seasonal unemployment, against oppressive charges of rent or interest, and against sharp fluctuations in the prices of the main commodities which they must sell or buy. They need instruction for themselves and education for their children. They need, in short, a wide range and large amounts of new government services.

These needs ordinarily cannot be met by traditional types of government, inherited from a precommercial and preindustrial age. Maharajahs, sultans, sheikhs, and chieftains all are quite unlikely to cope with these new problems, and traditional rule by land-owning oligarchies or long established religious bodies most often is apt to prove equally disappointing in the face of the new needs. Most of the attempts to change the characteristics of the traditional ruling families—perhaps by supplying them with foreign advisers or by having their children study in some foreign country—are likely to remain superficial in their effects, overshadowed by mounting pressures for more thoroughgoing changes.

In developing countries of today, however, the increasingly ineffective and unpopular traditional authorities cannot be replaced successfully by their historic successors in the Western world, the classic institutions of eighteenth and nineteenth century liberalism and laissez-faire. For the uprooted, impoverished and disoriented masses produced by social mobilization, it is surely untrue that that government is best that governs least. They are far more likely to need a direct transition from traditional government to the essentials of a modern welfare state. The developing countries of Asia, Africa, and parts of Latin America may have to accomplish, therefore, within a few decades a process of political change which in the history of Western Europe and North America took at least as many generations; and they may have to accomplish this accelerated change almost in the manner of a jump, omitting as impractical some of the historic stages of transition through a period of near laissez-faire that occurred in the West.

The growing need for new and old government services usually implies persistent political pressures for an increased scope of government and a greater relative size of the government sector in the national economy. In the mid-1950s, the total government budget—national, regional and local—tended to amount to roughly 10 per cent of the gross national product in the very poor and poorly mobilized countries with annual per capita gross national products at or below $100. For highly developed and highly mobilized countries, such as those with per capita gross national products at or above $900, the corresponding proportion of the total government sector was about 30 per cent. If one drew only the crudest and most provisional inference from these figures, one might expect something like a 2.5 per cent shift of national income into the government sector for every $100 gain in per capita gross national product in the course of economic development. It might be more plausible, however, to expect a somewhat more rapid expansion of the government sector during the earlier stages of economic development, but the elucidation of this entire problem—with all its obvious political implications—would require and reward a great deal more research.

The relationship between the total process of social mobilization and the growth of the national income, it should be recalled here, is by no means symmetrical. Sustained income growth is very unlikely without social mobilization, but a good deal of social mobilization may be going on even in the absence of per capita income growth, such as occurs in countries with poor resources or investment policies, and with rapid population growth. In such cases, social mobilization still would generate pressures for an expansion of government services and hence of the government sector, even in a relatively stagnant or conceivably retrograde economy. Stopping or reversing in such cases the expansion of government or the process of social mobilization behind it—even if this could be done—hardly would make matters much better. The more attractive course for such countries might rather be to use the capabilities of their expanding governments so as to bring about improvements in their resources and investment policies, and an eventual resumption of economic growth. To what extent this has been, or could be, brought about in cases of this kind, would make another fascinating topic for study.

The figures just given apply, of course, only to non-Communist countries; the inclusion of Communist states would make the average in each class of government sectors higher. It would be interesting to investigate, however, whether and to what extent the tendency toward the relative expansion of the government sector in the course of social mobilization applies also, *mutatis mutandis,* to the Communist countries.

A greater scope of governmental services and functions requires ordinarily an increase in the capabilities of government. Usually it requires an increase in the numbers and training of governmental personnel, an increase in governmental offices and institutions, and a significant improvement in administrative organization and efficiency. A rapid process of social mobilization thus tends to generate major pressures for political and administrative reform. Such reforms may include notably both a quantitative expansion of the bureaucracy and its qualitative improvement in the direction of a competent civil service—even though these two objectives at times may clash.

Similar to its impact on this specific area of government, social mobilization tends to generate also pressures for a more general transformation of the political elite. It tends to generate pressures for a broadening and partial transformation of elite functions, of elite recruitment, and of elite communications. On all these counts, the old elites of traditional chiefs, village headmen, and local notables are likely to prove ever more inadequate; and political leadership may tend to shift to the new political elite of party or quasi-party organizations, formal and informal, legal or illegal, but always led by the new "marginal men" who have been exposed more or less thoroughly to the impact of modern education and urban life.

Something similar applies to elite communications. The more broadly recruited elites must communicate among themselves, and they must do so more often impersonally and over greater distances. They must resort more often to writing and to paper work. At the same time they must direct a greater part of their communications output at the new political strata; this puts a premium on oratory and journalism, and on skill in the use of all mass media of communication. At the same time rapid social mobilization causes a critical problem in the communication intake of elites. It confronts them with the ever present risk of losing touch with the newly mobilized social strata which until recently still did not count in politics. Prime Minister Nehru's reluctance to take into account the strength and intensity of Mahratti sentiment in the language conflict of Bombay in the 1950s and his general tendency since the mid-1930s to underestimate the strength of communal and linguistic sentiment in India suggest the seriousness of this problem even for major democratic leaders.

The increasing numbers of the mobilized population, and the greater scope and urgency of their needs for political descisions and governmental services, tend to translate themselves, albeit with a time lag, into increased political participation. This may express itself informally through greater numbers of people taking part in crowds and riots, in meetings and demonstrations, in strikes and uprisings, or less dramatically, as members of a growing audience for political communications, written or by radio, or finally as members of a growing host of organizations. While many of these organizations are ostensibly non-political, such as improvement societies, study circles, singing clubs, gymnastic societies, agricultural and commercial associations, fraternal orders, workmen's benefit societies, and the like, they nevertheless tend to acquire a political tinge, particularly in countries where more open outlets for political activities are not available. But even where there are established political parties and elections, a network of seemingly non-political or marginally political organizations serves an important political function by providing a dependable social setting for the individuals who have been partly or wholly uprooted or alienated from their traditional communities. Such organizations may serve at the same time as marshalling grounds for the entry of these persons into political life.

Where people have the right to vote, the effects of social mobilization are likely to be reflected in the electoral statistics. This process finds its expression both through a tendency towards a higher voting participation of those already enfranchised and through an extension of the franchise itself to additional groups of the population. Often the increase in participation amongst those who already have the right to vote precedes the enfranchisement of new classes of voters, particularly in countries where the broadening of the franchise is occurring gradually. Thus in Norway between 1830 and 1860, voting participation remained near the level of about 10 per cent of the adult male population; in the 1870s and 1880s this participation rose rapidly among the enfranchised voters, followed by extensions of the franchise, until by the year 1900, 40 per cent of the Norwegian men were actually voting. This process was accompanied by a transformation of Norwegian politics, the rise to power of the radical peasant party *Venstre,* and a shift from the earlier acceptance of the existing Swedish-Norwegian Union to rising demands for full Norwegian independence.[10] These political changes had been preceded or accompanied by a rise in several of the usual indicators of social mobilization among the Norwegian people.

Another aspect of the process of social mobilization is the shift of emphasis away from the parochialism and internationalism of many tra-

---

[10]See Raymond Lindgren, *Norway-Sweden: Union, Disunion, Reunion* (Princeton, Princeton University Press, 1959); and K. W. Deutsch, *et al., Political Community and the North Atlantic Area* (Princeton University Press, 1957).

ditional cultures to a preoccupation with the supralocal but far less than worldwide unit of the territorial, and eventually national, state.

An as yet unpublished study of American communications before the American Revolution, which has been carried on by Richard Merritt, shows how during the years 1735–1775 in the colonial newspapers the percentage of American or all-colonial symbols rose from about 10 to about 40 per cent, at the cost, in the main, of a decline in the share of symbols referring to places or events in the world outside the colonies and Britain, while Britain's share in American news attention remained relatively unchanged. Within the group of American symbols, the main increase occurred among those which referred to America or to the colonies as a whole, rather than among those referring to particular colonies or sections.[11]

More recent experiences in some of the "development countries" also suggest a more rapid rise of attention devoted to national topics than of that given to world affairs, on the one hand, and to purely local matters, on the other. This, however, is at present largely an impression. The nature and extent of attention shifts in mass media, as well as in popular attitudes, in the course of social mobilization is a matter for research that should be as promising as it is needed.[12]

Some data on the flow of domestic and foreign mails point in a similar direction. Of five development countries for which data are readily available the ratio of domestic to foreign mail rose substantially in four—Egypt, Iran, Nigeria, and Turkey—from 1913 to 1946–51; the fifth, Indonesia, was an exception but was the scene of internal unrest and protracted warfare against the Dutch during much of the latter period. The trend for Egypt, Iran, Nigeria, and Turkey is confirmed in each case by data for the intermediate period 1928-34, which are also intermediate, in each case, between the low domestic-foreign mail ratio for 1913 and the high ratios for 1946–51. Many additional development countries—including the Gold Coast (now Ghana), the Belgian Congo, Malaya, French Morocco, Kenya-Uganda, Tanganyika, Mozambique, and Malaya—for which data were found only for the 1928–34 to 1946–51 comparison, show upward trends in their ratios of domestic to foreign mail.[13] Here again, a relatively moderate investment in the further collection and study of data might lead to interesting results.

---

[11]Richard Merritt's monograph, "Symbols of American Nationalism, 1735–1775," which is to cover eventually one or more newspapers from Massachusetts, New York, Pennsylvania, and Virginia, respectively, will be published in due course.

[12]For examples of pioneering contributions of this kind, see the series of Hoover Institute Studies by Harold Lasswell, Ithiel Pool, Daniel Lerner, and others, and particularly Pool, The Prestige Papers (Stanford, Stanford University Press, 1951).

[13]See charts 1, 3, and 4 in Karl W. Deutsch, "Shifts in the Balance of Communication Flows: A Problem of Measurement in International Relations," Public Opinion Quarterly, Vol. 20 (Spring, 1956), pp. 152–155, based on data of the Universal Postal Union.

According to some data from another recent study, a further side effect of social mobilization and economic development might possibly be first a substantial expansion, and then a lesser but significant reduction, of the share of the international trade sector in the national economy. Thus, in the course of British development, the proportion of total foreign trade (including trade to British overseas possessions) rose from an average of 20 per cent in 1830–40 to a peak of 60 per cent in 1870–79, remained close to that level until 1913, but declined subsequently and stood at less than 40 per cent in 1959. Similarly, the proportion of foreign trade to national income rose in Germany from about 28 per cent in 1802–1830 to a peak of 45 per cent in 1870–79, declined to 35 per cent in 1900–1909, and by 1957 had recovered, for the much smaller German Federal Republic, to only 42 per cent. In Japan, the early proportion of foreign trade to national income was 15 per cent in 1885–89, rising to peaks of 41 per cent in 1915–19 and 40 per cent in 1925–29; but by 1957 it stood at only 31 per cent. Data for Denmark, Norway, France and Argentina give a similar picture, while the same foreign-trade-to-national-income ratio in the United States fell, with minor fluctuations, from 23 per cent in 1799 to less than 9 per cent in 1958.[14] Here again the evidence is incomplete and partly contradictory, and the tentative interpretation, indicated at the beginning of this paragraph, still stands in need of confirmation and perhaps modification through additional research.

The problem of the ratio of the sector of internationally oriented economic activities relative to total national income—and thus indirectly the problem of the political power potential of internationally exposed or involved interest groups *vis-à-vis* the rest of the community—leads us to the problem of the size of states and of the scale of effective political communities. As we have seen, the process of social mobilization generates strong pressures towards increasing the capabilities of government, by increasing the volume and range of demands made upon the government and administration, and by widening the scope of politics and the membership of the politically relevant strata. The same process increases the frequency and the critical importance of direct communications between government and governed. It thus necessarily increases the importance of the language, the media, and the channels through which these communications are carried on.

Other things assumed equal, the stage of rapid social mobilization may be expected, therefore, to promote the consolidation of states whose peoples already share the same language, culture, and major social insti-

---

[14]See Karl W. Deutsch and Alexander Eckstein, "National Industrialization and the Declining Share of the International Economic Sector, 1890–1957," *World Politics*, Vol. 13 (January, 1961) pp. 267–299. See also Simon Kuznets, *Six Lectures on Economic Growth* (New York, Free Press, 1959), esp. the section on "The Problem of Size" and "Trends in Foreign Trade Ratios," pp. 89–107.

tutions; while the same process may tend to strain or destroy the unity of states whose population is already divided into several groups with different languages or cultures or basic ways of life. By the same token, social mobilization may tend to promote the merging of several smaller states, or political units such as cantons, principalities, sultanates or tribal areas, whose populations already share substantially the same language, culture and social system; and it may tend to inhibit, or at least to make more difficult, the merging of states or political units whose populations or ruling personnel differ substantially in regard to any of these matters. Social mobilization may thus assist to some extent in the consolidation of the United Arab Republic, but raise increasing problems for the politics and administration of multilingual India—problems which the federal government of India may have to meet or overcome by a series of creative adjustments.[15]

In the last analysis, however, the problem of the scale of states goes beyond the effects of language, culture, or institutions, important as all these are. In the period of rapid social mobilization, the acceptable scale of a political unit will tend to depend eventually upon its performance. If a government fails to meet the increasing burdens put upon it by the process of social mobilization, a growing proportion of the population is likely to become alienated and disaffected from the state, even if the same language, culture and basic social institutions were shared originally throughout the entire state territory by rulers and ruled alike. The secession of the United States and of Ireland from the British Empire, and of the Netherlands and of Switzerland from the German Empire may serve in part as examples. At bottom, the popular acceptance of a government in a period of social mobilization is most of all a matter of its capabilities and the manner in which they are used—that is, essentially a matter of its responsiveness to the felt needs of its population. If it proves persistently incapable or unresponsive, some or many of its subjects will cease to identify themselves with it psychologically; it will be reduced to ruling by force where it can no longer rule by display, example and persuasion; and if political alternatives to it appear, it will be replaced eventually by other political units, larger or smaller in extent, which at least promise to respond more effectively to the needs and expectations of their peoples.

---

[15]For more detailed arguments, see Deutsch, *Nationalism and Social Communication*, and Deutsch, *et al.*, *Political Community and the North Atlantic Area;* see also the discussions in Ernst B. Haas, "Regionalism, Functionalism and Universal Organization," *World Politics*, Vol. 8 (January, 1956), and "The Challenge of Regionalism," *International Organization*, Vol. 12 (1958), pp. 440–458; and in Stanley Hoffmann, *Contemporary Theory in International Relations* (Englewood Cliffs, N.J., Prentice-Hall, 1960), pp. 223–40.

In practice the results of social mobilization often have tended to increase the size of the state, well beyond the old tribal areas, petty principalities, or similar districts of the traditional era, while increasing the direct contact between government and governed far beyond the levels of the sociologically superficial and often half-shadowy empire of the past.

This growth in the size of modern states, capable of coping with the results of social mobilization, is counteracted and eventually inhibited, however, as their size increases, by their tendency to increasing preoccupation with their own internal affairs. There is considerable evidence for this trend toward a self-limitation in the growth of states through a decline in the attention, resources and responsiveness available for coping with the implicit needs and explicit messages of the next marginal unit of population and territory on the verge of being included in the expanding state.[16]

The remarks in this section may have sufficed to illustrate, though by no means to exhaust, the significance of the process of social mobilization in the economic and political development of countries. The main usefulness of the concept, however, should lie in the possibility of quantitative study which it offers. How much social mobilization, as measured by our seven indicators, has been occurring in some country per year or per decade during some period of its history, or during recent times? And what is the meaning of the differences between the rates at which some of the constituent subprocesses of social mobilization may have been going on? Although specific data will have to be found separately for each country, it should be possible to sketch a general quantitative model to show some of the interrelations and their possible significance.

III. A QUANTITATIVE MODEL OF THE SOCIAL MOBILIZATION PROCESS

For a quantitative description, it is convenient to express our first six indicators not in terms of the total percentage of the population which is literate, or exposed to modern life, etc., but in terms only of that average annual percentage of the total population which has been added to, or subtracted from, the total share of the population in that category. If for some country our indicator showed, say, 40 per cent exposed to significant aspects of modern life in 1940, and 60 per cent so exposed in 1950, the average annual percentage shift, dm_1 would be 2 per cent. The seventh indicator, per capita increase, may be broken up into two elements and written as the annual percentage of the total income added, dm_7 and the annual percentage of population growth, p.

Adopting these conventions, we may use in this model, for purposes of illustration, crudely estimated magnitudes from various collections of data. If we add indicators for the increase in voting participation, and in linguistic, cultural or political assimilation, we may write for a case of fairly rapid social mobilization a small table of the sort shown in Table 1. The case represented by this table is an imaginary one, but the different rates of sub-processes of social mobilization are not necessarily unrealistic, and neither are the consequences suggested by this model, for the stability of the government in any country to which these or similar assumptions would apply.

Before discussing these consequences more explicitly, it should be made clear that the annual rates of change are likely to be realistic, at most, only for countries during the rapid middle stages of the process of social mobilization and economic development—say, for a range of between 10 to 80 per cent literacy and for analogous ranges of other indicators of economic development. In the earliest stages, the annual percentages of the population shifting into a more mobilized state are apt to be much smaller, and in the late stages of the process something like a "ceiling effect" may be expected to appear—once 80 or 90 per cent of the population have become literate, any further annual gains in the percentage of literates in the population are likely to be small.

Within the middle stages of development, however, which are appropriate to the assumptions of the model, a cumulative strain on political stability may be expected. All the rates of change in group I tend to make for increased demands or burdens upon the government, and all of them have median values above 1 per cent per year. The rates of change in group II are related to the capabilities of the government for coping with these burdens, but the median values of all these rates, with only one exception, are well below 1 per cent. If it were not for this exception—the assumed 5 per cent annual increase in national income—one would have to predict from the model an annual shift of perhaps 1 per cent or more of the population into the category of at least partly socially mobilized but largely unassimilated and dissatisfied people.

If one assumes, in accordance with this model, an annual entry of 2.75 per cent of the population into the mass media audience and a shift of only 0.6 per cent into non-agricultural employment, then the expectable increase in the numbers of not adequately reemployed new members of the mass media audience might be as high as 2.15 per cent of the population per year, or more than one-fifth of the population within a decade. This might be the proportion of people newly participating in their imagination in the new opportunities and attractions of modern life, while still being denied most or all of these new opportunities in fact—

TABLE 1. A HYPOTHETICAL EXAMPLE OF A COUNTRY UNDERGOING RAPID SOCIAL MOBILIZATION: RATES OF CHANGE

Symbol of Indicator		Description	Average Annual % of Total Population or Income Added to Category	
			Range	Median
Group I:	dm_1	Shift into any substantial exposure to modernity, incl. rumors, demonstrations of machinery or merchandise, etc.	2.0 to 4.0	3.0
	dm_2	Shift into mass media audience (radio, movies, posters, press)	1.5 to 4.0	2.75
	dm_8	Increase in voting participation	0.2 to 4.0	2.1
	dm_6	Increase in literacy	1.0 to 1.4	1.2
	dm_3	Change of locality of residence	1.0 to 1.5	1.25
	p	Population growth	(1.9 to 3.3)	(2.6)
Group II:	dm_5	Occupational shift out of agriculture	0.4 to 1.0	0.7
	dm_4	Change from rural to urban residence	0.1 to 1.2	0.5
	a	Linguistic, cultural or political assimilation	—.05 to 1.0	0.25
	dy	Income growth	(2.0 to 8.0)	(5.0)
	dm_7	Income growth per capita	—	(2.3)

NOTE: Figures in parentheses refer to percentage increases against the previous year, and thus are not strictly comparable to percentage shifts among sub-categories of the total population. A shift of 1.2 per cent of all adults into the category of literates, for instance, would refer to the total adult population, including the part just added by population aging; etc.

something which should be a fairly effective prescription for accumulating political trouble. The spread of more effective methods of production and perhaps of improved patterns of land tenure, rural credit, and other betterments within the agricultural sector could do something to counteract this tendency; but short of major and sustained efforts at such agricultural improvements the dangerous gap between the fast-growing, mass media audience and the slow-growing circle of more adequately employed and equipped persons is likely to remain and to increase.

If linguistic, cultural or political assimilation—that is, the more or less permanent change of stable habits of language, culture, legitimacy and loyalty—is also a relevant problem in the country concerned, then the lag of the slow assimilation rate, put at only 0.25 per cent per year in our model, behind the far more rapid mobilization rates of 0.5 to 3.0 per cent for the various subprocesses in our model, might be even larger for some of them, and potentially more serious.

Table 2 shows some of the implications of our model for a hypothetical country of 10 million population, $100 per capita income, a principal language spoken by 35 per cent of its inhabitants, and a relatively low degree of social mobilization in 1950. Conditions somewhat similar to these can in fact be found in several countries in Africa and Asia. Table 2 then shows the expectable state of affairs for our imaginary country in 1960 and 1970, if we assume the rates of change given in our model, as set forth in Table 1, and their persistence over twenty years. As can be seen from Table 2, the cumulative effects of these changes from 1950 to 1960 will appear still moderate, but by 1970 these effects will have become so great that many of the political institutions and practices of 1950 might be no longer applicable to the new conditions.

As Table 2 shows, a major transformation of the underlying political and social structure of a country could occur—and could pose a potential threat to the stability of any insufficiently reform-minded government there—even during a period of substantially rising per capita income.

To be sure, many of these political and social difficulties could be assuaged with the help of the benefits potentially available through the 5 per cent increase in total national income, which was assumed for our model. Such a 5 per cent growth rate of total income is not necessarily unrealistic. It is close to the average of 5.3 per cent, found by Paul Studenski in a recent survey of data from a large number of non-Communist countries.[17] Since the rate of population growth, assumed for the model, was 2.6 per cent—which is well above the world average in recent years—the average per capita income might be expected to rise by slightly more than 2 per cent per year.[18] These additional amounts of available income might well go at least some part of the way to meet the new popular needs and expectations aroused by the mobilization process, if the income can be devoted to consumption and price levels remain stable. But any increments of income will also be needed for savings (in addition to loans and grants from abroad) to permit a high rate of investment and an adequate rate of expansion of opportunities for education, employment and consumption for the growing numbers of the mobilized population.

These beneficial consequences could only be expected, however, if we assume that an adequate share of the increase in income would go

---

[17]*Cf.* Paul Studenski, *The Income of Nations* (New York, New York University Press, 1958), p. 249; *cf.* also pp. 244–250.

[18]*Cf.* United Nations, Department of Social and Economic Affairs, Population Studies No. 28, "The Future Growth of World Population" (New York, 1958), and United Nations, Bureau of Social Affairs, *Report of the World Social Situation* (Sales No.: 1957. IV. 3) (New York, 1957), p. 5.

TABLE 2. HYPOTHETICAL EXAMPLE OF A COUNTRY UNDERGOING RAPID SOCIAL MOBILIZATION: ASSUMED LEVELS FOR 1950 AND EXPECTABLE LEVELS FOR 1960 AND 1970

Symbol of Indicator	Description	Per Cent of Total Population		
		1950	1960	1970
Group I: m_1	Population exposed to modernity	35	65	95
m_2	Mass media audience	20	47.5	75
m_8	Actual voting participation	20	41	62
m_6	Literates	15	27	39
m_3	Persons who changed locality of residence since birth	10	22.5	35
P	Total population (millions)	(10)	(12.9)	(16.7)
Group II: m_5	Population in non-agricultural occupations	18	25	32
m_4	Urban population	15	20	25
A	Linguistically assimilated population	35	37.5	40
Y	Total income (million $)	(1000)	(1629)	(2653)
m_7	Per capita income ($)	(100)	(126)	(159)

NOTE: Figures in parentheses refer to absolute numbers, not percentages. Because of rounding, calculations are approximate.

directly or indirectly to the newly mobilized groups and strata of the population. Unfortunately, no assumption of this kind would be realistic for many of the developing countries of Asia and Africa.

It would be far more realistic to assume that in most of these countries the top 10 per cent of income receivers are getting about 50 per cent of the total national income, if not more. If we assume further, as seems not implausible, that in the absence of specific social reforms the increase in income will be distributed among the various strata of the population roughly in proportion to the present share of each group in the total national income, then we may expect that the richest 10 per cent of the people will get about 50 per cent of the additional income produced by income growth. At the same time, since these richest 10 per cent are not likely to be much more fertile than the rest of the population, they are likely to get only 10 per cent of the population increase; and they will, therefore, on the average not only get richer in absolute terms, but they will also retain the full extent of their relative lead over the rest of the population; and so they will increase in absolute terms the gap in income that separates them from the mass of their countrymen. Under the same assumptions, however, we should expect that the poorest nine-tenths of the population will get only one-tenth of the total income gain, but that they will get up to nine-tenths of the entire population growth; and that on the average these poorest 90 per cent of the people will remain in relative terms as far below the level of the rich one-tenth as ever. The fact that the poorer majority will have become slightly richer in absolute terms may then in the main increase their awareness of the wide gap between their living standards and those of their rulers; and it might at the same time increase their ability to take political action.

Differently put, if for the entire country the *average* per capita income was assumed to rise, we must now add that under the assumptions stated, the "social gap"—the gap between the incomes of the poorest 90 per cent and those of the top 10 per cent—may well be expected to increase. Political stability, however, may well be more affected by changes in the income gap than by changes in the average which in this respect might be little more than a statistical abstraction. Our model would lead us to expect, therefore, on the whole the danger of a significant deterioration of political stability in any development country to which its assumptions might apply. Since these assumptions were chosen with an eye to making them parallel, as far as possible, to the more rapid among the actual rates found in countries of this type, the expectations of rising political tensions in countries undergoing rapid social mobilization may not be unrealistic.

To rely upon automatic developments in economic and political life in those countries of the Free World to which the assumptions of our model apply, would be to court mounting instability, the overthrow of existing governments and their replacement by no less unstable successors, or else their eventual absorption into the Communist bloc. Deliberate political and economic intervention into the social mobilization process, on the other hand, might open up some more hopeful perspectives. Such intervention should not aim at retarding economic and social development, in the manner of the policies of the regime of Prince Metternich in Austria during much of the first half of the nineteenth century. Those policies of slowing down social mobilization and economic development in the main only diminished the capabilities of the government, paved the way to domestic failures and international defeats and were followed over the course of three generations by the persistent backwardness and ultimate destruction of the state. A more promising policy might have to be, on the contrary, one of active intervention in favor of more rapid and more balanced growth; a somewhat more even distribution of income, related more closely to rewards for productive contributions rather than for status and inheritance; the more productive investment of available resources; and sustained growth in the political and administrative capabilities of government and of ever wider strata of the population.

The crude model outlined above may have some modest usefulness in surveying and presenting in quantitative terms some of the magnitudes and rates of change that would be relevant for understanding the basic problems of such a more constructive policy in developing countries.[19] Somewhat as the economic models of the late Lord Keynes drew attention to the need of keeping the national rates of spending and investment in a country in balance with the national propensity to save, so it may become possible some day for political scientists to suggest in what areas, in what respects, and to what extent the efforts of government will have to be kept abreast of the burdens generated by the processes of social mobilization. The first steps toward this distant goal might be taken through research which would replace the hypothetical figures of the model by actual data from specific countries, so that the model could be tested, revised, and advanced nearer toward application.

Any cooperation which social scientists and other students of cultural, political, and economic development and change could extend to this effort—by improving the design of the model or by suggesting more precise or refined definitions of some of its categories, or by furnishing specific data—would be very much appreciated.

FOR FURTHER READING

ARTHUR S. BANKS, "Modernization and Political Change: The Latin American and Amer-European Nations" (Comparative Political Studies, II, 4. January 1970, 405–418)

PHILLIPS CUTRIGHT, "National Political Development: Measurement and Analysis" (American Sociological Review, XXVIII, 2, April 1963, 253–264)

KARL W. DEUTSCH, Nationalism and Social Communication: An Inquiry into the Foundations of Nationality (Cambridge: M.I.T. Press, 1966, second edition)

KARL W. DEUTSCH, The Nerves of Government: Models of Political Communication and Control (New York: Free Press, 1963)

ERNEST A. DUFF AND JOHN F. MCCAMANT, "Measuring Social and Political Requirements for System Stability in Latin America" (American Political Science Review, LXII, 4, December 1968, 1125–1143)

RAYMOND F. HOPKINS, "Aggregate Data and the Study of Political Development" (Journal of Politics, XXXI, 1, February 1969, 71–94)

MICHAEL C. HUDSON, "A Case of Political Underdevelopment" (Journal of Politics, XXIX, 4, November 1967, 821–837)

---

[19] For other highly relevant approaches to these problems, see Almond and Coleman, eds., The Politics of the Developing Areas, esp. the discussion by Almond on pp. 58–64. The problem of rates of change and their acceleration is discussed explicitly by Coleman, Ibid., pp. 536–558. While this work presented extensive data on levels of development, it did not take the further step of using explicit quantitative rates of change, which would be needed for the type of dynamic and probabilistic models that seem implicit in the long-range predictions of the authors, as set forth on pp. 58–64, 535–544.

SEYMOUR MARTIN LIPSET, "Some Social Requisites of Democracy: Economic Development and Political Legitimacy" *(American Political Science Review,* LIII, 1, March 1959, 69–105)

DONALD J. MCCRONE AND CHARLES F. CNUDDE, "Toward a Communications Theory of Democratic Political Development: A Causal Model" *(American Political Science Review,* LXI, 1, March 1967, 72–79)

MARTIN C. NEEDLER, "Political Development and Socioeconomic Development: The Case of Latin America" *(American Political Science Review,* LXII, 3, September 1968, 889–897)

ANTHONY OBERSCHALL, "Communications, Information and Aspirations in Rural Uganda" *(Journal of Asian and African Studies,* IV, 1, January 1969, 30–50)

KENNETH S. SHERRILL, "The Attitudes of Modernity" *(Comparative Politics,* I, 2, January 1969, 184–210)

ARTHUR K. SMITH, JR., "Socio-Economic Development and Political Democracy: A Causal Analysis" *(Midwest Journal of Political Science,* XIII, 1, February 1969, 95–125)

4

MODERNIZATION AND
SOCIAL INTEGRATION

It is fashionable to speak of recently independent states as the "developing" countries. Perhaps a more accurate adjective would be "unintegrated." "Integration" is, in the opinion of many scholars and political leaders, the fundamental need of these states. Steady growth and development presupposes a minimum level of national unity, consensus, and political participation, all of which are aspects of integration.

Yet what, precisely, does integration entail? As Professor Weiner points out in the first reading in this section, the concept of "integration" is used to describe an extraordinarily wide range of phenomena. He identifies five of these phenomena—all of which are "attempts to define what it is *which holds a society and a political system together*": the development of a sense of nationality by subsuming various cultural loyalties; the integration of political units into a common territorial framework; the greater linkage of the rulers and the ruled; the integration of citizens into a common political process; and, finally, the working together of individuals for common goals. Integration, in all these senses, vitally affects the course of political modernization. A description of political modernization as an increase in the capabilities of men for association together has much to commend it.

Most new states have yet to complete what Professor A. F. K. Organski[1] describes as the first stage of political development—"primitive unification" similar to the tasks of integration already listed. During this stage, "the primary function of government is one: the creation of national unity."[2] There are, according to Organski, four difficulties the government must overcome in this stage of development: establishing central political rule over all the territories and peoples within the boundaries; maintaining this political rule in the face of ethnic antagonisms, separatism, and the like; bringing about some degree of national economic unification; and "expanding the meaning of nationhood to engage the efforts and the loyalty of the mass of the citizenry."[3] The effective unity of the population within a state—in short, the achievement of national integration within the state's frontiers—appears to be an unavoidable part of political modernization. The people who, physically and legally, are members of a political system must come to identify themselves as members of that system. Integration thus has a significant psychological component, a sense of identity with the political system. Sidney Verba has commented, "The development of a clear and unambiguous sense of identity is more than a *facilitating* factor in the creation of a nation; it may be in some sense the major *constituting* factor of a new nation."[4]

The second reading in this section, "The Integrative Revolution: Primordial Sentiments and Civil Politics in the New States," treats the question of "identity" in detail. Professor Geertz notes that in the recently independent countries there is a "search for identity." At the same time, however, there is a quest for progress—for a rising standard of living, greater social justice, and the like. These quests, Professor Geertz suggests, often conflict. The sense of identity "remains bound up in the gross actualities of blood, race, language, locality, religion, or tradition"—not in the would-be nation that incorporates such groups. The main agent for change and for the distribution of resources is the state. Where feelings of national identity remain weak, the population may view the state as controlled by "strangers." Psychological identification with the state as a whole has not sufficiently subsumed parochial identifications to permit orderly change. The result

[1]A. F. K. Organski, *The Stages of Political Development* (New York: Knopf, 1965).

[2]Organski, p. 8.

[3]Organski, p. 9.

[4]Lucian W. Pye and Sidney Verba, eds., *Political Culture and Political Development* (Princeton: Princeton University Press, 1965), p. 530. Emphasis supplied.

is a direct confrontation between "primordial" and "civil" sentiments. An excellent example of conflict and uncertainty about the nature of identity can be found in Ceylon, which achieved independence early in 1948. The first few years of self-government passed peacefully, but, in 1956, ethnic antagonisms were intensified during an electoral campaign. An Oxford-trained, English-speaking aristocrat appealed to the primordial sentiments of the Sinhalese-speaking group, about 70 percent of the island's population. His victory in the election and his subsequent decisions to promote the Sinhalese language and to give greater support to the Buddhists brought tensions and riots between the Sinhalese and the minority Tamil community. As Dr. Wriggins comments in "Impediments to Unity in New Nations: The Case of Ceylon," mutual understanding between the ethnic groups seemed to diminish after 1956. Awareness of differences increased. The Ceylonese population seemed "little aware of a public interest that must take priority if the national community is to solve its problems effectively and survive." The difficulties confronted in Ceylon effectively show why the "art of associating together" must increase rapidly in new states if they are to achieve long-run stability.

POLITICAL INTEGRATION AND POLITICAL DEVELOPMENT

Myron Weiner

Analysts of political development agree that integration is a necessary part of the process of modernization—but what, precisely, is meant by this term? Professor Weiner comments upon several definitions of integration and the importance of five types: national integration, territorial integration, value integration, elite-mass integration, and integrative behavior.

It is often said of the developing nations that they are "unintegrated" and that their central problem, often more pressing than that of economic development, is the achievement of "integration." The term "integration" is now widely used to cover an extraordinarily large range of political phenomena. It is the purpose of this article to analyze the various uses of this term, to show how they are related, then to suggest some of the alternative strategies pursued by governments to cope with each of these "integration" problems.

DEFINITIONS

(1) Integration may refer to the process of bringing together culturally and socially discrete groups into a single territorial unit and the establishment of a national identity. When used in this sense "integration" generally presumes the existence of an ethnically plural society in which each group is characterized by its own language or other self-conscious cultural qualities, but the problem may also exist in a political system which is made up of once distinct independent political units with which people identified. National integration thus refers specifically to the problem of creating a sense of territorial nationality

From *The Annals*, Vol. 358 (March 1965), pp. 52–64, by permission.

which overshadows—or eliminates—subordinate parochial loyalties.[1]

(2) Integration is often used in the related sense to refer to the problem of establishing national central authority over subordinate political units or regions which may or may not coincide with distinct cultural or social groups. While the term "national integration" is concerned with the subjective feelings which individuals belonging to different social groups or historically distinct political units have toward the nation, "territorial integration" refers to the objective control which central authority has over the entire territory under its claimed jurisdiction.[2]

(3) The term "integration" is often used to refer to the problem of linking government with the governed. Implied in this usage is the familiar notion of a "gap" between the elite and the mass, characterized by marked differences in aspirations and values.[3] The "gap" may be widest in society with a passive population and modernizing elite, but a relatively stable if frustrating relationship may exist. More often the masses are beginning to become organized and concerned with exercising influence, while the elite responds with attempts to coerce, persuade, or control the masses. It is under these conditions of conflict and often internal war that we customarily speak of "disintegration."

(4) Integration is sometimes used to refer to the minimum value consensus necessary to maintain a social order. These may be end values concerning justice and equity, the desirability of economic development as a goal, the sharing of a common history, heroes, and symbols, and,

---

[1] This is perhaps the most common use of the term. For a precise view of the many attempts to define "nationality," see Rupert Emerson, *From Empire to Nation* (Boston: Beacon Press, 1960), especially Part 2: "The Anatomy of the Nation." K. H. Silvert, the editor of a collection of studies of nationalism prepared by the American Universities Field Staff, *Expectant Peoples: Nationalism and Development* (New York: Random House, 1963), suggests as a working definition of nationalism "the acceptance of the state as the impersonal and ultimate arbiter of human affairs" (p. 19). See also Karl W. Deutsch, *Nationalism and Social Communication* (New York: John Wiley and Sons, 1953) and Karl W. Deutsch and William J. Foltz (eds.), *Nation-Building* (New York: Atherton Press, 1963).

[2] For a discussion on some of the problems of territorial control in Africa see James S. Coleman, "The Problem of Political Integration in Emergent Africa," *Western Political Quarterly* (March 1955), pp. 44–57.

[3] For an explanation of this use of the term integration in the literature see Leonard Binder, "National Integration and Political Development," *American Political Science Review* (September 1964), pp. 622–631. Elite-mass integration is also one of the usages in James S. Coleman and Carl G. Rosberg (eds.), *Political Parties and National Integration in Africa* (Berkeley: University of California, 1964). They use integration in two senses: "(1) political integration, which refers to the progressive bridging of the elite-mass gap on the vertical plane in the course of developing an integrated political process and a participant political community, and (2) territorial integration, which refers to the progressive reduction of cultural and regional tensions and discontinuities on the horizontal plane in the process of creating a homogeneous territorial political community" (p. 9). These two definitions correspond with our first and third definitions.

in general, an agreement as to what constitutes desirable and undesirable social ends. Or the values may center on means, that is, on the instrumentalities and procedures for the achievement of goals and for resolving conflicts. Here the concern is with legal norms, with the legitimacy of the constitutional framework and the procedures, by which it should operate—in short, on desirable and undesirable conduct.

(5) Finally, we may speak of "integrative behavior," referring to the capacity of people in a society to organize for some common purposes. At the most elementary level all societies have the capacity to create some kind of kinship organization—a device whereby societies propagate themselves and care for and socialize their young. As other needs and desires arise within a society we may ask whether the capacity grows to create new organizations to carry out new purposes. In some societies the capacity to organize is limited to a small elite and is only associated with those who have authority.[4] Only the state, therefore, has a capacity to expand for the carrying out of new functions. In still other societies organizational capacities are more evenly spread throughout the population, and individuals without coercive authority have the readiness to organize with others. Societies differ, therefore, in the extent to which organizational proclivities are pervasive or not, and whether organizations are simply expressive in character—that is, confined to kinship and status—or purposive.

The term "integration" thus covers a vast range of human relationships and attitudes—the integration of diverse and discrete cultural loyalties and the development of a sense of nationality; the integration of political units into a common territorial framework with a government which can exercise authority; the integration of the rulers and the ruled; the integration of the citizen into a common political process; and, finally, the integration of individuals into organizations for purposive activities. As diverse as these definitions are, they are united by a common thread. These are all attempts to define what it is *which holds a society and a political system together.* Scholars of the developing areas have groped for some such notions of integration, for they recognize that in one or more of these senses the political systems they are studying do not appear to hold together *at a level commensurate with what their political leadership needs to carry out their goals.* If each scholar has in his mind a different notion of "integration," it is often because he is generalizing from one or more specific societies with which

---

[4]For an analysis of the attitudes which inhibit organized activity see Edward Banfield, *The Moral Basis of a Backward Society* (Glencoe, Ill.: Free Press, 1958). Though Banfield's study is confined to a single village in Italy, he raises the general problem of analyzing the capacities of a people to organize for common purposes.

he is familiar and which is facing some kind of "integration" problem. Since there are many ways in which systems may fall apart, there are as many ways of defining "integration."

To avoid further confusion we shall use a qualifying adjective hereafter when we speak of one kind of integration problem. We shall thus speak of national integration, territorial integration, value integration, elite-mass integration, and integrative behavior and use the term integration alone when we are referring to the generalized problem of holding a system together.

FORMS AND STRATEGIES

Transitional or developing political systems are generally less integrated than either traditional or modern systems. This is because these systems cannot readily perform the functions which the national leadership—or in some instances, the populace too—expects them to perform. In other words, as the functions of a system expand or the political leadership aspires to expand the functions of the system—a new level of integration is required. When we speak of political development, therefore, we are concerned first with the expanding functions of the political system, secondly with the new level of integration thereby required to carry out these functions, and, finally, with the capacity of the political system to cope with these new problems of integration. It is necessary, therefore, that we now take a more concrete look at the kinds of expanding functions which occur in the course of political development, the specific integrative problems which these pose, and the public policy choices available to governmental elites for coping with each of these integrative problems.

National Integration

It is useful to ask why it is that new nations with pluralistic social orders require more national integration than did the colonial regimes which preceded them. The obvious answer is that colonial governments were not concerned with national loyalties but with creating classes who would be loyal to them as a colonial power. Colonial governments, therefore, paid little or no attention to the teaching of a "national" language or culture, but stressed instead the teaching of the colonial language and culture. We are all familiar with the fact that educated Vietnamese, Indonesians, Nigerians, Indians, and Algerians were educated in French, English, and Dutch rather than in their own languages and traditions. Although the colonialist viewed the development of national loyalties as a threat to his political authority, the new leadership views it as essential to its own maintenance. Moreover, since the colonial rulers permitted only limited participation, the parochial sentiments of local people rarely entered into the making of any significant decisions of essential interest to policy makers. Once the new nations permit a greater measure of public participation, then the integration requirements of the system are higher. Moreover, the new elite in the new nations have higher standards of national integration than those of their former colonial rulers and this, too, creates new integration problems.

So long, for example, as export-import duties were imposed by a colonial ruler whose primary concern was with the impact of commercial policies upon their trade and commerce, then no questions of national integration were involved. Once these areas of policy are in the hands of a national regime, then issues immediately arise as to which sections of the country—and therefore which communities—are to be affected adversely or in a beneficial fashion by trade policies. Once educational policy is determined by national rather than colonial needs, the issues of language policy, location of educational facilities, the levels of educational investment, and the question of who bears the costs of education all affect the relations of culturally discrete groups. Finally, once the state takes on new investment responsibilities—whether for roads and post offices or for steel mills and power dams—questions of equity are posed by the regions, tribes, and linguistic groups which make up plural societies. Even if the assent of constituent groups is not necessary for the making of such decisions—that is, if an authoritarian framework is maintained—at least acquiescence is called for.

How nations have handled the problems of national integration is a matter of historical record. Clifford Geertz[5] has pointed out that public policy in the first instance is effected by patterns of social organization in plural societies. These patterns include (1) countries in which a single group is dominant in numbers and authority and there are one or more minority groups; (2) countries in which a single group is dominant in authority but not numbers; (3) countries in which no single group by itself commands a majority nor is a single group politically dominant; and (4) countries of any combination in which one or more minorities cut across international boundaries. Examples of the first group are prewar Poland (68 per cent Polish), contemporary Ceylon (70 per cent Sinhalese), and Indonesia (53 per cent Javanese). The dominant minority case is best exemplified by South Africa (21 per cent "white"). The best examples of complete pluralism with no majori-

---

[5]See Clifford Geertz, "The Integrative Revolution: Primordial Sentiments and Civil Politics in the New States," *Old Societies and New Nations*, ed., Clifford Geertz (New York: Free Press of Glencoe, 1963). [Reprinted in this reader, p. 197.]

ties are India, Nigeria, and Malaya and, in Europe, Yugoslavia and Czechoslovakia. And finally, among the minorities which cross international boundaries, the most troublesome politically have been the Kurds, the Macedonians, and Basques, the Armenians, and the Pathans. In contemporary Africa, there are dozens of tribes which are cut by international boundaries, and in Southeast Asia there are substantial Chinese and Indian minorities.

In general there are two public policy strategies for the achievement of national integration: (1) the elimination of the distinctive cultural traits of minority communities into some kind of "national" culture, usually that of the dominant cultural group—a policy generally referred to as assimilationist: "Americanization," "Burmanization," "detribalization"; (2) the establishment of national loyalties without eliminating subordinate cultures—the policy of "unity in diversity," politically characterized by "ethnic arithmetic." In practice, of course, political systems rarely follow either policy in an unqualified manner but pursue policies on a spectrum somewhere in between, often simultaneously pursuing elements from both strategies.

The history of ethnic minorities in national states is full of tragedy. If today the future of the Watusi in East Africa, the Hindus in East Pakistan, the Turks in Cyprus and the Greeks in Turkey and Indians in Burma and Ceylon is uncertain, let us recall the fate of minorities in the heterogeneous areas of East Europe. Poland in 1921 had minorities totalling 32 per cent of the population. Since then 2.5 million Polish Jews have been killed or left the country and over 9 million Germans have been repatriated. Border shifts and population changes have also removed Ruthenian, white Russian, and Lithuanian minorities, so that today only 2 per cent of the population of Poland belongs to ethnic minorities. Similarly, the Turkish minority in Bulgaria was considerably reduced at the end of the Second World War when 250,000 Turks were forced to emigrate to Turkey in 1950; and three million Germans and 200,000 Hungarians have been repatriated from Czechoslovakia since the war. Killings, the transfers of populations, and territorial changes have made most Eastern European countries more homogeneous today than they were at the beginning of the Second World War. Yugoslavia and Czechoslovakia are the only remaining East European countries which lack a single numerically dominant ethnic group.[6]

It is sad to recount an unpleasant historical fact—that few countries have successfully separated political loyalties from cultural

---

[6]These figures are taken from Lewis M. Alexander, *World Political Patterns* (Chicago: Rand McNally), pp. 277–325.

loyalties. The dominant social groups have looked with suspicion upon the loyalty of those who are culturally different—generally, though not always (but here, too, we have self-fulfilling prophecies at work) with good reason. Where killings, population transfers, or territorial changes have not occurred, the typical pattern has been to absorb the ethnic minority into the dominant culture or to create a new amalgam culture. Where cultural and racial differences continue in Europe or the United States, they are generally accompanied by political tensions. No wonder that so many leaders of the new nations look upon assimilation and homogenization as desirable and that strong political movements press for population transfers in Cyprus, India, and Pakistan, and are likely to grow in importance in sub-Sahara Africa. It remains to be seen whether the ideal of unity and diversity, that is, *political* unity and *cultural* diversity, can be the foundation for modern states. Perhaps the most promising prospects are those in which no single ethnic group dominates—Nigeria, India, and Malaysia. The factors at work in prewar Eastern Europe seem tragically in the process of being duplicated in many of the developing nations: the drive by minorities for ethnic determination, the unsuccessful effort by newly established states to establish their own economic and political viability, the inability of states to establish integration without obliterating cultures—and often peoples—through assimilation, population transfers, or genocide, and, finally, the efforts of larger more powerful states to establish control or absorb unintegrated, fragile political systems.

Territorial Integration

The association of states with fixed territories is a relatively modern phenomenon. The fluctuating "boundaries" of historic empires, and the fuzziness at the peripheries where kinship ties and tributary arrangements marked the end of a state are no longer acceptable arrangements in a world where sovereignty is characterized by an exclusive control over territory. In time the control over territory may be accompanied by a feeling of common nationality—our "national integration," but there must first of all be territorial integration. For most new states—and historic ones as well—the establishment of a territory precedes the establishment of subjective loyalties. A Congo nation cannot be achieved, obviously, without there being a Congo state, and the first order of business in the Congo has been the establishment by the central government of its authority over constituent territorial units. Some scholars have distinguished between the state and the nation, the former referring to the existence of central authority with the capacity to control a given territory and the latter to the extent of subjective loyalty on the part of the population within that territory to the state. There are, of course, instances where the "nation" in this sense precedes the "state"—as in the case of Israel and, according to some, Pakistan—but more typically the "state" precedes the "nation." "Nation-building," to use the increasingly popular phrase, thus presumes the prior existence of a state in control of a specified—and, in most instances, internationally recognized—territory. Territorial integration is thus related to the problem of *state-building* as distinct from *nation-building*.

Colonial rulers did not always establish central authority over the entire territory under their *de jure* control. The filling of the gap between *de jure* and *de facto* control has, in most instances, been left to the new regimes which took power after independence. Thus, the areas under *indirect* control by colonial authorities have been placed under the *direct* control of the new governments—in India, Pakistan, Malaya and in many areas of Africa. This process has been accomplished with relatively little bloodshed and international disturbance—although the dispute over Kashmir is an important exception—largely because the colonial regimes denied these quasi-independent pockets of authority the right to create their own armies.

The more serious problem of territorial integration has been the efforts of the new regimes to take control over border areas which were, in effect, unadministered by the colonial governments. Since both sides of a boundary were often governed by the same colonial power— as in French West Africa—or by a weak independent power—as in the Indian-Tibetan and Indian-Chinese borders—the colonial government often made no effort to establish *de facto* authority. Moreover, some of these areas are often occupied by recalcitrant tribes who forcefully resisted efforts toward their incorporation in a larger nation-state.

Some of the new governments have wisely not sought to demonstrate that they can exercise control over all subordinate authorities— wisely, because their capacity to do so is often exceedingly limited. But no modern government can tolerate for long a situation in which its laws are not obeyed in portions of its territory. As the new regimes begin to expand their functions, their need to exercise control grows. As an internal market is established, there is a need for a uniform legal code enforceable in courts of law; as state expenditures grow, no area can be exempt from the tax collectors; with the growth in transportation and communication there is a need for postal officers and personnel for the regulation in the public interest of communication and transport facilities. Finally, there is pride, for no government claiming international recognition will willingly admit that it cannot exercise authority in areas under its recognized jurisdiction, for to do so is to invite the strong to penetrate into the territory of the weak.

Value Integration

The integration of values—whatever else it encompasses—at a minimum means that there are acceptable procedures for the resolution of conflict. All societies—including traditional societies—have conflicts, and all societies have procedures for their resolution. But as societies begin to modernize, conflicts multiply rapidly, and the procedures for the settlement of conflict are not always satisfactory. There are societies where the right of traditional authority to resolve conflict remained intact during the early phases of modernization—Japan comes readily to mind—and were thereby able to avoid large-scale violence. But these are the exceptions. Why does the system require a new level of value integration?

First of all, the scale and volume of conflict increase in societies experiencing modernization. The status of social groups is frequently changed, even reversed, as education opens new occupational opportunities, as the suffrage increases the political importance of numbers, and as industrial expansion provides new opportunities for employment and wealth. A caste or tribe, once low in status and wealth, may now rise or at least see the opportunity for mobility. And social groups once high in power, status, and wealth may now feel threatened. Traditional rivalries are aggravated, and new conflicts are created as social relationships change.

The modernization process also creates new occupational roles and these new roles often conflict with the old. The new local government officer may be opposed by the tribal and caste leader. The textile manufacturer may be opposed by producers of hand-loomed cloth. The doctor may be opposed by a traditional healer. To these, one could add an enormous list of conflicts associated with modernization; the conflicts between management and labor characteristic of the early stages of industrial development, the hostility of landlords to government land-reform legislation, the hostility of regions, tribes, and religious groups with one another as they find it necessary to compete—often for the first time—in a common political system where public policies have important consequences for their social and economic positions. Finally, we should note the importance of ideological conflicts so often found in developing societies as individuals try to find an intellectually and emotionally satisfying framework for re-creating order out of a world of change and conflict.

There are two modal strategies for integrating values in a developing society. One stresses the importance of consensus and is concerned with maximizing uniformity. This view of consensus, in its extreme, emphasizes as a goal the avoidance of both conflict and competition through either coercion or exhortation. A second view of the way integrative values may be maximized emphasizes the interplay of individual and group interests. Public policy is thus not the consequence of a "right" policy upon which all agree, but the best policy possible in a situation in which there are differences of interests and sentiments.

Since most developing societies lack integrative values, political leaders in new nations are often self-conscious of their strategies. In practice, of course, neither of these two strategies is pursued in a "pure" fashion, for a leadership which believes in consensus without conflict may be willing to permit the interplay of some competitive interests while, on the other hand, regimes committed to open competition often set limits as to which viewpoints can be publicly expressed.

Though movements often develop aimed at the elimination of conflict—Communists, for example, see class harmony as the culmination of a period of struggle—such movements in practice simply add another element of conflict. The problem has been one of finding acceptable procedures and institutions for the management of conflict. It is striking to note the growth of dispute-settling institutions in modern societies. When these bodies are successful, it is often possible to prevent conflicts from entering a country's political life. Here we have in mind the social work agencies, churches and other religious bodies, lawyers and the courts, labor-management conciliation bodies and employee councils, and interracial and interreligious bodies. The psychiatrist, the lawyer, the social worker, and the labor mediator all perform integrating roles in the modern society. In the absence of these or equivalent roles and institutions in rapidly changing societies in which conflict is growing, it is no wonder that conflicts move quickly from the factory, the university, and the village into political life.

A modern political system has no single mechanism, no single procedure, no single institution for the resolution of conflict; indeed, it is precisely the multiplicity of individuals, institutions, and procedures for dispute settlement that characterizes the modern political system—both democratic and totalitarian. In contrast, developing societies with an increasing range of internal conflict, typically lack such individuals, institutions, and procedures. It is as if mankind's capacity to generate conflict is greater than his capacity to find methods for resolving conflict; the lag is clearly greatest in societies in which fundamental economic and social relationships are rapidly changing.

Elite-Mass Integration

The mere existence of differences in goals and values between the governing elite and the governed mass hardly constitutes disintegration so long as those who are governed accept the right of the governors to govern. British political culture stresses the obligations of citizens toward their government; the American political culture stresses the importance of political participation. In both, a high degree of elite-mass integration exists. At the other extreme are societies faced with the problem of internal war, and in between are many countries whose governments are so cut off from the masses whom they govern that they can neither mobilize the masses nor be influenced by them. The integration of elite and mass, between governors and the governed, occurs not when differences among the two disappear, but when a pattern of authority and consent is established. In no society is consent so great that authority can be dispensed with, and in no society is government so powerful and so internally cohesive that it can survive for long only through the exercise of cohesive authority. We need to stress here that both totalitarian and democratic regimes are capable of establishing elite-mass integration and that the establishment of a new pattern of relations between government and populace is particularly important during the early phase of development when political participation on a large scale is beginning to take place.

It is commonplace to speak of the "gap" between governors and the governed in the new nations, implying that some fundamental cultural and attitudinal gaps exist between the "elite" and the "mass," the former being secular-minded, English- or French-speaking, and Western-educated, if not Western-oriented, while the latter remain oriented toward traditional values, are fundamentally religious, and are vernacular-speaking.[7] In more concrete political terms, the government may be concerned with increasing savings and investment and, in general, the postponement of immediate economic gratification in order to maximize long-range growth, while the public may be more concerned with immediate gains in income and, more fundamentally, equitable distribution or social justice irrespective of its developmental consequences. Often the governmental elite itself may be split with one section concerned with satisfying public demands in order to win popular support while the other is more concerned with maximizing growth rates, eliminating parochial sentiments, establishing a secular society, or achieving international recognition. The elite-mass gap also implies that com-

---

[7]For a critique of "gap" theories of political development, see Ann Ruth Willner, "The Underdeveloped Study of Political Development," *World Politics* (April 1964), pp. 468–482.

munications are inadequate, that is, that the elite is oriented toward persuading the mass to change their orientation, but the feedback of political demands is not heard or, if heard, not responded to.

Perhaps too much is made of the attitudinal "gap" between governors and governed; what is more important perhaps is the attitude of government toward its citizens. Nationalist leaders out of power are typically populist. They generally identify with the mass and see in the "simple peasant" and the "working class" qualities which will make a good society possible. But once the nationalist leadership takes power and satisfies its desire for social status it tends to view the mass as an impediment to its goals of establishing a "modern," "unified," and "powerful" state. From being the champion of the masses the elite often becomes their detractor.

In all political systems, those of developing as well as developed societies, there are differences in outlook between those who govern and those who are governed. In a developed system, however, those who govern are accessible to influence by those who are governed—even in a totalitarian system—and those who are governed are readily available for mobilization by the government. In modern societies governments are so engaged in effecting the economy, social welfare, and defense that there must be a closer interaction between government and the governed.[8] Governments must mobilize individuals to save, invest, pay taxes, serve in the army, obey laws. Modern governments must also know what the public will tolerate and must be able to anticipate, before policies are pursued, what the public reaction to a given policy might be. Moreover, the modern government is increasingly armed with sophisticated tools of economic analysis and public opinion surveys to increase its capacity to predict both the economic and political consequences of its actions. In contrast, the elites of new nations are constantly talking to the masses; it is not that they do not hear the masses, but what they hear is often so inappropriate to what they wish to do. To ban opposition parties, muzzle the press, and restrict freedom of speech and assembly does indeed close two-way channels of communication, but often this is precisely what is intended.

But whatever their fear of the masses, governmental elites in new nations cannot do without them. While the elite may be unsympathetic to mass efforts to exercise influence, the elite does want to mobilize the masses for its goals. In some developing societies an organizational revolution is already under way as men join together for increas-

---

[8]Karl Deutsch has pointed out that governments of industrial societies, whether totalitarian or democratic, spend a larger proportion of their GNP than do governments in underdeveloped economies, irrespective of their ideologies.

ingly complex tasks to create political parties, newspapers, corporations, trade unions, and caste and tribal associations. Governmental elites are confronted with a choice during the early stages of this development. Should they seek to make these new organizations instruments of the authoritative structures or should these organizations be permitted to become autonomous bodies, either politically neutral or concerned with influencing government? When the state is strong and the organizational structures of society weak—a condition often found in the early phases of postcolonial societies with a strong bureaucratic legacy—then government leadership clearly has such an option.[9] It is at this point that the classic issue of the relationship of liberty and authority arises, and the elite may choose to move in one direction rather than the other.

The choices made are often shaped by dramatic domestic or international crises of the moment. But they are also affected by the society's tradition of elite-mass relations. The traditional aloofness, for example, of the mandarin bureaucracy toward the Vietnamese populace and the traditional disdain of the Buddhist and Catholic Vietnamese toward the *montegnards* or "pagan" hill peoples have probably been more important factors affecting elite-mass relations in contemporary Vietnam than any strategic or ideological considerations on the part of the Vietnamese government. Similarly, the behavior of many African leaders can often be understood better by exploring the customary patterns of authority in traditional tribal society than by reference to any compulsions inherent in the development process.

In the analysis of elite-masses relations much attention is rightly given to the development of "infra-structures"—that is, political parties, newspapers, universities, and the like—which can provide a two-way communication channel between government and populace.[10] Much attention is also given to the development of "middle strata" of individuals who can serve as links—newspapermen, lobbyists, party bosses, and precinct workers. While in the long run these developments are of great importance, in the short run so much depends upon the attitude of the governmental elites, whether the elites fundamentally feel—and behave—as if they were alienated from and even antagonistic to the masses as they are, or whether the elites perceive the values of the masses as essentially being congruent to their own aims.

[9]This theme is amplified by Fred W. Riggs, "Bureaucrats and Political Development: A Paradoxical View," *Bureaucracy and Political Development*, ed., Joseph LaPalombara (Princeton, N. J.: Princeton University Press, 1963).

[10]For a discussion of the role of infra-structures in political development, see Edward Shils, *Political Development in the New States* (The Hague: Mouton, 1962).

Integrative Behavior

The readiness of individuals to work together in an organized fashion for common purposes and to behave in a fashion conducive to the achievement of these common purposes is an essential behavioral pattern of complex modern societies. Modern societies have all encountered organizational revolutions—in some respects as essential and as revolutionary as the technological revolution which has made the modern world. To send a missile into outer space, to produce millions of automobiles a year, to conduct research and development, to manage complex mass media all require new organizational skills. During the last few decades we have begun to understand the nature of managerial skills and the complexity of organizations—how they carry out their many purposes, how they adapt themselves to a changing environment, and how they change that environment. We know less about why some societies are more successful than others in creating men and women capable of establishing, maintaining, and adapting complex organizations for the achievement of common purposes.

The consequences of an organizational lag as an impediment to development are, however, quite apparent. The inability of many political leaders to maintain internal party and government unity in many new nations has resulted in the collapse of parliamentary government and the establishment of military dictatorships. The much vaunted organizational skill of the military has also often failed in many new nations. In Ceylon a planned military coup collapsed when several of the conspirators spoke of their plans so openly that even a disorganized civilian government had time to take action, and in many Latin-American countries, and now in Vietnam, the military has proven to be as incapable of maintaining cohesive authority as their civilian predecessors.

The capacity—or lack of capacity—to organize with one's fellow men may be a general quality of societies. A society with a high organizational capacity appears to be organizationally competent at creating industrial organizations, bureaucracies, political parties, universities, and the like. Germany, Japan, the United States, the Soviet Union, Great Britain come quickly to mind. In contrast, one is struck by a generalized incompetence in many new nations where organizational breakdowns seem to be greater bottlenecks to economic growth than breakdowns in machinery. In some new countries technological innovations—such as industrial plants, railways, telegraph and postal systems—have expanded more rapidly than the human capacities to make the technologies work, with the result that mail is lost, the transport system does not function with any regularity, industrial managers cannot implement their decisions, and government administrative regulations impede rather than facilitate the management of public sector plants. Though some scholars have argued that the skill to create complex institutions will accompany or follow technological innovation, there is good reason to think that organizational skills are a prerequisite for much political and economic development. In fact, the pattern of interpersonal relations appears to be more conducive to organization-building in some traditional societies than in others. Just as the presence of entrepreneurial talents in the traditional society is a key element in whether or not economic growth occurs, so may the presence of organizational talents be an important element in whether there emerges a leadership with the capacity to run a political party, an interest association, or a government.[11]

Surprisingly little is known about the conditions for the development of effectual political organizations. If the modernization process does produce political organizations, why is it that in some societies these organizations are effectual and in others they are not? By effectual, we mean the capacity of an organization to establish sufficient internal cohesion and external support to play some significant role in the decision-making or decision-implementing process. The multiplication of ineffectual political organizations tends to result either in a highly fragmented unintegrated political process in which government is unable to make or implement public policy, or in a political system in which the authoritative structures make all decisions completely independently of the political process outside of government. In the latter case we may have a dual political process, one inside of government which is meaningful and one outside of government which, in policy terms, is meaningless.

Some scholars have suggested that political organization is a consequence of increased occupational differentiation which in turn results from economic growth and technological change—an assumption, incidentally, of much foreign economic assistance. The difficulty with viewing political change as a consequence of social changes which in turn are the consequence of economic development is that, however logical this sequence may appear to be, in the history of change no such sequence can be uniformly found. Indeed, political organization often precedes large-scale economic change and may be an important factor in whether or not there is large-scale economic change.

---

[11]For an attempt to relate traditional patterns of social and political relations to modern party-building, see Myron Weiner, "Traditional Role Performance and the Development of Modern Political Parties: The Indian Case," *Journal of Politics* (November 1964). The problems of party-building in a new nation are treated in my *Party-Building in a New Nation: The Indian National Congress* (in preparation).

In recent years greater attention has been given to the psycho-cultural components of political organization. Attention is given to the existence of trust and distrust and the capacity of individuals to relate personal ambition with some notion of the public good and of moral behavior. For explanations, psychologists focus on the process of primary socialization.

While psychologists focus on the working of the mind, sociologists and social anthropologists have been concerned with the working of society, and focus on the rules that affect the relationship among men—why they are kept and why they are broken. Sociologists have given attention to the complex of rules that organize social relationships, the patterns of superordination and subordination as among and between groups and individuals, how these change, and what effects they have on political and social relationships. While psychologists give attention to the primary process of socialization, sociologists and social anthropologists are concerned with the way in which the individual, during his entire life, comes to learn the rules and, under certain circumstances, to break them. It is from these two complementary views of man that we may expect the more systematic study of politically integrative and disintegrative behavior.

CONCLUSION

We have tried to suggest in this essay that there are many different kinds of integration problems faced by developing nations, for there are innumerable ways in which societies and political systems can fall apart. A high rate of social and economic change creates new demands and new tasks for government which are often malintegrative. The desire of the governing elite or the governed masses, for whatever reasons, to increase the functions of government are often causes of integration problems. Since modern states as well as modernizing states are often taking on new functions, it would be quite inappropriate to view integration as some terminal state. Moreover, the problems of integration in the developing areas are particularly acute because so many fundamentally new tasks or major enlargements of old tasks are now being taken on. Once the state actively becomes concerned with the mobilization and allocation of resources, new patterns of integration between elite and mass are called for. Once the state takes on the responsibilities of public education and invokes sentiments of "national" solidarity, then the integration of social groups to one another becomes an issue. And once men endeavor to create corporations, newspapers, political parties, and professional associations because they perceive their individual interests served by common actions, a new set of values is called for which provides for the integration of new structures into the political process. The challenges of integration thus arise out of the new tasks which men create for themselves.

FOR FURTHER READING

CLAUDE AKE, *A Theory of Political Integration* (Homewood, Illinois: Dorsey, 1967)

LEONARD BINDER, "National Integration and Political Development" (*American Political Science Review*, LVIII, 3, September 1964, 622–631)

JAMES S. COLEMAN AND CARL G. ROSBERG, JR., eds., *Political Parties and National Integration in Tropical Africa* (Berkeley and Los Angeles: University of California Press, 1964)

JAMES S. COLEMAN, "The Problem of Political Integration in Emergent Africa" (*Western Political Quarterly*, VIII, 1, March 1955, 44–57)

KARL W. DEUTSCH, *Nationalism and Social Communication: An Inquiry into the Foundations of Nationality* (Cambridge: M. I. T. Press, 1953)

PHILIP E. JACOB AND JAMES V. TOSCANO, eds., *The Integration of Political Communities* (Philadelphia: Lippincott, 1964)

WILLARD R. JOHNSON, *The Cameroon Federation: Political Integration in a Fragmentary Society* (Princeton: Princeton University Press, 1970)

LUCIAN W. PYE, *Politics, Personality and Nation-Building: Burma's Quest for Identity* (New Haven: Yale University Press, 1962)

LUCIAN W. PYE AND SIDNEY VERBA, eds., *Political Culture and Political Development* (Princeton: Princeton University Press, 1965)

IMMANUEL WALLERSTEIN, "Ethnicity and National Integration in West Africa" (*Cahiers d'Etudes Africaines*, II, 3, October 1960, 129–138)

ARISTIDE R. ZOLBERG, "Patterns of National Integration" (*Journal of Modern African Studies*, V, 4, December 1967, 449–467)

ARISTIDE R. ZOLBERG, "Mass Parties and National Integration: The Case of the Ivory Coast" (*Journal of Politics*, XXV, 1, February 1963, 36–48)

THE INTEGRATIVE REVOLUTION: PRIMORDIAL SENTIMENTS AND CIVIC POLITICS IN THE NEW STATES

Clifford Geertz

The search for identity in multi-ethnic states shows many complexities. Which is more important to an individual: his long-standing ties of "blood, race, language, locality, religion, or tradition"; or the relatively new and less familiar attachment to the impersonal legal order of the state? Professor Geertz suggests that the conflict between primordial sentiments and civil sentiments cannot be easily avoided. The search for identity and the demand for progress bring about severe tensions in new states.

I

... The peoples of the new states are simultaneously animated by two powerful, thoroughly interdependent, yet distinct and often actually opposed motives—the desire to be recognized as responsible agents whose wishes, acts, hopes, and opinions "matter," and the desire to build an efficient, dynamic modern state. The one aim is to be noticed: it is a search for an identity, and a demand that the identity be publicly acknowledged as having import, a social assertion of the self as "being somebody in the world."[1] The other aim is practical: it is a demand for progress, for a rising standard of living, more effective political order, greater social justice, and beyond that of "playing a part in the larger

Reprinted with permission of The Free Press from *Old Societies and New States: The Quest for Modernity in Asia and Africa*, edited by Clifford Geertz. Copyright © 1963 by The Free Press of Glencoe, a division of The Macmillan Company.

[1] I. Berlin, *Two Concepts of Liberty*, New York, Oxford University Press, 1958, p. 42.

arena of world politics," of "exercising influence among the nations."[2] The two motives are, again, most intimately related, because citizenship in a truly modern state has more and more become the most broadly negotiable claim to personal significance, and because what Mazzini called the demand to exist and have a name is to such a great extent fired by a humiliating sense of exclusion from the important centers of power in world society. But they are not the same thing. They stem from different sources and respond to different pressures. It is, in fact, the tension between them that is one of the central driving forces in the national evolution of the new states; as it is, at the same time, one of the greatest obstacles to such evolution.

This tension takes a peculiarly severe and chronic form in the new states, both because of the great extent to which their peoples' sense of self remains bound up in the gross actualities of blood, race, language, locality, religion, or tradition, and because of the steadily accelerating importance in this century of the sovereign state as a positive instrument for the realization of collective aims. Multiethnic, usually multilinguistic, and sometimes multiracial, the populations of the new states tend to regard the immediate, concrete, and to them inherently meaningful sorting implicit in such "natural" diversity as the substantial content of their individuality. To subordinate these specific and familiar identifications in favor of a generalized commitment to an overarching and somewhat alien civil order is to risk a loss of definition as an autonomous person, either through absorption into a culturally undifferentiated mass or, what is even worse, through domination by some other rival ethnic, racial, or linguistic community that is able to imbue that order with the temper of its own personality. But at the same time, all but the most unenlightened members of such societies are at least dimly aware—and their leaders are acutely aware—that the possibilities for social reform and material progress they so intensely desire and are so determined to achieve rest with increasing weight on their being enclosed in a reasonably large, independent, powerful, well-ordered polity. The insistence on recognition as someone who is visible and matters and the will to be modern and dynamic thus tend to diverge, and much of the political process in the new states pivots around an heroic effort to keep them aligned.

II

A more exact phrasing of the nature of the problem involved here is that, considered as societies, the new states are abnormally suscep-

---

[2]E. Shils, "Political Development in the New States," *Comparative Studies in Society and History*, 2: 265–292; 379–411, 1960.

tible to serious disaffection based on primordial attachments.[3] By a primordial attachment is meant one that stems from the "givens"—or, more precisely, as culture is inevitably involved in such matters, the assumed "givens"—of social existence: immediate contiguity and kin connection mainly, but beyond them the givenness that stems from being born into a particular religious community, speaking a particular language, or even a dialect of a language, and following particular social practices. These congruities of blood, speech, custom, and so on, are seen to have an ineffable, and at times overpowering, coerciveness in and of themselves. One is bound to one's kinsman, one's neighbor, one's fellow believer, *ipso facto;* as the result not merely of personal affection, practical necessity, common interest, or incurred obligation, but at least in great part by virtue of some unaccountable absolute import attributed to the very tie itself. The general strength of such primordial bonds, and the types of them that are important, differ from person to person, from society to society, and from time to time. But for virtually every person, in every society, at almost all times, some attachments seem to flow more from a sense of natural—some would say spiritual—affinity than from social interaction.

In modern societies the lifting of such ties to the level of political supremacy—though it has, of course, occurred and may again occur—has more and more come to be deplored as pathological. To an increasing degree national unity is maintained not by calls to blood and land but by a vague, intermittent, and routine allegiance to a civil state, supplemented to a greater or lesser extent by governmental use of police powers and ideological exhortation. The havoc wreaked, both upon themselves and others, by those modern (or semimodern) states that did passionately seek to become primordial rather than civil political communities, as well as a growing realization of the practical advantages of a wider-ranging pattern of social integration than primordial ties can usually produce or even permit, have only strengthened the reluctance publicly to advance race, language, religion, and the like as bases for the definition of a terminal community. But in modernizing societies, where the tradition of civil politics is weak and where the technical requirements for an effective welfare government are poorly understood, primordial attachments tend, as Nehru discovered, to be repeatedly, in some cases almost continually, proposed and widely acclaimed as preferred bases for the demarcation of autonomous political units. And the thesis that truly legitimate authority flows only from the inherent co-

---

[3]E. Shils, "Primordial, Personal, Sacred and Civil Ties," *The British Journal of Sociology,* June 1957.

erciveness such attachments are conceived somehow to possess is frankly, energetically, and artlessly defended:

> The reasons why a unilingual state is stable and a multilingual state unstable are quite obvious. A state is built on fellow feeling. What is this fellow feeling? To state briefly it is a feeling of a corporate sentiment of oneness which makes those who are charged with it feel that they are kith and kin. This feeling is a double-edged feeling. It is at once a feeling of "consciousness of kind" which, on the one hand, binds together those who have it so strongly that it overrides all differences arising out of economic conflicts or social gradations and, on the other, severs them from those who are not of their kind. It is a longing not to belong to any other group. The existence of this fellow feeling is the foundation of a stable and democratic state.[4]

It is this crystallization of a direct conflict between primordial and civil sentiments—this "longing not to belong to any other group"— that gives to the problem variously called tribalism, parochialism, communalism, and so on, a more ominous and deeply threatening quality than most of the other also very serious and intractable problems the new states face. Here we have not just competing loyalties, but competing loyalties of the same general order, on the same level of integration. There are many other competing loyalties in the new states, as in any state—ties to class, party, business, union, profession, or whatever. But groups formed of such ties are virtually never considered as possible selfstanding, maximal social units, as candidates for nationhood. Conflicts among them occur only within a more or less fully accepted terminal community whose political integrity they do not, as a rule, put into question. No matter how severe they become they do not threaten governments, or even forms of government, but they rarely at best— and then usually when they have become infused with primordial sentiments—threaten to undermine the nation itself, because they do not involve alternative definitions of what the nation is, of what its scope of reference is. Economic or class or intellectual disaffection threatens revolution, but disaffection based on race, language, or culture threatens partition, irredentism, or merger, a redrawing of the very limits of the state, a new definition of its domain. Civil discontent finds its natural outlet in the seizing, legally or illegally, of the state apparatus. Primordial discontent strives more deeply and is satisfied less easily. If

---

[4]B. R. Ambedkar, *Thoughts on Linguistic States*, Delhi, B. R. Ambedkar Co., 1955, p. 11. Noting that the modern bilingual states of Canada, Switzerland, and (white) South Africa might be quoted against him, Ambedkar adds: "It must not be forgotten that the genius of India is quite different than the genius of Canada, Switzerland, and South Africa. The genius of India is to divide—the genius of Switzerland, South Africa and Canada to unite."

severe enough, it wants not just Sukarno's or Nehru's or Moulay Hassan's head; it wants Indonesia's or India's or Morocco's.

The actual foci around which such discontent tends to crystallize are various, and in any given case several are usually involved concurrently, sometimes at cross-purposes with one another. On a merely descriptive level they are, nevertheless, fairly readily enumerable:[5]

1] *Assumed Blood Ties.* Here the defining elements in quasi-kinship. "Quasi" because kin units formed around known biological relationship (extended families, lineages, and so on) are too small for even the most tradition-bound to regard them as having more than limited significance, and the referent is, consequently, to a notion of untraceable but yet sociologically real kinship, as in a tribe. Nigeria, the Congo, and the greater part of sub-Saharan Africa are characterized by a prominence of this sort of primordialism. But so also are the nomads or seminomads of the Middle East—the Kurds, Baluchis, Pathans, and so on; the Nagas, Mundas, Santals, and so on, of India; and most of the so-called "hill tribes" of Southeast Asia.

2] *Race.* Clearly, race is similar to assumed kinship, in that it involves an ethnobiological theory. But it is not quite the same thing. Here, the reference is to phenotypical physical features—especially, of course, skin color, but also facial form, stature, hair type, and so on—rather than any very definite sense of common descent as such. The communal problems of Malaya in large part focus around these sorts of differences, between, in fact, two phenotypically very similar Mongoloid peoples. "Negritude" clearly draws much, though perhaps not all, of its force from the notion of race as a significant primordial property, and the pariah commercial minorities—like the Chinese in Southeast Asia or the Indians and Lebanese in Africa—are similarly demarcated.

3] *Language.* Linguism—for some yet to be adequately explained reasons—is particularly intense in the Indian subcontinent, has been something of an issue in Malaya, and has appeared sporadically elsewhere. But as language has sometimes been held to be the altogether essential axis of nationality conflicts, it is worth stressing that linguism is not an inevitable outcome of linguistic diversity. As indeed kinship, race, and the other factors to be listed below, language differences need not in themselves be particularly divisive: they have not been so for the most part in Tanganyika, Iran (not a new state in the strict sense, perhaps), the Philippines, or even in Indonesia, where despite a great confusion of tongues linguistic conflict seems to be the one social prob-

---

[5]For a similar but rather differently conceived and organized listing, see R. Emerson, *From Empire to Nation,* Cambridge, Mass., Harvard University Press, 1960, Chapters 6, 7, and 8.

lem the country has somehow omitted to demonstrate in extreme form. Furthermore, primordial conflicts can occur where no marked linguistic differences are involved, as in Lebanon, among the various sorts of Batak-speakers in Indonesia, and to a lesser extent perhaps between the Fulani and Hausa in northern Nigeria.

4] *Region.* Although a factor nearly everywhere, regionalism naturally tends to be especially troublesome in geographically heterogeneous areas. Tonkin, Annam, and Cochin in prepartitioned Vietnam, the two baskets on the long pole, were opposed almost purely in regional terms, sharing language, culture, race, etc. The tension between East and West Pakistan involves differences in language and culture too, but the geographic element is of great prominence owing to the territorial discontinuity of the country. Java versus the Outer Islands in archipelagic Indonesia; the Northeast versus the West Coast in mountain-bisected Malaya, are perhaps other examples in which regionalism has been an important primordial factor in national politics.

5] *Religion.* Indian partition is the outstanding case of the operation of this type of attachment. But Lebanon, the Karens and the Moslem Arakenese in Burma, the Toba Bataks, Ambonese, and Minahassans in Indonesia, the Moros in the Philippines, the Sikhs in Indian Punjab and the Ahmadiyas in Pakistan, and the Hausa in Nigeria are other well-known examples of its force in undermining or inhibiting a comprehensive civil sense.

6] *Custom.* Again, differences in custom form a basis for a certain amount of national disunity almost everywhere and are of especial prominence in those cases in which an intellectually and/or artistically rather sophisticated group sees itself as the bearer of a "civilization" amid a largely barbarian population that would be well advised to model itself upon it: the Bengalis in India, the Javanese in Indonesia, the Arabs (as against the Berbers) in Morocco, the Amhara in—another "old" new state—Ethiopia, etc. But it is important also to point out that even vitally opposed groups may differ rather little in their general style of life: Hindu Gujeratis and Maharashtrians in India; Baganda and Bunyoro in Uganda; Javanese and Sundanese in Indonesia. And the reverse holds also: the Balinese have far and away the most divergent pattern of customs in Indonesia, but they have been, so far, notable for the absence of any sense of primordial discontent at all . . .

Initially, a useful analytic distinction can be made with respect to this matter of classification between those allegiances that operate more or less wholly within the confines of a single civil state and those that do not but which run across them. Or, put somewhat differently, one can contrast those cases in which the racial, tribal, linguistic, and so on, reference group that is charged with a "corporate sentiment of oneness" is smaller than the existing civil state, and those where it is larger, or at least transgresses its borders in some fashion. In the first instance primordial discontent arises from a sense of political suffocation; in the second, from a sense of political dismemberment. Karen separatism in Burma, Ashanti in Ghana, or Baganda in Uganda are examples of the former; pan-Arabism, greater Somaliism, pan-Africanism, of the latter.

Many of the new states are plagued by both these sorts of problems at once. In the first place, most interstate primordial movements do not involve entire separate countries, as the pan-movements at least tend to do, but rather minorities scattered through several, for example: the Kurdistan movement to unite Kurds in Iran, Syria, Turkey, and the Soviet Union, perhaps the most unlikely-to-succeed political movement of all time; the Abako movement of Kasavubu and his Republic of the Congo and Angola allies; the Dravidistan movement, in so far as it comes to see itself as extending across Palk Strait from South India into Ceylon; the movement—or perhaps it is so far only a formless sentiment—for a unified and sovereign Bengal independent of both India and Pakistan. And there are even a few classical irredentist-type problems scattered among the new states—the Malays in South Thailand, the Pushtu speakers along the Afghan border of Pakistan, and so on; and when political boundaries become more firmly established in sub-Saharan Africa there will be a great many more of them. In all these cases, there is—or there may develop—both a desire to escape the established civil state and a longing to reunite a politically divided primordial community.

In the second place, interstate and intrastate primordial attachments often cross-cut one another in a complex network of balanced— if most precariously balanced—commitments. In Malaya one of the more effective binding forces that has, so far at least, held Chinese and Malays together in a single state despite the tremendous centrifugal tendencies the racial and cultural difference generates is the fear on the part of either group that should the Federation dissolve they may become a clearly submerged minority in some other political framework: the Malays through the turn of the Chinese to Singapore and China; the Chinese through the turn of the Malays to Indonesia. In a similar way, in Ceylon both the Tamils and Sinhalese manage to see themselves as minorities: the Tamils because 70 per cent of the Ceylonese are Sinhalese; the Sinhalese because the eight million of them in Ceylon are all there are, while in addition to the two million Tamils on the island there are 28 million more in South India. In Morocco, there has tended to be both a within-state split between Arab and Berber, and an extra-state split between partisans of Nasser's pan-Arabism and of Bourguiba's and Balafrej's *regroupement maghrebin.* And Nasser himself, until the Syrian debacle perhaps the new States' most accomplished virtuoso in the primordial arts, is absorbed in juggling pan-Arabist, pan-Islamic, and pan-African sentiments in the interests of Egyptian hegemony among the Bandung powers.

But whether the relevant attachments outrun state boundaries or not, most of the major primordial battles are for the moment being fought within them. A certain amount of international conflict focusing around, or at least animated by, primordial issues does exist among the new states. The hostility between Israel and her Arab neighbors and the quarrel of India and Pakistan over Kashmir are the most prominent cases, of course. But the embroilment of two older states, Greece and Turkey, over Cyprus is another; the impending clash between Somalia and Ethiopia concerning an essentially irredentist problem a third; the Indonesian difficulties vis-à-vis Peking with respect to the issue of "dual citizenship" for Chinese residents of Indonesia a mild fourth, and so on. As the new states solidify politically, such disputes may well grow both more frequent and more intense. But as of now they have not yet become—with the exception of the Israeli-Arab conflict and, sporadically, the Kashmir problem—paramount political issues and the immediate significance of primordial differences is almost everywhere primarily domestic, though this is not to say that they are therefore without important international implications.[6]

The construction of a typology of the concrete patterns of primordial diversity that are found within the various new states is severely hampered, however, by the simple lack of detailed and reliable information in the overwhelming majority of the cases. But, again, a gross and merely empirical classification can nonetheless fairly easily be devised, and should prove useful as a rough-and-ready guide to a wilderness otherwise uncharted, and facilitate a more incisive analysis of the role of primordial sentiments in civil politics than is possi-

---

[6]Nor does the interstate significance of primordial sentiments lie wholly in their divisive power. Pan-African attitudes, weak and ill-defined as they may be, have provided a useful context of mild solidarity for the confrontation of leaders of major African countries—Arab and Negro alike—as at Casablanca in January, 1961. Burma's strenuous (and expensive) efforts to strengthen and revitalize international Buddhism, as in the Sixth Great Council and Yegu in 1954, have served to link her more effectively with the other Theravada countries—Ceylon, Thailand, Laos, and Cambodia. And a vague, mainly racial, feeling of common "Malayness" has played a positive role in the relations between Malaya and Indonesia and Malaya and the Philippines (though not, as yet, between Indonesia and the Philippines).

ble in terms of "pluralism," "tribalism," "parochialism," "communal-ism," and the other clichés of commonsense sociology:

1] One common and, relatively speaking, simple pattern seems to be that of a single dominant and usually, though not inevitably, larger group set over against a single strong and chronically troublesome minority: Cyprus with Greeks and Turks; Ceylon with Sinhalese and Tamils; Jordan with Jordanians and Palestinians, though in this last case the dominant group is the smaller.

2] Similar in some ways to this first pattern, but more complex, is that of one central—often enough in a geographic sense as well as a political—group and several mediumly large and at least somewhat opposed peripheral groups: the Javanese versus the Outer Island peoples in Indonesia; the Irrawaddy Valley Burmese versus the various hill tribes and upland valley peoples in Burma; the central plateau Persians and the various tribes in Iran (though, again, this is not strictly a new state); the Atlantic Plain Arabs encircled by the diverse Berber tribes of the Rif, the Atlas, and the Sous; the Mekong Lao and the tribal peoples in Laos; and so on. How far such a pattern is to be found in black Africa is unclear. The one case where it might have crystallized, with the Ashanti in Ghana, the power of the central group seems to have, at least temporarily, been broken. And whether in a new state the Baganda will be able to maintain their dominant position vis-à-vis the other Uganda groups through their greater education, political sophistication, and so on, and despite their comprising but about a fifth of the population, remains to be seen.

3] Another pattern that forms an internally even less homogeneous type is a bipolar one of two nearly evenly balanced major groups: Malays and Chinese in Malaya (though there is also a smaller Indian group); or Christians and Moslems in Lebanon (though here both groups are actually aggregates of smaller sects); or Sunnis and Shiis in Iraq. Perhaps the two regions of Pakistan, although the Western region is far from wholly homogeneous within itself, gives that state a somewhat bipolar primordial pattern. Vietnam before partition tended to take this form—Tonkin versus Cochin—this problem now having been solved with the assistance of the great powers. Even Libya, which has scarcely enough people to develop decent group conflicts, has something of this pattern with the Cyrenaica-Tripolitania contrast.

4] Next, there is the pattern of a relatively even gradation of groups in importance, from several large ones through several medium-sized ones to a number of small ones, with no clearly dominant ones and no sharp cut-off points. India, the Philippines, Nigeria, Kenya are perhaps examples.

5] Finally, there is simple ethnic fragmentation, as Wallerstein has called it, with multiple small groups, into which somewhat residual category it is necessary to toss much of Africa, at least until more is known about it.[7] One proposal, issuing from the nothing if not experimental Leopoldville Government, suggesting a grouping of the Congo Republic's estimated 250 or so separate tribal-linguistic groups into eighty autonomous tribal regions, which would then be organized into twelve federated states, gives something of an indication of the extent to which such fragmentation can go, and the complexity of primordial allegiances it may involve. . . .

III

The reduction of primordial sentiments to civil order is rendered more difficult, however, by the fact that political modernization tends initially not to quiet such sentiments but to quicken them. The transfer of sovereignty from a colonial regime to an independent one is more than a mere shift of power from foreign hands to native ones; it is a transformation of the whole pattern of political life, a metamorphosis of subjects into citizens. Colonial governments, like the aristocratic governments of premodern Europe in whose image they were fashioned, are aloof and unresponsive; they stand outside the societies they rule, and act upon them arbitrarily, unevenly, and unsystematically. But the governments of the new states, though oligarchic, are popular and attentive; they are located in the midst of the societies they rule, and as they develop act upon them in progressively more continuous, comprehensive, and purposeful manner. For the Ashanti cocoa farmer, the Gujerati shopkeeper, or the Malayan Chinese tin miner, his country's attainment of political independence is also his own attainment, willy-nilly, of modern political status, no matter how culturally traditional he may remain nor how ineffectively and anachronistically the new state may in practice function. He now becomes an integral part of an autonomous and differentiated policy that begins to touch his life at every point except the most strictly private. "The same people which has hitherto been kept as far as possible from government affairs must now be drawn into them," the Indonesian nationalist Sjahrir wrote on the eve of World War II, defining exactly the character of the "revolution" that was in fact to follow in the Indies over the next decade—"That people must be made politically conscious. Its political interest must be stimulated and maintained."[8]

[7]I. Wallerstein, "The Emergence of Two West African Nations: Ghana and the Ivory Coast," unpublished Ph.D. thesis, Columbia University, 1959.
[8]S. Sjahrir, *Out of Exile*, New York, John Day, 1949, p. 215.

This thrusting of a modern political consciousness upon the mass of a still largely unmodernized population does indeed tend to lead to the stimulation and maintenance of a very intense popular interest in the affairs of government. But, as a primordially based "corporate feeling of oneness" remains for many the *fons et origo* of legitimate authority—the meaning of the term "self" in "self-rule"—much of this interest takes the form of an obsessive concern with the relation of one's tribe, region, sect, or whatever to a center of power that, while growing rapidly more active, is not easily either insulated from the web of primordial attachments, as was the remote colonial regime, or assimilated to them as are the workaday authority systems of the "little community." Thus, it is the very process of the formation of a sovereign civil state that, among other things, stimulates sentiments of parochialism, communalism, racialism, and so on, because it introduces into society a valuable new prize over which to fight and a frightening new force with which to contend.[9] The doctrines of the nationalist propagandists to the contrary notwithstanding, Indonesian regionalism, Malayan racialism, Indian linguism, or Nigerian tribalism are, in their political dimensions, not so much the heritage of colonial divide-and-rule policies as they are products of the replacement of a colonial regime by an independent, domestically anchored, purposeful unitary state. Though they rest on historically developed distinctions, some of which colonial rule helped to accentuate (and others of which it helped to moderate), they are part and parcel of the very process of the creation of a new polity and a new citizenship.

For a telling example in this connection one may look to Ceylon, which having made one of the quietest of entries into the family of new states is now the scene of one of its noisiest communal uproars. Ceylonese independence was won largely without struggle; in fact, without even very much effort. There was no embittered nationalist mass movement, as in most of the other new states, no loudly passionate hero-leader, no diehard colonial opposition, no violence, no arrests—no revolution really, for the 1947 transfer of sovereignty consisted of the replacement of conservative, moderate, aloof British civil servants by con-

---

[9]As Talcott Parson has pointed out, power, defined as the capacity to mobilize social resources for social goals, is not a "zero-sum" quantity within a social system, but, like wealth, is generated by the working of particular, in this case political rather than economic, institutions. "The Distribution of Power in American Society," *World Politics*, 10: 123–143, 1957. The growth of a modern state within a traditional social context represents, therefore, not merely the shifting or transfer of a fixed quantity of power between groups in such a manner that aggregatively the gains of certain groups or individuals match the losses of others, but rather the creation of a new and more efficient machine for the production of power itself, and thus an increase in the general political capacity of the society. This is a much more genuinely "revolutionary" phenomenon than a mere redistribution, however radical, of power with a given system.

servative, moderate, aloof British-educated Ceylonese notables who, to more nativistic eyes at least, "resembled the former colonial rulers in everything but the color of their skin."[10] The revolution was to come later, nearly a decade after formal independence, and the British governor's valedictory expression of "profound satisfaction that Ceylon has reached its goal of freedom without strife or bloodshed along the path of peaceful negotiation,"[11] proved to be somewhat premature: in 1956 wild Tamil-Sinhalese riots claimed more than a hundred lives, in 1958, perhaps as many as two thousand.

The country, 70 per cent Sinhalese, 23 per cent Tamil, has been marked by a certain amount of group tension for centuries.[12] But such tension has taken the distinctively modern form of an implacable, comprehensive, and ideologically instigated mass hatred mainly since the late S. W. R. D. Bandaranaike was swept into the premiership on a sudden wave of Sinhalese cultural, religious and linguistic revivalism in 1956. Himself Oxford-educated, vaguely Marxist and essentially secularist in civil matters, Bandaranaike undermined the authority of the English-speaking (and bi-ethnic Colombo) patriciate by appealing openly, and one suspects somewhat cynically, to the primordial sentiments of the Sinhalese, promising a "Sinhala-only" linguistic policy, a place of pride for Buddhism and the Buddhist clergy, and a radical reversal of the supposed policy of "pampering" the Tamils, as well as rejecting Western dress for the traditional "cloth and banian" of the Sinhalese countryman.[13] And if, as one of his more uncritical apologists claims, his "supreme ambition" was not "to set up an outmoded, parochial, racialist government," but to "stabilize democracy and convert his country into a modern welfare state based on Nehru-style socialism,"[14] he soon found himself the helpless victim of a rising tide of primordial fervor, and his death, after thirty hectic and frustrating

---

[10]D. K. Rangenekar, "The Nationalist Revolution in Ceylon," *Pacific Affairs*, 33: 361–374, 1960.

[11]Quoted in M. Weiner, "The Politics of South Asia," in G. Almond and J. Coleman, *The Politics of the Developing Areas*, Princeton, N. J., Princeton University Press, 1960, pp. 153–246.

[12]About half the Tamils are stateless "Indian Tamils"—that is, individuals transported to Ceylon in the nineteenth century to work on British tea estates, and now rejected as citizens by India on the ground that they live in Ceylon, and by Ceylon on the ground that they are but sojourners from India.

[13]Commenting on the spectacular failure of Sir Ivor Jennings's 1954 prediction that Bandaranaike was unlikely to win the leadership of the nationalist movement because he was a "political Buddhist," having been educated as a Christian, Rangenekar shrewdly remarks, "In an Asian setting a Western-educated politician who renounces his Westernization and upholds indigenous culture and civilization wields a much greater influence than the most dynamic local thoroughbred can ever hope to do." Rangenekar, *op. cit.*

[14]Rangenekar, *op. cit.*

months in power, at the hands of an obscurely motivated Buddhist monk was merely that much more ironic.

The first definite move toward a resolute, popularly based, social reform government led, therefore, not to heightened national unity, but to the reverse—increased linguistic, racial, regional, and religious parochialism, a strange dialectic whose actual workings have been well described by Wriggins.[15] The institution of universal suffrage made the temptation to court the masses by appealing to traditional loyalties virtually irresistible, and led Bandaranaike and his followers to gamble, unsuccessfully as it turned out, on being able to tune primordial sentiments up before elections and down after them. The modernizing efforts of his government in the fields of health, education, administration, and so on, threatened the status of consequential rural personages—monks, ayurvedic doctors, village schoolteachers, local officials—who were thereby rendered that much more nativistic and insistent upon communal tokens of reassurance in exchange for their political support. The search for a common cultural tradition to serve as the content of the country's identity as a nation now that it had become, somehow, a state, led only to the revivification of ancient, and better forgotten, Tamil-Sinhalese treacheries, atrocities, insults, and wars. The eclipse of the Western-educated urban elite, within which class loyalties and old-school ties tended to override primordial differences, removed one of the few important points of amicable contact between the two communities. The first stirrings of fundamental economic change aroused fears that the position of the industrious, frugal, aggressive Tamils would be strengthened at the expense of the less methodical Sinhalese. The intensified competition for government jobs, the increasing importance of the vernacular press, and even government-instituted land-reclamation programs—because they threatened to alter population distribution and so communal representation in the parliament—all acted in a similarly provocative manner. Ceylon's aggravated primordial problem is not a mere legacy, an inherited impediment to her political, social, and economic modernization; it is a direct and immediate reflex of her first serious—if still rather ineffective—attempt to achieve such modernization.

And this dialectic, variously expressed, is a generic characteristic of new state politics. In Indonesia, the establishment of an indigenous unitary state made the fact that the thinly populated but mineral-rich Outer Islands produced the bulk of the country's foreign-ex-

[15]H. Wriggins, "Impediments to Unity in New Nations: The Case of Ceylon." [Reprinted in this reader, p. 219.]

change earnings, while densely populated, resource-poor Java consumed the bulk of its income, painfully apparent in a way it could never become in the colonial era, and a pattern of regional jealousy developed and hardened to the point of armed revolt.[16] In Ghana, hurt Ashanti pride burst into open separatism when, in order to accumulate development funds, Nkrumah's new national government fixed the cocoa price lower than what Ashanti cocoa growers wished it to be.[17] In Morocco, Riffian Berbers, offended when their substantial military contribution to the struggle for independence was not followed by greater governmental assistance in the form of schools, jobs, improved communications facilities, and so on, revived a classic pattern of tribal insolence—refusal to pay taxes, boycott of market places, retreat to a predatory mountain life—in order to gain Rabat's regard.[18] In Jordan, Abdullah's desperate attempt to strengthen his newly sovereign civil state through the annexation of Cis-Jordan, negotiation with Israel, and modernization of the army provoked his assassination by an ethnically humiliated pan-Arab Palestinian.[19] Even in those new states where such discontent has not progressed to the point of open dissidence, there has almost universally arisen around the developing struggle for governmental power as such a broad penumbra of primordial strife. Alongside of, and interacting with, the usual politics of party and parliament, cabinet and bureaucracy, or monarch and army, there exists, nearly everywhere, a sort of parapolitics of clashing public identities and quickening ethnocratic aspirations.

What is more, this parapolitical warfare seems to have its own characteristic battlegrounds; there are certain specific institutional contexts outside the customary arenas of political combat into which it has a strong inclination to settle. Though primordial issues do, of course, turn up from time to time in parliamentary debates, cabinet deliberations, judicial decisions and, more often, in electoral cam-

---

[16]H. Feith, "Indonesia," in G. McT. Kahin (ed.), *Government and Politics of Southeast Asia*, Ithaca, N. Y., Cornell University Press, 1959, pp. 155–238; and G. McT. Kahin. (ed.), *Major Governments of Asia*, Ithaca, N. Y., Cornell University Press, 1958, pp. 471–592. This is not to say that the crystallization of regional enmities was the sole motivating force in the Padang rebellion, nor that the Java-Outer Islands contrast was the only axis of opposition. In all the quoted examples in this essay, the desire to be recognized as a responsible agent whose wishes, acts, hopes, and opinions matter is intertwined with the more familiar desires for wealth, power, prestige, and so on. Simple primordial determinism is no more defensible a position than economic determinism.

[17]D. Apter, *The Gold Coast in Transition*, Princeton, N. J., Princeton University Press, 1955, p. 68.

[18]W. Lewis, "Feuding and Social Change in Morocco," *Journal of Conflict Resolution*, 5: 43–54, 1961.

[19]R. Nolte, "The Arab Solidarity Agreement," American University Field Staff Letter, Southwest Asia Series, 1957.

paigns, they show a persistent tendency to emerge in purer, more explicit, and more virulent form in some places where other sorts of
social issues do not ordinarily, or at least so often or so acutely, appear.

One of the most obvious of these is the school system. Linguistic conflicts, in particular, tend to emerge in the form of school
crises—witness the fierce dispute between Malay and Chinese teachers' unions over the degree to which Malay should replace Chinese in
Chinese schools in Malaya, the three-way guerrilla war between partisans of English, Hindi, and various local vernaculars as instruction
media in India, or the bloody riots staged by Bengali-speaking university students to block the imposition of Urdu by West on East Pakistan. But religious issues, too, tend to penetrate educational contexts
quite readily. In Moslem countries there is the enduring question of the
reform of traditional Koranic schools toward Western forms; in the
Philippines there is the clash between the American-introduced tradition of the secular public school and the intensified clerical effort to
increase the teaching of religion in such schools; and in Madras there
are the Dravidian separatists announcing sanctimoniously that "education must be free from political, religious or communal bias," by
which they in fact mean that it "must not stress Hindu writings such
as the epic Ramayana."[20] Even largely regional struggles tend to
engulf the school system: in Indonesia the rise of provincial discontent
was accompanied by a competitive multiplication of local institutions of
higher learning to the point where, despite the extreme shortage of
qualified instructors, there is now a faculty in nearly every major
region of the country, monuments to past resentments and perhaps
cradles for future ones; and a similar pattern may now be developing in Nigeria. If the general strike is the classical political expression of class warfare, and the coup d'état of the struggle between militarism and parliamentarianism, then the school crisis is perhaps becoming the classical political—or parapolitical—expression of the clash
of primordial loyalties.

There are a number of other poles around which parapolitical
vortices tend to form, but so far as the literature is concerned they
have been more noted in passing than analyzed in detail. Social statistics, for example. In Lebanon there has not been a census since 1932,
for fear that taking one would reveal such changes in the religious composition of the population as to make the marvelously intricate political
arrangements designed to balance sectarian interests unviable. In India,
with its national language problem, just what constitutes a Hindi

speaker has been a matter of some rather acrimonious dispute, because it depends upon the rules of counting: Hindi enthusiasts use census figures to prove that as many as a half of India's people speak "Hindi" (including Urdu and Punjabi), while anti-Hindiists force the figure down as low as 30 per cent by considering such matters as script differences, and evidently even religious affiliation of the speaker, as linguistically significant. Then, too, there is the closely related problem of what, in connection with the strange fact that according to the 1941 census of India there were 25 million tribal peoples but in the 1951 one only 1.7 million, Weiner has aptly called "genocide by census redefinition."[21] In Morocco, published figures for the percentage of the population that is Berber run all the way from 35 to 60 per cent, and some nationalist leaders would like to believe, or have others believe, that the Berbers are a French invention altogether.[22] Statistics, real or fancied, concerning the ethnic composition of the civil service are a favorite weapon of primordial demagogues virtually everywhere, being particularly effective where a number of local officials are members of a group other than the one they administrate. And in Indonesia a leading newspaper was banned, at the height of the regionalist crisis, for printing, in mock innocence, a simple bar graph depicting export earnings and government expenditure by province.

Dress (in Burma hundreds of frontier tribesmen brought to Rangoon for Union day to improve their patriotism are cannily sent home with gifts of Burmese clothing), historiography (in Nigeria a sudden proliferation of tendentious tribal histories threatens to strengthen the already very powerful centrifugal tendencies plaguing the country), and the official insignia of public authority (in Ceylon, Tamils have refused to use automobile license plates marked with Sinhala characters, and in South India they have painted over Hindi railroad signs) are other as yet but impressionistically observed spheres of parapolitical controversy.[23] So, also, is the rapidly expanding complex of tribal unions, caste organizations, ethnic fraternities, regional asso-

---

[21]M. Weiner, "Community Associations in Indian Politics," unpublished MS. The reverse process, "ethnogenesis by census redefinition," also occurs, as when in Libreville, the Gabon capital, Togolese and Dahomeans are lumped statistically into a new category, "the Popo," or in Northern Rhodesia copperbelt towns Henga, Tonga, Tambuka, and so on, are "by common consent" grouped together as Nyasalanders, these manufactured groupings then taking on a real "ethnic" existence. I. Wallerstein, "Ethnicity and National Integration in West Africa," *Cahiers d'etudes africaines*, 3: 129–139 October, 1960.
[22]The 35 per cent figure can be found in N. Barbour (ed.), *A Survey of North West Africa*, New York, Oxford University Press, 1959, p. 79; the 60 per cent figure in D. Rustow, "The Politics of the Near East," in Almond and Coleman, *op. cit.*, pp. 369–453.
[23]On Burmese dress, see H. Tinker, *The Union of Burma*, New York, Oxford University Press, 1957, p. 184. On Nigerian tribal histories, see Coleman, *op. cit.*,

ciations, and religious sodalities that seems to be accompanying urbanization in virtually all the new states, and has made the major cities in some of them—Lagos, Beirut, Bombay, Medan—caldrons of communal tension.[24] But, details aside, the point is that there swirls around the emerging governmental institutions of the new states, and the specialized politics they tend to support, a whole host of self-reinforcing whirlpools of primordial discontent, and that this parapolitical maelstrom is in great part an outcome—to continue the metaphor, a backwash—of that process of political development itself. The growing capacity of the state to mobilize social resources for public ends, its expanding power, roils primordial sentiments because, given the doctrine that legitimate authority is but an extension of the inherent moral coerciveness such sentiments possess, to permit oneself to be ruled by men of other tribes, other races, or other religions is to submit not merely to oppression but to degradation—to exclusion from the moral community as a lesser order of being whose opinions, attitudes, wishes, and so on, simply do not fully count, as those of children, the simple-minded and the insane do not fully count in the eyes of those who regard themselves as mature, intelligent, and sane.

Though it can be moderated, this tension between primordial sentiments and civil politics probably cannot be entirely dissolved. The power of the "givens" of place, tongue, blood, looks, and way-of-life to shape an individual's notion of who, at bottom, he is and with whom, indissolubly, he belongs is rooted in the nonrational foundations of personality. And, once established, some degree of involvement of this unreflective sense of collective selfhood in the steadily broadening political process of the national state is certain, because that process seems to touch on such an extraordinarily wide range of matters. Thus, what the new states—or their leaders—must somehow contrive to do as far as primordial attachments are concerned is not, as they have so often tried to do, wish them out of existence by belittling them or even denying their reality, but domesticate them. They must reconcile them with the unfolding civil order by divesting them of their legitimizing force with respect to governmental authority, by neutralizing the apparatus of the state in relationship to them, and by channeling discontent arising out of their dislocation into properly political rather than parapolitical forms of expression. This goal, too, is not fully achievable or at

---

pp. 327–328. On Ceylonese license plates, see Wriggins, "Ceylon's Time of Troubles, 1956–8," *Far Eastern Survey*, 28: 33–38 (1959). On Hindi railroad signs, see Weiner, "Community Associations . . . ," *op. cit.*

[24]For a general discussion of the role of voluntary associations in the urbanization process in modernizing societies, see Wallerstein, "The Emergence of Two West African Nations," *op. cit.*, pp. 144–230.

least has never yet been achieved—even in Mr. Ambedkar's Canada and Switzerland (the less said of South Africa in this connection, the better) with their admitted "genius to unite." But it is relatively so, and it is upon the possibility of such relative achievement that the hope of the new states to turn the attack upon their integrity and their legitimacy by unfettered primordial enthusiasm rests. As with industrialization, urbanization, restratification, and the various other social and cultural "revolutions" these states seem fated to undergo, the containment of diverse primordial communities under a single sovereignty promises to tax the political capacity of their peoples to its utmost limits—in some cases, no doubt, beyond them. . . .

IV

Over the cases reviewed here, at least one common developmental tendency does stand out: the aggregation of independently defined, specifically outlined traditional primordial groups into larger, more diffuse units whose implicit frame of reference is not the local scene but the "nation"—in the sense of the whole society encompassed by the new civil state . . . the process . . . is a progressive extension of the sense of primordial similarity and difference generated from the direct and protracted encounter of culturally diverse groups in local contexts to more broadly defined groups of a similar sort interacting within the framework of the entire national society, an extension Freedman has described particularly well for Malaya:

> Malaya was and remains a culturally plural society. Paradoxically, from a purely structural point of view, its plural nature is more marked today than ever before. Nationalism and political independence in their early phases have tended to define, on a pan-Malayan basis, ethnic blocs which in former times were merely categories. Then the social map of Malaya was, so to speak, made up of a kaleidoscope of small culturally defined units rearranging themselves in accordance with local conditions. "The Malays" did not interact with "the Chinese" and "the Indians." Some Malays interacted with some Chinese and some Indians. But as "Malays," "Chinese," and "Indians" come to be realized as structural entities on a nation-wide scale, they can begin to have total relations with one another.[25]

The emergence of a nation-wide system of "ethnic-blocs" engaged in "total relations with one another" sets the stage for a direct clash between personal identity and political integrity in the new states. By generalizing and extending tribal, racial, linguistic, or other principles of primordial solidarity, such a system permits the main-

[25]M. Freedman, "The Growth of a Plural Society in Malaya," *Pacific Affairs*, 33: 158–167, 1960.

tenance of a profoundly rooted "consciousness of kind," and relates that consciousness to the developing civil order. It allows one to continue to claim public acknowledgement of one's existence and import in terms of the familiar symbols of group uniqueness, while at the same time becoming more and more drawn into a political society cast in a wholly different mold than the "natural" community those symbols define. But, on the other hand, it also simplifies and concentrates group antagonisms, raises the specter of separatism by superimposing a comprehensive political significance upon those antagonisms, and, particularly, when the crystallizing ethnic blocs outrun state boundaries, stirs international controversies. The integrative revolution does not do away with ethnocentrism; it merely modernizes it.

Yet modernizing ethnocentrism does render it more easily reconciled to the presence of developed national political institutions. The effective operation of such institutions does not require the simple replacement of primordial ties and identifications by civil ones. In all probability, such a replacement is a sheer impossibility. What it does demand is an adjustment between them, an adjustment such that the processes of government can proceed freely without seriously threatening the cultural framework of personal identity, and such that whatever discontinuities in "consciousness of kind" happen to exist in the general society do not radically distort political functioning. At least as they have been conceived here, primordial and civil sentiments are not ranged in direct and implicitly evolutionary opposition to one another in the manner of so many of the theoretical dichotomies of classical sociology—*Gemeinschaft* and *Gesellschaft,* mechanical and organic solidarity, folk and urban society; the history of their development does not consist simply of the expansion of the one at the expense of the other. Their marked tendency to interfere with one another in the new states stems not from any natural and irremovable antipathy between them but rather from dislocations arising from the differing patterns of change intrinsic to each of them as they respond to the disequilibrating forces of the mid-twentieth century. Their clash is an outcome of the contrasting sorts of transformation that traditional political institutions and traditional modes of self-perception undergo as they move along their separate paths toward modernity.

On the self-perception side, the nature of the modernizing process is virtually uninvestigated; it is not usually even recognized that such a process exists. The already mentioned aggregation of narrowly circumscribed tribal, linguistic, religious, and so on, groups into larger more generalized ethnic blocs set within the context of a common social frame is certainly a crucial part of it. A simple, coherent, broadly defined ethnic structure, such as is found in most industrial societies, is not an undissolved residue of traditionalism but an earmark of modernity. But how this reconstruction of the system of primordial affiliation takes place, the stages through which it passes, the forces that advance or retard it, the transformations in personality structure it involves, all are largely unknown. The comparative sociology (or social psychology) of ethnic change remains to be written.

With respect to the political side, it can hardly be said that the problem is unrecognized, for the notion of a civil society, of the nature of citizenship and the diffuse social sentiments on which it rests, has been a central concern of political science since Aristotle. But it remains none the less vague; much easier to point to than describe; much easier to sense than to analyze. What the civic sense more than anything else seems to involve is a definite concept of the public as a separate and distinct body and an attendant notion of a genuine public interest, which though not necessarily superior to, is independent of and at times even in conflict with, both private and other sorts of collective interest. When we talk about the changing forms of civil politics in the new states or elsewhere, it is the vicissitudes of just this sense of the public and the public interest, its waxings and wanings, its alterations in mode of expression, to which we refer. Again, however, though we have at least a general idea of the nature of civility and the range of forms through which it is materialized in industrial states, very little is known about the processes by which the present patterns have come to be what they are. A genuine civil sense is often even denied—incorrectly in my opinion—to traditional states at all. In any case, the stages through which a modern sense of political community arises out of a traditional one have been at best but impressionistically traced, and thus both the roots and the character of civility remain obscure.

A satisfactory understanding of the reasons for the chronic tension in the new states between the need to maintain a socially ratified personal identity and the desire to construct a powerful national community demands, therefore, a more circumstantial tracing of the stages through which their relationship to one another passes as each proceeds along the special lines of its own development. And it is in the histories of those states as they unfold before our eyes that such a tracing is most readily to be accomplished. The diverse constitutional, quasi-constitutional, or simply *ad hoc* experiments in government that characterize at least those new states described here represent, among other things, an attempt to establish a pattern of politics in which the looming headlong clash of primordial and civil loyalties can be averted. Whether ethnic differentiation is given its political expression in terms of territorial sub-units, political parties, government posts, executive leadership, or, as is most common, one or another combination of these, the effort is everywhere to find a formula that will keep the pace of modernization of the nation's sense of selfhood in step with the parallel modernization not only of its political, but of its economic, stratificatory, domestic, and so on, institutions as well. It is by watching the integrative revolution happen that we shall understand it. This may seem like a mere wait-and-see policy, inappropriate to the predictive ambitions of science. But such a policy is at least preferable, and more scientific, to waiting and not seeing, which has been largely the case to date.

In any case, the success of the efforts to find a formula for balance in the midst of change now taking place in the new states is nowhere assured. A high degree of governmental immobilism resulting from the attempt to reconcile divergent primordial groups is everywhere apparent. The mere prejudices that must be tolerated in order to effect such reconciliations are often repugnant. But as the alternatives to such attempts as these to construct a civil politics of primordial compromise would seem to be either Balkanization, *Herrenvolk* fanaticism, or the forcible suppression of ethnic assertion by a leviathan state, can they be viewed, especially by members of a society that has notably failed to resolve its own most troublesome primordial problem, with either indifference or contempt?

FOR FURTHER READING

ROBERT J. ALEXANDER, "Nationalism, Latin America's Predominant Ideology" (*Journal of International Affairs*, XV, 2, [1961], 108–114)

FRANCIS CARNELL, "South Asian Nationalism and the West," in G. F. Hudson, ed., *Far Eastern Affairs, Number Two*, St. Antony's Papers, Number Seven (London: Chatto & Windus, 1960), 62–87

JAMES S. COLEMAN, "Nationalism in Tropical Africa" (*American Political Science Review*, XLVIII, 2, June 1954, 404–426)

KARL W. DEUTSCH, *Nationalism and Social Communications: An Inquiry into the Foundations of Nationality* (Cambridge: M.I.T. Press, 1953)

RUPERT EMERSON, *From Empire to Nation: The Rise to Self-Assertion of Asian and African Peoples* (Cambridge: Harvard University Press, 1960)

RUPERT EMERSON, "Nationalism and Political Development" (*Journal of Politics*, XXII, 1, February 1960, 3–28)

THOMAS HODGKIN, *Nationalism in Colonial Africa* (New York: New York University Press, 1957)

ELIE KEDOURIE, *Nationalism*, revised edition (London: Hutchinson, 1961)

HANS KOHN, *The Idea of Nationalism: A Study in Its Origins and Background* (New York: Macmillan, 1961)

ARNOLD RIVKIN, "The Politics of Nation-Building: Problems and Preconditions" (*Journal of International Affairs*, XVI, 2, [1962], 131–143)

ROYAL INSTITUTE OF INTERNATIONAL AFFAIRS, *Nationalism* (London: Oxford University Press, 1939)

KALMAN H. SILVERT, "The Strategy of the Study of Nationalism," in K. H. Silvert, ed., *Expectant Peoples: Nationalism and Development* (New York: Random House, 1963), 3–38

HISHAM B. SHARABI, *Nationalism and Revolution in the Arab World* (Princeton: Van Nostrand, 1965)

BARBARA WARD, *Nationalism and Ideology* (New York: Norton, 1966)

IMPEDIMENTS TO UNITY
IN NEW NATIONS:
THE CASE OF CEYLON

W. Howard Wriggins

The conflict between linguistic groups in Ceylon seems to bear out the thesis that modernization may increase tension. According to Dr. Wriggins, the attempt by Ceylonese politicians to exploit the language issue helped touch off riots; the unity brought by the quest for independence diminished once self-government was achieved. A strong sense of Ceylonese identity has yet to transcend the split between the Sinhalese and Tamil communities.

In their search for nationhood since World War II, many peoples of Asia and Africa have discovered that independence from western rule is only the first and perhaps the easiest step. Once the foreigner has gone, the larger problem looms of creating a viable political society. Divisions and competitive strivings held in check when outsiders controlled affairs are suddenly released. Ethnic, religious and regional differences, that seemed less important so long as colonial administrators ruled, boil up after independence and more often than not come to dominate the loyalties and inspire the ambitions that move men in politics. To their dismay, responsible leaders find themselves heading not the homogeneous, modern nation state they dreamed of before independence, but a congeries of separate groups. The simple, unifying purpose of the independence struggle fades away, leaving a host of contradictions and cleavages.

Indonesia is wracked by repeated resistance to Jakarta. Burma has been beset by periodic insurrection, supported in part by regional and ethnic hostility to Rangoon. The nightmare of India's Nehru is the

From *The American Political Science Review*, Vol. LV, No. 2 (1961), pp. 313–320, by permission of the author and publisher.

growth of regional and linguistic differences. Imminent disintegration of the ex-Belgian Congo dramatizes the extreme case.

Are the difficulties impeding national consolidation mainly the fruit of irresponsible political leadership, as ex-colonial administrators are tempted to allege? Are ill-considered linguistic and educational reforms to blame, reforms that wiser statesmanship could have avoided? What other social and political developments sharpen antagonisms and impede the building of a viable nation state? Would more rapid economic development solve the problems of marked diversity, as the proponents of take-off aid programs often assert?

I. THE PRICE OF THE UNION

No doubt repeated appeals to regional, ethnic or traditional differences stunt the growth of a sense of common nationhood. Yet political leaders usually have substantial reasons for stressing their attachment to such divisions in the body politic. Unlike the colonial administrator who preceded him, the elected politician must elicit support; he cannot impose allegiance. So long as the bulk of citizens are moved by appeals to local or traditional ties, there is no surer way of winning political backing than by demonstrating attachment to parochial loyalties. It remains an essential part of political campaigning in Scotland or Wales, as it does in Louisiana or in Maine. In Great Britain and the United States, to be sure, tacit understandings by now set bounds beyond which regional or certain other special interests cannot profitably be pressed at the expense of an overriding national interest. In new countries, the pressures for asserting regional, ethnic or traditional values are many times greater, tacit understandings of the proper limits as not yet agreed upon, and people are little aware of a public interest that must take priority if the national community is to solve its problems effectively and survive.

In India, as Selig Harrison reminds us, many members of the Congress Party—and even the Communist Party—draw their strength mainly from regional or traditional interests so insistent that an overarching identity with policies of concern to all of India in many instances is not possible. In Indonesia, many politicians and administrators feel impelled to insist upon regional interest, reenforced by traditional attachments and religious differences. Not even Sukarno can count any more upon a freely given nationwide support; he has had to reach adjustment with the army to help him hold the nation's multiplicity together. In Pakistan, differences between Urdu-speaking, Moghul-influenced West Pakistan and Bengali-speaking, Hindu-influenced

East Pakistan are profound. Any political man from East Pakistan who does not speak out for his region's peculiar interests is likely to lose indispensable political support at home. However understandable these political imperatives may be, it often appears that spokesmen for parochial interests press their claims excessively, disregarding the likely disruptive consequences to the whole of what they seek to achieve for the part.

In nearly all the countries of South and Southeast Asia, linguistic legislation and educational reform have had high priority. Yet governments and legislators on the side of the largest language group have persistently and seriously underestimated the strength of linguistic loyalties among minorities. In India, for example, legislation provides that Hindi shall replace English as the official language, at a pace defined by an official time-table. At the same time, the efforts to promote Hindi have sharpened minority anxieties about the larger ambitions of the Hindi-speaking segments of the population, and consolidated their loyalties to their own languages. In Malaya, Chinese are antagonized by Malay efforts to strengthen the position of Malay. In Ceylon, Tamils have bitterly opposed efforts of the Sinhalese majority to raise the status of Sinhalese. Each such measure may promote national consolidation in the long run, but it usually favors immediately one group more than another, and changes the terms on which groups compete for opportunity, wealth and power. Those who promote the reforms find it hard to imagine why the minorities should feel so bitter, a lack of empathy that impedes taking steps to assuage minority anxieties, or otherwise to ease what may be an unavoidable transition.

Educational reforms adopted on grounds of excellent principles—the right to universal education, for example, or the right to have children taught in the language of their parents—may have disruptive side effects which can be foreseen but are not taken seriously. A rapidly expanded school system without appropriate changes in the curriculum produces large numbers of educated citizens who are ambitious for status but for whom there are no proper jobs. Teaching children only in the vernaculars segregates them into ethnic groups from the outset and weakens communication between communities. A leadership which transcends the traditional differences such as developed, with all its inequities, under the British and to a more limited extent, under the French colonial systems is no longer produced. Neither by-product is examined with care, and sufficient counter-measures are not taken, with the result that communal awareness is heightened and competition for all-too-scarce opportunities is sharpened.

Economic development providing new opportunities and greater hope for the future would be likely to mitigate this competition in the long run, but in the politically crucial short run it does not eliminate the attachment to old divisions. At the outset, development is likely to favor those most adaptable and ready to seize new opportunities, who are often ethnic and linguistic minorities such as the Marwaris in India or aliens, like the Chinese, in Indonesia. If this process is allowed to run its course, divisions and antagonisms are aggravated. If it is interrupted by political intervention in favor of the majority, resentments among these minorities are heightened. Improved means of communication may at first arouse more perception of group differences and sharpen conflicting ambitions.

Modernization may provoke its own reaction, as traditionalist groups organize to oppose innovation and to weaken the power of those who are responsible for it. Thus, in the short run, at least, modernization may increase group tensions. However much urbanization and industrialization may eventually free men from their traditional loyalties and make a new basis for integration possible, the transition is more likely to be immediately disruptive than to ease group relations.

The struggle for independence provokes the turning back to prewestern cultural roots. But as the early history of each country is explored, it is discovered that the ancestors of those presently engaged in common opposition to the European fought one another in bloody wars or gradual incursions upon one another's territory. When independence is finally achieved, these historical struggles take on a new urgency as groups compete for opportunity and status in the new country.

Hence, the task of national consolidation, however urgent it may be, poses very difficult problems. A close look at Ceylon's experience with relations between its majority and minority populations will illustrate these observations. The country's small size permits clearer analysis of interacting social, political, and economic factors than is possible in massive India or less organized Burma or Indonesia. Of all the new Asian countries, Ceylon seemed to have the best chance of making a successful transition to modern statehood. It began its independence most auspiciously with seasoned leadership drawn from nearly all important ethnic groups. The population was sixty percent literate at independence. It had longer experience with nationwide elections on the basis of a universal franchise to represent single-member, territorial constituencies than any other country. Per capita GNP was higher than in any other country in the area apart from Japan. Its recent experience of relative harmony among classes and racial groups was such that there had been no insurrection, no partition, no sharp class struggle. Yet in 1956 and 1958, unprecedented riots left deep antagonisms that will be hard to soften in the future; the hitherto orderly processes of representative government were interrupted by emergency governor's rule, and the Prime Minister was assassinated.

A detailed examination of this deterioration where high hopes were entertained may shed some light on what other countries have in store. For despite their many differences, virtually all the former colonial countries on the edge of Asia share certain fundamental characteristics that complicate their search for national consolidation. First, there are fissures in the indigenous social order, often regionally defined, that separate ethnic, linguistic and religious groups from one another. In most there are also important minorities who have come to the country within the past century, brought by European enterprisers or drawn by economic opportunities during the colonial period. Indian Tamils in Ceylon, Bengalis in Burma, Chinese in Thailand, Vietnam and Indonesia are the legacy that must be dealt with. Both of these impediments to national unity are usually identified as "communal" differences, creating a "plural" or "mosaic" society. Second, the horizontal stratifications are no less important, dividing socio-economic classes sharply from one another. By education, language and culture, the leading elements are in many respects alien to the masses they must lead. The nearest analogues to this stratification in the contemporary West are perhaps to be found in Latin America, Spain or southern Italy.

II. IMPEDIMENTS TO UNITY IN CEYLON

The Social Structure. The social structure of Asian countries provides an underlying element of disunity; the plural society in Ceylon is simpler than most others in the area. The majority Sinhalese community comprises nearly 70 percent of the total population. There are two Tamil-speaking minorities: approximately 12 percent of the population have lived on the island for many centuries; another 10 percent are relative newcomers who arrived during the colonial period to man the tea and rubber estates and develop wholesale businesses. A Muslim minority of some 5 percent and a Burgher community descended from mixed European and Ceylonese marriages form the balance.

The Sinhalese are largely Buddhists and speak Sinhalese, an Aryan language related to Bengali; the Tamils are Hindus who speak the Dravidian language Tamil. The Muslims, descendants of Arab traders, speak Sinhalese or Tamil and perhaps English as well, depending upon where they live. The Burghers claim English as their mother-tongue, though many speak Sinhalese too. Perhaps 8 percent of the population are Christians, divided between Sinhalese and Tamils, though nearly all the Burghers are Christians. There are also caste groupings, less strict than in India, which need not detain us. These are the gross contours of the plural society in Ceylon.

Members of the Sinhalese and Tamil communities speak different languages, lead different lives, and follow differing family customs. Although many individuals in both communities are fully accepted within the other, the two groups hold unflattering views of each other. Their attitudes show clearly differentiated and mutually critical stereotypes. Sinhalese and Tamils consider themselves to be markedly different. Each sees in the other traits it does not admire. Group distrust lies not far beneath the surface. Each community tends to form a network of mutual confidence and assistance when a member is faced with harm from those outside his own community. Some, though by no means all, trade unions, the Christian churches, larger business enterprises and the public service have provided opportunities for mingling and common activity. The army, though drawing on all communities, remains small and professionalized, playing only a minor role in national integration. The communities are therefore brought together by few institutions.

Other divisions in the society complicate the fundamental Sinhalese-Tamil difference. In many ways as profound is the fissure that separates the mass of the population from the English-speaking, western educated elite who represent roughly 8 percent of the total. An exact appraisal of this social distance is difficult, since the man who appears most at home in the western offices or salons of the capital may quickly shed his western ways when he returns to the family village. There are, of course, gradations in the degree of westernization, from the Oxford graduate raised in an English-speaking Ceylonese family, at one extreme, to the graduate of grammar school who has learned his English after primary school, on the other. Yet the division between the trousered men who command English and the rest is a visible, striking reality, and one profoundly felt by the millions who are not part of that elite. It is significant because the distribution of wealth, opportunity and power no longer depends alone upon family ties and family relations to the land, as in the traditional society. This is still important. But today, and for several generations already, real influence on the national state and often wealth have depended in addition upon the acquired skills of English education and western social ways.

Regardless of whether they were Sinhalese, Tamils, or Burghers in origin, the English-educated formed a stratum that lay across the ethnic and linguistic differences. These Tamils and Sinhalese had many close friendships that ignored communal lines. The English-educated articulated the desire for independence. Their vision usually encompassed all communities living in some degree of mutual acceptance in a gradually modernizing, unifying Ceylonese nationhood. As elsewhere in Asia, they inherited political power when the colonial rulers withdrew, in 1948.

But they were not politically homogeneous. Indeed, they competed among themselves for the opportunities of office. They were divided on political-ideological as well as religious grounds, and visions were accentuated as their leading position in the society became less sure.

Growing Awareness of Differences. Awareness of mutual differences has increased rather than diminished since independence. First, a cultural revival came to Ceylon only after independence, expressing the need to assert a cultural idiom distinct from western ways. As Sinhalese and Tamils each explored their own pasts, they recalled battles won from the other; they gained a sense of inferiority or superiority toward each other. In their search, they found no common Ceylonese tradition, only separate Sinhalese and Tamil pasts. The state-wide alien rule no longer formed a common opponent uniting the different groups.

Second, an expanded educational system carried schooling to ever higher grades in the vernacular languages. More and more young people graduated from upper levels of the school system, reared entirely within one or the other vernacular culture without the unifying experience of English education.

Third, mutual understanding between the ethnic communities seemed to diminish. The vernacular press, for example, gained importance as literacy increased and as the wider masses became more actively concerned with public issues. This enhanced the distance between the Sinhalese and Tamils, since each vernacular paper tended to stress those aspects of public issues and cultural traditions which editors believed would appeal to their differentiated audiences. The press thus tended to provide contrasting and often contradictory interpretations of public problems to the different ethnic communities, hardening differences and sharpening distrust.

Fourth, with independence the Sinhalese majority expected that the Tamil and other minorities would assimilate to the Sinhalese way of life. But a sense of cultural superiority among the Tamils led them to resist the majority's effort to realize this expectation. Tamils feel a part of the capacious Indian tradition; they believe they have a culture rich in art, literature and religious insight. Becoming part of the Sinhalese cultural world is taken to mean abandoning this great tradition. Conversely, a sense of Sinhalese cultural inferiority has made many in the majority community unusually sensitive. There are only 8 million Sinhalese in all the world. In Ceylon itself reside 2 million Tamil-speaking people; across in India there are some 28 million more. The Sinhalese are often fearful of being overwhelmed by their Tamil neighbors; the Ceylon Tamils fear being swamped by the island's majority Sinhalese. Ironically, both groups are beset with something akin to minority feelings, each oversensitive to the other's criticisms and fearful of the other's ambitions.

These differences set the stage for invidious communal comparisons. Moreover, modernization has not gone so far that an individual's professional or financial achievement is seen as his personal accomplishment. On the contrary, an individual's achievement still reflects more upon the position of his communal group. When communal differences become projected into politics, every act of members of one community is looked at for its political significance—to see, that is, whether it enhances or diminishes the relative political influence of his own community. Past political contests between communities are disinterred and over-elaborate political strategies and tactics are attributed to moves made by members of the other community that often had no political intention behind them.

Fifth, a growing awareness among the masses concerning the privileged position of the westernized elite and a clearer cultural consciousness led to an increasing resentment against that elite. Articulate leaders of the independence movement from among the westernized talked of welfare, of democracy and of majority rule. But positions of control in the society were still filled by men of high birth or those fortunate enough to have been able to learn English. In a period of growing cultural self-awareness, this was not the democracy that had been preached by the leadership for many decades. The country still seemed to be ruled by an oligarchy of men alienated from indigenous traditions and cultures.

Moreover, their efforts to modernize their country, though cautious, provoked anxiety and resentment in important groups in the countryside who were among the intermediaries between the urban politicians and the rural masses. Practitioners of traditional *ayurvedic* medicine resented the resources invested in modern, western-type medical services; Buddhist monks, keepers of the Sinhalese tradition, opposed the growing emphasis on materialistic values; vernacular teachers protested against their second-class professional status by comparison with the higher pay and respect accorded to English-speaking teachers; local officials opposed the growing influence and size of the capital's bureaucracy.

Economic Competition. Awareness of economic competition increased as the population grew. The expanding school system turned out more liberal arts graduates who aspired to enter the coveted public service than the service could absorb. After an initial expansion to replace colonial officials and provide new economic and social service functions, public service hiring fell off just as more graduates began to enter the job market.

The students who could not find work form an articulate group, with time on their hands and an acute sense of grievance. They possess the skills necessary for political activity. Had there been other job opportunities, their frustrated ambitions for public service careers would not have mattered so desperately. But economic development that produced white collar jobs was disappointingly slow. The jobs they sought were not to be found in the government or elsewhere, and their liberal arts education had not fitted them for much else.

This increased the potentiality for tension between communities in part because the communal structure of Ceylon is relatively simple and readily lends itself to statistical comparisons. It was possible to argue, for example, that although the Sinhalese represented some 70 percent of the population, they held only 60–65 percent of the public service jobs, while the Ceylon Tamils, representing only 12 percent of the population, held some 20 percent of the jobs. In a time of growing unemployment in lower jobs as well, a politician could prove his devotion to the majority community by pointing the finger at the Tamils who had "usurped" more than their fair share of the best jobs.

Clearing and irrigating jungle land to be settled by peasants from the overcrowded Sinhalese and Tamil areas became a bitter apple of discord between the two communities. The land had lain under the rule of malaria, empty and desolate, until DDT made its reconquest possible. Tamils consider these new lands to be areas they have traditionally inhabited. The Sinhalese see much historical evidence to prove that Buddhist civilization once flourished before the jungle and malaria made their conquest. Both argue that settlement of peasants from the other community represents encroachment. And since political representation goes according to territorial constituencies, a significant change in the population structure of such areas would alter the balance of communal representation in the House of Representatives. Hence, even land development has sharpened group conflict.

Political Imperatives. The background of political leaders and the electoral imperatives provided other potentialities for social tension.

The principal political figures have come from the westernized elite. Broadly speaking, national electoral politics has been a struggle for office between men of this socio-economic class. Each has sought those relationships and issues that would carry influence and "project his image" across the social and linguistic gulf that separated him from the mass of voters. A convenient way of identifying himself with the voters was to demonstrate that he was more closely attached to the cultural and religious values of his constituents than his opponent, who could usually be charged with being too much like the former colonial rulers in style of life and language.

After independence, Ceylon was ruled by a coalition of moderately conservative men from the English-educated, land-owning, professional families in both Sinhalese and Tamil communities. Their support in the countryside was reenforced by the semi-feudal fact that the rural masses tended to vote the way the rural notable, landowner or employer wished. But as new men from lesser origins entered the westernized elite, as cultural revival accented indigenous virtues often flouted by the more modern, westernized man, as democratic ideology penetrated the countryside, the westernized could not assume that their ruling position would continue. Their right to control affairs was bound to be tested. More direct appeals to mass sentiments often seemed the way to ensure continued political success.

Until 1956 the opposition parties were splintered, as in India, and the majority party could not be effectively challenged on the floor of the House of Representatives or at the hustings. The urban population was relatively small and underrepresented in a House designed to give greater representation to backward rural areas. Only if the opposition could undercut the government party in the countryside could it hope to displace the men who had ruled since independence.

In rural areas, between the notables and landowners who dominated national politics and the peasant and town masses, is a rural middle class of men who are prominent in their towns and villages. Buddhist monks, elected village officials, teachers skilled in the vernacular languages, practitioners of traditional *ayurvedic* medicine are such men. Opposition agitation in 1956 drew them into political activity that contributed decisively to the opposition's electoral victory that year. This agitation precipitated the elements of potential disunity into communal discord and violent conflict. The particular issue of import to them all concerned the matter of language.

III. LANGUAGE AND POLITICS

The "Language Question." It is difficult in the United States, where one language predominates, to appreciate the intensity of emotions that the "language question" can arouse. In a plural society, language distinguishes one man from his neighbor, gives him access to his own cultural tradition, is the canonical representation of his religion and the instrument for communicating about it. English had been the colonial ruler's language. Language differences had much to do with the distribution of opportunity, wealth and political power. Widespread resentment against the airs and privileges of the English-educated, the power and aloofness of the English-speaking public service, the cultural snobbishness of the westernized city man, made the demotion of English virtually inevitable.

As independence neared, two vexed questions of government policy toward the country's languages had to be answered. In what language should the children be taught and what should be the country's official language (or languages) of government?

After sharp and protracted debates, it was decided that Sinhalese and Tamil children should learn in their own language, while English would be taught as a second language. The policy solution was obvious enough, but the debates on the matter added to communal sensitivities. Each year they were renewed as the Opposition accused the government of not pressing ahead rapidly enough with the necessary language changeover in the higher grades of the schools. As a by-product of this decision—and significant for the long run—there would no longer be produced an island-wide elite from all communities who had passed together through the same educational experience.

Electoral Politics. Intense feelings were provoked over the issue of the language or languages to be designated as official languages of state. Seeking to undercut the ruling coalition, the political opposition found the language question an unusually effective means for mobilizing the rural middle class in the majority community—the teachers, native physicians, the *bhikkhus* and local elected officials. Each one, for different reasons, experienced some sense of threat from westernizing, modernizing changes or some resentment against the westernized elite. Each rallied behind traditional communal symbols. They all believed that if Sinhalese were made the sole official language, their cultural and religious tradition would receive greater attention and their opportunities and status would be commensurately improved.

All who opposed making Sinhalese the sole official language were held to be standing in the way of legitimate—and national—aspirations. The Tamils opposed such a change and were therefore considered opponents. In the excitement of platform polemics, which were remarkably colorful and keyed to traditional allusions and indigenous fancy, many politicians made no distinction between Tamil invaders of 1,000 years ago and contemporary Ceylon Tamils. Ancient antagonisms were thus revived and combined with contemporary competition for scarce opportunity and uncertain status.

Many among the western-educated Sinhalese were generally opposed to the changes. But their will and power were sapped by two circumstances. In the first place, they feared that speaking out on behalf of moderation and a gradual transition to Sinhalese as the official language would turn the wrath of ardent Sinhalese against them, leading to the accusation that they were allies of the Tamils in a cause which they felt was all but lost already. Secondly, many experienced a growing sense of guilt that they had allowed themselves to become so alienated from their own tradition. In the name of their community's tradition, which they now sensed they had neglected, they were prepared to acquiesce in the changes even though these would seriously undermine their hitherto privileged position and risk bringing on dramatic communal difficulties.

As the Tamils saw it, to make Sinhalese the sole official language put Tamil in an inferior position and would no doubt give the Sinhalese-speaking people a competitive advantage as entrants to the public service, to teaching, university and other desirable careers. Pride in their culture was hurt; even their status as accepted inhabitants of Ceylon seemed brought in doubt.

In the 1956 election, the Sinhalese opposition, skilfully led by Bandaranaike, was successful in displacing the formerly ruling United National Party by a landslide vote. The ruling party had been vulnerable on other counts as well, but it was primarily linguistic politics that brought it down.

Electoral By-products. As a by-product of the campaign, communal antagonisms were at a new high for the country. The successful Prime Minister—like his defeated opponents—had assumed that communal antagonism could be turned up for tactical purposes and then turned down when the political need was gone. But new pressure groups organized among extremist Sinhalese and a vigorous minority of the clergy were not prepared to allow the new Prime Minister to moderate these antagonisms until their full aspirations were met. The Tamils, frightened by the upsurge of anti-Tamil sentiment, became more rigid.

Riots in 1956 followed close on the heels of the election and the debate in the House of Representatives over a language bill designed to give Sinhalese sole official standing. In the face of dramatic activities by the newly organized pressure groups, all provisions designed to safeguard Tamil interests were removed from the bill before it was submitted to debate. Starting in Colombo, vicious riots spread rapidly and over 100 were killed.

If bold political leadership, putting extremists on both sides in their place, might have cut through the fear and tension of communal intransigence, none appeared.

In 1958 more serious riots occurred. The police had become demoralized as a result of politically inspired transfers and because of restraining orders pressed upon the Prime Minister by his Marxist cabinet colleagues with political trade union interests to promote. The police were unable to restore order as rioting, looting, and burning spread. Several hundreds were killed—some say as many as 2,000. In the end, 10,000 Tamils and 2,000 Sinhalese sought refuge in army-managed refugee camps. When the army was finally called out, order was quickly restored. But a deeper gulf of fear now separated the minority Ceylon Tamil community from the majority Sinhalese.

As a tragic climax to these events, the Prime Minister was assassinated on his own verandah in September 1959 by a monk, a student of *ayurvedic* medicine. The case is under adjudication and there may be obscure political or even economic foundations for what at first appeared to be an act of a religious and cultural enthusiast who found the Prime Minister unable to carry out the promises he had made in the heat of political campaigning.

IV. CONCLUSIONS

Apart from the tragedy of the hundreds killed during the riots and the assassination of the Prime Minister himself, the two rounds of communal riots left the country divided as it had not been for centuries. What conclusions can be drawn from these unhappy events?

(1) The social structure of the plural society remains a stubborn social and political fact. Modernizing currents have not yet undermined the primary loyalty of the mass voters to traditional linguistic communities. A sense of Ceylonese nationhood is not yet clear.

(2) Efforts to assert cultural independence from the West lead to explorations of the country's tradition. But this reaffirms diverse traditions and a past of local conflict which enlivens communal awareness and antagonisms. These differences increase after independence is achieved when the common opponent, the western ruler, no longer provides a focus for unifying antagonism.

(3) Important rural middle class figures feel sufficiently threatened by modern, secular influences to be particularly susceptible to traditional appeals that have, as their by-products, profound communal implications. These men are potential intermediaries between the westernized political leaders and opposition and the rural voters. They can therefore play an important role in politics when they are drawn into political activity, and they are by no means always carriers of modernization to the rural masses.

(4) The earlier equation between education and opportunity has been disrupted and ever-higher levels of education are conducted in the vernaculars. Economic diversification and growth have not kept pace with expanding educational opportunities, resulting in a middle-class unemployment. This contributes particularly and directly to communal competition. Since the newly educated middle classes are largely trained in the vernacular languages, they identify only with their own parochial community. They do not comprehend a wider loyalty to the country as a whole, and they see their job futures in terms of their language community only.

(5) Unavoidable decisions have to be made regarding the language or languages to replace English in the schools and in the government. These are bound to cause communal discord unless handled with great finesse.

(6) Where a ruling elite is at a notable linguistic and cultural distance from the masses in a representative political system, those who seek to replace elected representatives may easily evoke communal and ethnic enthusiasms as a means of enlisting mass political support.

(7) As one side effect of such electoral politics, communal anxieties may be greatly increased and new pressure groups develop to further press communal and religious claims. This stiffens the inflexibility of minority leaders and leaves a new government relatively little room for maneuver as it seeks an adjustment of contradictory claims.

(8) A new government that is indecisive in domestic affairs and allows the vigor of the police to deteriorate unwittingly encourages extremists in both camps. Outbreaks of mob violence create further anxiety and antagonism for the future.

(9) Rapid economic growth providing new opportunities to the most frustrated probably would mitigate such conflicts. In itself, however, it would not be sufficient to prevent them, and in the short run, at least, it may provide additional grounds for group antagonism.

In sum, those forces which divide, which separate one group from another grow in strength after independence—in school, in political activity and sometimes in economic life. Cultural revival enlivens the recollection of historic divisions and group conflicts; steps toward modernization arouse resistance from traditionalists who, feeling threatened, fall back on vernacular cultural values as protection. Rapidly expanding the liberal arts school system in the vernaculars at a time when the colonial administrator's *lingua franca* must be replaced produces educated unemployed, stops the creation of a nation-wide elite, and provokes minority anxieties about their own future opportunities. Simultaneously, a westernized elite at a cultural distance from the masses and not having solved important public problems is an easy target of criticism and scorn for those who would use ethnic enthusiasm as a means of replacing the leaders who gained power at independence. As a result of such political developments, new pressure groups form around divisive, parochial purposes while new leadership may only encourage extremists if it is indecisive.

In the Ceylon setting, the westernized elite no longer can be as self-assured as it used to be. Consolidation of ethnic communities into one nation is farther away today than it was ten years ago. The task of mending the social fabric will tax the skill and statesmanship of the new government of Mrs. Sirimavo Bandaranaike, widow of the former Prime Minister, whose electoral coalition won handsomely in June 1960. In other new countries, too, national consolidation remains one of the crucial problems of the future, demanding quite as much courage and foresight as the more familiar problems of economic development.

FOR FURTHER READING

BERTRAM HUGHES FARMER, *Ceylon: A Divided Nation* (London: Oxford University Press, 1963)

JAMES JUPP, "Constitutional Developments in Ceylon Since Independence," *(Pacific Affairs, XLI, 1, Spring 1968, 34–50)*

ROBERT N. KEARNEY, "Sinhalese Nationalism and Social Conflict in Ceylon" *(Pacific Affairs, XXXVII, 2, Summer 1964, 125–136)*

SIDNEY ARNOLD PAKEMAN, *Ceylon* (New York: Praeger, 1964)

D. K. RANGNEKAR, "The Nationalist Revolution in Ceylon" *(Pacific Affairs, XXXIII, 4, December 1960, 361–374)*

BRUCE RYAN, *Sinhalese Village* (Coral Gables: University of Miami Press, 1958)

MARSHALL R. SINGER, *The Emerging Elite: A Study of Political Leadership in Ceylon* (Cambridge: M. I. T. Press, 1964)

MARSHALL R. SINGER, "Group Perception and Social Change in Ceylon" *(International Journal of Comparative Sociology, VII, 1-2, March 1966, 209–226)*

W. HOWARD WRIGGINS, *Ceylon: Dilemmas of a New Nation* (Princeton: Princeton University Press, 1960)

5

MODERNIZATION AND
POLITICAL INSTITUTIONS

The nature and pace of social change interact with political modernization in several ways. The previous readings have dealt with the effects of social change on political institutions, and particularly with the weakening of traditional ways of life and the growth of political participation. In this section, rather than examining social issues and their impacts—the clash of primordial and civil sentiments, the effects of social mobilization, the problem of identity with the state—we shall examine the ways in which government actions directly influence modernization. How does government organization affect the speed and direction of change? What organs of government seem best able to meet the growing tasks created by modernization? Are specific political institutions required for modernization?

The explosive growth of political participation in recently independent countries significantly affects governmental effectiveness. As Professor Huntington comments in the first reading, "Rapid increases in mobilization and participation, the principal political aspects of modernization, undermine political institutions. Rapid modernization, in brief, produces not political development, but political decay." The institutionalization of political organization and procedures is exceedingly difficult; it may require slowing the rate of social change and creating a strong single party as "the source of legitimacy and authority." Effective political organization must be consciously sought lest the forces unleashed by modernization help topple governments—as in coups d'etat.

In 1958, General Ayub Khan seized power in Pakistan. Disgruntled by parliamentary wrangling, Ayub sought both to evoke and to control political participation through Basic Democracies. However, his efforts were complicated by other factors. New tasks, notably in economic development, strained the abilities of the bureaucracy. The scope of government activities increased. The Basic Democracies represented an effort to mobilize the populace, but because of demands made on them, also to control the populace. Pakistan, like other modernizing countries, must establish common values within severe constraints, as Professor Wilcox suggests in the second selection. The Ayub government did not succeed in this effort—perhaps its time was too short—and was supplanted by a new military-based government in 1969.

The third selection in this section, "Building the Newest Nations: Short-Run Strategies and Long-Run Problems," centers on the "politically relevant strata" of recently independent countries. In the pre-independence period, both elite and mass worked through broadly based nationalist parties to achieve self-government. "The mass party," Professor Foltz notes, "became the framework within which ethnic, caste, and regional differences among the population at large could be submerged in the search for a common goal. It both embodied and promoted a preliminary sense of national unity and identity." When self-government was attained, however, the mass party lost its unifying slogan of "Independence"; competition among members of the elite grew; the monolithic unity of the mass party declined. Short-run stability through party cohesiveness, even at the cost of repression, may be necessary for the long-run building of the nation.

The burdens of nation-building place great strains on the governments of newly independent states. One result, analyzed in the third selection, is corruption. As patterns of political interaction shift, uncertainties arise. In some respects, corruption helps retain institutional fluidity and responsiveness in periods of alteration. Corruption reflects a disjunction between the social system and the formal political system— a disjunction that might, were it not for corruption, lead to violence.

Two studies based on post-independence Africa conclude this section. As Professors Coleman and Rosberg point out, strong government, centralized control, and single-party supremacy attracted African leaders when their countries gained self-government. In particular, the lack of national unity seemed to justify centralization of political power. Primordial sentiments have remained strong, possibly enhanced by social mobilization; popular identity with the state as a whole, though growing, remains relatively weak. Coleman and Rosberg see two likely paths for single-party-dominant systems: a fusion of party and government in a "party-state," in which neither party nor state would wither away; or a "no-party state" induced by a decline of the party as the center of power and decision making—whether by the dominance of bureaucracy or by military seizure of control. Striking confirmation of their hypothesis came in late 1965 and early 1966, when, within a few weeks, the armies of the Congo, Dahomey, Upper Volta, Central African Republic, Nigeria, and Ghana ousted politicians from office.

Can military officers make significant contributions to political modernization? Armies obviously are "modern" institutions—but it seems unlikely that they can move entire societies toward modernity. The concluding reading suggests that military leaders lack bargaining skills and cannot readily build legitimate political institutions.

The lesson to be drawn from this section is that long-range stability and effectively functioning political institutions *can* be attained, though the odds may seem unfavorable. The ways in which the governments and political parties of new states influence political modernization —especially by building institutions or by increasing social mobilization —may bring development or may bring decay.

POLITICAL DEVELOPMENT
AND POLITICAL DECAY

Samuel P. Huntington

Many studies of new states have neglected the growth of political institutions and have concentrated instead upon alterations in society. Professor Huntington criticizes this tendency, since rapid social change may undermine political development. Strong parties could be the only alternatives to instability resulting from rapid social change.

"Among the laws that rule human societies," de Tocqueville said, "there is one which seems to be more precise and clear than all others. If men are to remain civilized or to become so, the art of associating together must grow and improve in the same ratio in which the equality of conditions is increased."[1] In much of the world today, equality of political participation is growing much more rapidly than is the "art of associating together." The rates of mobilization and participation are high; the rates of organization and institutionalization are low. De Tocqueville's precondition for civilized society is in danger, if it is not already undermined. In these societies, the conflict between mobilization and institutionalization is the crux of politics. Yet in the fast-growing literature on the politics of the developing areas, political institutionalization usually receives scant treatment. Writers on political development emphasize the processes of modernization and the closely related phenomena of social mobilization and increasing political participation. A balanced view of the politics of contemporary Asia, Africa, and Latin America requires more attention to the "art of associating together" and the growth of political institutions. For this purpose, it is useful to distinguish political development from modernization and to

From *World Politics*, Vol. XVII, No. 3 (1965), pp. 386–430, by permission. Text and footnotes abridged by the editor.

[1]*Democracy in America* (Phillips Bradley edn., New York, 1955), II, 118.

identify political development with the institutionalization of political organizations and procedures. Rapid increases in mobilization and participation, the principal political aspects of modernization, undermine political institutions. Rapid modernization, in brief, produces not political development, but political decay.

I. POLITICAL DEVELOPMENT AS MODERNIZATION

Definitions of political development are legion. Most, however, share two closely related characteristics. First, political development is identified as one aspect of, or as intimately connected with, the broader processes of modernization in society as a whole. Modernization affects all segments of society; its political aspects constitute political development. Indeed, many authors seem to prefer the phrase "political modernization" as more descriptive of their primary concern. Second, if political development is linked with modernization, it is necessarily a broad and complex process. Hence most authors argue that political development must be measured by many criteria. The "multi-functional character of politics," Lucian Pye has said, "... means that no single scale can be used for measuring the degree of political development."[2] It thus differs from economic development, on the character of which there seems to be more general agreement and which is measurable through fairly precise indices such as per capita national income. Definitions of political development hence tend to itemize a number of criteria. Ward and Rustow list eight characteristics of the modern polity; Emerson has five. Pye identifies four major aspects of political development plus half a dozen additional "factors." Eisenstadt finds four characteristics of political modernization.[3]

The definitions are many and multiple; but, with a few exceptions, the characteristics which they identify with political development are all aspects of the processes of modernization. Four sets of categories recur continuously in the definitions. One set, focusing on the Parsonian pattern variables, can perhaps best be summed up as *rationalization*. This involves movement from particularism to universalism, from diffuseness to specificity, from ascription to achievement, and from affectivity to affective neutrality. In terms of political development, functional differentiation and achievement criteria are partic-

---

[2]Lucian W. Pye, ed., *Communications and Political Development* (Princeton 1963), 16.

[3]Robert E. Ward and Dankwart A. Rustow, eds., *Political Modernization in Japan and Turkey* (Princeton 1964), 6–7; Rupert Emerson, *Political Modernization: The Single-Party System* (Denver 1963), 7–8; Pye, ed., *Communications and Political Development*, 17–18; S. N. Eisenstadt, "Bureaucracy and Political Development," in Joseph LaPalombara, ed., *Bureaucracy and Political Development* (Princeton 1963), 99.

ularly emphasized.[4] A second set of characteristics identified with development involves nationalism and *national integration*. Almost all writers recognize the problem of the "crisis of national identity" and the necessity of establishing a firmly delimited ethnic basis for the political community.[5] A developed polity, it is usually assumed, must, with rare exception, be a nation-state. "Nation-building" is a key aspect of political development. A third approach focuses on *democratization*: pluralism, competitiveness, equalization of power, and similar qualities. "Competitiveness," says Coleman, "is an essential aspect of political modernity." Hence, "the Anglo-American polities most closely approximate the model of a modern political system. . . . "[6] Frey argues that "the most common notion of political development in intellectual American circles is that of movement towards democracy." He finds this a congenial notion and offers his own definition of political development as "changes in the direction of greater distribution and reciprocity of power."[7]

Rationalization, integration, and democratization thus commonly appear in definitions of political development. The characteristic of political development or political modernization which is most frequently emphasized, however, is *mobilization,* or *participation*. Modernization, Karl Deutsch has emphasized, involves social mobilization, and "this complex of processes of social change is significantly correlated with major changes in politics." Increases in literacy, urbanization, exposure to mass media, industrialization, and per capita income expand "the politically relevant strata of the population," multiply the demands for government services, and thus stimulate an increase in governmental capabilities, a broadening of the elite, increased political participation, and shifts in attention from the local level to the national level.[8] Modernization means mass mobilization; mass mobilization means increased political development. Participation distinguishes modern politics from traditional politics. "Traditional society," says Lerner, "is non-participant—it deploys people by kinship into communities isolated from each

[4]James S. Coleman, in Gabriel A. Almond and Coleman, eds., *The Politics of the Developing Areas* (Princeton, 1960), 532; Fred W. Riggs, "Bureaucracy and Political Development: A Paradoxical View," in LaPalombara, ed., *Bureaucracy and Political Development*, 122; Eisenstadt, in *ibid.*, 99; Ward and Rustow, eds., *Political Modernization*, 7.

[5]See, e.g., Gabriel A. Almond, "Political Systems and Political Change," *American Behavioral Scientist*, VI (June 1963), 3–10; Ward and Rustow, eds., *Political Modernization*, 7.

[6]Coleman, in Almond and Coleman, eds., *Politics of Developing Areas*, 533.

[7]Frederick W. Frey, "Political Development, Power, and Communications in Turkey," in Pye, ed., *Communications and Political Development*, 301.

[8]Karl W. Deutsch, "Social Mobilization and Political Development," *American Political Science Review*, LV (September 1961), 493ff. [Reprinted in this reader, p. 153.]

other and from a center . . ." Modern society, in contrast, is "participant society."[9] The "new world political culture," say Almond and Verba, "will be a political culture of participation. If there is a political revolution going on throughout the world, it is what might be called the participation explosion. In all the new nations of the world the belief that the ordinary man is politically relevant—that he ought to be an involved participant in the political system—is widespread. Large groups of people who have been outside politics are demanding entrance into the political system."[10] Political development, Rustow argues, may be defined as "(1) an increasing national political unity plus (2) a broadening base of political participation." Similarly, Riggs declares that political development "refers to the process of politicization: increasing participation or involvement of the citizen in state activities, in power calculations, and consequences."[11]

All definitions are arbitrary. These definitions of political development as some combination or permutation of participation, rationalization, democratization, and nation-building are just as legitimate as any other definitions. While all definitions may be equally arbitrary and equally legitimate, they do vary greatly, however, in their relevance to particular problems and their usefulness for particular ends. Presumably one major purpose of concepts of political development is to facilitate understanding of the political processes in contemporary Asian, African, and Latin American societies. To be analytically useful, a concept must be precise and relevant. It must also have sufficient generality of application to permit comparative analysis of differing situations. Many approaches to political development suffer from one or more of the following difficulties.

First, the identification of political development with modernization or with factors usually associated with modernization drastically limits the applicability of the concept in both time and space. It is defined in parochial and immediate terms, its relevance limited to modern nation-states or the emergence of modern nation-states. It becomes impossible to speak of a politically developed tribal authority, city-state, feudal monarchy, or bureaucratic empire. Development is identified with one type of political system, rather than as a quality which might characterize any type of political system. All systems which are not modern are underdeveloped, including presumably fifth-century Athens, the third-century B.C. Roman republic, the second-century A.D. Roman

[9]Daniel Lerner, The Passing of Traditional Society (Glencoe 1958), 48–50.
[10]Gabriel A. Almond and Sidney Verba, The Civic Culture (Princeton 1963), 4.
[11]Dankwart A. Rustow, "The Vanishing Dream of Stability," AID Digest (August 1962), 13; Riggs, in LaPalombara, ed., Bureaucracy and Political Development, 139.

empire, the Han and T'ang empires in China, or even eighteenth-century America. None of these political systems was modern. Is it also useful to consider them underdeveloped? Would it not be more appropriate to consider development or underdevelopment as a characteristic which might be found in any type of political system? City-states could be developed or underdeveloped; so also could be bureaucratic empires or modern nation-states. This approach would cast additional light on contemporary modernizing societies by furnishing a second set of categories (in addition to the traditional-modern set) for comparing the processes of change in those societies with the processes of change in other types of societies. Such an approach, of course, would also liberate the concept of development from even more limited identification of it with the Western, constitutional, democratic nation-state.

The second problem with many definitions of political development is the obverse but also the corollary of the first. On the one hand, development is limited to the characteristics of the modern nation-state. On the other, it is also broadened to include almost all politically relevant aspects of the modernization process. It acquires comprehensiveness at the cost of precision. There is a natural tendency to assume that political development is all of a piece, that one "good thing" is compatible with another. In addition, studies of modernization have shown a very high degree of correlation among such indices as literacy, urbanization, media participation, and political participation.[12] Hence, it is easy to assume that a similar correlation exists among the various elements identified as contributing to political development. In fact, however, the four, eight, or twelve criteria of development may or may not have any systematic relation to each other. They may indeed be negatively correlated. There is no particular reason, for instance, why more participation and more structural differentiation should go together; in fact, there is some a priori reason to assume that more of one might mean less of the other. If this be the case, two contradictory tendencies (A, —B; —A, B) could both be labeled "political development." The broader the definition of development, moreover, the more inevitable development becomes. The all-encompassing definitions make development seem easy by making it seem inescapable. Development becomes an omnipresent first cause, which explains everything but distinguishes nothing. Almost anything that happens in the "developing" countries—coups, ethnic struggles, revolutionary wars—becomes part of the process of development, however contradictory or retrogressive this may appear on the surface. Political development thus loses its

---

[12]Lerner, Passing of Traditional Society, chap. 2.

analytical content and acquires simply a geographic one. At the extreme, it becomes synonymous with the political history of Asia, Africa, and Latin America.[13]

Thirdly, many definitions of political development fail to distinguish clearly the empirical relevance of the components going into the definition. Concepts of "developed" and "undeveloped" as ideal types or states of being are confused with concepts of "development" as a process which are, in turn, identified with the politics of the areas commonly called "developing." The line between actuality and aspiration is fogged. Things which are in fact occurring in the "developing" areas become hopelessly intertwined with things which the theorist thinks should occur there. Here again the tendency has been to assume that what is true for the broader processes of social modernization is also true for political changes. Modernization, in some degree, is a fact in Asia, Africa, Latin America: urbanization is rapid; literacy is slowly increasing; industrialization is being pushed; per capita gross national product is inching upward; mass media circulation is expanding; political participation is broadening. All these are facts. In contrast, progress toward many of the other goals identified with political development—democracy, stability, structural differentiation, achievement patterns, national integration—often is dubious at best. Yet the tendency is to think that because modernization is taking place, political development also must be taking place. As a result, many of the sympathetic Western writings about the underdeveloped areas today have the same air of hopeful unreality which characterized much of the sympathetic Western writing about the Soviet Union in the 1920's and 1930's. They are suffused with what can only be described as "Webbism": that is, the tendency to ascribe to a political system qualities which are assumed to be its ultimate goals rather than qualities which actually characterize its processes and functions.[14]

---

[13]For the *reductio in absurdum*, see Majid Khadduri, *Modern Libya: A Study in Political Development* (Baltimore 1963), and J. Clagett Taylor, *The Political Development of Tanganyika* (Stanford 1963). In the titles and content of both, "political development" has no analytical meaning. It is simply a synonym (euphemism?) for "political history." Both books are good history, but they are not social science.

[14]See, e.g., Milton J. Esman, "The Politics of Development Administration," to be published in John D. Montgomery and William Siffin, eds., *Politics, Administration, and Change: Approaches to Development* (New York 1965). Esman bases his analysis on the assumption that the political leaders of modernizing societies are motivated by the goals of nation-building and social-economic progress and not by desire for personal power, wealth, status, or the territorial expansion of their countries. This assumption has about the same degree of truth and usefulness in explaining politics in the contemporary "developing" areas as the assumption that Stalin's policies were devoted to building communism has to the explanation of Soviet politics in the 1930's.

In actuality, only some of the tendencies frequently encompassed in the concept "political development" appear to be characteristic of the "developing" areas. Instead of a trend toward competitiveness and democracy, there has been an "erosion of democracy" and a tendency to autocratic military regimes and one-party regimes. Instead of stability, there have been repeated coups and revolts. Instead of a unifying nationalism and nation-building, there have been repeated ethnic conflicts and civil wars. Instead of institutional rationalization and differentiation, there has frequently been a decay of the administrative organizations inherited from the colonial era and a weakening and disruption of the political organizations developed during the struggle for independence.[15] Only the concept of political development as mobilization and participation appears to be generally applicable to the "developing" world. Rationalization, competitiveness, and nation-building, in contrast, seem to have only a dim relation to reality.

This gap between theory and reality suggests a fourth difficulty in many concepts of political development. They are usually one-way concepts. Little or no provision is made for their reversibility. If political development is thought to involve the mobilization of people into politics, account should also be taken of the possibility that political de-development can take place and people can be demobilized out of politics. Structural differentiation may occur, but so also may structural homogenization. National disintegration is a phenomenon as much as national integration. A concept of political development should be reversible. It should define both political development and the circumstances under which political decay is encouraged.

The failure to think of political development as a reversible process apparently stems from two sources. Insofar as development is identified with modernization, many aspects of modernization do appear to be practically irreversible. Urbanization is not likely to give way to ruralization. Increases in literacy are not normally followed by sharp declines. Capital once invested in factories or power plants stays invested. Even increases in per capita gross national product are, more often than not, permanent, except for minor dips or destruction caused by war or natural catastrophe. With varying slopes, with hesitancy in some sectors but with strength and steady progress in others, virtually all the indices of modernization progress steadily upward on the charts. But political changes have no such irreversibility.

---

[15]On the "erosion of democracy" and political instability, see Rupert Emerson, *From Empire to Nation* (Cambridge, Mass., 1960), chap. 15; and Michael Brecher, *The New States of Asia* (London 1963), chap. 2.

In other instances, one feels that an underlying commitment to the theory of progress is so overwhelming as to exclude political decay as a possible concept. Political decay, like thermonuclear war, becomes unthinkable. Almond, for instance, measures not just political development but *political change* by "the acquisition by a political system of some new capability."[16] The specific capabilities he has in mind are those for national integration, international accommodation, political participation, and welfare distribution. Before the Renaissance, Almond argues, political systems "acquired and lost capabilities . . . in anything but a unilinear, evolutionary way." Modernization, however, reduces "the independence of man's political experiments." Change is "far from unilinear," but it is toward "the emergence of world culture." Surely, however, modern and modernizing states can change by losing capabilities as well as by gaining them. In addition, a gain in any one capability usually involves costs in others. A theory of political development needs to be mated to a theory of political decay. Indeed, as was suggested above, theories of instability, corruption, authoritarianism, domestic violence, institutional decline, and political disintegration may tell us a lot more about the "developing" areas than their more hopefully defined opposites.

II. POLITICAL DEVELOPMENT AS INSTITUTIONALIZATION

There is thus much to be gained (as well as something to be lost) by conceiving of political development as a process independent of, although obviously affected by, the process of modernization. In view of the crucial importance of the relationship between mobilization and participation, on the one hand, and the growth of political organizations, on the other, it is useful for many purposes to define political development as the institutionalization of political organizations and procedures. This concept liberates development from modernization. It can be applied to the analysis of political systems of any sort, not just modern ones. It can be defined in reasonably precise ways which are at least theoretically capable of measurement. As a concept, it does not suggest that movement is likely to be in only one direction: institutions, we know, decay and dissolve as well as grow and mature. Most significantly, it focuses attention on the reciprocal interaction between the on-going social processes of modernization, on the one hand, and the strength, stability, or weakness of political structures, traditional, transitional, or modern, on the other.[17]

---

[16]Almond, *American Behavioral Scientist*, VI, 6.

[17]The concept of institutionalization has, of course, been used by other writers concerned with political development—most notably, S. N. Eisenstadt. His definition, however, differs significantly from my approach here. See, in particular, his "Initial

The strength of political organizations and procedures varies with their *scope of support* and their *level of institutionalization*. Scope refers simply to the extent to which the political organizations and procedures encompass activity in the society. If only a small upper-class group belongs to political organizations and behaves in terms of a set of procedures, the scope is limited. If, on the other hand, a large segment of the population is politically organized and follows the political procedures, the scope is broad. Institutions are stable, valued, recurring patterns of behavior. Organizations and procedures vary in their degree of institutionalization. Harvard University and the newly opened suburban high school are both organizations, but Harvard is much more of an institution than is the high school. The seniority system in Congress and President Johnson's select press conferences are both procedures, but seniority is much more institutionalized than are Mr. Johnson's methods of dealing with the press. Institutionalization is the process by which organizations and procedures acquire value and stability. The level of institutionalization of any political system can be defined by the adaptability, complexity, autonomy, and coherence of its organizations and procedures. So also, the level of institutionalization of any particular organization or procedure can be measured by its adaptability, complexity, autonomy, and coherence. If these criteria can be identified and measured, political systems can be compared in terms of their levels of institutionalization. Furthermore, it will be possible to measure increases and decreases in the institutionalization of particular organizations and procedures within a political system.

Adaptability-Rigidity

The more adaptable an organization or procedure is, the more highly institutionalized it is; the less adaptable and more rigid it is, the lower its level of institutionalization. Adaptability is an acquired organizational characteristic. It is, in a rough sense, a function of environmental challenge and age. The more challenges which have arisen in its environment and the greater its age, the more adaptable it is. Rigidity is more characteristic of young organizations than of old ones. Old organizations and procedures, however, are not necessarily adaptable if they have existed in a static environment. In addition, if over a period of time an organization has developed a set of responses for dealing effectively with one type of problem, and if it is then confronted with an entirely different type of problem requiring a different response, the

Institutional Patterns of Political Modernisation," *Civilisations*, XII, 4, 461–72, XIII, 1, 15–26; "Institutionalization and Change,"*American Sociological Review*, XXIX (April 1964), 235–47; "Social Change, Differentiation and Evolution," *ibid.*, XXIX (June 1964), 375–86.

organization may well be a victim of its past successes and be unable to adjust to the new challenge. In general, however, the first hurdle is the biggest one. Success in adapting to one environmental challenge paves the way for successful adaptation to subsequent environmental challenges. If, for instance, the probability of successful adjustment to the first challenge is 50 per cent, the probability of successful adjustment to the second challenge might be 75 per cent, to the third challenge 87½ per cent, to the fourth 93¾ per cent, and so on. Some changes in environment, moreover, such as changes in personnel, are inevitable for all organizations. Other changes in environment may be produced by the organization itself; if, for instance, it successfully completes the task which it was originally created to accomplish. So long as it is recognized that environments can differ in the challenges which they pose to organizations, the adaptability of an organization can in a rough sense be measured by its age. Its age, in turn, can be measured in three ways.

One is simply chronological: the longer an organization or procedure has been in existence, the higher the level of institutionalization. The older an organization is, the more likely it is to continue to exist through any specified future time period. The probability that an organization which is one hundred years old will survive one additional year, it might be hypothesized, is perhaps one hundred times greater than the probability that an organization one year old will survive one additional year. Political institutions are thus not created overnight. Political development, in this sense, is slow, particularly when compared with the seemingly much more rapid pace of economic development. In some instances, particular types of experience may substitute for time: fierce conflict or other serious challenges may transform organizations into institutions much more rapidly than normal circumstances. But such intensive experiences are rare, and even with such experiences time is still required. "A major party," Ashoka Mehta has observed, in commenting on why communism is helpless in India, "cannot be created in a day. In China a great party was forged by the revolution. Other major parties can be or are born of revolutions in other countries. But it is simply impossible, through normal channels, to forge a great party, to reach and galvanize millions of men in half a million villages."[18]

A second measure of adaptability is generational age. So long as an organization still has its first set of leaders, so long as a proced-

---

[18]Ashoka Mehta, in Raymond Aron, ed., *World Technology and Human Destiny* (Ann Arbor 1963), 133.

ure is still performed by those who first performed it, its adaptability is still in doubt. The more often the organization has surmounted the problem of peaceful succession and replaced one set of leaders with another, the more highly institutionalized it is. In considerable measure, of course, generational age is a function of chronological age. But political parties and governments may continue for decades under the leadership of one generation. The founders of organizations—whether parties, governments, or business corporations—are often young. Hence the gap between chronological age and generational age is apt to be greater in the early history of an organization than later in its career. This gap produces tensions between the first leaders of the organization and the next generation immediately behind them, which can look forward to a lifetime in the shadow of the first generation. In the middle of the 1960's the Chinese Communist Party was forty-five years old, but in large part it was still led by its first generation of leaders. An organization may also change leadership without changing generations of leadership. One generation differs from another in terms of its formative experiences. Simple replacement of one set of leaders by another, i.e., surmounting a succession crisis, counts for something in terms of institutional adaptability, but it is not as significant as a shift in leadership generations, i.e., the replacement of one set of leaders by another set with significantly different organizational experiences. The shift from Lenin to Stalin was an intra-generation succession; the shift from Stalin to Khrushchev was an inter-generation succession.

Thirdly, organizational adaptability can be measured in functional terms. An organization's functions, of course, can be defined in an almost infinite number of ways. (This is a major appeal and a major limitation of the functional approach to organizations.) Usually an organization is created to perform one particular function. When that function is no longer needed, the organization faces a major crisis. It either finds a new function or reconciles itself to a lingering death. An organization which has adapted itself to changes in its environment and has survived one or more changes in its principal functions is more highly institutionalized than one which has not. Not functional specificity but functional adaptability is the true measure of a highly developed organization. Institutionalization makes the organization more than simply an instrument to achieve certain purposes.[19] Instead its leaders and members come to value it for its own sake, and it develops a life of its own quite apart from the specific functions it may perform at any given time. The organization triumphs over its function.

---

[19]See the very useful discussion in Philip Selznick's small classic, *Leadership in Administration* (New York 1957), 5ff.

Organizations and individuals thus differ significantly in their cumulative capacity to adapt to changes. . . . Organizations . . . are usually created to perform very specific functions. When the organization confronts a changing environment, it must, if it is to survive, weaken its commitment to its original functions. As the organization matures, it becomes "unset" in its ways. . . .

A political party gains in functional age when it shifts its function from the representation of one constituency to the representation of another; it also gains in functional age when it shifts from opposition to government. A party which is unable to change constituencies or to acquire power is less of an institution than one which is able to make these changes. A nationalist party whose function has been the promotion of independence from colonial rule faces a major crisis when it achieves its goal and has to adapt itself to the somewhat different function of governing a country. It may find this functional transition so difficult that it will, even after independence, continue to devote a large portion of its efforts to fighting colonialism. A party which acts this way is less of an institution than one, like the Congress Party, which after achieving independence drops its anti-colonialism and quite rapidly adapts itself to the tasks of governing. Industrialization has been a major function of the Communist Party of the Soviet Union. A major test of the institutionalization of the Communist Party will be its success in developing new functions now that the major industrializing effort is behind it. A governmental organ which can successfully adapt itself to changed functions, such as the British Crown in the eighteenth and nineteenth centuries, is more of an institution than one which cannot, such as the French monarchy in the same period.

Complexity-Simplicity

The more complicated an organization is, the more highly institutionalized it is. Complexity may involve both multiplication of organizational subunits, hierarchically and functionally, and differentiation of separate types of organizational subunits. The greater the number and variety of subunits, the greater the ability of the organization to secure and maintain the loyalties of its members. In addition, an organization which has many purposes is better able to adjust itself to the loss of any one purpose than an organization which has only one purpose. . . .

Relatively primitive and simple traditional political systems are usually overwhelmed and destroyed in the modernization process. More complex traditional systems are more likely to adapt to these new demands. Japan, for instance, was able to adjust its traditional political institutions to the modern world because of their relative complexity. For two and a half centuries before 1868, the emperor had reigned and the Tokugawa shogun had ruled. The stability of the political order, however, did not depend solely on the stability of the shogunate. When the authority of the shogunate decayed, another traditional institution, the emperor, was available to become the instrument of the modernizing samurai. The collapse of the shogun involved not the overthrow of the political order but the "restoration" of the emperor.

The simplest political system is that which depends on one individual. It is also, of course, the least stable. Tyrannies, Aristotle pointed out, are virtually all "quite short-lived."[20] A political system with several different political institutions, on the other hand, is much more likely to adapt. The needs of one age may be met by one set of institutions; the needs of the next by a different set. The system possesses within itself the means of its own renewal and adaptation. . . .

Complexity produces stability. "The simple governments," Burke echoed two thousand years later, "are fundamentally defective, to say no worse of them."[21]

Autonomy-Subordination

A third measure of institutionalization is the extent to which political organizations and procedures exist independently of other social groupings and methods of behavior. How well is the political sphere differentiated from other spheres? In a highly developed political system, political organizations have an integrity which they lack in less developed systems. In some measure, they are insulated from the impact of non-political groups and procedures. In less developed political systems, they are highly vulnerable to outside influences.

At its most concrete level, autonomy involves the relations between social forces, on the one hand, and political organizations, on the other. Social forces include the groupings of men for social and economic activities: families, clans, work groups, churches, ethnic and linguistic groupings. Political institutionalization, in the sense of autonomy, means the development of political organizations and procedures which are not simply expressions of the interests of particular social groups. A political organization which is the instrument of a social group—family, clan, class—lacks autonomy and institutionalization. If the state, in the traditional Marxist claim, is really the "executive committee of the bourgeoisie," then it is not much of an institution. A ju-

---

[20]*Politics* (Ernest Barker trans., London 1946), 254.
[21]*Reflection on the Revolution in France* (Gateway edn., Chicago 1955), 92.

diciary is independent to the extent that it adheres to distinctly judicial norms and to the extent that its perspectives and behavior are independent of those of other political institutions and social groupings. As with the judiciary, the autonomy of political institutions is measured by the extent to which they have their own interests and values distinguishable from those of other social forces. As with the judiciary, the autonomy of political institutions is likely to be the result of competition among social forces. A political party, for instance, which expresses the interests of only one group in society—whether labor, business, or farmers—is less autonomous than one which articulates and aggregates the interests of several social groups. The latter type of party has a clearly defined existence apart from particular social forces. So also with legislatures, executives, and bureaucracies. Political procedures, like political organizations, also have varying degrees of autonomy. A highly developed political system has procedures to minimize, if not to eliminate, the role of violence in the system and to restrict to explicitly defined channels the influence of wealth in the system. To the extent that political officials can be toppled by a few soldiers or influenced by a few dollars, the organizations and procedures lack autonomy. Political organizations and procedures which lack autonomy are, in common parlance, said to be corrupt.

Political organizations and procedures which are vulnerable to non-political influences from within the society are also usually vulnerable to influences from outside the society. They are easily penetrated by agents, groups, and ideas from other political systems. Thus, a *coup d'état* in one political system may easily "trigger" a *coup d'état* by similar groups in other less-developed political systems.[22] In some instances, apparently, a regime can be overthrown by smuggling into the country a few agents and a handful of weapons. In other instances, a regime may be overthrown by the exchange of a few words and a few thousand dollars between a foreign ambassador and some disaffected colonials. The Soviet and American governments presumably spend substantial sums attempting to bribe high officials of less well-insulated political systems which they would not think of wasting in attempting to influence high officials in each other's political system.

In every society affected by social change, new groups arise to participate in politics. Where the political system lacks autonomy, these groups gain entry into politics without becoming identified with the established political organizations or acquiescing in the established political procedures. The political organizations and procedures are un-

---

[22]See Samuel P. Huntington, "Patterns of Violence in World Politics," in Huntington, ed., *Changing Patterns of Military Politics* (New York 1962), 44–47.

able to stand up against the impact of a new social force. Conversely, in a developed political system, the autonomy of the system is protected by mechanisms which restrict and moderate the impact of new groups. These mechanisms either slow down the entry of new groups into politics or, through a process of political socialization, impel changes in the attitudes and behavior of the most politically active members of the new group. In a highly institutionalized political system, the most important positions of leadership can normally be achieved only by those who have served an apprenticeship in less important positions. The complexity of a political system contributes to its autonomy by providing a variety of organizations and positions in which individuals are prepared for the highest offices. In a sense, the top positions of leadership are the inner core of the political system; the less powerful positions, the peripheral organizations, and the semi-political organizations are the filters through which individuals desiring access to the core must pass. Thus the political system assimilates new social forces and new personnel without sacrificing its institutional integrity. In a political system which lacks such defenses, new men, new viewpoints, new social groups may replace each other at the core of the system with bewildering rapidity.

Coherence-Disunity

The more unified and coherent an organization is, the more highly institutionalized it is; the greater the disunity of the organization, the less its institutionalization. Some measure of consensus, of course, is a prerequisite for any social group. An effective organization requires, at a minimum, substantial consensus on the functional boundaries of the group and on the procedures for resolving disputes on issues which come up within those boundaries. The consensus must extend to those active in the system. Non-participants or those only sporadically and marginally participant in the system do not have to share the consensus and usually, in fact, do not share it to the same extent as the participants.[23] In theory, an organization can be autonomous without being coherent and coherent without being autonomous. In actuality, however, the two are often closely linked together. Autonomy becomes a means to coherence, enabling the organization to develop an esprit and style which become distinctive marks of its behavior. Autonomy also prevents the intrusion of disruptive external forces, although, of course, it does not protect against disruption from internal sources. Rapid or substantial expan-

---

[23]See, e.g., Herbert McCloskey, "Consensus and Ideology in American Politics," *American Political Science Review*, XVIII (June 1964), 361ff; Samuel Stouffer, *Communism, Conformity, and Civil Liberties* (New York 1955), *passim*.

sions in the membership of an organization or in the participants in a system tend to weaken coherence. The Ottoman Ruling Institution, for instance, retained its vitality and coherence as long as admission was restricted and recruits were "put through an elaborate education, with selection and specialization at every stage." The Institution perished when "everybody pressed in to share its privileges ... numbers were increased; discipline and efficiency declined."[24]

Unity, esprit, morale, and discipline are needed in governments as well as in regiments. Numbers, weapons, and strategy all count in war, but major deficiencies in any one of those may still be counter-balanced by superior coherence and discipline. So also in politics. The problems of creating coherent political organizations are more difficult but not fundamentally different from those involved in the creation of coherent military organizations. "The sustaining sentiment of a military force," David Rapoport has argued, "has much in common with that which cements any group of men engaged in politics—the willingness of most individuals to bridle private or personal impulses for the sake of general social objectives. Comrades must trust each other's ability to resist the innumerable temptations that threaten the group's solidarity; otherwise, in trying social situations the desire to fend for oneself becomes overwhelming."[25] The capacities for coordination and discipline are crucial to both war and politics, and historically societies which have been skilled at organizing the one have also been adept at organizing the other. "The relationship of efficient social organization in the arts of peace and in the arts of group conflict," one anthropologist has observed, "is almost absolute, whether one is speaking of civilization or subcivilization. Successful war depends upon team work and consensus, both of which require command and discipline. Command and discipline, furthermore, can eventually be no more than symbols of something deeper and more real than they themselves."[26] Societies, such as Sparta, Rome, and Britain, which have been admired by their contemporaries for the authority and justice of their laws have also been admired for the coherence and discipline of their armies. Discipline and development go hand in hand. . . .

Experience tells us that levels of institutionalization differ. Measuring that difference may be difficult, but it is not impossible. Only by measuring institutionalization will we be able to buttress or disprove

[24]Arnold J. Toynbee, *A Study of History* (Abridgement of Vols. I-VI by D. C. Somervell, New York 1947), 176–77.

[25]David C. Rapoport, "A Comparative Theory of Military and Political Types," in Huntington, ed., *Changing Patterns of Military Politics*, 79.

[26]Harry Holbert Turney-High, *Primitive War* (Columbia, S. C., 1949), 235–36.

hypotheses about the relation between social, economic, and demographic changes, on the one hand, and variations in political structure, on the other.

III. MOBILIZATION VS. INSTITUTIONALIZATION: PUBLIC INTERESTS, DEGENERATION, AND THE CORRUPT POLITY

Mobilization and Institutionalization

Social mobilization and political participation are rapidly increasing in Asia, Africa, and Latin America. These processes, in turn, are directly responsible for the deterioration of political institutions in these areas. As Kornhauser has conclusively demonstrated for the Western world, rapid industrialization and urbanization create discontinuities which give rise to mass society. "The *rapid* influx of large numbers of people into *newly* developing urban areas invites mass movements."[27] In areas and industries with very rapid industrial growth, the creation and institutionalization of unions lag, and mass movements are likely among the workers. As unions are organized, they are highly vulnerable to outside influences in their early stages. "The rapid influx of large numbers of people into a new organization (as well as a new area) provides opportunities for mass-oriented elites to penetrate the organization. This is particularly true during the formative periods of organizations, for at such times external constraints must carry the burden of social control until the new participants have come to internalize the values of the organization."[28]

So also in politics. Rapid economic growth breeds political instability.[29] Political mobilization, moreover, does not necessarily require the building of factories or even movement to the cities. It may result simply from increases in communications, which can stimulate major increases in aspirations that may be only partially, if at all, satisfied. The result is a "revolution of rising frustrations."[30] Increase in literacy and education may bring more political instability. By Asian standards, Burma, Ceylon, and the Republic of Korea are all highly literate, but no one of them is a model of political stability. Nor does literacy necessarily stimulate democracy: with roughly 75 per cent

---

[27]William Kornhauser, *The Politics of Mass Society* (Glencoe 1959), 145.
[28]Kornhauser, 146.
[29]See Mancur Olson, Jr., "Rapid Growth as a Destabilizing Force," *Journal of Economic History*, XXVII (December 1963), 529–52; and Bert F. Hoselitz and Myron Weiner, "Economic Development and Political Stability in India," *Dissent*, VIII (Spring 1961), 172–79.
[30]See Daniel Lerner, "Toward a Communication Theory of Modernization," in Pye, ed., *Communications and Political Development*, 330ff.

literacy, Cuba was the fifth most literate country in Latin America (ranking behind Argentina, Uruguay, Chile, and Costa Rica), but the first to go Communist; so also Kerala, with one of the highest literacy rates in India, was the first Indian state to elect a Communist government.[31] Literacy, as Daniel Lerner has suggested, "may be dysfunctional—indeed a serious impediment—to modernization in the societies now seeking (all too rapidly) to transform their institutions."[32]

Increased communication may thus generate demands for more "modernity" than can be delivered. It may also stimulate a reaction against modernity and activate traditional forces. Since the political arena is normally dominated by the more modern groups, it can bring into the arena new, anti-modern groups and break whatever consensus exists among the leading political participants. It may also mobilize minority ethnic groups who had been indifferent to politics but who now acquire a self-consciousness and divide the political system along ethnic lines. Nationalism, it has often been assumed, makes for national integration. But in actuality, nationalism and other forms of ethnic consciousness often stimulate political disintegration, tearing apart the body politic.

Sharp increases in voting and other forms of political participation can also have deleterious effects on political institutions. In Latin America since the 1930's, increases in voting and increases in political instability have gone hand in hand. "Age requirements were lowered, property and literacy requirements were reduced or discarded, and the unscrubbed, unschooled millions on the farms were enfranchised in the name of democracy. They were swept into the political life of the republics so rapidly that existing parties could not absorb many of them, and they learned little about working within the existing political system."[33] The personal identity crises of the elites, caught between traditional and modern cultures, may create additional problems: "In transitional countries the political process often has to bear to an inordinate degree the stresses and strains of people responding to personal needs and seeking solutions to intensely personal problems."[34] Rapid social and economic change calls into question existing values and behavior patterns. It thus often breeds personal corruption. In some circumstances this corruption may play a positive role in the modernizing process, enabling dynamic new groups to get things done which would have

---

[31]Cf. Deutsch, *American Political Science Review*, LV, 496.

[32] Daniel Lerner, "The Transformation of Institutions" (mimeo.), 19.

[33]John J. Johnson, *The Military and Society in Latin America* (Stanford 1964), 98–99.

[34]Lucian W. Pye, *Politics, Personality and Nation Building* (New Haven 1962), 4–5.

been blocked by the existing value system and social structure. At the same time, however, corruption undermines the autonomy and coherence of political institutions. It is hardly accidental that in the 1870's and 1880's a high rate of American economic development coincided with a low point in American governmental integrity.[35]

Institutional decay has become a common phenomenon of the modernizing countries. *Coups d'état* and military interventions in politics are one index of low levels of political institutionalization: they occur where political institutions lack autonomy and coherence. According to one calculation, eleven of twelve modernizing states outside Latin America which were independent before World War II experienced *coups d'état* or attempted coups after World War II. Of twenty states which became independent between World War II and 1959, fourteen had coups or coup attempts by 1963. Of twenty-four states which became independent between 1960 and 1963, seven experienced coups or attempted coups before the end of 1963.[36] Instability in Latin America was less frequent early in the twentieth century than it was in the middle of the century. In the decade from 1917 to 1927, military men occupied the presidencies of the twenty Latin American republics 28.7 per cent of the time; in the decade from 1947 to 1957, military men were presidents 45.5 per cent of the time.[37] In the 1930's and 1940's in countries like Argentina and Colombia, military intervention in politics occurred for the first time in this century. Seventeen of the twenty Latin American states experienced coups or coup attempts between 1945 and 1964, only Chile, Mexico, and Uruguay having clean records of political stability.

In many states the decline of party organizations is reflected in the rise of charismatic leaders who personalize power and weaken institutions which might limit that power. The increasing despotism of Nkrumah, for instance, was accompanied by a marked decline in the institutional strength of the Convention People's Party. In Turkey, Pakistan, and Burma, the Republican People's Party, Muslim League, and AFPFL deteriorated and military intervention eventually ensued. In party organizations and bureaucracies, marked increases in corruption often accompanied significant declines in the effectiveness of governmental services. Particularistic groups—tribal, ethnic, religious—fre-

---

[35]See, in general, Ronald E. Wraith and Edgar Simpkins, *Corruption in Developing Countries* (London 1963).

[36]These figures are calculated from the data in the Appendix of Fred R. von der Mehden, *Politics of the Developing Nations* (Englewood Cliffs, N. J., 1964).

[37]Computed from figures in R. W. Fitzgibbon, "Armies and Politics in Latin America," paper, 7th Round Table, International Political Science Association, Opatija, Yugoslavia (September 1959), 8–9.

quently reasserted themselves and further undermined the authority and coherence of political institutions. The legitimacy of post-colonial regimes among their own people was often less than that of the colonial regimes of the Europeans. Economists have argued that the gap between the level of economic well-being of the underdeveloped countries and that of highly developed countries is widening as the absolute increases and even percentage increases of the latter exceed those of the former. Something comparable and perhaps even more marked is occurring in the political field. The level of political institutionalization of the advanced countries has, with a few exceptions such as France, remained relatively stable. The level of political institutionalization of most other countries has declined. As a result, the political gap between them has broadened. In terms of institutional strength, many if not most of the new states reached their peak of political development at the moment of independence.

The differences which may exist in mobilization and institutionalization suggest four ideal-types of politics (see Table 1). Modern, developed, civic polities (the United States, the Soviet Union) have high levels of both mobilization and institutionalization. Primitive polities (such as Banfield's backward society) have low levels of both. Contained polities are highly institutionalized but have low levels of mobili-

TABLE 1.

TYPES OF POLITICAL SYSTEMS

Social Mobilization	Political Institutionalization	
	High	Low
High	Civic	Corrupt
Low	Contained	Primitive

zation and participation. The dominant political institutions of contained polities may be either traditional (e.g., monarchies) or modern (e.g., political parties). If they are the former, such polities may well confront great difficulties in adjusting to rising levels of social mobilization. The traditional institutions may wither or collapse, and the result would be a corrupt polity with a high rate of participation but a low level of institutionalization. In the corrupt society, politics is, in Macaulay's phrase, "all sail and no anchor."[38] This type of polity characterizes

---

[38]Thomas B. Macaulay, letter to Henry S. Randall, Courtlandt Village, New York, May 23, 1857, printed in "What Did Macaulay Say About America?" *Bulletin of the New York Public Library*, XXIX (July 1925), 477–79.

much, if not most, of the modernizing world. Many of the more advanced Latin American countries, for instance, have achieved comparatively high indices of literacy, per capita national income, and urbanization. But their politics remains notably underdeveloped. Distrust and hatred have produced a continuing low level of political institutionalization. "There is no good faith in America, either among men or among nations," Bolivar once lamented. "Treaties are paper, constitutions books, elections battles, liberty anarchy, and life a torment. The only thing one can do in America is emigrate."[39] Over a century later, the same complaint was heard: "We are not, or do not represent a respectable nation . . . and without organization we cannot merit or attain respect from other nations."[40] So long as a country like Argentina retains a politics of coup and countercoup and a feeble state surrounded by massive social forces, it cannot be considered politically developed, no matter how urbane and prosperous and educated are its citizens.

In reverse fashion, a country may be politically highly developed, with modern political institutions, while still very backward in terms of modernization. India, for instance, is typically held to be the epitome of the underdeveloped society. Judged by the usual criteria of modernization, it was at the bottom of the ladder during the 1950's: per capita GNP of $72, 80 per cent illiterate, over 80 per cent of the population in rural areas, 70 per cent of the work force in agriculture, a dozen major languages, deep caste and religious differences. Yet in terms of political institutionalization, India was far from backward. Indeed, it ranked high not only in comparison with other modernizing countries in Asia, Africa, and Latin America, but also in comparison with many much more modern European countries. A well-developed political system has strong and distinct institutions to perform both the "input" and the "output" functions of politics. India entered independence with not only two organizations, but two highly developed—adaptable, complex, autonomous, and coherent—institutions ready to assume primary responsibility for these functions. The Congress Party, founded in 1885, was one of the oldest and best-organized political parties in the world; the Indian Civil Service, dating from the early nineteenth century, has been appropriately hailed as "one of the greatest administrative systems of all time."[41] The stable, effective, and democratic government of India during the first fifteen years of

---

[39]Simon Bolivar, quoted in K. H. Silvert, ed., *Expectant Peoples: Nationalism and Development* (New York 1963), 347.

[40]*El Dia*, Quito, November 27, 1943, quoted in Bryce Wood, *The Making of the Good Neighbor Policy* (New York 1961), 318.

[41]Ralph Braibanti, "Public Bureaucracy and Judiciary in Pakistan," in LaPalombara, ed., *Bureaucracy and Political Development*, 373.

independence rested far more on this institutional inheritance than it did on the charisma of Nehru. In addition, the relatively slow pace of modernization and social mobilization in India did not create demands and strains which the Party and the bureaucracy were unable to handle. So long as these two organizations maintain their institutional strength, it is ridiculous to think of India as politically underdeveloped, no matter how low her per capita income or how high her illiteracy rate.

Almost no other country which became independent after World War II was institutionally as well prepared as India for self-government. In countries like Pakistan and the Sudan, institutional evolution was unbalanced; the civil and military bureaucracies were more highly developed than the political parties, and the military had strong incentives to move into the institutional vacuum on the input side of the political system and to attempt to perform interest aggregation functions. This pattern, of course, has also been common in Latin America. In countries like Guatemala, El Salvador, Peru, and Argentina, John J. Johnson has pointed out, the military is "the country's best organized institution and is thus in a better position to give objective expression to the national will" than are parties or interest groups.[42] In a very different category is a country like North Vietnam, which fought its way into independence with a highly disciplined political organization but which was distinctly weak on the administrative side. The Latin American parallel here would be Mexico, where, as Johnson puts it, "not the armed forces but the PRI is the best organized institution, and the party rather than the armed forces has been the unifying force at the national level." In yet a fourth category are those unfortunate states, such as the Congo, which were born with neither political nor administrative institutions. Many of these new states deficient at independence in one or both types of institutions have also been confronted by high rates of social mobilization and rapidly increasing demands on the political system (see Table 2).

TABLE 2.

INSTITUTIONAL DEVELOPMENT AT MOMENT OF INDEPENDENCE

Input Institutions	Output Institutions	
	High	*Low*
High	India	North Vietnam
Low	Sudan	Congo

[42]Johnson, *Military and Society*, 143.

Political Institutions and Public Interests

A society with weak political institutions lacks the ability to curb the excesses of personal and parochial desires. Politics is a Hobbesian world of unrelenting competition among social forces—between man and man, family and family, clan and clan, region and region, class and class—a competition unmediated by more comprehensive political organizations. The "amoral familism" of Banfield's village has its counterparts in amoral clanism, amoral groupism, and amoral classism. Without strong political institutions, society lacks the means of defining and realizing its common interests. The capacity to create political institutions is the capacity to create public interests.

Traditionally the public interest has been approached in three ways.[43] It has been identified either with abstract, substantive ideal values and norms such as natural law, justice, or right reason; or with the specific interest of a particular individual ("L'état, c'est moi"), group, class (Marxism), or majority; or with the result of a competitive process among individuals (classic liberalism) or groups (Bentleyism). The problem in all these approaches is to arrive at a definition which is concrete rather than nebulous and general rather than particular. Unfortunately, in most cases what is concrete lacks generality and what is general lacks concreteness. One partial way out of the problem is to define the public interest in terms of the concrete interests of the governing institutions. A society with highly institutionalized governing organizations and procedures is, in this sense, more able to articulate and achieve its public interests. "Organized (institutionalized) political communities," as Friedrich argues, "are *better adapted* to reaching decisions and developing policies than unorganized communities."[44] The public interest, in this sense, is not something which exists *a priori* in natural law or the will of the people. Nor is it simply whatever results from the political process. Rather it is whatever strengthens governmental institutionalization of government organizations. In a complex political system, many governmental organizations and procedures represent many different aspects of the public interest. The public interest of a complex society is a complex matter.

We are accustomed to think of our primary governing institutions as having representative functions—that is, as expressing the in-

---

[43]See, in general, Glendon Schubert, *The Public Interest* (Glencoe 1960); Carl J. Friedrich, ed., *Nomos V: The Public Interest* (New York 1962); Douglas Price, "Theories of the Public Interest," in Lynton K. Caldwell, ed., *Politics and Public Affairs* (Bloomington, Ind., 1962), 141–60.
[44]Carl J. Friedrich, *Man and His Government* (New York 1963), 150; italics in original.

terests of some other set of groups (their constituency). Hence, we tend to forget that governmental institutions have interests of their own. These interests not only exist; they are also reasonably concrete. The questions, "What is the interest of the Presidency? What is the interest of the Senate? What is the interest of the House of Representatives? What are the interests of the Supreme Court?" are difficult but not completely impossible to answer. The answers would furnish a fairly close approximation of the "public interest" of the United States. Similarly, the public interest of Great Britain might be approximated by the specific institutional interests of the Crown, Cabinet, and Parliament. In the Soviet Union, the answer would involve the specific institutional interests of the Presidium, Secretariat, and Central Committee of the Communist Party.

Institutional interests differ from the interests of individuals who are in the institutions. Keynes's percipient remark that "In the long run, we are all dead" applies to individuals, not institutions. Individual interests are necessarily short-run interests. Institutional interests, however, exist through time: the proponent of the institution has to look to its welfare through an indefinite future. This consideration often means a limiting of immediate goals. The "true policy," Aristotle remarked, "for democracy and oligarchy alike, is not one which ensures the greatest possible amount of either, but one which will ensure the longest possible life for both."[45] The official who attempts to maximize power or other values in the short run often weakens his institution in the long run. . . .

In terms of the theory of natural law, governmental actions are legitimate to the extent that they are in accord with the "public philosophy."[46] According to democratic theory, they derive their legitimacy from the extent to which they embody the will of the people. According to the procedural concept, they are legitimate if they represent the outcome of a process of conflict and compromise in which all interested groups have participated. In another sense, however, the legitimacy of governmental actions can be sought in the extent to which they reflect the interests of governmental institutions. In contrast to the theory of representative government, under this concept governmental institutions derive their legitimacy and authority not from the extent to which they represent the interests of the people or of any other group, but from the extent to which they have distinct interests of their

---

[45]*Politics* (Ernest Barker trans., London 1946), 267.
[46]See Walter Lippmann, *The Public Philosophy* (Boston 1955), esp. 42, for his definition of the public interest as "what men would choose if they saw clearly, thought rationally, acted disinterestedly and benevolently."

own apart from all other groups. Politicians frequently remark that things "look different" after they obtain office than they did when they were competing for office. This difference is a measure of the institutional demands of office. It is precisely this difference in perspective which legitimizes the demands which the officeholder makes on his fellow citizens. The interests of the President, for instance, may coincide partially and temporarily first with those of one group and then with those of another. But the interest of the Presidency, as Neustadt has emphasized,[47] coincides with that of no one else. The President's power derives not from his representation of class, group, regional, or popular interests, but rather from the fact that he represents none of these. The Presidential perspective is unique to the Presidency. Precisely for this reason, it is both a lonely office and a powerful one. Its authority is rooted in its loneliness.

The existence of political institutions (such as the Presidency or Presidium) capable of giving substance to public interests distinguishes politically developed societies from undeveloped ones. The "ultimate test of development," as Lucian Pye has said, "is the capacity of a people to establish and maintain large, complex, but flexible organizational forms."[48] The level of organization in much of the world, however, is low. "Except in Europe and America," Banfield notes, "the concerting of behavior in political associations and corporate organizations is a rare and recent thing."[49] The ability to create public organizations and political institutions is in short supply in the world today. It is this ability which, above all else, the Communists offer modernizing countries.

Degeneration and the Corrupt Polity

Most modernizing countries are buying rapid social modernization at the price of political degeneration. This process of decay in political institutions, however, has been neglected or overlooked in much of the literature on modernization. As a result, models and concepts which are hopefully entitled "developing" or "modernizing" are often only partially relevant to the countries to which they are applied. More relevant in many cases would be models of corrupt or degenerating societies, highlighting the decay of political organization and the increasing dominance of disruptive social forces. Who, however, has advanced

---

[47]See Richard E. Neustadt, *Presidential Power* (New York 1960), *passim*, but esp. 33–37, 150–51.

[48]Pye, *Politics, Personality and Nation Building*, 51.

[49]Edward C. Banfield, *The Moral Basis of a Backward Society* (Glencoe, Ill., 1958) 7–9, 15ff.

such a theory of political decay or a model of a corrupt political order which might be useful in analyzing the political processes of the countries that are usually called "developing"? Perhaps the most relevant ideas are the most ancient ones. The evolution of many contemporary new states, once the colonial guardians have departed, has not deviated extensively from the Platonic model. Independence is followed by military coups as the "auxiliaries" take over.[50] Corruption by the oligarchy inflames the envy of rising groups. Conflict between oligarchy and masses erupts into civil strife. Demagogues and street mobs pave the way for the despot. Plato's description of the means by which the despot appeals to the people, isolates and eliminates his enemies, and builds up his personal strength is a far less misleading guide to what has taken place in Ghana and other new states than many things written yesterday.[51]

Plato is one of the few theorists, ancient or contemporary, with a highly explicit theory of political degeneration.[52] The concept of a "corrupt society," however, is a more familiar one in political theory. Typically it refers to a society which lacks law, authority, cohesion, discipline, and consensus, where private interests dominate public ones, where there is an absence of civic obligation and civic duty, where, in short, political institutions are weak and social forces strong. Plato's degenerate states are dominated by various forms of appetite: by force, wealth, numbers, and charisma. "Those constitutions," says Aristotle, "which consider only the personal interest of the rulers are all wrong constitutions, or perversions of the right forms."[53] So also, Machiavelli's concept of the corrupt state, in the words of one commentator, "includes all sorts of license and violence, great inequalities of wealth and power, the destruction of peace and justice, the growth of disorderly ambition, disunion, lawlessness, dishonesty, and contempt for reli-

---

[50]For comments on the short time lag between independence and the first coup, see Dankwart A. Rustow, "The Military in Middle Eastern Society and Politics," in Sidney N. Fisher, ed., *The Military in the Middle East: Problems in Society and Government* (Columbus, Ohio, 1963), 10.

[51]See, in general, *The Republic*, Book VIII, and especially the description of the despotic regime (Cornford trans., New York 1945), 291-93.

[52]Perhaps the closest contemporary model comes not from a social scientist but from a novelist: William Golding. The schoolboys (newly independent elites) of *The Lord of the Flies* initially attempt to imitate the behavior patterns of adults (former Western rulers). Discipline and consensus, however, disintegrate. A demagogic military leader and his follower gain or coerce the support of a majority. The symbol of authority (the conch) is broken. The voices of responsibility (Ralph) and reason (Piggy) are deserted and harassed, and reason is destroyed. In the end, the naval officer (British Marine Commandos) arrives just in time to save Ralph (Nyerere) from the "hunters" (mutinous troops).

[53]*Politics*, 112.

gion."[54] Modern equivalents of the classical corrupt society are Kornhauser's theory of the mass society (where, in the absence of institutions, elites are accessible to masses and masses are available for mobilization by the elite) and Rapoport's concept of the praetorian state where "private ambitions are rarely restrained by a sense of public authority; [and] the role of power (i.e., wealth and force) is maximized."[55] Typical of the corrupt, praetorian, or mass societies is the violent oscillation between extreme democracy and tyranny. "Where the pre-established political authority is highly autocratic," says Kornhauser, "rapid and violent displacement of that authority by a democratic regime is highly favorable to the emergence of extremist mass movements that tend to transform the new democracy in anti-democratic directions."[56] Aristotle and Plato saw despotism emerging out of the extremes of mob rule. Rapoport finds in Gibbon an apt summary of the constitutional rhythms of the praetorian state, which "floats between the extremes of absolute monarchy and wild democracy."[57] Such instability is the hallmark of a society where mobilization has outrun institutionalization.

IV. STRATEGIES OF INSTITUTIONAL DEVELOPMENT

If decay of political institutions is a widespread phenomenon in the "developing" countries and if a major cause of this decay is the high rate of social mobilization, it behooves us, as social scientists, to call a spade a spade and to incorporate these tendencies into any general model of political change which we employ to understand the politics of these areas. If effective political institutions are necessary for stable and eventually democratic government and if they are also a precondition of sustained economic growth, it behooves us, as policy analysts, to suggest strategies of institutional development. In doing this, we should recognize two general considerations affecting probabilities of success in institution-building.

First, the psychological and cultural characteristics of peoples differ markedly and with them their abilities at developing political

---

[54]George H. Sabine, *A History of Political Thought* (rev. edn., New York 1950), 343.

[55]Kornhauser, *Politics of Mass Society, passim*; David C. Rapoport, "Praetorianism: Government Without Consensus" (Ph.D. dissertation, University of California, Berkeley, 1959): and Rapoport in Huntington, ed., *Changing Patterns of Military Politics*, 72 where the quotation occurs.

[56]Kornhauser, *Politics of Mass Society*, 125.

[57]Edward Gibbon, *The Decline and Fall of the Roman Empire* (New York 1899) I, 235, quoted by Rapoport in Huntington, ed., *Changing Patterns of Military Politics*, 98.

institutions. Where age-old patterns of thought and behavior have to be changed, quite obviously the creation of political institutions is a far more difficult task than otherwise. "The Tokugawa Japanese could not, as did the Chinese, put family above government," one expert has observed. "The samurai was expected to be loyal to his official superior first, his family second. In mores generally the primacy of the organization over the person was constantly reiterated."[58] This difference in Japanese and Chinese attitudes toward authority undoubtedly accounts in part for their differences in modernization and development. The Japanese peacefully and smoothly created new political institutions and amalgamated them with old ones. The weakness of traditional Chinese political institutions, on the other hand, led to forty years of revolution and civil war before modern political institutions could be developed and extended throughout Chinese society.

Second, the potentialities for institution-building differ markedly from society to society, but in all societies political organizations can be built. Institutions result from the slow interaction of conscious effort and existing culture. Organizations, however, are the product of conscious, purposeful effort. The forms of this effort may vary from a Meiji Restoration to a Communist Revolution. But in each case a distinct group of identifiable people set about adapting old organizations or building new ones. "Nation-building" has recently become a popular subject, and doubts have been raised about whether nations can be "built."[59] These doubts have a fairly solid basis. Nations are one type of social force, and historically they have emerged over long periods of time. Organization-building, however, differs from nation-building. Political organizations require time for development, but they do not require as much time as national communities. Indeed, most of those who speak of nation-building in such places as tropical Africa see organization-building as the first step in this process. Political parties have to be welded out of tribal groups; the parties create governments; and the governments may, eventually, bring into existence nations. Many of the doubts which people have about the possibilities of nation-building do not apply to organization-building.

Given our hypotheses about the relation of social mobilization to institutionalization, there are two obvious methods of furthering institutional development. First, anything which slows social mobilization presumably creates conditions more favorable to the preservation

---

[58]John Whitney Hall, "The Nature of Traditional Society: Japan," in Ward and Rustow, eds., *Political Modernization in Japan and Turkey*, 19.

[59]See Karl W. Deutsch and William J. Foltz, eds., *Nation-Building* (New York 1963), *passim*, but especially the contributions of Joseph R. Strayer and Carl J. Friedrich.

and strengthening of institutions. Secondly, strategies can be developed and applied directly to the problem of institution-building.

Slowing Mobilization

Social mobilization can be moderated in many ways. Three methods are: to increase the complexity of social structure; to limit or reduce communications in society; and to minimize competition among segments of the political elite.[60]

In general, the more highly stratified a society is and the more complicated its social structure, the more gradual is the process of political mobilization. The divisions between class and class, occupation and occupation, rural and urban, constitute a series of breakwaters which divide the society and permit the political mobilization of one group at a time. On the other hand, a highly homogeneous society, or a society which has only a single horizontal line of division between an oligarchy that has everything and a peasantry that has nothing, or a society which is divided not horizontally but vertically into ethnic and communal groups, has more difficulty moderating the process of mobilization. Thus, mobilization should be slower in India than in the new African states where horizontal divisions are weak and tribal divisions strong, or in those Latin-American countries when the middle strata are weak and a small oligarchy confronts a peasant mass. A society with many horizontal divisions gains through the slower entry of social groups into politics. It may, however, also lose something in that political organizations, when they do develop, may form along class and stratum lines and thus lack the autonomy of more broadly based political organizations. Political parties in countries like Chile and Sweden have been largely the spokesmen for distinct classes; caste associations seem destined to play a significant role in Indian politics. The disruptive effects of political organizations identified with social strata may be reduced if other political institutions exist which appeal to loyalties across class or caste lines. In Sweden, loyalty to the monarchy and the Riksdag mitigates the effects of class-based parties, and in India the caste associations must, in general, seek their goals within the much more extensive framework of the Congress Party. In most societies the social structure must be largely accepted as given. Where it is subject to governmental manipulation and influence, mobilization

---

[60]These are not, of course, the only ways of slowing mobilization. Myron Weiner for instance, has suggested that one practical method is "localization": channeling political interests and activity away from the great issues of national politics to the more immediate and concrete problems of the village and community. This is certainly one motive behind both community development programs and "basic democracies."

will be slowed by government policies which enhance the complexity of social stratification.

The communications network of a society is undoubtedly much more subject to governmental influence. Rapid gains in some of the most desired areas of modernization—such as mass media exposure, literacy, and education—may have to be purchased at the price of severe losses in political stability. This is not to argue that political institutionalization as a value should take precedence over all others: if this were the case, modernization would never be good. It is simply to argue that governments must balance the values won through rapid increases in communications against the values jeopardized by losses in political stability. Thus, governmental policies may be wisely directed to reducing the number of university graduates, particularly those with skills which are not in demand in the society. Students and unemployed university graduates have been a concern common to the nationalistic military regime in South Korea, the socialist military regime in Burma, and the traditional military regime in Thailand. The efforts by General Ne Win in Burma to cut back the number of university graduates may well be imitated by other governments facing similar challenges. Much has been made of the problems caused by the extension of the suffrage to large numbers of illiterates. But limited political participation by illiterates may well, as in India, be less dangerous to political institutions than participation by literates. The latter typically have higher aspirations and make more demands on government. Political participation by illiterates, moreover, is more likely to remain limited, whereas participation by literates is much more likely to snowball with potentially disastrous effects on political stability. A governing elite may also affect the intensity of communications and the rate of political mobilization by its policies on economic development. Large, isolated factories, as Kornhauser has shown, are more likely to give rise to extremist movements than smaller plants more closely integrated into the surrounding community.[61] Self-interest in political survival may lead governing elites to decrease the priority of rapid economic change.

The uncontrolled mobilization of people into politics is also slowed by minimizing the competition among political elites. Hence mobilization is likely to have less disturbing effects on political institutions in one-party systems than in two-party or multiparty systems. In many new states and modernizing countries, a vast gap exists between the modernized elite and the tradition-oriented mass. If the elite divides against itself, its factions appeal to the masses for support. This pro-

---

[61]Kornhauser, *Politics of Mass Society*, 150–58.

duces rapid mobilization of the masses into politics at the same time that it destroys whatever consensus previously existed among the politically active on the need for modernization. Mobilization frequently means the mobilization of tradition; modern politics become the vehicle of traditional purposes. In Burma during the first part of this century, the "general pattern was one in which the modernizers first fell out among themselves whenever they were confronted with demanding choices of policy, and then tended to seek support from among the more traditional elements, which in time gained the ascendency."[62] In Turkey a rough balance between the mobilization of people into politics and the development of political institutions existed so long as the Republican People's Party retained a political monopoly. The conscious decision to permit an opposition party, however, broadened the scope of political competition beyond the urban, Westernized elite. The Democratic Party mobilized the peasants into politics, strengthened the forces of traditionalism, and broke the previous consensus. This led the party leaders to attempt to maintain themselves in power through semi-legal means and to induce the army to join them in suppressing the Republican opposition. The army, however, was committed to modernization and seized power in a *coup d'état,* dissolving the Democratic Party and executing many of its top leaders. In due course, the military withdrew from direct conduct of the government, and democratic elections led to a multiparty system in which no party has a clear majority. Thus from a relatively stable one-party system, Turkey passed through a brief two-party era to military rule and a multiparty system: the familiar syndrome of states where mobilization has outrun institutionalization. In the process, not only were political institutions weakened, but the traditional-minded were brought into politics in such a way as to create obstacles to the achievement of many modernizing goals.

Creating Institutions

"Dans la naissance des sociétés ce sont les chefs des républiques qui font l'institution; et c'est ensuite l'institution qui forme les chefs des républiques," said Montesquieu.[63] But in the contemporary world political leaders prefer modernization to institution-building, and no matter who leads modernization, the process itself generates conflicting

---

[62]Pye, *Politics, Personality and Nation Building,* 114.

[63]Charles de Secondat, Baron Montesquieu, *Considérations sur les causes de la grandeur des romains et de leur décadence,* in *Oeuvres,* I (Paris 1828), 119–20. ["In the birth of societies, it is the leaders of republics who create the institution; it is afterwards the institution that forms the leaders of republics."—Ed.]

demands and inducements which obstruct the growth of political institutions. Where modernization is undertaken by traditional leaders working through traditional political institutions, the efforts of the traditional leaders to reform can unleash and stimulate social forces which threaten the traditional political institutions. Traditional leaders can modernize and reform their realms, but, where substantial social elements oppose reform, they have yet to demonstrate they can put through reforms without undermining the institutions through which they are working. The problem is: how can the traditional political institutions be adapted to accommodate the social forces unleashed by modernization? Historically, except for Japan, traditional political institutions have been adapted to the modern world only where a high degree of political centralization was not required for modernization and where traditional (i.e., feudal) representative institutions retained their vitality (as in Great Britain and Sweden). If modernization requires the centralization of power in a "reform monarch" or "revolutionary emperor," it means the weakening or destruction of whatever traditional representative institutions may exist and thus complicates still further the assimilation of those social forces created by modernization. The concentration of power also makes the traditional regime (like the eighteenth-century French monarchy) more vulnerable to forcible overthrow. *The vulnerability of a traditional regime to revolution varies directly with the capability of the regime for modernization.* For traditional rulers, the imperatives of modernization conflict with the imperatives of institution-building.

If the traditional political institutions are weak, or if they have been displaced and suppressed during periods of colonial rule, adaptation is impossible. In societies which have undergone colonial rule, incubation can serve as a substitute for adaptation. Unfortunately, the opportunity for incubation was missed in most colonial societies, with a few prominent exceptions such as India and the Philippines. Incubation requires a colonial administration which is willing to permit and *to contend with* a nationalist movement for many years, thus furnishing the time, the struggle, and the slowly increasing responsibility which are the ingredients of institution-building. In general, however, colonial powers tend to postpone incubation for as long as possible and then, when they see independence as inevitable, to bring it about as quickly as possible. Consequently, most of the states which became independent in the 1950's and 1960's had little opportunity to incubate political institutions while still under colonial tutelage.

Where traditional political institutions are weak, or collapse, or are overthrown, authority frequently comes to rest with charismatic leaders who attempt to bridge the gap between tradition and modernity by a highly personal appeal. To the extent that these leaders are able to concentrate power in themselves, it might be supposed that they would be in a position to push institutional development and to perform the role of "Great Legislator" or "Founding Father." The reform of corrupt states or the creation of new ones, Machiavelli argued, must be the work of one man alone. A conflict exists, however, between the interests of the individual and the interests of institutionalization. Institutionalization of power means the limitation of power which might otherwise be wielded personally and arbitrarily. The would-be institution-builder needs personal power to create institutions but he cannot create institutions without relinquishing personal power. Resolving this dilemma is not easy. It can be done only by leaders who combine rare political skill and rare devotion to purpose. It was done by Mustafa Kemal who, for almost two decades, managed to maintain his own personal power, to push through major modernizing reforms, and to create a political institution to carry on the government after his death. Atatürk has been a conscious model for many contemporary modernizing leaders, but few, if any, seem likely to duplicate his achievement.

The military junta or military dictatorship is another type of regime common in modernizing countries. It too confronts a distinct set of problems in the conflict between its own impulses to modernization and the needs of institution-building. The military officers who seize power in a modernizing country frequently do so in reaction to the "chaos," "stalemate," "corruption," and "reactionary" character of the civilian regimes which preceded them. The officers are usually passionately devoted to measures of social reform, particularly those which benefit the peasantry (whose interests have frequently been overlooked by the anterior civilian regime). A rationalistic approach to societal problems often makes the officers modernizers par excellence. At the same time, however, they are frequently indifferent or hostile to the needs of political institution-building. The military typically assert that they have taken over the government only temporarily until conditions can be "cleaned up" and authority restored to a purified civilian regime. The officers thus confront an organizational dilemma. They can eliminate or exclude from politics individual civilian politicians, but they are ill-prepared to make fundamental changes in political processes and institutions. If they turn back power to the civilians, the same conditions to which they originally objected tend to reappear (Burma). If they attempt to restore civilian government and to continue in power as a civilian political group (Turkey, South Korea), they open themselves to these same corrupting influences and may pave the way for a second military takeover by a younger generation of colonels who purge the civilianized generals, just as the generals had earlier purged the civilians. Finally, if the military leaders retain power indefinitely, they need to create authoritative political organizations which legitimize and institutionalize their power. Concern with their own personal authority and unfamiliarity with the needs of political institution-building create problems in the fulfillment of this task. It is still too early to say for certain what sort of authoritative political institutions, if any, will be produced by regimes led by miliary officers such as Nasser and Ayub Khan.

The Primacy of Party

Charismatic leaders and military chiefs have thus had little success in building modern political institutions. The reason lies in the nature of modern politics. In the absence of traditional political institutions, the only modern organization which can become a source of authority and which can be effectively institutionalized is the political party. *The importance of the political party in providing legitimacy and stability in a modernizing political system varies inversely with the institutional inheritance of the system from traditional society.* Traditional systems do not have political parties. Unlike bureaucracy, the party is a distinctly modern form of political organization. Where traditional political institutions (such as monarchies and feudal parliaments) are carried over into the modern era, parties play secondary, supplementary roles in the political system. The other institutions are the primary source of continuity and legitimacy. Parties typically originate within the legislatures and then gradually extend themselves into society. They adapt themselves to the existing framework of the political system and typically reflect in their own operations the organizational and procedural principles embodied in that system. They broaden participation in the traditional institutions, thus adapting those institutions to the requirements of the modern polity. They help make the traditional institutions legitimate in terms of popular sovereignty, but they are not themselves a source of legitimacy. Their own legitimacy derives from the contributions they make to the political system.

Where traditional political institutions collapse or are weak or nonexistent, the role of the party is entirely different from what it is in those polities with institutional continuity. In such situations, strong party organization is the only long-run alternative to the instability of a corrupt or praetorian or mass society. The party is not just a supplementary organization; it is instead the source of legitimacy and authority. In the absence of traditional sources of legitimacy, legitimacy is sought in ideology, charisma, popular sovereignty. To be lasting, each of these principles of legitimacy must be embodied in a party. Instead of the party reflecting the state, the state becomes the creation of the party and the instrument of the party. The actions of government are legitimate to the extent that they reflect the will of the party. The party is the source of legitimacy because it is the institutional embodiment of national sovereignty, the popular will, or the dictatorship of the proletariat.

Where traditional political institutions are weak or nonexistent, the prerequisite of stability is at least one highly institutionalized political party. States with one such party are markedly more stable than states which lack such a party. States with no parties or many weak parties are the least stable. Where traditional political institutions are smashed by revolution, post-revolutionary order depends on the emergence of one strong party: witness the otherwise very different histories of the Chinese, Mexican, Russian, and Turkish revolutions. Where new states emerge from colonialism with one strong party, the problem is to maintain the strength of that party. In many African countries the nationalist party was the single important modern organization to exist before independence. The party "was generally well organized. The conditions of the political struggle and the dedication of the top elite to the party as the prime instrument of political change led the elite to give the major portion of their energies and resources to building a solid, responsive organization capable of disciplined action in response to directives from the top and able to ferret out and exploit feelings of dissatisfaction among the masses for political ends."[64] After independence, however, the dominant political party is often weakened by the many competing demands on organizational resources. A marked dispersion of resources means a decline in the overall level of political instutionalization. "Talents that once were available for the crucial work of party organization," one observer has warned, "may now be preoccupied with running a ministry or government bureau . . . unless new sources of loyal organizational and administrative talents can be found immediately, the party's organization—and, therefore, the major link between the regime and the masses—is likely to be weakened."[65]

The need for concentration applies not only to the allocation of resources among types of organizations but also to the scope of organization. In many modernizing countries, the political leaders attempt

---

[64]William J. Foltz, "Building the Newest Nations: Short-Run Strategies and Long-Run Problems" p. 122. [Reprinted in this reader, p. 293.]

[65]Foltz, p. 123–124.

too much too fast; they try to build mass organizations when they should concentrate on elite organizations. Organizations do not have to be large to be effective and to play a crucial role in the political process: the Bolshevik Party in 1917 is one example; the Indian Civil Service (which numbered only 1,157 men at independence) is another. Overextension of one's resources in organization-building is as dangerous as overextension of one's troops in a military campaign. (The strategic hamlet program in South Vietnam is an example of both.) Concentration is a key principle of politics as well as strategy. The pressures for broad organizational support, however, seem to push towards the all-inclusive organization. In his efforts to create a political structure to bolster his military regime in Egypt, for instance, Nasser first created the Liberation Rally in 1953, which soon came to have from 5 to 6 million members. The organization was simply too big to be effective and to achieve its purpose. After the adoption of a new constitution in 1956, the Liberation Rally was replaced by the National Union, which was designed to be the school of the nation and also to be universal in membership (except for reactionaries). Again the organization was too broad to be effective. Hence in 1962, after the break with Syria, a new organization, the Arab Socialist Union, was organized with the advice of organizational and ideological experts from Yugoslavia. It was designed to be a more exclusive, more tightly organized body, its membership limited to 10 per cent of the population. Inevitably, however, it also mushroomed in size, and after two years it had 5 million members. In a fourth effort, early in 1964 President Nasser reportedly formed still another group limited to only 4,000 members and called the "Government Party," which would form the core of the Arab Socialist Union. The new organization was to be designed by Nasser "to enforce a peaceful transfer of power and a continuation of his policies if anything happens to him."[66] Whether this organization, unlike its predecessors, becomes an institution remains to be seen. Its likelihood of success depends upon its limitation in size.

American social scientists have devoted much attention to the competitiveness of political systems, devising various ways of measuring that competitiveness and classifying systems according to their degree of competitiveness.[67] The more parties which exist within a system, presumably the more competitive it is. Yet the proliferation of par-

---

[66]*Washington Post*, February 9, 1964, p. A–17.
[67]See James S. Coleman, in Almond and Coleman, eds., *Politics of the Developing Areas*, Conclusion; Phillips Cutright, "National Political Development: Its Measurement and Social Correlates," in Nelson W. Polsby, Robert A. Dentler, and Paul A. Smith, eds., *Politics and Social Life* (Boston 1963), 569–82; von der Mehden, *Politics of the Developing Nations*, 54–64.

ties usually means the dispersion of organization and leadership talents and the existence of a large number of weak parties. If sufficient resources are available to support more than one well-organized party, this is all to the good. But most modernizing countries will be well off if they can create just one strong party organization. *In modernizing systems, party institutionalization usually varies inversely with party competitiveness.* Modernizing states with multiparty systems are much more unstable and prone to military intervention than modernizing states with one party, with one dominant party, or with two parties. The most unstable systems and those most prone to military interven-

TABLE 3. DISTRIBUTION OF COUPS AND COUP ATTEMPTS IN MODERNIZING COUNTRIES SINCE INDEPENDENCE

Type of Political System	Number of Countries	Countries with Coups Number	Countries with Coups Per cent
Communist	3	0	0
One-party	18	2	11
One-party dominant	12	3	25
Two-party	11	5	45
Multiparty	22	15	68
No effective parties	17	14	83

SOURCE: Figures are somewhat revised and adapted from the similar table in Fred R. von der Mehden, *Politics of the Developing Nations* (Englewood Cliffs, N. J., 1964), 65.

tion are the multiparty systems and the no-party systems. The weak institutionalization of parties in the multiparty system makes that system extremely fragile. The step from many parties to no parties and from no parties to many parties is an easy one. In their institutional weakness, the no-party system and the multiparty system closely resemble each other.

Political Development and American Policy

The Bolshevik concept of the political party is directly relevant to modernizing countries. It provides a conscious and explicit answer to the problem of mobilization vs. institutionalization. The Communists actively attempt to expand political participation. At the same time they are the most energetic and intense contemporary students of de Tocqueville's "art of associating together." Their specialty is organization, their goal the mobilization of the masses into their organizations. For them mobilization and organization go hand in hand. "There are only two kinds of political tasks," a leading Chinese Communist theorist has said: "one is the task of propaganda and education, the saysay, Diem, or Ayub Khan. Alternatively, the American government has stressed adherence to particular structural forms, such as free elections.

All of these approaches are doomed to failure. Neither military juntas nor charismatic personalities nor free elections can be a long-term substitute for effective political organization. Charismatic leaders are reluctant to substitute party control for personal control. Military officers are usually even more explicitly anti-party. They contrast the venal party politics of the civilians with the honest devotion to the nation of the military. Military coups and military juntas may spur modernization, but they cannot produce a stable political order. Instead of relying on the military, American policy should be directed to the creation within modernizing countries of at least one strong non-Communist political party. If such a party already exists and is in a dominant position, support of that party should be the keystone of policy. Where political life is fragmented and many small parties exist, American backing should go to the strongest of the parties whose goals are compatible with ours. If it is a choice between a party and a personality, choose the party: better the Baath than Nasser. Where no parties exist and the government (whether traditional, military, or charismatic) is reasonably cooperative with the United States, American military, economic, and technical assistance should be conditioned upon the government's making efforts to develop a strong supporting party organization.

Several years ago Guy Pauker warned that "What is most urgently needed in Southeast Asia today is organizational strength."[72] Organizational strength is also the most urgent need in southern Asia, the Middle East, Africa, and Latin America. Unless that need is met with American support, the alternatives in those areas remain a corrupt political system or a Communist one.

other is the task of organization."[68] The party is initially a highly select group of those who have achieved the proper degree of revolutionary consciousness. It expands gradually as it is able to win the support and participation of others. Peripheral organizations and front groups provide an organizational ladder for the gradual mobilization and indoctrination of those who in due course become full-fledged party members. If the political struggle takes the form of revolutionary war, mobilization occurs on a gradual territorial basis as village after village shifts in status from hostile control to contested area to guerrilla area to base area. The theory is selective mobilization; the political involve-

---

[68]Ai Ssu-chi, quoted in Frederick T. C. Yu, "Communications and Politics in Communist China," in Pye, ed., *Communications and Political Development*, 261-62.

ment of masses who have not reached the proper level of revolutionary consciousness can only benefit reaction. The "opportunist" Menshevik, Lenin warned, "strives to proceed from the bottom upward, and, therefore, wherever possible and as far as possible, upholds autonomism and 'democracy'." The Bolshevik, on the other hand, "strives to proceed from the top downward, and upholds an extension of the rights and powers of the center in relation to the parts."[69]

Communist doctrine thus recognizes the need to balance mobilization and organization and stresses the party as the key to political stability. The American approach, on the other hand, tends to ignore the requirements of political organization and to deprecate the importance of party. American attitudes are rooted in the secondary, instrumental role of party in the American constitutional system. In addition, American distaste for politics leads to an emphasis on the output aspects of the political system. The stress, as Lucian Pye has pointed out, has been on the efficient administrator rather than the wily politician.[70] Aid missions advise governments on administrative organization and economic planning, but seldom do they advise political leaders on how to create a strong party. To meet the problems of interest aggregation, Americans have resorted to a variety of alternatives to political organization. Some Americans have urged that the military, as the strongest organization in many modernizing countries, should assume a major role in the responsibilities of government.[71] At times American policy has relied on individual political leaders, such as Magsaysay, Diem, or Ayub Khan. Alternatively, the American government has stressed adherence to particular structural forms, such as free elections.

All of these approaches are doomed to failure. Neither military juntas nor charismatic personalities nor free elections can be a long-term substitute for effective political organization. Charismatic leaders are reluctant to substitute party control for personal control. Military officers are usually even more explicitly anti-party. They contrast the venal party politics of the civilians with the honest devotion to the nation of the military. Military coups and military juntas may spur modernization, but they cannot produce a stable political order. Instead of

---

[69]V. I. Lenin, *One Step Forward, Two Steps Back* (*The Crisis in Our Party*), in *Collected Works* (Fineberg and Jochel trans., London 1961), 396–97.

[70]Pye, *Politics, Personality and Nation Building*, 297–301; and Pye, "The Policy Implications of Social Change in Non-Western Societies" (M.I.T. Center for International Studies, Cambridge 1957, mimeo.), 69–80.

[71]Guy J. Pauker, "Southeast Asia as a Problem Area in the Next Decade," *World Politics*, XI (April 1959), 325–45; Lucian W. Pye, "Armies in the Process of Political Modernization," in Johnson, ed., *The Role of the Military in Underdeveloped Countries* (Princeton 1962), 69–89.

relying on the military, American policy should be directed to the creation within modernizing countries of at least one strong non-Communist political party. If such a party already exists and is in a dominant position, support of that party should be the keystone of policy. Where political life is fragmented and many small parties exist, American backing should go to the strongest of the parties whose goals are compatible with ours. If it is a choice between a party and a personality, choose the party: better the Baath than Nasser. Where no parties exist and the government (whether traditional, military, or charismatic) is reasonably cooperative with the United States, American military, economic, and technical assistance should be conditioned upon the government's making efforts to develop a strong supporting party organization.

Several years ago Guy Pauker warned that "What is most urgently needed in Southeast Asia today is organizational strength."[72] Organizational strength is also the most urgent need in southern Asia, the Middle East, Africa, and Latin America. Unless that need is met with American support, the alternatives in those areas remain a corrupt political system or a Communist one.

FOR FURTHER READING

C. E. BLACK, *The Dynamics of Modernization: A Study in Comparative History* (New York: Harper & Row, 1966)

BERNARD E. BROWN, "The French Experience of Modernization" *(World Politics, XXI, 3, April 1969, 366–391)*

S. N. EISENSTADT, "Initial Institutional Patterns of Political Modernization" *(Civilisations, XII, 4, 461–472; XIII, 1, 15–26)*

S. N. EISENSTADT, "Modernization and Conditions of Sustained Growth" *(World Politics, XVI, 4, July 1964, 576–594)*

GINO GERMANI, "Stages of Modernization" *(International Journal, XXIV, 3, Summer 1969, 463–485)*

ROBERT T. HOLT AND JOHN E. TURNER, *The Political Basis of Economic Development: An Exploration in Comparative Political Analysis* (New York: Van Nostrand-Reinhold, 1966)

SAMUEL P. HUNTINGTON, *Political Order in Changing Societies* (New Haven: Yale University Press, 1968)

JOSEPH LA PALOMBARA, ed., *Bureaucracy and Political Development* (Princeton: Princeton University Press, 1963)

JOSEPH LA PALOMBARA AND MYRON WEINER, eds., *Political Parties and Political Development* (Princeton: Princeton University Press, 1966)

JOHN D. MONTGOMERY AND WILLIAM J. SIFFIN, eds., *Approaches to Development: Politics, Administration and Change* (New York: McGraw-Hill, 1966)

A. F. K. ORGANSKI, *The Stages of Political Development* (New York: Knopf, 1965)

FRED W. RIGGS, *Administration in Developing Countries: The Theory of Prismatic Society* (Boston: Houghton Mifflin, 1964)

---

[72]Pauker, *World Politics*, XI, 343.

POLITICAL CHANGE IN PAKISTAN: STRUCTURES, FUNCTIONS, CONSTRAINTS AND GOALS

Wayne Wilcox

Created as Great Britain precipitously withdrew from South Asia, Pakistan has confronted enormous obstacles to modernization. Military intervention brought efforts to establish Basic Democracies and increase the government's role. As Professor Wilcox notes, increased social mobilization weakens political institutions by threatening anarchy; but on the other hand, narrow control by an elite denies the mass support requisite for change.

Few governments created since World War II had greater problems in establishing and maintaining their authority than Pakistan. The nationalist movement that contributed to its creation was remarkably weak, narrowly-based and divided. Mohammad Ali Jinnah, its great leader, was the only figure who had the perspective and skill to focus conflicting factions and competing groups on common tasks. The cadre of experienced politicians in the Muslim League were scarcely more than a handful, and they were from provinces that were to be included in India, not Pakistan. The administrative reach of the British Indian government was weakest in Eastern Bengal, later East Pakistan, and only about 140 elite Indian Civil Service and Indian Police Service Officers were Muslim and willing to transfer to Pakistan state service.[1] None of the infrastructure of a national government existed in the dividing provinces that became Pakis-

From *Pacific Affairs*, Vol. XLI, No. 3 (1968), pp. 341–54, by permission. This article was presented as a paper at the Asian Studies on the Pacific Coast Conference, University of Hawaii, Honolulu, June 12, 1968. Views expressed in the article are those of the author and should not be interpreted as reflecting the views of The RAND Corporation as the official opinion or policy of any of its governmental or private research sponsors.
[1] The exact numbers and training of the officers is recounted in great detail in Ralph Braibanti, "Public Bureaucracy and Judiciary in Pakistan," in Joseph LaPalombara, (ed.) *Bureaucracy and Political Development*, Princeton, N.J.: Princeton University Press, 1967, pp. 364–369.

tan and the precipitant timing of the creation of the state forced an almost impossible operation—partition and independence—into a clearly impossible time frame, seventy-two days.[2]

I

In the eighteen tenuous months after its independence, Pakistan experienced four crises that nearly destroyed the new state: war with India over Kashmir; communal rioting, urban destruction and a massive influx of refugees into West Punjab; disputes with India over the transfer of Pakistan's share of British Indian assets, especially currency and military stores; and the death of the only truly national leader, Jinnah, before the new political order could be stabilized. The nature of each of these disputes is well known, but it needs to be remembered that they were faced almost simultaneously by very few men, none of them with great political experience, and certainly with nothing in their training and background to prepare them for the awesome magnitude of the challenges. Pakistan somehow survived, but the business of establishing an orderly political system was set back years and certain aspects of public life were permanently distorted.

The principal legacy of the first years of independence was a profound sense of insecurity. The Muslim League's propaganda had painted the Hindus and Sikhs in vivid hues but even the jingos were surprised and frightened by the incredible violence of the great killings in the Punjab. The war for Kashmir tended to confirm the popular view of Indian perfidy, and once the British were gone from Delhi the leaders in Karachi saw Sardar Patel's iron fist behind Jawaharlal Nehru's velvet glove. When Gandhi was assassinated by an anti-Muslim rightist, most Pakistanis believed that the only man from whom they could expect tolerance was gone and that India would move to eliminate Pakistan. These several unwelcome thoughts and fears, reinforced by the eight to nine million refugees who had fled the terror of the North Indian plains, coincided with the death of Pakistan's *Quaid-i-Azam* (great leader). Gone from the helm was the sole symbol of confidence and will who had carried the community and the new country through the hardest of anxious and uncertain days. Jinnah's successor, Liaquat Ali Khan, was more a mediator than a protagonist and his harsh learning experience as Prime Minister of the bereft country was cut short by an assassin's bullet in 1951.

Thus, after four years, Pakistan's political system was without vital leadership. The confused environment of government after 1948

---

[2]Some of the consequences of the partition to the economic life of the two successor states are described in my article "The Economic Consequences of Partition: India and Pakistan," *Journal of International Affairs*, XVIII (2) 1964, pp. 188–197.

was characterized by an abortive military *coup d'état,* political charges that Liaquat's death had been bought by his provincial rivals, unstable coalition politics, the breakdown of the tenuous unity of the nationalist leadership, and the unsettling effects of quite rapid social, political, and economic change.

The second principal legacy of the first years of independence was a fundamental disagreement about the organization and purposes of the Pakistan state. Cabinets changed rapidly, rarely lasting for more than two years. Party loyalties were transient and party discipline in the legislatures almost non-existent. Without confident leadership and disciplined support, no national government could clearly define the alternatives and push forward on constitutional issues. The four great conflicts of the period—the role of Islam in the state, the system of electoral procedures, the nature of the executive branch of government, and the federal structure—were truly fundamental questions.

The third principal legacy of the early disorganization and confusion of Pakistan's public life was the autonomy and primacy of the civil and military bureaucracy. While emerging political forces and weak political institutions characterized the ambiguous politics of constitution-making, the civil and military services were ruling. Bureaucrats assumed new functions because their opportunities were greatly expanded and because it was necessary to do so to maintain Pakistan. The so-called law and order bureaucrats of the colonial *raj* found themselves knee deep in developmental planning, economic operations, and political decision-making even before the ink was dry on the Indian Independence Act.

The military officer corps, having been indoctrinated in a system that was allegedly innocent of politics, almost immediately were drawn into new areas of operation that involved them in decision-making in security and foreign policy. Pakistan's needs at its birth were stability and security, the twin mandates of the praetorian civil and military services.

The tragedy in Pakistan's early history was that everyone agreed on the necessity of a strong state but no one agreed on its form or proper role. Muslim culture is, ideally, corporatist rather than individualistic; it enshrines the virtues of creative conformity in its doctrine, history, and ideals.[3] Yet the social, economic, and political differentiation begun under British rule and accelerated by World War II had shattered the relevance of traditional symbols of common purpose and identity between the various Muslim groups. The resultant ideational diversity and increased social

---

[3]Amplification of these arguments may be found in the several contributions on Pakistan in Donald E. Smith (ed.), *South Asian Politics and Religion,* Princeton N. J.: Princeton University Press, 1966, pp. 337–450.

distance meant that Islamic society was very different things to different people, and while its saliency and importance could not be denied, its operational prescriptions for political life were uncertain. Each mobilized group in the society believed that Islam should have a major role that enhanced unity in the community of believers, but they disagreed on the model of the society that would reflect the Muslim *corpus mysticum.*

Since agreement was impossible and no constitutional settlement seemed stable, most aspects of public life were de-politicized. The administration went its own way toward bureaucratic incrementalism. The military services searched for external suppliers of arms and training. The economy, which should have been very sensitive to Muslim notions of distributional justice, ideas moreover that were reinforced by Western norms of democratic equalitarianism, was in fact dominated by entrepreneurs who in their immense profits and reinvestments demonstrated "the social utility of greed."[4] Pakistan's national life in its first years therefore found the praetorian guard manning the parapets while public men disagreed on fundamentals of national life; it found common citizens pitting themselves against desperate poverty while men new to business took their first risks and began to profit. These developments kept the country together but they left the constitutional configurations of power fluid and ambiguous.

II

In 1958 in the midst of continuing federal, economic, electoral, and cabinet dissonance the Army commander-in-chief, General Mohammad Ayub Khan, seized power.[5] There were many factors in the seizure, but *the general cause of military intervention seems to have been that the increasingly radical effects of social and economic change threatened the whole structure of administration in Pakistan.* Many civil and military bureaucrats had concluded that their work, in stabilizing the country's administration and ensuring its security, was in danger of being undercut by political developments. They saw the imperative needs of the second decade of independence as more discipline, stability, and security rather than mobilization and experimentation.[6] And since the relatively weak political forces of the country were incapable of resisting the army's

---

[4]Gustav Papanek's apt phrase from his *Pakistan's Development: Social Goals and Private Incentives,* Cambridge, Mass.: Harvard University Press, 1967, p. 226.
[5]See *Friends Not Masters: A Political Biography,* New York: Oxford University Press, 1967, especially pp. 70–76. I have attempted a detailed analysis of the period in an earlier article "The Pakistan Coup D'Etat of 1958," *Pacific Affairs,* XXXVIII (2), Summer, 1965, pp. 142–163.
[6]Thus, L. R. Rushbrook-Williams quotes one senior bureaucrat as saying, in the wake of the *coup d'état,* "Thank Goodness, we can now get on with our job without interference from those wretched politicians." *The State of Pakistan,* London, Faber, 1962, p. 189.

power, its leadership could undertake the operation without worrying about its possible high cost, uncertainty, or bloodshed.

Curiously enough, the coup d'état reflected the increasing confidence and strength of the Pakistan state. The administration's outreach and influence, the normal habits of compliance with authority, the going and successful concern of the economy, the commitment of citizens to their somewhat more secure country and their children's future in it, and their trust in the army leadership made possible an undemocratic change of authority under peaceful conditions. It also made possible a return to non-military government in a very short period of time after the coup.

It was not that the commitment to democracy was weak in Pakistan; indeed, even the cabalists proclaimed its virtues and could hardly wait to reinstate it. It was rather that *the political forms of expressing democratic values could not be related to the solution of the fundamental problems of the political society.* There was no majority in Pakistan, and the search for one had exaggerated the disturbing uncertainty with which the state had been born. Citizens of General Ayub Khan's Pakistan could both damn his undemocratic mandate and yet feel relief in the fact that the ambiguous constitutional quest of the past was ended. It is this combination of attitudes that continues to characterize the dialogue in Pakistan, and that leads to the paradox of open, general, and radical criticism of the government matched by confused, fragmented, and powerless opposition to it.

All of the major issues that have baffled and distracted Pakistan's elites since independence continue to exist. President Ayub Khan's government has not resolved them and probably cannot resolve them. What it has done is to reduce political mobilization based on them, and compartmentalize the dissent at relatively low levels of the political system. Thus the role of Islam troubles this government because it is the most salient problem; it touches so many otherwise unmobilized groups in the country. And after some initial Ataturk-like secular statements, the government has retreated into a generalized, ambiguous posture in a very low key.

The electoral system continues to be very controversial, no longer because of the problem of Hindu and Muslim voting lists, but because universal direct adult suffrage has been abridged. With the expansion of the electoral college of Basic Democrats to 120,000, the indirect system of elections has probably reached its maximum limit. The government is temporizing about future channels of participation.

Under the 1962 constitution, the division of powers that confused the previous fundamental laws of the country was ended; the President f the Republic now combines both the symbolic and establishment affairs ole of the Governor-General with the policy responsibility of the Prime Iinister. But the more significant change of the constitution was the eduction of autonomy and power of the legislatures *vis-à-vis* the executive. The cabinet is responsible solely to a fixed-term chief executive, and arty discipline is secured because crossing the floor entails a new election or the defector. The key amendments to the constitution that have een proposed deal not with the executive powers but with the relative ower of the executive and the legislatures. The government is making aste slowly in modifying the present relationships.

Finally the federal politics of Pakistan continue to be very important. East Pakistan's size, condition, and physical and linguistic solation from West Pakistan pose great problems under the best of onditions. So long as a West Pakistani is President, many East Pakistanis do not think that the country is witnessing the best of conditions. he federal problem may be even greater for President Ayub Khan than or his parliamentary predecessors since it has been more difficult for im to configure a power-sharing federal system with major East 'akistan politicians.

In the two decades of Pakistan's evolution, therefore, very different forms and conditions of national government have pertained, but *he fundamental nature of the polity remains unclear.* Political institutions are unsettled, and the *mechanisms for orderly democratic transfers f authority have not been evolved.* On the four fundamental issues that he country has faced there is no policy consensus. And given the nature f the society and the effects of modernization, there can be no general onsensus for some time, if ever. In this situation, the study of political hange is especially revealing because the importance of structures, unctions, constraints, and goals and their interrelationships in the olitical system stand out in greater relief and fidelity than in more ettled polities where continuity introduces distortions between historical nyth and operational reality.

III

Political change may be viewed as a change in political transctions (functions), and/or the transactive mechanisms (structures), nd/or the parameters of political transactions within a social system constraints) and/or changes in political elites or elite preferences goals). As Ernest Hocking once put it, much more simply, *politics is he process by which men set the conditions of their common association.*

Political elites, in their attempt to realize shared goals, mobilize esources that become "means" in the public policy process. These means or capacities to further political goals deal with behavioral compliance. Since elite preferences and mass behavior differ, especially in modernizing post-colonial societies, *governments must develop three capacities: the ability to wield administrative capacity (directed compliance); the ability to evoke widespread popular support (voluntary compliance); and the ability to maintain coherence and confidence in the various segments of the political elite.*

Elite discipline, administrative competence, and popular support are complementary necessities for effective policy but they rarely exist, in strength, in any political society. Where one requisite is weak, the other two tend to be correspondingly strong, or else the policy goals or political performance correspondingly modest. Thus "modern" governments like "traditional" ones work under constraints imposed by weak administrations, tenuous popular support, and quarreling elites. The difference between the two, as between liberal and totalitarian forms as well, is partially in the "mix" between elements, which might be called the compensatory balance of the political system. But a more fundamental difference is in the number and scope of transactions that the political system processes, a quality that tends to be a function of the magnitude of social mobilization in the society.

It follows from this typological analysis that the politics of a country like Pakistan, characterized by low mobilization, will consequently witness a limited scope of state activity. The public policy process will be further constrained by elite disunity and administrative weakness, such constraints leading to unambitious public policy that does not purposefully stimulate increasing demands on the system. Empirical analysis should therefore focus on the interdependence of structures, functions, constraints, and goals to attempt to locate the sources of greatest dynamism and therefore explain the quality of political changes in Pakistan since 1947.

IV

It is not accurate to suggest that Pakistan was created from whole cloth. It inherited a viceregal organization of authority. The British colonial system in India had many facets, but the democratic participatory culture was limited in its extent to the great port cities while rural India and the provinces were ruled autocratically. Pakistan inherited rural areas and the rural idiom of politics. Lahore was its only genuine city, and it was the capital of the most bureaucratized and carefully controlled province in India, the Punjab. The only Muslims of the subcontinent who enjoyed the benefits of the capitalist participatory system of British rule were the commercial minorities of Western India

(Mohammad Ali Jinnah among them), the English-literate, secular moderns of the cities who had lost their "Muslimness" in their mobility (H.S. Suhrawardy among them), and the *zamindars* of the United Provinces who were a part of the rural feudal order (Liaquat Ali Khan among them).

These three groups provided the leadership for the Pakistan movement and for parliamentary government in Pakistan, but they were all alien to the provinces that became Pakistan. Their claim to lead had to be found in a democratic mandate, yet they were without constituencies in the promised land. And they were few in number.

The sons of the soil in Pakistan's provinces were part of the other political culture. The Punjab and Sind were ruled by feudal landowning families who were jealous of their autocratic prerogatives and scornful of populist politics. They owned not land, but villages, including the villagers. And while they ridiculed the notions of the adult franchise, they controlled villages and hence majority votes. The other significant elite from the Muslim provinces was the civil and military bureaucracy which also scorned the notion that the masses should direct the activities of the state.

The incongruity and cruelty of historical chance is clear. The democrats could win only if they could reconcile their democratic values with majority votes to maintain the mandate of the nationalist movement. Their autocratic rivals, however, controlled the masses even though, while not valuing a mass mandate, could use it against the "alien" nationalist leadership. And since politics is always areally focused, and since the institutions of authority were controlled by representative bureaucratic and military elites, the outcome, both the participatory system and for the nature of elite dominance, was prejudiced against the democrats. *Thus the strongest traditions and structures of politics that were inherited by Pakistan were autocratic and viceregal.*

When, in 1958, the (Punjabi-led) army came to power, it was more declaratory than revolutionary. Since 1953, the civil and military services had, through the Governor-General's office, exercised paramount influence in the political system. The coup foreclosed what might truly have been a revolution, the national elections scheduled for early 1959 that would probably have seen H.S. Suhrawardy (a Bengali politician) Prime Minister and a much more representative legislature supporting the cabinet.

What had been a marked trend within British India, the increasing influence of political parties, provinces, and parliaments over administration was reversed in Pakistan. The martial law period, 1958-1962, was a return to early twentieth century imperial practice, and the constitution of 1962 in many ways is similar to the Government of India Acts of 1919 and 1935. The nearly autonomous power of the executive at the center and the devolution of subjects to the provinces and localities for operational control was once called dyarchy. Popular mobilization around issues, a major role of political parties, is explicitly consigned to legislative caucus. The direct participation of the voters in choosing their national and provincial leaders, previously screened and organized by the parties, is disaggregated and transferred to the local leadership that is part of community power structures in rural Pakistan.

In temporal comparative perspective, this development is clearly backward. This is not to make a normative judgment but only a chronological one. And perhaps the structural stability and continuity of the system in Pakistan is little more than the confirmation of one of the great truths of anthropology: *structures change more slowly than functions* and often continue to be the vessels in which very different wine is held.

V

By emphasizing structures in the analysis of Pakistan's changing political system, the impression to be gained is that there has been very little change since 1947, or even 1937, a view clearly at variance with observed reality. *What has changed is not the mechanisms by which political transactions are processed but the transactions themselves. Literally hundreds of new undertakings by the state characterize modern Pakistan.*[7] Indeed, the proliferation of government corporations, academies, experimental programs, research bodies and economic operations has become the hallmark of the present regime. What is noteworthy, however, is that *the new functions undertaken by the state have been undertaken within the inherited structure; they are bureaucratic variations responsive to changing goals and problems, not participatory associations created out of the non-governmental processes of the society.*[7a]

For example, Pakistan's economic development has proceeded more rapidly than most observers expected, supposedly because of the talent of the entrepreneurs, the presence of large amounts of foreign aid, and the weakness of the bureaucracy in attempting to over-administer economic development. By the time that the government possessed the capacity to

---

[7] Even as assiduous a bibliographer as Ralph Braibanti could hardly manage to catalog and document the extraordinary number of commissions, reports, and programs that were within the bureaucratic experience of only 20 years. See his *Research on the Bureaucracy of Pakistan*, Durham, N. C.: Duke University Press, 1966, *passim.*

[7a] This pattern corresponds almost completely with Fred Rigg's model of the bureaucratic state.

play a more active regulatory role, the economy was shaped in favor of continued autonomy within overall government guidance for the private entrepreneur. Yet Government has played a major role in the economy, even if it allowed private business to be the main engine of growth. As in most countries, the "public sector" responded to needs for infrastructural development: the transport, electricity, banking and capital market, foreign exchange and licensing procedures, policing, export performance and other necessary public facilities that allow a private sector to develop and prosper. These functions were thrust upon the government because they were not profitable, or because their scale was beyond the capital resources of business, or because they required foreign exchange that only governments could find in the world economy, but they were accepted because the bureaucracy wanted to play a significant economic role. The mid-twentieth century world economy requires governments in all states to conduct a certain amount of planning and business regardless of the social system.

And government has played a more active role in the directly productive part of the economy than many observers notice. Thus the Pakistan Industrial Development Corporation (PIDC) uses public funds to establish basic industries, some of which may be sold to private firms but some are kept as part of bureaucratic and status politics.[8] Similarly the new Agricultural Development Corporations (ADC) that are supposed to "administer" agricultural growth in the country moved into a field in which profits were limited, holdings atomized, and investments limited to cash crops, but they did so with much older bureaucratic attitudes. The ever present tendency is to favor the use of administrative controls rather than market incentives to produce desired ends.

At a certain point, obviously, the expanded range of transactions being processed by inherited structures constitutes a qualitative change in the political system. An increased scale of governmental operations tends to widen the jurisdiction of the state, and such a change implies either enhanced administrative capacity or increased social mobilization or both. In analyzing the data from Pakistan, the question to be asked is whether the new variants of administrative institutions processing expanded transactions in the society constitute a structural change *in the process* by which men set the conditions of their common association. *It is clear in Pakistan that there has been extensive change in the scope of government operations, but little intensive change in the procedures and mechanisms of political management.* Meanwhile, elite unity has been

---

[8]Papanek, *op. cit.*, has a very detailed acount of PIDC economics and the problems of administrative politics, political inefficiency and misplaced capital investment.

maintained by reducing participation in decision-making, administrative capacity has grown rapidly, and popular support has been elicited only grudgingly.

VI

At low levels of goal-pursuit, governments can afford to make minimum demands for mass compliance. But as economic development proceeds and social differentiation increases, demands for the state as a coordinating and planning mechanism increase. *Pakistan's economic growth is starting to revolutionize group relationships in the country, and the political system, to maintain equilibrium and promote the goal of relatively peaceful growth, must extend the parameters of state influence in the society. It must pursue deliberate policies of mobilization and social control.*

One of the important attempts of Ayub Khan's government to develop participatory and compliance institutions is the Basic Democracies scheme.[9] Since its inception, it has been in the process of constant flux as it added more important functions. It was created primarily to improve administrative access and capacity in rural areas and shortly thereafter, to validate President Ayub Khan's political legitimacy. The next stage witnessed its evolution into a permanent electoral college and rural intelligence system, and that was followed by its conversion into an agency for government public works. Thereupon it became the major arena for political recruitment, competition, and patronage and has recently been expanded into a 120,000-strong council of national notables. None of the stages has been distinct since attributes of one period have not been discarded with subsequent accretions. The central feature of the system—the symbiosis between local leadership and local administration—continues to be the most important characteristic but its operational consequences are unclear.

Does intimate contact with the local bureaucracy make local leadership more compliant to central direction, or does local leadership use its access in the administrative structure to frustrate government policy? Do the BD's "sell" government policy to their fellows, tenants, and neighbors? Do they keep the administration informed of major developments of national and provincial importance in their localities?

---

[9]The structure of the system, resting on 120,000 local Basic Democrats, extends upward in pyramidal layers to the division. The BD's also constitute the electoral college for offices in the legislature and for the chief executive. There has not been a meaningful and full analysis of the system, in the first instance because most observers thought it to be a fig leaf for a near-monarchy. but perhaps more importantly, the system has been changing so rapidly that the few social scientists who have been in the field have been unable to complete a major study.

Are they mobilizing young talent into patterns of politics that can be absorbed by the narrow arenas of legitimate competition now allowed in the system? The returns are not in, but the ability of the system to survive and grow in importance testifies to its relevance to contemporary Pakistan. The direction of capital flow—from the central government to the BD's—rather than the reverse suggests that the institution is not *solely* another aspect of the administration, even though funds are allocated to BD's on the basis of development plans.

Without more analysis or more time in which to observe, it is difficult to judge whether the system is a new embodiment of a rural development bureaucracy with some political functions, or whether it is a local participatory political system with some rural development attributes. In either case, it is clear that the BD system is expanding participation in the political system and therefore expanding the parameter set by the relative absence of mobilization.

Under the principle of compensating balances, the expansion of rural BD participation entails changed strengths of the bureaucracy or of elite discipline and coherence. As the BD system has developed, elite dissent has in fact been reduced. The press and mass media no longer offer a forum for radical dissent,[10] the universities are more carefully controlled and monitored and police surveillance has been more visible, if not more active. The strength of the BD's has been at the expense of the urban middle class professionals in general, and the present coalition of effective mobilized groups includes only the civil and military bureaucracy, business, and the Basic Democrats. Just as the government has expanded its access and central apparatus in the rural areas, its policy in the cities has set more narrow parameters. The dissent of the intellectuals, the "brain drain" associated with low morale and lower status, the frustration of powerlessness and the weakening of the universities are, however, producing severe problems in such diverse areas as manpower, urban control, and the expressive arts, not to say in the training and recruitment into public life of the urban intelligentsia. The only path to influence and participation in the present system for the urbanite is via the bureaucracy.

While examples may be multiplied of the problems of mobilization and constraints, *the essence of the policy dilemma is that full mobilization in a country as diverse as Pakistan threatens to lead to anarchy, while narrow elite control denies government the support necessary* to undertake mass tasks. Thus, under martial law when President Ayub Khan gave his administrative subordinates full freedom to investigate problems and

---

[10]Dacca's *Holiday* is the only exception that I find, and its editor is one of the sons of the Speaker of the National Assembly, an ally of the present government and one of its most influential Bengalis.

propose solutions, the results were unimpressive not because of the quality of the research but because the administration was unable to implement the recommendations. Popular opposition, elite opposition, paucity of financial resources, incapacity of administration, inadequate data, and any number of other constraints were clear for all to see.[11] In response to army pressure to do more, President Ayub Khan criticized young activists by noting, "What they did not understand was that civil action was subject to the limitation of the law and had to take into account currents and cross currents of public opinion."[12] In short, they did not understand the constraints of politics.

Popular support for policies will always be a function of the difference between legislative or executive intent and popular behavior. And if the political system allows mobilization in the rural areas—and mobilization always implies shared power and influence—and if the national government chooses to call for changes that would run counter to the interests of the mobilized, enfranchised, and powerful local leaders, the policy is unlikely to be implemented and support will be denied. Under almost any set of circumstances, therefore, the parameters of public policy remain narrow. If external resources can be mobilized through diplomacy, or if the society tolerates the use of coercion in pursuit of public policy, some otherwise impractical policies can be enacted. But political change is the change of relationships between actors and goals in the system, and therefore external influences have no fundamental effect.

VII

Just as problems create new pressures for government action, and just as government action may have structural effects on the organization of authority, historical change and the impact of world developments set into motion new ideas and forces that reshape the goals of elites. The "international demonstration effect" of Nurkse does not concern only economics. The magnitude of the personal and generational changes in attitudes and goals that are implied for the Pakistan elite in choices between, say, a reasonably comfortable, low-key, elitist British nineteenth century state and a high pressure, richly uncomfortable, mass American style society is apparent. With the world generating alternatives not only in London and New York, but Peking, Moscow, Delhi, Tokyo, and Paris, the range of choice and alternative objects for emulation are legion.

---

[11]This aspect of Pakistan's public life is superbly documented in Karl Von Vorys, *Political Development in Pakistan*, Princeton, N. J.: Princeton University Press, 1966.
[12]In *Friends Not Masters*, p. 78.

Pakistan evolved from a threatened sense of distinct identity that would have been exaggerated by remaining part of a democratic, socialist Hindustan. Islam dictated separation, but not the pattern of future development. The inherited viceregal system of structures and functions seemed to serve Pakistan well when the task was survival but seems to serve it less as a model for the future. Neo-Islamists like Maulana Maudoodi preach a return to something that never was; a pristine but autocratic Muslim puritanism. The present Pakistani leadership calls for patient, incremental change on the basis of the present system that has served Pakistan well. The younger generation is more attentive to a wider range of possibilities, be they internationally inspired or part of the liberal, pluralist versus directed, socialist dogmas of our era. And since the younger generation is not experienced in the political culture that is so sensitive to constraints, its advocacy is more radically fulsome than it might otherwise be.

The ideational and generational diversity in the country is immense, and the social institutions of parliamentary democracy or historic Islam do not address themselves to the problem of resolving differences in public preferences. *Pakistan has been successful in creating new working relationships for large segments of the population and relating the work to a common state. But it has not been able to establish a common set of values that undergird either the polity or any specific set of institutions in the society or economy. Every government finds itself a minority government and thus strengthens autocratic controls. Autocratic controls tend to enfranchise administrators whose problem-solving biases reinforce existing institutions. New ideas and social forces are unable to assert themselves in corporate activity because the society is unresponsive and organizationally incapable of accepting participant mobilization outside limited administrative channels.*

Yet new ideas do shape the goals of the elite, inside and outside administration. The impact of foreign economic and military assistance triggers changes in procedures and outlooks, especially within the government. Occupational diversity tends to bring new insights into the public policy process as governments become involved in wide operations. The changes, since they are attitudinal, take place relatively rapidly but their social effect requires much more time. Every new idea that finds embodiment in a goal also sets into motion the political process by which elites attempt to win support from masses for new forms of common activity.

Politics is too complex a human activity to lend itself to simple portrayal or summary. To the question: *How* are Pakistan's politics changing? the general answer can be given that its dominant bureaucratic structures are assuming a wider jurisdiction, and in the process involving more people in the decision-making and implementing process. To the general question: *Why* are Pakistan's politics changing? the answer is also clear, in its broadest dimensions, because of the increasing role of the state in coordinating an increasingly differentiated and complex common society. *Why* is the political system changing *so slowly?* President Ayub Khan and his agents have opted for a slowly changing political system to avoid the worse consequences of unchecked advocacy and dissonance, and have been constrained in their choice of approaches both by the inherited structures and by the lack of consensual support of the society.

And a final question: is change a very useful category of either analysis or description, and the answer is, of course, no. Change is a condition and not a category.

FOR FURTHER READING

W. M. DOBELL, "Ayub Khan as President of Pakistan" *(Pacific Affairs,* XLII, 2, Fall 1969, 244–310)

AYUB KHAN, *Friends Not Masters: A Political Biography* (New York: Oxford University Press, 1967)

TALUKDER MANIRUZZAMAN, "National Integration and Political Development In Pakistan" *(Asian Survey,* VII, 12, December 1967, 876–885)

RAYMOND A. MOORE, "The Army as a Vehicle for Social Change in Pakistan" *(Journal of Developing Areas,* II, 1, October 1967, 57–74)

M. RASHIDUZZAMAN, "Election Politics in Pakistan Villages" *(Journal of Commonwealth Political Studies,* IV, 3, November 1966, 191–200)

KARL VON VORYS, *Political Development in Pakistan* (Princeton: Princeton University Press, 1966)

BUILDING THE NEWEST NATIONS: SHORT-RUN STRATEGIES AND LONG-RUN PROBLEMS

William J. Foltz

Winning independence is far more exciting and far less onerous than building a nation. The mass party that has won self-government, Professor Foltz notes, may be weakened by the day-to-day burdens of governing; its preeminence may be challenged by new administrative and technical elites. The author concludes with a question: Can the restrictive consolidation of power in the hands of a few give way to a more balanced, pluralistic distribution of power?

Obtaining even the sort of cooperation necessary for the regular functioning of a state apparatus may be dependent on the prior establishment of a strong sense of common identity and a common outlook among the "politically relevant strata" of a society on a wide variety of issues. A glance around today's globe suffices to show, however, that in many new states forceful governmental structures have been established that do not approach the level of internal communication and mutual comprehension of the thirteen American colonies on the eve of the Revolution. The problem here, it seems to me, is the composition and extent of the "politically relevant strata." A large proportion of the eighteenth-century American population not only possessed the skills requisite for participation in political decision-making, but also energetically insisted on such participation. Few rural hamlets were so small or isolated that they did not contain one voice whose words had to be reckoned with at some distant center of government. In contrast, most of the nations that have achieved their independence since World War

From W. J. Foltz, "Building the Newest Nations: Short-Run Strategies and Long-Run Problems," in K. W. Deutsch and W. J. Foltz, Editors, *Nation-Building*. Reprinted by permission of the publishers, Atherton Press, Inc. Copyright © 1966, Atherton Press, Inc., New York. All rights reserved.

II have had what is, from a short-range point of view at least, the good fortune to possess a narrowly constricted and homogeneous set of politically relevant strata. Furthermore, the large gap separating these people from the masses has permitted them to maintain themselves as a stable and nearly self-sufficient political elite during the most trying periods of political transition.

In most cases, this is not a gap of inherited traditional status, but one of modern achievement, most significantly educational achievement.[1] This, if anything, makes the gap more permanent, for ascribed status distinctions can sometimes be abolished overnight for political purposes, but most of the population cannot be taught overnight, or even in a few generations, the skills necessary to participate meaningfully and effectively in politics. The gap is between those living in the modern world and participating in the crucial decisions of the political arena and those living essentially as did their ancestors; bereft not only of skills for modern politics and other modern occupations, but, in some cases, of even a minimal sense of identity with political structures and the people animating them. Although this gap provides the greatest long-run challenge to those who would build an integrated nation, in the short run it has given the elite the great flexibility of maneuver that is necessary to seize and consolidate the power of the state.

The educational structures of the newest states tend to reinforce polarization between elite and mass. Typically, there exists a great mass of people with no or only primary education and then, at the other extreme, a small but significant number of people with university-level training. What is lacking are people educated to the intermediate high school and junior high levels that characterize the bulk of the population in most advanced societies.[2] The reason for this gap is, on the surface, a good one. Because of the lack of educational funds, students for post-primary education must be rigorously selected at the sixth grade level. Those that succeed are then pushed to the limit of their abilities, which may be very great indeed. Without a large intermediate sector of reasonably competent and educated mid-elites, however, complex issues of government and administration are not interpreted and transmitted throughout society in meaningful terms that the masses can easily grasp. At the top, issues are faced in all their complexity; at the bottom,

---

[1]For a similar educational distinction of elite from mass, see Claude Tardits, *Porto Novo* (Paris: Mouton, 1958), p. 11.

[2]In Ghana, for instance, only about 12 per cent of those finishing primary school are admitted to advanced secondary training. Similarly, in the Ivory Coast in 1957 "only 750 out of 5,739 who completed primary school continued their education." At least half of these then went on to university training. Both countries have recently taken steps to expand secondary education. See Ruth Sloan Associates, *The Educated African* (New York: Praeger, 1962), esp. pp. 334–340, 460–469.

they are grouped and boiled down to simple slogans—"Independence now!" "One man, one vote!" Issues cannot be meaningfully debated within the populace at large, and votes tend to become mere approving plebiscites.

If, in society as a whole, there are few individuals in everyday life prepared to interpret and relate the problems of the elite to the masses, there are also few institutions capable of bridging the gap. In most African, and some Asian countries, the single, mass political party (*parti unique*) has played this role and has been the primary means of bringing the masses into contact with the political culture and inducting individuals into political roles.[3] Where the political party apparatus has been strong and active, the greatest political acculturation of the masses has taken place, as a comparison of, say, Guinea with Upper Volta or Ghana with Sierra Leone would show. However, the limits of this political acculturation should be noted. The masses are, for the most part, still associated with the receiving end of the political order. As Professor Scott put it, they are still "subjects," and their participation is ideally limited to applause on cue and, at most, to sullen foot-dragging when changes appear to be for the worse. Since the single, mass political parties, more than formal governmental or purely social organizations, often seem to be the prime mediators between elite and mass, they may, as Professor Emerson suggests, hold out the best hope for building the newest nations. We shall, therefore, take a more thorough look at their past successes and future possibilities.

Most of the currently ruling political parties in the newest states grew up under the late colonial regimes as instruments for attaining national independence. Particularly in the British and French colonial empires, the single, mass parties were singularly successful in leading the way to independence and quickly consolidating control over the government and administrative apparatuses once independence was achieved. The strength and success of these parties have rested on four principal factors. First, in "Independence!" they had a rallying cry of universal appeal. Typically, in any competitive party situation, the party that first proclaimed, "Freedom now," "Uhuru," or "N'dépendence" ended up on top once it had made itself the recognized spokesman for the feelings of vague revolt and common identity that usually make up modern nationalism in the underdeveloped countries. Its es-

---

[3]"The *parti unique* is both an elite and a link.... The *parti unique* has as a goal to forge new elites, to create a new governing class, to unite and train political leaders capable of organizing the country, for the masses cannot govern themselves.... The party establishes a direct and permanent contact between [the political elite] and the country." Maurice Duverger, *Les Partis politiques* (Paris: Armand Colin, 1958), p. 288.

pousal of national independence provided a focus around which both elite and mass could unite. Second, the single, mass party usually included virtually all the modern elite. These men were united by ties of personal friendship, frequently reinforced by common educational and agitational experiences and by dedication to the nationalist cause. Those members of the modern elite who did not join the mass party initially were generally co-opted at a later date or were so compromised by association with the colonial administration that they were ineffective as opposition leaders. Third, because of the dominance of the nationalist issue and because of the general lack of other modern structures, the single political party had no serious competition from other modern associations as a focus for popular loyalties. Finally, the single, mass party was generally well organized. The conditions of the political struggle and the dedication of the top elite to the party as the prime instrument of political change led the elite to give the major portion of their energies and resources to building a solid, responsive organization capable of disciplined action in response to directives from the top and able to ferret out and exploit feelings of dissatisfaction among the masses for political ends. The mass party became the framework within which ethnic, caste, and regional differences among the population at large could be submerged in the search for a common goal. It both embodied and promoted a preliminary sense of national unity and identity.

But winning independence, although it may be a necessary condition, is only the first and perhaps easiest step in building a nation. The new state apparatus must then be solidly implanted and extended, and the loyalty of the people to a stable governing regime, not to an agitational opposition movement, must be assured. However, the very factors making the mass party such an effective tool in the struggle for independence and permitting it to take over governmental power may be weakened by the day-to-day exercise of governmental responsibilities and by the nation-building process itself. Once formal independence is won, the unifying slogan of "Independence" has lost its magic force, and it is unlikely that anything quite so dramatic and effective can be found to replace it. Defending a revolution is always a less exciting and more onerous task than making it. Frequently, newly independent states seize on a new derivative slogan or goal to replace "independence" as a means of unifying both elite and mass. These secondary goals have frequently involved transforming the world outside the state to bring it more into line with the desires and presumed advantages of the new state, thus symbolically continuing the movement of independence. Such movements have sometimes, but not always, sought to export a national revolution or, as in Africa recently, to continue the independence movement to areas not yet favored by an enlightened colonial master. Of the same sort are the many irredentist movements designed to annex a lost or related territory or region, as, for example, the recent disputes between Morocco and Mauritania or Ghana and Togo. With such direct extensions of the goal of "national independence," governments frequently may promote a regional or federal unity movement of some sort, which may seek to reactivate popular emotions by redirecting them toward a greater whole. Pan-Africanism and Pan-Arabism are well-known examples.

Although turning to the outside world may provoke as strong an emotional yearning for unity as did the simpler search for national political unity and independence formerly, it may, in the short run, simply dilute or confuse more specific national sentiment. To the degree that it makes the success of the territorial nationalist movement dependent on that of a greater whole, it may in the long run succeed only in calling into question the worth of the national regime when the larger unity proves unrealizable.

The new state may try to unite its people by focusing animosities and frustrations on some external enemy, just as the nationalist movement focused its resentments on the colonial power or previous ruling class. To this end, the term "neocolonialism" has recently been invented. Those who brandish "neocolonialism" as a political slogan warn against continued domination by the former masters, now presumably operating behind the scenes through control of indigenous puppets and the new state's economy. Moise Tshombe's regime in Katanga is generally presented as the most blatant example of neocolonialism, but domestic difficulties in the most anti-imperialist states may be blamed on secret neocolonialists. "Neocolonialism" as a political slogan does have the great advantage of being almost universally applicable. By definition, neocolonialism operates behind the scenes, so virtually anything can be blamed on it. At the same time, however, its very ethereality means that neocolonialism is not directly experienced by the man in the street as was foreign political or military control, and it may, thereby, be a less effective political slogan.

Finally, the new state may choose some purely internal, nonsymbolic goal to replace national independence as a national rallying cry. The "battle for economic development" is the most common and significant such goal today, as one would expect. However praiseworthy economic development may be as a national goal and however important it may be for long-term nation-building, it is still not likely to have the political potency of "independence." No matter how it is explained to them, few people are likely to make voluntarily and happily the sacrifices required in order to increase the gross national product by 3 per cent per annum or whatever else the goal might be. Furthermore, to the extent that most of the new states are primarily agricultural countries, the new regimes are obliged to earn precious domestic developmental capital from the sweat of peasantry fulfilling and over-fulfilling their quotas. Thus, the first results of the drive for economic development may be a tougher lot for the very people for whom the new regime was brought into power—a fact which is unlikely to increase the masses' esteem for the regime.

As the mass party in the newly independent state is deprived of "independence" as a national rallying cry, so, too, its organization may suffer once it has passed from systematic opposition to coping with the demands of day-to-day administration. Talents that once were available for the crucial work of party organization may now be preoccupied with running a ministry or government bureau. This will be particularly true where the conditions under which independence was obtained led to the withdrawal of European advisors and technicians and threw the whole technical and administrative burden on the shoulders of the young indigenous politicians. Unless new sources of loyal organizational and administrative talents can be found immediately, the party's organization—and, therefore, the major link between the regime and the masses—is likely to be weakened.

If, in the days of nationalist agitation for independence, the mass party provided the unique and inclusive instrument for popular political participation, this is not likely to be the case after independence is attained. Governing an independent country requires indigenous participation in a great variety of new, formally constituted units. A civil service and national army are only the minimal, though most essential, organizations that must be staffed. Although these, like the governmental apparatus, will formally be brought under the control of the mass party, they can be expected to become new focuses of loyalty and to develop new goals, priorities, and methods that are at variance with those of the mass party. With increased specialization of function, the elite will share fewer and fewer common perspectives and experiences and will develop personal and group interests that could well produce internal scissions that were absent when the mass political party was the single organ of political expression, participation, and planning.

Of course, in theory, the new organizations should complement the mass party as the means of bridging the gap between the elite and the masses. However, if a struggle for influence pitting army or administration against the party develops, the very contacts of the new organizations with the masses may serve to divide the people more deeply than they were when only the party undertook to link them with the realm of modern politics. This will be particularly the case in cultures where personal leadership is important, and an army general, top administrator, or cabinet minister may build a personal following among the population at large.

The dispersion of leadership talents and the competition of different decision-making units may be further accentuated if economic development is given top priority by the ruling elite. It is in part to prevent the creation of autonomous domestic decision-making units with a basis of economic power that many new states have refused to expand the private sector of the economy, even when such expansion would clearly contribute to economic development. It is not, in this sense, paradoxical that one of the most "revolutionary" new states, Guinea, should have tried repressing all domestic free enterprise while signing major contracts for exploitation of her natural resources with a consortium of Western private concerns. As the Guineans saw it, the foreigners would remain outside the sphere of domestic politics, but any Guinean private enterprise might augment fissiparous tendencies in the body politic. Elsewhere in the new states, governments have promoted or insisted upon partnership with private capital in all major economic enterprises to ensure the regime's control over the decisions and credit for any success.

Even where economic planning and execution remain firmly in governmental hands, however, one may expect to find a new center of power created in the planning ministry, allied or not allied with the civil service against the party and regime. This would seem almost inevitable if economic development is to be given serious priority. On almost every level, the demands of economic efficiency are sure to conflict at some point with the demands of political expediency or orthodoxy. Since their independence, Indonesia and Ghana have continually faced such conflicts. This type of conflict was illustrated most dramatically in December, 1962, when the Senegalese party leaders felt obliged to remove the prime minister and dismantle the planning and administrative apparatus under his control when they seemed to threaten party primacy.

But this is a realm in which the single-party regime must tread lightly, for the outcome of the struggle for pre-eminence is not at all foreordained. The further development has gone, the more opposition the regime will arouse among the technically oriented younger elites if the party chooses to slow down or stop change as a means of maintaining political control. This has, of course, been particularly the case in Burma, Pakistan, and Sudan, where technical military elites have seized power from the politicians. . . .

In a somewhat broader perspective, the implementation of rapid economic and social change and, in particular, of educational development can open a whole range of new problems centered around controlling the burgeoning new elites. In part this is simply a qualitative problem. The promising young men who are trained after independence has been won will have quite different associations, perceptions, and preoccupations from those of their elders of the nationalist generation. Furthermore, since the nationalist generation is likely to come into power around age forty at the most, it is unlikely to fade from the scene so quickly as the new generation would like. On the other hand, the new generation is likely to have more formal education than its elders, particularly in technical domains. Also, since it will in all probability be trained abroad for the most part, it will escape the direct influence of the single-party regime during the crucial formative years of adolescence. It is not surprising that a recent survey of African students in France revealed that 63 per cent considered themselves in serious conflict with their governments.[4] After their return to home, one would naturally expect these young men to side with one of the alternative loci of power in the country, particularly if they are blocked, as they must be if the single-party regime's continuity is to be maintained, in their attempt to accede immediately to posts of high responsibility and power. This clash of interests was emphasized in Guinea in 1962, when several of the young intellectuals sought to impose their political vision on the single-party regime. In a direct confrontation, the party leaders jailed the intellectual leaders, recalled Guinean students from abroad, locked rebellious *lycée* students in their school, sent in the loyal party youth group, made up of the educationally underprivileged, to teach the students a lesson—something they did with considerable gusto. In this state, as in other new states, the regime has, in time of stress, tended to fall back on loyal, if uneducated, political cadres rather than on the new elites. Although this may be a proper response to a short-run problem, it may have adverse effects on long-run political development.

But the rapid creation of new elites has a quantitative dimension of equal importance. It is one thing to integrate smoothly ten, twenty, or fifty returning students a year into the single-party regime and to inculcate in them the established political values and perceptions, but it is quite another to integrate a hundred or five hundred, particularly if they cannot be given the positions of top leadership to which they aspire because their fathers or older brothers are reluctant

---

[4]J. P. N'Diaye, *Enquête sur les étudiants noirs en France* (Paris: Réalités Africaines, 1962), p. 223.

to step down. Without the clear necessity of pulling together to achieve independence and with a wider range of choices than faced the nationalist generation, these young men are unlikely to melt quietly into the previously established single-party regime. Nor are they so likely as were their elders to make the attempt to bridge the gap separating them from the masses, since by doing so they may only diminish the distinctiveness of their personal elite position without necessarily gaining corresponding political advantage. With no provisions for a loyal open opposition, a disloyal covert opposition may seem the only choice.

The emphasis on rapid social and economic change also poses problems for the single-party state on the level of the masses. If, through economic and social planning, one increases the rate of popular mobilization,[5] one also increases the demands made on the government. Although this mobilization is essential for building national sentiment among the masses, it may also threaten the regime if the government cannot keep pace with the new demands. Although in most cases this social mobilization was begun under the colonial regime, the colonial power was seldom attentive to these demands, even if it had been capable of responding. The nationalist single-party movement learned to be attentive to the masses' demands and used the colonial regime's reluctance to respond as an argument for seizing power. The independent single-party regime may continue to be attentive, but it is unlikely to possess the resources for responding effectively if mobilization proceeds at too great a pace. Alternatively, it may emphasize building an effective response capability by giving the younger technical elites their head and playing down the political party structure. But, in doing this, it may end by making the new regime less well attuned to the immediate wants of the mobilized and dissatisfied masses, thereby inadvertently re-creating a situation analogous to that of the colonial era. A rigid new bureaucracy, even if technically competent and filled with good intentions, may open the possibility of new popular revolts led, perhaps, by disaffected politicians of the older nationalist generation who have maintained their links with the masses. Such a conflict between a distant technical bureaucracy and politicians of the nationalist generation has been particularly acute in the new states where the military has seized power.[6]

The new states will increasingly be obliged to make some hard

---

[5]On the concept of mobilization, see Karl W. Deutsch, "Social Mobilization and Political Development," *American Political Science Review*, LV, No. 3 (1961), 493–514. [Reprinted in this reader, p. 153.]

[6]See Lucian W. Pye, "The Army in Burmese Politics," in John J. Johnson, ed., *The Role of the Military in Underdeveloped Countries* (Princeton: Princeton University Press, 1962), pp. 231–251.

long-range decisions for which the experience and habits acquired in the period of nationalist agitation will provide little guidance. Stated most baldly, the polar choices open to the new states hold terrors equal to those of Scylla and Charybdis. At one extreme, a state may choose to ride the tiger of exacerbated pluralism and possible internal strife and disintegration, and, at the other extreme, it may choose to restrain social and economic change to a level that can be handled by the existing political structures. Similarly, the new regimes face a choice between transforming themselves completely to the profit of the new post-nationalist elites, with the attendant danger of losing political attentiveness to popular demands and what remains of the prestige (and personnel) of the nationalist movement, and, on the other hand, constricting access to the political elite, with the possibilities of political stagnation and turning the younger generation of elites against the regime.

It is difficult to predict at what point a given regime will succeed in striking a balance between these extremes. In general, it would seem that the closer to either extreme a regime comes, the poorer its chance of maintaining political integrity and eventually building a nation. Long-run pressures, especially those of an economic sort, would seem to be on the side of a more pluralist political process permitting entry of at least some new elites into the legitimate political arena and associating at least some newly mobilized sectors of the population with these elites through structures more or less outside the existing single-party framework. If this increase in political and social pluralism does not seriously weaken central governmental authority and create focuses of loyalty that challenge the legitimacy of the nation itself, rather than just a particular group of leaders or a specific policy, the nation-building process should be considerably advanced. For such a dynamic compromise to be maintained over the long run, the existing regime in most of the newest states must first feel itself secure enough from disruptive internal and external pressures to permit it to accept the necessary loosening of direct political control. At least in the short run, most such regimes will require absolute loyalty from new elites and acquiescence from the population at large, if only as evidence that the state is firmly enough established to permit the nation to be built.

Ensuring the short-run stability of the new states has led many regimes into practices which appear particularly objectionable to most people with a liberal democratic tradition. The "cult of personality" built around the national hero, the mouthing of seemingly senseless revolutionary slogans after the apparent revolution has been won, and the suppression of opposition groups and leaders are among the practices most commonly noted in the Western press. Although the disadvantages of these practices are readily apparent—at least to the outside observer with no immediate policy responsibilities—they may also serve useful functions in permitting the regimes to survive the initial period of building the state and make a successful transition to building a nation. Popular identification with a national hero and commitment to a revolutionary program, whether or not confined purely to the verbal level, both have the advantage of dissociating the state from a particular group of individuals making up the nationalist regime and permitting the people at large or new elites to serve and identify with a specific leader or set of policies. The national hero can retain not only the loyalty of the mass of the people, who are perhaps annoyed at specific government agents for specific causes, but can also go against his own lieutenants and bring new elites into the regime. Both Nasser and Nkrumah have used their positions in this way. Similarly, concentration on some sort of ideology, even if only symbolic, permits popular recognition of particular governmental functions above and beyond the specific individuals fulfilling those functions. At the same time, it holds up a national goal for younger elites to follow, and, by their acceptance of such a goal, they may more easily be brought into smoothly-functioning relationships with the incumbent elite.

Finally, the suppression of opposition leaders, and even of some of the new elites, may, with luck, permit the new states to get over the most trying period of postrevolutionary letdown without a collapse of the ruling regime, either through internal bickering or outside attacks. To the extent that the new state concentrates on building a more continuous educational system at home and to the extent that it has time to indoctrinate the younger elites in loyalty to the new political order, succeeding elites should pose fewer problems to the regime than does the immediate postrevolutionary generation.

The ability of the newest states to grow out of their initial periods of restrictive consolidation of power and into a more balanced society-wide pattern of national growth will depend in part on the willingness of the leaders to envisage fundamental revisions in the relations between the regime and its people and also on whether the adoption of less restrictive policies brings with it sufficient rewards to make the risk of pluralism worth taking. Certainly, if economic and social development seem impossible no matter what course of action is adopted or if the nations in the best position to assist a new state turn a deaf ear to a regime's initial pleas for assistance, the sterile pattern of repression, stagnation, and revolt will become the lot of most states. Instead of profiting from the West's arduous history of nation-building, the newest nations may then be condemned to repeat the long apprenticeship of "coups, conquests, revolutions, and wars" before they, too, evolve viable national societies.

FOR FURTHER READING

HARRY J. BENDA, "Non-Western Intelligentsias as Political Elites" (*Australian Journal of Politics and History*, VI, 2, November 1960, 205-218)

MORROE BERGER, *Bureaucracy and Society in Modern Egypt* (Princeton: Princeton University Press, 1957)

RALPH BRAIBANTI, "The Civil Service of Pakistan: A Theoretical Analysis" (*South Atlantic Quarterly*, LVIII, 2, Spring 1959, 258-304)

JOHN FRIEDMANN, "Intellectuals in Developing Societies" (*Kyklos*, XIII, 4, [1960], 513-544)

JOSEPH LA PALOMBARA, *Bureaucracy and Political Development* (Princeton: Princeton University Press, 1963)

WILLIAM H. LEWIS, "Traditional and Emerging Elites," in William H. Lewis, ed., *Emerging Africa* (Washington: Public Affairs Press, 1963), pp. 1-11

GEORGE E. LICHTBLAU, "The Politics of Trade Union Leadership in Southern Asia" (*World Politics*, VII, 1, October 1954, 84-101)

KHALID B. SAYEED, "The Political Role of Pakistan's Civil Service" (*Pacific Affairs*, XXXI, 2, June 1958, 131-146)

EDWARD SHILS, "The Intellectuals in the Political Development of the New States" (*World Politics*, XII, 3, April 1960, 329-368)

AN ESSAY ON THE POLITICAL FUNCTIONS OF CORRUPTION

James C. Scott

Is corruption directly linked to particular stages of economic development? Professor Scott suggests that corruption in new states may not
differ substantially in extent from that in Western states earlier in
their economic growth. Corruption provides a useful measure of the
disjunctions between the social system and the formal political system
—and may reduce the likelihood of violence.

INTRODUCTION

Most discussions of corruption in developing nations have generated vast quantities of heat and righteous indignation while shedding
little light on the phenomenon itself. Observers from Western nations,
often quite oblivious of their own recent history, have contributed more
than their share to the resulting confusion and moralizing. Only recently
have a handful of American and English economists and political scientists
—profiting perhaps from their respective nations' long experience in
this area—begun to examine corruption, in a more systematic, dispas-
sionate, and comparative manner.[1]

In this new spirit an attempt is made here to examine in some
detail the political functions of corruption. Before plunging in, however,
we must have a working definition of corruption, a difficult task in view
of the immense variety of entrepreneurial skill which has been devoted
to its actual practice. Profiting from the definitional efforts of J. S. Nye,
we may, with one caveat, subscribe to the statement that, "Corruption is
behavior which deviates from the formal duties of a public role because

From *Asian Studies*, Vol. V, No. 3 (1967), pp. 501–23, by permission.

[1]See for example, Nathaniel Leff, "Economic Development Through Bureau-
cratic Corruption," *The American Behavioral Scientist* (November, 1964), pp. 8–14; J. S.
Nye, "Corruption and Political Development, A Cost-Benefit Analysis," *The American
Political Science Review* (June, 1967), pp. 417–427; Ronald Wraith and Edgar Simkins,
Corruption in Developing Countries (London: Oxford U. Press, 1963); and Robert K.
Merton, *Social Theory and Social Structure*. (Glencoe, Ill.: Free Press, 1949), pp. 71–81.

of private regarding (personal, close family, private clique) pecuniary or status gains; or violates rules against the exercise of certain types of private-regarding influence."[2] The only problem with this definition is that with the meaning it attaches to the term, "private regarding," it seems to exclude illegal favors done without reward by public officials on behalf of, say, their ethnic or religious group. Perhaps the term "non-public" would be more appropriate here as it includes, within the definition, deviations which favor longer groupings. With this qualification, the term covers most of what is meant when people speak of corruption among public officials. It includes behavior ranging from a peasant's minute payment to the government hospital orderly so that he might be examined by the physician more quickly to a large firm's generous contribution to a politician in return for his fiddling with the tax laws to its advantage. It includes not only favors done for cash, but illegal favors done for motives of loyalty or kinship.

About the actual causes of corruption we shall have very little to say except as they touch on its political function. But one point should be clear; while there may well be a greater incidence of *illegal* corrupt acts in the developing nations than in the West at a similar stage of economic development, *there is no reason to suppose that the actual behavior we are referring to*—forgetting for a moment its legal status—*is any more widespread in the new nations than in the West at a comparable epoch.* Judgments which imply otherwise are not simply cases of Westerners forgetting their own past and wagging their fingers at developing nations. The misunderstanding is usually more subtle and involves: a) a failure to compare legal systems at analogous periods and b) a failure to distinguish between the private and public sectors.[3]

1. *The gap between the legal system and social practice:* The development of the legal system in most Western nations was a more or less internal affair. At any given time, there were a host of governmental and non-governmental practices the legal standing of which had not yet been determined. In Great Britain, for example, before civil service reforms were instituted a tremendous number of sinecures—"officers without employment"—and pensions were distributed or sold by the crown. Although even contemporary observers called this corruption,[4] such patronage did not contravene any existing law until the Whigs found it to their political advantage to pass one.

---

[2]J. S. Nye, *op. cit.*, p. 419.
[3]See Wraith and Simkins, *op. cit.*, pp. 12, 13.
[4]See John Wade, *The Black Book*, (1820) cited in J.F.C. Harrison, ed., *Society and Politics in England: 1780–1960* (New York: Harper, 1965), pp. 93–98.

The new nations, by contrast, have often adopted a system of laws and general orders which give expression to reforms which were the product of long political struggle in the West. Consequently, the Malaysian politician, for example, finds himself denied much of the patronage which helped build strong political parties in England and the United States. Acts which were at one stage in Britain or the U.S. quite legal, or at least legally ambiguous, are now expressly forbidden by the laws and regulations of new nations. The behavior is the same in each case, but the legal status of the act has made corruption seem more widespread in developing areas.[5]

2. *Private morality and public morality:* It is quite obvious that, *even today the standards of behavior for the public sector are more puritanical than those of the private sector.* The president of a business firm may appoint his inept son assistant vice president and, although he may regret the appointment from a financial point of view and be accused of bad taste, he is quite within the limits of the law. Similarly, if he lets an overpriced supply contract to a close friend, the market may punish him but not the law. Should a politician Smith or bureaucrat Smith feel inclined likewise, however, he is likely to find himself without office and perhaps the object of the State-vs-Smith criminal action.

Whether a given act takes place within the public or private sector thus makes all the difference in the world as to whether it is defined legally as corruption or not. Restraints in the one case are the responsibility of law enforcement agencies and, in the other, it is the discipline of the market which checks such behavior. The point here is simply that *the larger the relative size and scope of the public sector, the greater is the proportion of certain acts which will be legally considered corrupt. And this is precisely the case in new nations where the role of the public sector is comparatively more important than it was in the West.* Many of the acts which we are considering took place within the confines of the private sector in developed nations and therefore fell outside the formal definition of corruption. By contrast, the public sector's size in developing areas changes what were private concerns in the West into public concerns, making the incidence of corruption—legally defined—that much greater.

The restrictiveness of the legal system and the expansion of the public sector, then, turn what might otherwise be simply bad taste or stupidity into corruption. But we should keep in mind that the incidence

---

[5] In fact, many new nations regulate public appointments in a more stringent manner than nations like the U.S. If a Nigerian were told about the political considerations involved in the appointments of postmasters in America he would undoubtedly call it corruption. The fact that it is now institutionalized, "legal" patronage and accepted practice would not change his view of it.

of such behavior in the national community as a whole may well have been as high or higher in the West than in the new nations although its legal status is vastly different.[6]

INPUT INFLUENCE-VS-OUTPUT INFLUENCE

1. The Distortion of Formal Analysis

By now political scientists are well acquainted with a growing body of theoretical and empirical literature which examines the process by which interest groups influence legislation. The strategies of influence, the nature of the relationship between elected officials and pressure groups, and the independent effects of the legislative process itself are among the subjects in this area which have received considerable scrutiny. Using the common distinction between input and output functions, the studies referred to are concerned with a portion of the input functions of a political system.

In contrast to the well developed structures for interest articulation and aggregation found in industrialized Western nations, students who have attempted similar analyses in less developed nations have encountered slim pickings indeed. The picture which has emerged from such attempts most often emphasizes: 1) the lack of subjective civic competence which inhibits the expression of demands; 2) the weakness of interest structures which might organize and clarify previously inchoate interests; and 3) the relative absence of institutionalized forms through which political demands might be communicated to political decision-makers. In this context, *the weakness of interest structures when coupled with the personalistic character of political loyalty allows national leaders to formulate policy free from many of the restraints imposed by party interest groups in the Western setting.*[7]

Even given competitive elections, then, the very weakness of political interest structures means that demands originating outside elite circles will not have nearly the degree of influence on legislation which they do in more highly organized political systems. As far as it goes, this seems to be an accurate analysis. It would be a grave mistake, how-

---

[6]One further distorting factor concerns the greater attention paid to corruption at the national level. In the West, although there are wide differences here, local and/or state governments were more powerful than they are in developing areas generally, and a great deal of the total "volume" of corruption took place at this level. By comparison then, the national governments in the West may have seemed less corrupt than in the new nations since local units were an equally attractive source of plunder in the West.

[7]See Lucian W. Pye, *Politics, Personality and Nation Building: Burma's Search for Identity* (New Haven: Yale University Press, 1962), pp. 19, 26, 27.

ever, to assume that because legislation is often drawn up in an atmosphere free from the organized pressure of interest groups, that therefore the public has little or no effect on the eventual "output" of government.

My point is simply that much of the interest articulation in the new states has been disregarded because Westerners, accustomed to their own polities, have been looking in the wrong place. A sizeable proportion of individual, and occasionally group, demands in less developed nations reach the political system, not before laws are passed, but rather at the enforcement stage. Influence before legislation is passed is generally called "pressure-group politics" and is the frequent object of examination by political scientists: influence at the enforcement stage is generally called "corruption" and has seldom been treated as the alternative means of interest articulation which it in fact constitutes.

2. Rational Impulses to Corruption

The peasants who avoid their land taxes by making a smaller and illegal payment which supplements the Assistant District Officers' disposable income, are as surely influencing policy outcomes as they would if they formed a peasant union and agitated for the reduction of land taxes. In a similar fashion, businessmen who protect their black market sales by buying   protection   from   civil servants   are   changing   policy outcomes as effectively as they might by working as a pressure group through Chambers of Commerce for an end to government price controls. A strong case can be made as well that, within the context of certain political systems, *it may be more "rational"—and here we use the term "rational" in its economizing sense—to protect one's interests when laws are being implemented rather than when they are still being debated by politicians.* Three examples of situations in which corruption may well conserve scarce resources are suggested below:

a. Where organizational skills are scarce and where, as a result, interest group associations are either weak or non-existent, the corruption of law enforcement may be a more economizing way to exert influence over policy outcomes. The divisive loyalties of peasants to their ethnic, village, religious or caste grouping create enormous organizational barriers which all but preclude their induction into an association which would seek to advance their interests *qua* peasants. Given this situation, it is more rational for the individual peasant or for the peasants of one village, say, to influence the laws which disadvantage them by bribing local government officials.

b. Where legislative acts tend to be formalistic—where the administration of law is so loose and erratic that existing law has little relation to eventual governmental outputs, it may well be more rational to make demands known at the enforcement stage than at the legislative stage. Businessmen in a developing nation may realize that, although the government has passed what they consider to be an unfair tax law, their actual administration bears little or no resemblance to what is called for by the statutes. This may occur because enforcement personnel are unwilling or unable to follow its directives or because politicians do not allow them to. Under the circumstances, it may make more sense for each firm to "buy" precisely what it needs in terms of enforcement rather than financing a campaign to press for a new law that would be as formalistic as the present one.

　　c. Where a minority is discriminated against politically and regarded more as a "subject" than a "citizen" group by the general population, its members may well feel that pressure group action would destroy what little political credit they enjoy and thus turn to the corruption of enforcement officials to avoid damaging political attacks from more powerful groups. Throughout much of Southeast Asia and East Africa, a large proportion of commerce and industry is in the hands of groups which, even if they have managed to acquire local citizenship, are considered as aliens by large sections of the local population. It would be foolish, even suicidal in some cases, for these so-called "pariah" capitalists to seek influence openly as an organized pressure group. A healthy regard for their property and skin alike forces them as a group to rely upon illegal payments to strategically placed bureaucrats if they are to safeguard their economic interests.

　　At least two of the conditions (a and c above) under which influence at the enforcement stage becomes "rational" are oft-cited characteristics of the less developed nations.[8] We have already remarked on the relative absence of associational interest groups which might bring the demands of their constituency to bear on the legislative process. Quite by itself this deficiency in organization makes the resort to corruption a rational strategy for many. And in underdeveloped areas there are groups which are virtually denied access to the open political area whether for ethnic reasons (the Chinese in Southeast Asia) or for ideological reasons (the private business sector in nations where the political elite champions public sector enterprise) or both, who thus exert their influence via more informal routes or else forego the effort to shape policy altogether.

---

[8]The remaining situation (b) where, because the laws are formalistic, influence at the enforcement stage would be more rational is fairly common among new nations, but not so general that one could call it "characteristic".

The reader will note, however, that the specified conditions under which it would be rational—other things equal—to seek influence at the enforcement stage have applied only to the seeker (buyer) of influence. The ultimate success of the transaction, of course, depends on the bureaucrat(s) or politician(s) in question. Provided that the civil servants' concern for the law or the nation at large does not impose restraints upon him,[9] we may say that the probability of him refusing, say a bribe, will be equal to the product of the probability of being punished times the severity of the penalty if punished.[10] Thus a severe penalty coupled with a very small probability of being caught and punished is roughly equivalent in its disincentive effects as a quite small penalty coupled to a high probability of being found out. Looking at things from the government side for a moment, then, there are *three factors at work determining the probability of corruption* (assuming the value of the reward to be constant) :

1. *The extent to which loyalty to the law, to the government, or to the nation has become a private value.*
2. *The probability of being caught.*
3. *The severity of the penalty if caught.*

As regards the initial factor, *the growth of concern for the national community, law, or to government policy* per se *is a slow process* and, although such concern has begun to take root quite firmly in many new nations, the leaders of these nations would be the first to concede that it has not yet rendered their civil establishments immune to corruption. The crucial importance of whether one's loyalties are engaged or not can be seen by the fact that corruption by the officials of clan associations among the Chinese of Southeast Asia or of tribal associations in Dakar or Kinshasa is rare in comparison with corruption among public servants in the same areas.[11] In the one case group loyalties are firmly engaged and in the other, group loyalties are less strongly at work. *Given the predominance of familial and parochial loyalties in the less developed areas, restraints, for the short-run at least, are often more a function of the penalties involved and the likelihood of being apprehended.* In most new nations the penalties are quite severe—involving at least the loss of

---

[9] The value of the "reward" for a corrupt act is the other factor here, but we are assuming, for the moment, a "constant" reward.

[10] Similar restraints are of course applicable to the case of the "buyer" of influence too, although we have thus far assumed the buyer to be a pure *homo economicus*.

[11] See Ronald Wraith and Edgar Simkins, *Corruption in Developing Countries* (London: Allen and Unwin Ltd., 1963), p. 50.

a relatively secure, high-paying, high-status post and, at most, loss of life. The probability of being apprehended, however, although it varies considerably from nation to nation, is generally quite low. The disincentive effects of severe penalties are therefore largely vitiated by the small likelihood of prosecution.

Under the circumstances we have described—circumstances which apply to most developing nations— it is not only rational for individuals and groups to seek influence at the enforcement stage but it is also rational for government officials to admit such influence.

CORRUPTION AND THE PROCESS OF POLITICAL INCLUSION

In a piece that challenges many of the assumptions commonly held by students of *political development,* Samuel Huntington proposes an alternative theory of *political decay.*[12] Briefly put, Huntington's argument is that the rapid social mobilization—urbanization, politicization, etc.—characteristic of new nations has placed an all but impossible burden on their new and frail political institutions and has led to the decline of political competition, political instability, national disintegration, corruption, and institutional decay. The new nations are, accordingly, "buying rapid social modernization at the price of political degeneration."[13]

I would like to suggest, however, that what we have called *corruption represents an effort—albeit informal—of the political system to cope with a rate of social change which chokes the formal channels of political influence.* Thus we can view corruption as an *index* of the disjunction between the social system and the formal political system; a subversive effort by the social system to bend the political system to its demands. In fact, the extent and variety of corruption in a new nation is a fairly accurate reflection of the failure of the formal political system to aggregate and meet the demands of important sectors of the society. Groups or individuals who seek influence through corruption have what they feel are essential interests which the open political system has failed to meet or perhaps even regards as illegitimate. In this way corruption supplements the capacity of a formal political system which is unable to process demands created by social mobilization.

The fact of corruption means that, while the formal political system may seem rigid and restrictive, the informal political system represented by corruption may add a substantial openness and flexibility to ultimate policy outputs. Political competitiveness may, if you will,

[12]Samuel P. Huntington, "Political Development and Political Decay," reprinted in this reader, p. 238.
[13]*Ibid.*

TABLE I. GROUPS AND THEIR MEANS OF ACCESS TO THE
POLITICAL SYSTEM IN LESS DEVELOPED NATIONS

Granted Access to Formal Political System	Groups Resorting to Informal (Corrupt) Political System Because Denied Formal Access by virtue of:		
	Ideological Reasons	Parochial Reasons	Lack of Organization
a. Political elites	a. Indigenous business groups	a. Minority ethnic or religious groups	a. Unorganized peasants
b. Party branches			
c. Civil servant ass'ns	b. Foreign business interests		b. Unorganized urban lower classes
d. Professional ass'ns	c. Political opposition		
e. Trade unions			

enter unobtrusively through the back door. An empirical assessment of the interests represented by policy outputs would be quite inadequate if it stopped at the content of laws and failed to ask in what direction and to what extent corruption in fact altered the implementation of policy. The table below is an effort to distinguish between those groups which achieve access to political influence via the formal political system and those groups which, for a variety of reasons, must enter the competition at a more informal level.

This categorization is rather sketchy and cannot do complete justice to any single developing nation but it is sufficiently descriptive of the situation in most to alert us to the variety of interests which make their surreptitious way through the political back door. Aside from those groups which are blocked from formal participation by ideological reasons—and which are often well organized—the formal political system is *par excellence* the domain, the monopoly, of the modern social sector. *The very nature of the formal political system places the unorganized and the minority communities at a tremendous disadvantage* such that their interests are seldom represented in the content of legislation. *This imbalance is, if not rectified, at least mitigated by the influence at the enforcement stage which constitutes virtually the only access to the political system afforded these groups.* Thus corruption serves as an important corrective to the competitive advantage enjoyed by the modern sector in a formally modern political system.

CORRUPTION AS AN ALTERNATIVE TO VIOLENCE

As we have indicated, the incidence of corruption in a developing nation is one indicator of a lack of integration in the formal political system. To the extent that corruption admits important interests which are blocked from formal participation, we may say that it seems as a deterrent to politically motivated violence.[14]

The political history of the West is rich in occasions where the timeliness of corruption allowed a new group to secure a measure of influence denied them by the formal political system and thereby diverted them from what might have become revolutionary pursuits into more mundane calculations of advantage. England may well owe the relatively peaceful inclusion of her bourgeoisie to the venality of her public officials while in France, on the other hand, the relative efficiency of the centralized bureaucracy under the monarchy left open only the revolutionary path to political power. Fattened by the West Indian trade, the British *nouveaux riches* were able to outbid rural landlords for seats in Parliament and to secure, by bribery, the conditions under which commerce might flourish. Urban and rural capitalists in France were less fortunate in this regard and resorted to a successful frontal assault on the system itself.[15]

In a similar vein, the corruption of the big city machines secured a measure of influence for the European immigrants who arrived in the United States in the late 19th and early 20th centuries. In return for their political support of the machine boss the newly arrived received patronage employment, favored treatment in court, and loans and welfare payments which were often quite outside the bounds of strict legality. Thus groups which might have otherwise become susceptible to more radical, not to say revolutionary, doctrines were effectively domesticated and given a stake in the system.[16]

Much of what we have said about the West is true as well for underdeveloped areas: the villagers who have recently arrived in the cities of West Africa, the Chinese or Indian businessman in Southeast Asia, have all been attached, in greater or lesser degree, to the informal political system which attempts to meet their needs and demands. Corruption acts on these groups as essentially a conservative force which, by granting them influence over policy outputs, weds them more firmly to the political system and dilutes the impulse toward more radical solutions. In this limited sense, then, corruption is also a democratizing

---

[14]Cf. Martin C. Needler, "The Political Development of Mexico," *American Political Science Review* (June, 1961), pp. 308–312.

[15]Nathaniel Leff, "Economic Development through Bureaucratic Corruption," *The American Behavioral Scientist* (November, 1964), pp. 8–14.

[16]For one group, and an important one, widespread corruption may well increase political alienation and the attractiveness of radical solution. The urban, Westernized, middle class have often incorporated current Western notions of governmental probity and are thus likely to view corruption as a symptom of the nation's moral turpitude. The same comment might apply to a lesser extent to the military officer corps.

TABLE II. A POLITICAL SYSTEM'S CAPACITY FOR INTEGRATION DEMANDS OVER TIME

Non-Integration	Informal Integration	Formal Integration
Violence — — — —→ Corruption — — — —→		Constitutionality (i.e. institutionalization of demands)
e.g. Congo	Thailand	England/USSR

influence inasmuch as it allows for the participation of interest groups beyond what the formal political system alone can presently manage.

Referring again to Huntington's theory of political decay, it would perhaps be more accurate to *look at corruption as a sort of half-way house between violence and constitutionality, a means by which some of the new demands produced by rapid social change are accommodated within a political system whose formal institutions are inadequate to the task.* If the concept of political development includes the capacity of a political system to respond to new demands in such a way as to reduce the potential for violence, then corruption and political development are not at all incompatible. Viewing corruption from this angle, the following paradigm might represent an appropriate developmental sequence.

Any existing political system will, of course, exhibit all three tendencies and one must ask by what means the *preponderance* of political conflict is managed. Thus, within the United States, one can find violence where the demands of Negroes are frustrated and corruption as the avenue by which illegal gambling and prostitution are represented,[17] but the preponderance of political demands are now processed at the formal, institutional level.

When violence becomes less common in a political system, corruption often becomes more common. The relationship is not simply fortuitous, but rather represents the substitution of bargaining for raw contests of strength. In this context, one might say that in England violence was beginning to give way to corruption around the period of the Glorious Revolution and that corruption became less prominent than institutional politics by the reform period of the 1830's. In the United States the apogee of violence represented by the Civil War—where fellow citizens slew one another on a scale not equalled before or since—gave way to corruption of similarly Texas style proportions through the 1880's and 90's and well into the first portion of the 20th century.

---

[17]As the growth of a nation's political institutions continues, much of the residual corruption represents the effort of business interests which are *per se* illegal, such as gambling and prostitution in the U.S., to protect themselves from prosecution.

It is important to understand that the conservative effects of corruption are a direct consequence of the fact that corruption places influence in the hands of individuals and groups which are most likely to be non-participants in the formal political system,[18] that is, *corruption is conservative to the degree it is democratizing.* In spite of the fact that corruption is often particularistic—dispensing favors to certain sections of the community more than others—and that when it is not particularistic it usually benefits wealth elites more than other groups, *the question is historically not one of choosing between the formal political system and corruption. Either because of their lack of organization or their outright exclusion from formal influence by the dominant elites, the groups which acquire influence at the enforcement stage are exercising the only means of influence open to them. Thus the choice is usually between no access or else limited, imperfect access which corruption at least provides.*

POLITICAL ADJUSTMENT BY SELF-INTEREST

The question of loyalties sheds further light on the function of corruption. In most developing nations the loyalties of the great proportion of citizens are restricted largely to parochial groupings and to close kinsmen. In the absence of the wider loyalties which would facilitate both the growth of effective parties and a measure of consensus on national goals, a system of political influence which emphasizes narrow self-interest—and corruption does precisely this—may well succeed in producing a degree of cooperation that would otherwise not be possible.[19] The "man in the street" in Bangkok or Bogota cares a good deal less whether the actions of the politician or bureaucrat conform to standards of due process than whether the outcomes benefit him or not. What is suggested here is that the *system of self-interest represented by corruption is perhaps the only viable basis of political adjustment during the early stages of political development when narrow loyalties predominate.* Later, the growth of wider loyalties leads to an increase of participation in the formal political system and a consequent decline in the level of corruption.

---

[18]One must, of course, assess the openness and effectiveness of the informal political system as well. Often some groups are excluded from both the formal *and* informal channels of influence, a problem we shall examine later.
    [19]David Greenstone suggested this in his article, "Corruption and Self Interest in Kampala and Nairobi," *Comparative Studies in Society and History* (January, 1966), p. 208. "The crucial function of self interest in politics is to replace a mutual dedication to the goals of 'good government' with a mutual if more selfish loyalty to a system of specific material incentives. Some of the decline in political capacity is offset by a modified and politicized version of the invisible hand."

Where the interests of one's family dwarf wider loyalties[20] and where political and economic life are seen as a zero-sum game, then, the cement which binds a group together must come from the individual rewards each receives by virtue of his participation. Operating in such circumstances, political parties in new nations are generally not so suicidal as to assume a high degree of loyalty to the political system *per se* or to modest interest groups. If a competitive political party wishes either to maintain or enlarge its basis of support it will of necessity have to turn to those inducements which motivate a good portion of its cadre and those whose electoral support it hopes to attract. In this setting, the resort to particularistic rewards (including patronage, exemption from prosecution, contracts, and land grants) is quite understandable. Some of these rewards can be distributed quite legally (through the "pork barrel", for example, in the Philippines) but many must be obtained in a less formal manner. In the short run, competitive political parties are more likely to respond to the incentives which motivate their clientele than to alter the nature of those incentives. Thus, as long as the circumstances we have described persist, political competition will always be associated with a certain amount of corruption.

WHO BENEFITS MOST?

A. Parochial-vs-Market Corruption

Determining which groups benefit from corruption is quite a complex task. One might begin by recognizing that most corruption involves the trading of a resource like wealth or family connections for power; that is, it involves the "purchase" of an authoritative governmental decision by some individual or group not legally entitled to enter into such a transaction. Both the buyer and the seller benefit in this "black market government"[21] since the buyer pays something less than what he estimates the benefits of the decision to be for him, while the power-holder, as a monopolist, charges what the traffic will bear and at least enough to compensate himself for the risks he runs.

Aside from the power-holder, be he politician or bureaucrat, who always benefits as a necessary partner in the transaction, the nature of the beneficiary depends to a great extent on whether the power holder is motivated more strongly by parochial loyalties to kinsmen, friends,

[20] . . . . "Amoral Familism," to use Banfield's term, Cf., *The Moral Basis of a Backward Society* (Chicago: The Free Press, 1958).

[21] A term borrowed from Robert O. Tilman's unpublished paper, "Administrative Corruption: An Interpretation".

or ethnic group or whether he is more impersonal and market oriented. Both play a role—sometimes simultaneously when say a politician will only do favors for his ethnic group but nonetheless exacts from them what he can in terms of cash, goods, or services. *To the extent that parochial considerations predominate, however, the beneficiaries will be those with "connections" such as kinship, friendship, ethnicity, etc. Where market considerations prevail, on the other hand, wealth elites will benefit more since they are in a position to make the most lucrative bids.* The two by two table below illustrates the relationship we have just discussed.

TABLE III.

Type of Corruption	Major Beneficiary
1. "Parochial"	Individuals and groups with "connections"
2. "Market"	Individuals and groups with wealth

South Vietnam under Diem would tend to fall in the "parochial" category given the favoritism shown northern Catholics, the Philippines would approach the "market" variety of corruption, while Thailand would have to be termed a "mixed" system.

B.   Political Competition and the Beneficiaries of Corruption

Two other important factors which determine who profits from corruption are the balance of political-vs-bureaucratic power within the polity and the degree to which politics is competitive in the electoral sense.

In the table we assume that realistically those persons and groups closely identified with members of the ruling elite will always profit to some extent from corruption. If corruption exists at all, it will be difficult to deny the persuasive claims of family and friends.

The probable patterning of rewards for each type of political system is explained at greater length below:

1. *Where parties are either weak or non-existent and where the bureaucrats—perhaps in league with the military—dominate, it is clear that bureaucrats and wealth elites will be the chief recipients of corruption's fruits.* This pattern is typical of Thailand where the reigning military/bureaucratic elite is relieved of electoral anxieties and where non-parochial corruption consequently centers largely around payments made by local and foreign business concerns to secure licenses, tax relief, government contracts, etc.

TABLE IV. LEVEL OF BENEFITS FROM CORRUPTION BY SOCIAL GROUP AND TYPE OF REGIME

	Recipients of Benefits and Type of Regime e.g. Indiv. & Groups with Parochial Connections to Elite	Wealth Elites	Bureaucrats	Party Leaders Cadre	Voters
1. Bureaucracy Polity (non-traditional— Thailand)	x	X	X		
Type of Regime 2. Party-dominated Polity non-competitive—Tunisia	x	x	x	X	
3. Party-dominated Polity competitive-Philippines	x	X	x	X	X
investment/consumption/ orientation	Uncertain	Investment	Uncertain	Uncertain	Consumption

Large X's indicate the probable major beneficiaries of corruption in each type of regime, while small x's indicate minor beneficiaries.

The bureaucracy-dominated polity and the sort of corruption which characterizes it are becoming, if anything, increasingly common as the decline of political parties coupled with a restive officer corps and a strong central bureaucracy conspire to create them. New nations such as Pakistan, Indonesia, Ghana, Burma, Dahomey, and perhaps even Nigeria, to mention but a few, fall into this classification at present.

2. Non-competitive, party-dominated regimes often have a strong ideological cast and a program for national reconstruction which has led some analysts to refer to them as "movement" regimes. Although the durability of such regimes is now rather questionable, Tunisia, Tanzania, Kenya and precoup Ghana, come to mind as examples of this system of government.

The need of such regimes to strengthen the party as the engine of economic and social change means that, *to the extent corruption exists, a portion of its benefits will flow to party cadre and supporters.*[22] Whereas

[22]To the degree such regimes are successful in creating national loyalty they will most likely reduce the *overall* level of corruption, although the direction of benefits will remain as we have indicated.

for the bureaucratic regime only parochial considerations are likely to interfere with "market" corruption, for the "movement" regime, the need to build the party organization also becomes a factor in determining who gets what. Virtually, by definition, a larger portion of corruption in a non-competitive party-dominated system is processed by the party elite with the bureaucracy becoming, as it were, a junior partner.

In actual practice during the 20th century, "movement" regimes have generally been motivated by socialist preferences for the public sector. The greater their success in propagating this doctrine, the less likely it is that wealth elites in the private sector will profit from corruption.

3. *Political systems dominated by competitive parties further widen the range of beneficiaries of corruption to include the voters themselves.* When elections are hard fought, those who control votes possess a power resource as surely as those who control wealth and can thus bargain in the informal political system. The access of wealth elites to the fruits of corruption is as evident in this regime as in a bureaucratic one and perhaps even greater since parties and politicians must have bonds for campaign purposes. But unlike the bureaucratic regime where there is no particular reason for the power holder to disburse his proceeds, the politicians in a competitive political system have great incentives to distribute a portion of their gains in buying votes and/or doing illegal favors for those who control votes which may influence the outcome of elections. Thus the competitive party regime, although it may encourage a greater amount of corruption, includes voters and vote brokers within the range of beneficiaries simply because the electoral process places bargaining resources in their hands.[23]

The outstanding example of this system and the corruption which typifies it is the Philippines, while nations such as Ceylon, Malaysia, Uruguay, Chile, Colombia, and Venezuela are possible candidates for inclusion here too. In the Philippines, which boasts the world's highest *per capita* cost for electoral campaigns, businessmen have easy access to politicians, and, the powerful "sugar bloc" virtually provides salaries for a certain number of senators and congressmen who protect its interests. The very competitiveness of the system, however, means that politicians find it useful to buy votes or perform illegal favors for local influentials.

What occurs in the Philippines is quite comparable to what happened in England, particularly before legislation against rotten boroughs, or in the immigrant choked cities of the U.S. Furthermore, one can

---

[23]This is not to say that wealth elites or bureaucrats profit less *in an absolute sense* from corruption since the level of corruption could, hypothetically, be so much higher than in another system that both groups might have higher absolute gains.

already see in the Philippines the growth of institutionalized means to reward voters and the consequent decline of more particularistic, illegal rewards—a process already experienced in much of the West. Two mechanisms are notable in this respect: first, pork-barrel legislation which enables the politician to channel employment, goods, and services to his constituents and remain within the law; and second, a legal patronage system which allows the successful candidate in the ruling party to nominate a number of his supporters for positions in the executive branch.[24]

The transfer of rewards from the informal to the formal political system—from illegality to legality—in this fashion presupposes certain changes in the nature of the electorate. For one thing, many of the rewards of "pork-barrel" legislation include indivisible benefits such as schools and public works and thus require a measure of community identification since voters must see themselves sharing in the gains of the entire community.[25] A system of legal rewards, in addition, necessitates a higher level of trust between voters and new candidates because pork-barrel funds and legal patronage can only be distributed after the nominee has won election while under pre-election bribery, the voter is paid off before he casts his ballot. Inasmuch as the transformation from outright corruption to the institutionalized rewards we have described requires the growth of both wider loyalties and political trust, we would not be inaccurate to describe it as a step in political development.

ECONOMIC GROWTH AND THE BENEFICIARIES OF CORRUPTION

The relative success or failure of a nation to achieve a high rate of economic growth depends on a host of factors beside corruption. The motivation of the ruling elite, the skills and resources at its disposal, and its capacity for carrying out agreed policies are more central to the question of capital formation than corruption. Nevertheless, corruption may have some independent influence on economic growth which merits examination.

A. Non-Distortive Corruption

Here it is useful to distinguish between corruption which distorts formal government policy, as it generally does, and corruption which has no appreciable effect on policy. In the latter category we would include

---

[24]See Gregoria A. Francisco and Paul de Guzman, "The 50–50 Agreement: A Political Administrative Case," *Philippine Journal of Public Administration* (October, 1960), pp. 328–347. The institutionalized political appointment of local postmasters and the nomination of cadets to the armed forces academies are instances of the same process in the United States.

[25]The conditions of "amoral familism" in the Southern Italian town Banfield, *(op. cit.,)* describes would render the pork-barrel an ineffective means of winning voter support.

what might be called "payments for speed". Such "speed money" may either add economic growth or have no effect on it, but only rarely would such corruption have a negative influence on growth. The citizen who pays a small illegal fee to a government clerk to receive his radio license more quickly is probably having no influence on economic activity.[26] Government policy is not changed since the citizen would have received his license anyway after, say, a half hour wait. On the other hand, the business firm which bribes a civil servant to secure a license to begin operation without a lengthy wait has decided that the wait would cost it more than the "bakshish" or "dash" needed to avoid such a delay. Providing the firm's calculations are accurate in this respect, corruption here has a net beneficial effect on the rate of economic growth.

B.   Distortive Corruption: The Private Sector

Most of what we call corruption, however, involves not merely a payment for speed but a real distortion of official government policy. The peasant who bribes to avoid his taxes and the businessman who receives an overpriced contract through a highly placed relative are both changing government policy: the peasant escapes his legal tax obligation and the entrepreneur secures a contract he would not otherwise be granted.

If we are interested in economic growth this "distortive" type of corruption impels us to ask whether the policy which results from such corruption is more likely to contribute to economic growth than the original governmental policy which is being distorted. *Here again the distinction between "parochial" and "market" corruption is central.* In the case of parochial corruption, only an examination of the marginal propensity to save of groups with "connections" will begin to reveal whether this distortion will promote economic growth more than formal government policy. There is some evidence, however, that "market" corruption, inasmuch as it benefits wealth elites, is likely to have a greater multiplier effect than the formal economic policy of most new nations.

The case for market corruption can be made persuasively for Southeast Asia. The nations which have made the most economic progress to date are the Philippines, Thailand, and Malaysia while Burma and Indonesia have hardly reached pre-war standards of real *per capita* income.[27] Although it is risky to generalize from only five cases, we would suggest that the size of the private sector is significant here. Both pre-

---

[26]The act, however, increases the clerk's income and decreases the citizen's by an equal amount and if there is a difference in their marginal propensity to save, this may have some effect on economic growth.

[27] See Douglas S. Paauw, "Economic Progress in Southeast Asia," *Journal of Asian Studies* (November, 1963), pp. 69–91. We have omitted the Indo-Chinese states from consideration here for obvious reasons.

coup Indonesia and Burma have opted for a largely state-run economy while Malaysia, Thailand, and the Philippines have imposed fewer restraints on the private sector. What few restrictions there are on private sector activity in the three more successful nations have been partly vitiated by corruption—the Philippines and Thailand would rank fairly high on anyone's scale of corruption—while ever widespread corruption in Burma and Indonesia failed to protect the private sector from state control or operation. In spite of the best intentions and a declared policy of economic growth, the state-run economies have performed significantly less well than those where the private sector predominates. Indications are that Southeast Asia is not an exception in this respect.[28]

If this analysis is correct, it follows that, *other things being equal corruption which secures greater freedom of operation for the private sector will generally promote economic growth.* The impetus to such corruption would, of course, be less if government policy imposed fewer restrictions on the private sector. But since we are speaking of the real world where most new nations are inclined to severely circumscribe or eliminate the private sector, "market" corruption may well enhance the possibilities for economic growth.

C. Effects of Political Competition on Corruption and Growth

Leaving aside for the moment the question of how effectively government policy promotes economic growth, one can distinguish between the groups which profit from corruption in terms of their marginal propensity to save. To the extent that corruption places power or money at the disposal of groups with a high marginal propensity to save it will clearly contribute more to economic growth than if it benefits groups with low marginal propensities to save (MPS). Using the list of groups in Table IV we can make but a few provisional judgments of this nature.

For those with parochial ties to the elite, bureaucrats, and politicians we cannot estimate *a priori* their MPS. It will vary greatly from country to country. In Malaysia one might suspect that bureaucrats have a higher MPS than politicians, and politicians a higher MPS than groups with parochial connections to the elite. Even if this is accurate, the order could well be reversed in other national settings. For voters and wealth elites, however, one can say with some confidence that the MPS

[28]One might compare the performance of Ghana or Guinea (state-run economies), to that of the Ivory Coast, for example. Albert O. Hirschman has argued too, that the concern for balanced growth and the creation of the economic infrastructure, both of which require greater government intervention, are perhaps less conducive to growth than orthodox theorists would suppose. Our generalization is meant to apply to non-communist state-run economies. How much better, however, is the subject of some dispute.

TABLE V. RECIPIENT GROUPS

	Individual and Parochial	Groups with Connections to Elite	Wealth Elites	Bureau-cratic Elites	Pol. Leaders & Pol. Cadre	Voters
MPS Estimate		uncertain		high	uncer-tain	uncer-tain	low

of voters is relatively low and that of wealth elites relatively high. Thus, if we were concerned exclusively with economic growth, corruption which benefited wealth elites more than voters would be of greater benefit than corruption which favored voters. The fact that competitive political systems are more likely to include voters among the beneficiaries of corruption implies that corruption here is less favorable to growth— other things equal—than corruption in a non-competitive political system where voters are not among the beneficiaries. Under conditions of political competition the gains of voters from corruption will probably spread the wealth more evenly—an egalitarian income effect—but may well have less salutary growth effects since voters are more likely to consume than to save their gains. Corruption in a non-competitive system, on the other hand, does not have this levelling effect but may well contribute more to economic growth by favoring groups with a higher MPS. This is not to say that corruption amidst political competition necessarily retards economic growth but rather that it is not as likely to assist economic growth as much as corruption in a non-competitive setting.[29]

D. Qualifications

The proposition that "market" corruption which benefits wealth elites will contribute to economic growth is, alas, subject to a few other qualifications which bear enumeration.

1. Not all of those who argue for the possible benefits of certain kinds of corruption in certain circumstances realize that, if carried too far, corruption is apt to be counter productive. There are at least two reasons for this.[30]

First, most forms of corruption, in fact, constitute a tax on economic activity. The payments for a license to do business, a construction

---

[29]Corruption in a competitive political system may marginally assist growth by subverting the bias of the electorate for present consumption and welfare.
[30]Leff, *op. cit.*, is an example of an analysis which errs, unlike traditional discussions, in its virtually unqualified praise for "market" corruption as a path to economic growth.

permit, etc., are part of the costs of doing business to the merchant or entrepreneur. When such costs are relatively modest they are more than outweighed by the bureaucratic obstacles which they overcome and the incentive which they may provide for efficient operation. At some level, however, corruption may become so costly that many businesses which could otherwise operate at a profit become marginal or clearly unprofitable. One might imagine that politicians and bureaucrats would realize the point at which they are killing the goose which lays their golden eggs —and while the Philippines seems to appreciate these limits, it appears that in Indonesia, quite apart from the policy of nationalization, the race for spoils becomes so wild that many potentially profitable enterprises were either not begun or were actually forced to close down. In such circumstances, many Indonesians preferred to deposit their holdings in foreign banks.

The level of corruption leads us to a second, and related, problem of uncertainty. Many of the bribes paid to bureaucrats and politicians by businessmen were in effect efforts to reduce somewhat the high risk factor which surrounds investment decisions in underdeveloped areas. In this context businessmen would prefer a predictable system of corruption which assures them of the service or decision for which they are paying and sets known limits on the costs they will have to bear. A strong, cohesive party often creates these conditions of certainty by acting as a central clearing house for corruption of this kind. But when uncertainty prevails, when the payment for a decision offers little assurance that it will actually be carried out or if the full cost of a needed decision cannot be known, the businessman may prefer to remain "liquid" rather than running risks of such magnitude. Thus, the greater the extent of corruption (the costliness of a decision) or the greater the uncertainties involved (the risk factor) the less likely that corruption by wealth elites will have a positive effect on economic growth.

2.   Until now we have assumed that most of the corrupt transactions between businessmen and bureaucrats or politicians expand the freedom of the private sector to respond to market forces. Some transactions, however, may actually restrict or distort market forces and have negative effects on economic growth. For example, a firm may secure a contract to supply materials to the government by bribing selected officials who are then unable to complain when he delivers materials well below contract standards or fails to observe other terms of the agreement. Similarly, an import or export enterprise might pay politicians or bureaucrats to enact laws or regulations which will give it a monopoly in a certain area or place obstacles in the path of its competitors. In such cases, corruption has the effect of inhibiting normal competitive pressures which

serve to encourage more efficient operation. Economic growth is more likely to be retarded than accelerated when corruption follows this pattern.

E. Corruption and Growth

Throughout this discussion we have suggested a number of conditions under which corruption may actually promote the process of economic growth. For the sake of convenience, most of these propositions are stated more succinctly below.

Corruption is more likely to have a positive influence on economic growth when:

1. National rulers are either uninterested or hostile to economic growth.
2. The government lacks the skills, capacity, or resources to effectively promote economic growth.

and when:

3. Corruption is "market" corruption where all "buyers" of influence have equal access to bureaucrats and politicians. (The assumption here is that if parochial considerations are weak, only the ability to pay will count and efficient producers will gain an advantage).
4. Corruption benefits groups with a high marginal propensity to save (*e.g.* wealth elites) more than groups with a low marginal propensity to save (voters).[31]
   — this situation is, in turn, more likely in a non-competitive political system than in a competitive one where votes can be traded for influence.
5. The cost of a unit of influence is not so high as to discourage otherwise profitable undertakings.
   — this situation is more likely when there is price competition among politicians and bureaucrats who sell influence.
6. There is greater certainty as to the price of a unit of influence and a high probability of receiving the paid-for "decision".
   — this is more likely when:
   a. The political and bureaucratic elites are strong *and* cohesive.
   b. Corruption has become "regularized"—even institutionalized after a fashion—by long practice.

---

[31]For this reason Nye (*op. cit.*, pp. 424–425) feels corruption among the upper levels of the elite is more likely to be beneficial for economic development than corruption at lower levels.

7. Corruption serves to increase competition in the private sector rather than to secure a special advantage or monopolistic position for any one competitor.

This listing is, of course, far from complete although it does represent many of the major considerations involved in determining whether corruption will have a net positive or negative effect on economic growth. The greater the number of these enumerated conditions which a system of corruption satisfies, the greater the likelihood that corruption will contribute to economic growth.

CONCLUSION

The preconditions for corruption are the existence of a government monopoly over goods, services, or posts and a level of demand for these benefits which outstrips available supply.[32] When the value of the scarce benefit is driven up by demand pressure to a level that exceeds the price the government has set (in many cases the government price is zero), offers to purchase it illegally are likely to occur. One writer has approximately called corruption a form of "black market bureaucracy".[33]

Since much corruption thus represents the penetration of the free market into areas where it is legally forbidden it becomes important to ask how "perfect" the bureaucratic and political "black market" is. A "perfect" market, among other things, responds only to cash and not to voting strength or kinship ties; its prices are determined solely by the interaction of demand and supply, and information as to product and price are available to all.

To the extent that this black market approaches "perfection" in this sense, it will be more likely to contribute to economic growth. A good many of the conditions we enumerated in the previous section reflect the fact that the freer the corruption market is, the higher the probability that wealth elites with their high marginal propensity to save will dominate the market. As beneficial as this might be for economic growth, chances are that it will restrict the equally important process of political inclusion or integration.

What we are suggesting is that, *when it comes to corruption, political integration and economic growth may work against each other.* The kind of corruption which most accelerates economic growth favors wealth elites and largely excludes voters and those with parochial ties

---

[32]This excludes, for the moment, corruption which involves avoiding the enforcement of laws (*e.g.* tax laws, criminal laws) by a lesser "payment" to enforcement officials.
[33]Robert O. Tilman, "Administrative Corruption: An Interpretation," unpublished paper, p. 7.

to the elite from the market. Pure market corruption, then, may wed the wealth elite to the regime while excluding voters and "parochials". On the other hand, corruption which distributes the fruits of corruption not only to wealth elites but also to voters and "parochials" is surely more beneficial for political inclusion but is, at the same time, likely to spread rewards among consumers who are less apt to use these rewards as productively as investors. Which variety of corruption is considered "better" therefore depends whether economic development or political integration is deemed to be the most crucial systemic problem. The Congo, one might say, would be better off with corruption which maximizes political integration while Tunisia or the Philippines might be better off with corruption that maximizes economic growth.

Regardless of the potential economic benefits of market corruption, there are important objections to such corruption which relate to the adequacy of the price system in allocating values. Market corruption suffers from all the recognized shortcomings of any free market pricing system. First, claims in the market must be backed with money and distribution is therefore highly unequal. Such goods and services as education, health care, etc., for example, are subject to government intervention because the distribution which would result from the price system is considered by almost all as unsatisfactory.[34] Secondly, the price system often involves third party damages or costs which are not a part of the market's calculations. Examples such as pollution or the depletion of natural resources come to mind where the community attempts collectively to restrict the price system so as to protect third party interests. Market allocation may finally result in the private control of functions which the community has decided to collectively allocate. Private control over courts or military units, for example, are results of market penetration into government services which could impose tremendous costs on the community at large. The importance of such considerations as these may be great enough to warrant centralized decisions rather than market decisions (in this case corruption) whether or not the political system is democratic and whether or not corruption might promote economic growth.

In concluding, it is well to remember that the fundamental objection to corruption is that it always assigns greater importance to wealth and/or "connections" than to votes. This is presumably the democratic response to corruption in public life. If as in many developing nations, however, the political system is closed or oligarchic, the democratic

[34]This and succeeding points are taken from Robert A. Dahl and Charles E. Lindblom, *Politics, Economics and Welfare* (New York: Harper, 1953), pp. 387–391.

objection to corruption becomes less valid since corruption may, in such instances, serve as an informal democratizing force.

FOR FURTHER READING

DAVID H. BAYLEY, "The Effects of Corruption in a Developing Nation" *(Western Political Quarterly, XIX, 4, December 1966, 719–732)*

O. P. DWIVEDI, "Bureaucratic Corruption in Developing Countries" *(Asian Survey, VII, 4, April 1967, 245–253)*

J. DAVID GREENSTONE, "Corruption and Self-Interest in Kampala and Uganda" *(Comparative Studies in Society and History, VIII, 2, January 1966, 199–210)*

ARNOLD J. HEIDENHEIMER, *Political Corruption: Readings in Comparative Analysis* (New York: Holt, Rinehart and Winston, 1970)

SAMUEL P. HUNTINGTON, *Political Order in Changing Societies* (New Haven: Yale University Press, 1968)

COLIN LEYS, "What is the Problem about Corruption?" *(Journal of Modern African Studies, III, 2, August 1965, 215–224)*

M. McMULLAN, "A Theory of Corruption" *(Sociological Review, IX, 2, June 1961, 181–200)*

JOSEPH S. NYE, JR., "Corruption and Political Development: A Cost-Benefit Analysis" *(American Political Science Review, LXI, 2, June 1967, 417–427)*

JAMES C. SCOTT, "Corruption, Machine Politics, and Social Change" *(American Political Science Review, LXIII, 4, December 1969, 1142–1158)*

W. F. WERTHEIM, "Sociological Aspects of Corruption in Southeast Asia" *(Sociologica Neerlandica, I, 2, Autumn 1963, 129–153)*

AFRICAN ONE-PARTY STATES AND MODERNIZATION

James S. Coleman and Carl G. Rosberg, Jr.

Given the tremendous burdens placed upon the new governments in Africa, single-party dominance and centralized administrative control seem necessary. According to Professors Coleman and Rosberg, African leaders believe that modernization requires "a central and unitary organization of power within the state, and . . . Africa's parties are the only structures available for this purpose." However, the governing single parties are vulnerable for several reasons, and their replacement by other forms of government is likely.

When their countries achieved independence, African leaders confronted a situation that was not only conducive to the consolidation of one-party dominance, but also made strong government attractive, if not necessary. They inherited the plenitude of autocratic power possessed by the departing colonial government, with few institutionalized restraints upon its exercise. Divisive and separatist tendencies, unchecked by any countervailing sense of national loyalty, threatened the geographic integrity and the internal security of the state, and even the authority of government itself. Political opposition groups tended to be suspect either because they were closely identified with the former colonial power, because they were based upon tribal, ethnic, or regional sentiment, or because they were linked with hostile regimes or movements in neighboring states. The leaders also faced the enormous task of modernization which, if not tackled vigorously and successfully, could convert the revolution of rising expectations, which had helped catapult them to power, into a counterrevolution of rising frustrations, which

---

From James S. Coleman and Carl G. Rosberg, Jr., eds., *Political Parties and National Integration in Tropical Africa* (Berkeley and Los Angeles: University of California Press, 1964), pp. 655–680, by permission. Text and footnotes abridged by the editor.

would most certainly ensure their demise. These and other aspects of the postcolonial period are now commonplace. The point here is that they created a situation favorable to the growth of one-party-dominant systems.

Two particularly significant aspects of the immediate postcolonial situation are (1) the heavy functional load thrown upon the new polity the state builders are seeking to stabilize and legitimate, and (2) the fact that, initially at least, the party is, or is rationalized as being, the most visible, immediately available, national organization for the performance of many, if not most, of the functions involved.

The magnitude of the functional load a particular governing party may carry is only partly the result of the character of the particular mélange of peoples out of which it seeks to make a nation, and for which it must stabilize a polity and develop an economy. It is also a result of the compulsiveness and the determination with which the dominant party desires to achieve modernizing objectives. The load is manifestly heavier in revolutionary-centralizing one-party-dominant states whose leaders seek simultaneously to extinguish the *corps intermédiares* between the central government and the individual; to assimilate the structures of party, government, and all functional associations into one vast monolithic unity; to plan and direct the total economy; to launch a vigorous foreign policy; and to reduce the dependence of their countries upon the external world.

Traditional Africa has exerted a variable influence upon the emergence of systems in which one party is dominant. In most instances it has played an obstructive role, as evidenced by the fact that traditionalism in all its forms and manifestations has been one of the principal targets of leaders in most one-party states of the revolutionary-centralizing persuasion. Yet, in several contexts, particularly in Sierra Leone, the Cameroun, and northern Nigeria, traditional factors have strongly supported the pragmatic-pluralistic pattern of one-party development. In all three instances the traditional authority systems, preserved and adapted as they were during the colonial period, provided an organizational infrastructure which modern territorial parties favorable to the traditionalists could use to penetrate and control the rural areas. Given the inexorable erosion of chiefly power, and of traditional symbols and sanctions, the tenure of the parties that have depended upon such power remains very much an open question. The presumption is that their days are numbered. Much will depend upon their skill in consolidating their authoritative position, in immobilizing the opposition, in developing their organizational structure, and in finding new social bases for support. Very much in point is the perpetuative power acquired by the Northern Peoples' Congress in Nigeria through its vigorous action against powerful traditional rulers who have been corrupt, its absorption of most of the leaders of the dissident Middle Belt groups, and its development of an organizational structure independent of the traditional systems.

The relevance of traditional authority structures in the development of one-party-dominant systems, whether they were supportive or obstructive, is a function of two factors: (1) their inherent strength, resilience, and adaptability, and (2) the character of the colonial legacy, that is, whether they were protected and supported, or neglected and ignored, during the colonial period. In most British areas they were protected, and, where possible, were made units of local government, in accordance with the principle of indirect rule. Although in some French territories they were shown some deference (for example, the chiefs of northern Togo and Cameroun, and the Marabouts in Senegal), French policy in general accelerated the demise of the traditional order. This difference in the colonial legacy helps to explain why national integration and the consolidation of one-party rule have been comparatively easier in former French territories than in those previously under British administration.

Closely related to the foregoing is the influence of the highly centralized, even quasi-military, systems of colonial administration upon African political perspectives and attitudes. Modern colonialism in Africa everywhere tended toward bureaucratic authoritarianism, even though it was paternalistic in motivation. Although colonial powers endeavored to establish democratic parliamentary government in the period preceding the grant of independence to their African territories, the fact remains that the exposure to pluralistic democracy was relatively brief, and that the present generation of Africans—whether party elites or the masses—were subjected during most of their lives to an authoritarian political order. However different the political socialization patterns of their respective traditional societies may have been—and these varied from virtually pure egalitarianism to sheer autocracy—it is believed that in most instances the really determinative factor in the orientation of the present party elites to the political order has been their exposure to bureaucratic centralism during the colonial period. In a sense, one-party rule and "national party" government are simply postcolonial terms for the same phenomenon. In the realm of government and administration in Africa, there is far more continuity than innovation.

A third element in the colonial legacy facilitating one-party development has been the so-called "aura of legitimacy" with which many of the governing parties were endowed at the time of independence. . . .

parties such as the Parti Démocratique de Guinée (PDG) and the Union Soudanaise established themselves in the public image, through ceaseless nationalist agitation before independence, as the true carriers of the African revolution. Even such parties as the Parti Démocratique de la Côte d'Ivoire (PDCI) and the Convention People's Party (CPP) in Ghana, which actively collaborated with the colonial governments during a protracted period of diarchy (1950 to 1960 for the PDCI, and 1951 to 1957 for the CPP), were able to perpetuate and to capitalize on a popular belief that they were also the parties of revolution. During a brief period in the late 1940's, each of these parties was more militantly nationalist than its competitors. Like the National Convention of Nigerian Citizens (NCNC), they were thereby endowed with the special mantle of grace. Once the CPP had won a majority, it was able to consolidate its power in the Ghanaian political system with the protection, support, and collaboration of the British government; at the same time it was vigorously denouncing imperialism and demanding "Self-Government Now!" Thus the critical element in the legitimating power of revolutionary imagery is not necessarily ceaseless struggle and uncompromising resistance until the final full surrender of imperial power—although leaders and supporters in the PDG and the Union Soudanaise continue to be fortified by their memories of sacrifice and martyrdom—but the establishment by a party of a favorable image in the public mind at that point in time when the imperial power seriously launched the protracted process of disengagement and withdrawal. Strengthened by an early revolutionary popularity which chastened and indulgent colonial powers allowed to be kept alive, protected from the opposition by the full support of the imperial government, and progressively endowed with real power enabling it to consolidate its position of primacy within the state, the governing party in many new states entered the era of independence not only with its aura of legitimacy virtually untarnished, but also with decisive control over the authoritative structures of government.

The consolidation of a party's position of primacy was frequently facilitated in the crucial phase of terminal colonialism by electoral systems based upon the single-member constituency, or the single-list principle, as well as by parliamentary forms of government based upon the sovereignty of the majority. The operation of these factors, both singly and in combination, tended in practice to give relatively unfettered control to a victorious party, although it may have won no more than a plurality of the popular vote or only a bare majority of the total constituencies. . . . In more developed countries such a system is rationalized and defended in terms of its capacity to produce strong leadership and effective government. Given the highly fragmented and unintegrated character of most new African states, and the consequent need for strong and effective government, the argument in favor of such a majoritarian system is logically even more persuasive. Yet there is a difference: in more highly developed countries there are structural and psychological restraints upon the arbitrary use of the relatively unlimited governmental power enjoyed by a party commanding a parliamentary majority. All aspects of this interesting and important issue obviously cannot be discussed here; suffice it to note that electoral and other institutional innovations in the terminal colonial period disproportionately favored the majority party, and that these were, in some instances, strongly determinative factors in the process of consolidation and maximization of its perpetuative power.

Imperial countries were not only the source of electoral systems and parliamentary models; party organization in Africa also reflected the strong influence of Socialist and Communist parties.... The strength and the pervasiveness of these various influences upon party organization were the result not only of the special efforts made by European parties of the Left to give support and guidance to African parties on organization, strategy, and tactics, but also of a determined effort by African leaders to secure advice and assistance in the development of a revolutionary organization. Even had left-wing European parties been indifferent or uncoöperative, African leaders would still probably have borrowed heavily from them because the monolithic and penetrative character of those parties was manifestly appropriate to the creation of an independent power base from which to launch their assault upon the colonial regime. Thus, whether European parties of the Left deliberately influenced African political groups, as the French Socialist Party (SFIO) did in Senegal, or were deliberately emulated, as President Kwame Nkrumah claims was true in the initial organization of the CPP, they were a not irrelevant part of the total colonial legacy.

These aspects of traditional society and of the colonial experience undoubtedly facilitated the development of one-party-dominant systems, but they are not full explanations. They become meaningful only when situational factors are favorable, and only when one-party predispositions are present among governing party elites.

The political culture of the new African elites has probably been the decisive factor in the general trend toward the one-party polity, although the contributions of traditional society and colonialism and the "ripe situation" were essential preconditions. By elite political culture, we refer to attitudes, beliefs, values, orientation toward authority, and self-images of the leaders of new states regarding their political roles and capacities.[1] This culture reflects the socializing influences both of traditional society and of the colonial period, as well as the post-colonial perceptions and evaluations of the elite, and their estimate as to what should, and realistically could, be done to realize elite objectives. Although there are numerous exceptions and qualifications to any generalization about African political phenomena, there are at least three rather common elements in the political culture of African party leaders: elitism, statism, and nationalism. These are all interrelated and mutually reinforcing, and each is supportive of one or another aspect of the one-party syndrome.

The elitism of African political leaders is manifested in many ways: through their perception and definition of their own roles in the political system; through the suggestion that in a population mainly illiterate the "educated" have a special claim to leadership, either because of superior enlightenment or because of a greater capacity to handle the complex affairs of a modern state; and through the "elect" pretensions and the paternalism which frequently creep into their references to their "people." It is not an ascriptive, aristocratic or closed elitism; indeed, the political culture is saturated with achievement norms, ultrapopulistic slogans, and egalitarian assumptions. Nor is it an arrogant, condescending elitism crudely flaunted before the people. On the contrary, political leaders are fortified in their elitist proclivities by the deference accorded them by the masses. Elitism has, however, clearly furthered the one-party tendency, because it carries the implicit presumption that the governing group possesses a monopoly of wisdom and legitimacy. It follows, therefore, that in their view an opposition group recruited from the nonelite is incompetent and illegitimate and that one recruited from the same social strata as the elite is either frivolous and irrelevant, or dangerously subversive because its members seek only power.

The statism in the African elite political culture reflects three facts: (1) the present generation of Africans has been politically socialized within the framework of a society whose private sector was extremely undeveloped, and consequently the state was dominant in all modern sectors of the society (e.g., the economy, the educational system, public works and utilities) and was as well the main employer, the source of all amenities, and the initiator and manager of most aspects of social and economic development—in a word, it was

---

[1]The term "political culture" is here used essentially as it is in Gabriel Almond and Sidney Verba, *The Civic Culture* (Princeton: Princeton University Press, 1963).

"socialist"; (2) the leaders inherited this system from the colonial powers, and by default it must serve them as the instrument for rapid modernization; and (3) Marxism has strongly influenced a substantial segment of the present generation of Africans, partly because of the appeal of the Leninist interpretation of modern imperialism, and partly because of the courting and indoctrination of Africans by European parties of the Left. Yet none of the governments of the new African states are totalitarian; indeed, large segments of their populations only partially or intermittently participate in the modern sectors. This fact, coupled with the extreme weakness of the authoritative governmental structures, makes African one-party-dominant systems a species of the larger genus of movement-regime.[2] A statist society is essentially a bureaucratic society; and, the more bureaucratic a society, the more difficult, if not illogical, it is to envisage a competitive political process, because of the normative and structural incompatibilities of the two systems.[3] It is in this sense that statism in contemporary Africa has supported the one-party tendency.

The African elite political culture is "nationalist" in that party leaders in African one-party-dominant states have been basically committed to "national unity" as the supreme value and goal. They either condemn or reluctantly tolerate (under firm central control) tribalism, ethnicity, regional autonomy, and other manifestations of subnational sentiment. They are also nationalist in that they rule out all forms of political opposition which threaten, actually or symbolically, the integrity of the nation they are seeking to build. Throughout Africa, political opposition has tended to be stigmatized by its link with external or subnational forces or influences. As a consequence, opposition is regarded as anti-nationalist, and therefore illegal in spirit, if not by statute. Yet this particular strand in elite political culture is not simply suppressive; it also reflects a widely held belief among African leaders that what is needed at this stage is a national party, a *parti unifié*, or, indeed, no party at all. Here it is pertinent to recall George Washington's opposition to political parties during the first decade of America's independence as the first "new nation." A penetrating analysis of the obstacles to party development in the early postcolonial period in the United States points out that,

> For men like Washington or Hamilton, . . . [doubts about the wisdom of parties] were concentrated around the question of the legiti-

[2]Robert C. Tucker, "Towards a Comparative Politics of Movement-Regimes," *American Political Science Review*, LV (June 1961), 281–289.
[3]Cf. Joseph A. Schumpeter, *Capitalism, Socialism and Democracy* (New York: Harper and Brothers, 1950), pp. 205–209.

macy of an opposition party. A man of forceful presence, a balancing and unifying force in politics, and the supreme hero of the Revolutionary War, Washington was convinced that once the new national government had been put in his hands, it was up to him and his chosen aides to manage it. Filled with determination to join the struggling states into a great and powerful nation, a far-seeing leader of determined purpose, Hamilton also was impatient with criticism, intolerant of democratic demands or the very idea of opposition.[4]

Yet, despite the historical similarity, there is a striking difference between postcolonial parties in the United States and postcolonial parties in the new African states. In the United States, parties as we know them today had yet to be created. In the new African states, however, parties existed as organized associations before national independence; moreover, constitutional norms, procedures, and institutions presumed their existence as sources for the recruitment of national political leadership. Thus, although the leaders of all new states have tended to be hostile toward political opposition in the interest of national unity, the problems they have confronted have been markedly different. The problem of Washington and Hamilton was to prevent the emergence of parties, whereas the problem of Kwame Nkrumah and Modibo Keita, and most of their contemporaries, has been to consolidate the primacy of one party over all others. It is this process of consolidation of one-party dominance with which we are primarily concerned here. . . .

The process of consolidation has encompassed four types of activity. One is the explicit actions taken by ruling party elites to convert, neutralize, or eliminate overt political opposition, actions so persuasive that they also deterred the later manifestation of opposition by dissident elements. Second, ruling party elites, in their effort to achieve structural unity, have "nationalized" all nonparty associations and made them either integral parts or adjuncts of the national party. A third set of measures includes those postcolonial constitutional and electoral innovations designed to strengthen unitary one-party rule. Fourth, party leaders have set forth a body of ideas—a political theory if you will—defending, rationalizing, or affirming the virtues of a one-party system. These elements in the consolidation process—opposition conversion or neutralization, associational integration, constitutional innovation, and ideological rationalizations—will be briefly examined in the following sections.

A wide variety of consolidation techniques have been available to governing party elites both in neutralizing existing opposition and in

---

[4]William Nisbet Chambers, *Political Parties in a New Nation: The American Experience, 1776–1809* (New York: Oxford University Press, 1963), p. 5.

preventing the emergence of potential opposition. These techniques fall roughly into two categories: rewarding those who support, or at least do not resist, the governing party, and punishing those who oppose it. Rewards include patronage, educational opportunities, developmental amenities, and preferential treatment in the award of government contracts and licenses. Punishments include deprivation of the foregoing rewards, of course, and, more directly, range from harassment by local chiefs, police, and courts to physical incarceration or deportation. None of the techniques are peculiarly African. Many are time-honored stratagems used with varying degrees of crudeness or subtlety by governing parties everywhere. Others, such as deportation, or physical restriction and punishment, are part of the colonial legacy, and therefore represent continuity in the governmental treatment of opposition rather than post-colonial African innovations.

The selective use of patronage to assimilate or control political opposition, or to enlist the support of potentially dissident elements, has been an extremely powerful weapon. It has extraordinary importance in the new African states because of the strongly statist character of their societies. Because government is deeply involved in all aspects of the modern sector of the economy, because it is the chief employer of labor and the only source of capital grants for modern amenities, and because it is the sole channel through which massive inputs of foreign assistance enter the society, African ruling parties are able to pursue with remarkable effectiveness the old Latin-American custom of *continuismo*. . . . With continuing expansion in public works and economic development programs, and the corollary insignificance of the private sector in providing employment and career opportunities, government patronage will remain a subtle and effective means of perpetuating the power of the present ruling party elites, provided, of course, their parties remain united.

The preferential awarding of government scholarships for higher education has been, and will continue to be, an enormously effective instrument of one-party consolidation. Very few African parents are financially able to give their children the higher and professional education necessary for their advancement in the new African societies. Although during the terminal colonial period government sought to minimize political manipulation of scholarship programs, since independence party elites have used these programs as a source of patronage as well as a means of controlling entry into the elite ranks. The implications of this are clear. An African parent or guardian will be very careful not to jeopardize the educational opportunities of his dependents. By accepting government largess he will be forced into a position either of political passivity or of dutiful support of the dominant party. As long as higher education provides the most rapid and direct access to high status, as it tends to do in contemporary Africa, the dominant party's power of self-perpetuation through allocation of educational opportunities is greatly enhanced.

The selective areal allocation of public funds and grants for modern amenities (piped water, electricity, hospitals, schools, etc.) and for the development of the country's infrastructure (communications, energy, roads, transportation facilities, etc.) has also been an important instrument of consolidation. In many new states the phenomenon known as the "vanishing opposition" is in large measure explained by the strong pressures placed upon opposition leaders by their constituents to join the governing party and share in this preferential treatment. It is a phenomenon manifested in a variety of contexts. Immediately after elections there is frequently a massive shift of elected members of a defeated party, or of independents, to the government party, under the time-honored rationale, "If you can't beat them, join them." This propensity is strengthened by the sense of futility engendered by the conviction that the party in power is impregnable.

Groups, as well as individuals, have abandoned the role of opposition, for the same reasons and in response to the same pressures discussed above. Among French-speaking African states voluntary mergers and fusions of political parties have been widespread, usually taking the form of assimilation of all parties into the dominant party. Between 1952 and 1957 the governing PDCI in the Ivory Coast absorbed all significant opposition parties; in Guinea, immediately after independence was achieved in 1958, the last of the opposition groups voluntarily merged with the dominant PDG; and in 1959 the Parti Soudanais Progressiste, the leading opposition party in the former French Soudan, was absorbed into the Union Soudanaise. The spirit of merger or integration has stemmed partly from the manifest advantages of a comprehensive "national front" (usually expressed in French as a *parti unifié*) in tackling the problems of independence and modernization. For opposition groups that were being absorbed, the impulse to merge was in part a response to the known wishes, or the determination, of the dominant party that opposition cease. But it also reflected the desire of opposition leaders that their groups not be excluded from all the benefits accruing from participation in the government. This issue was for some time at the heart of the argument among the leaders of the principal opposition party in Nigeria: Would not abandonment of the role of opposition contribute to the unity of the country and, at the same time, help the people of the Western Region, who have been denied access to federal patronage and amenities?

Although the dominant ruling parties in Africa's new states have preferred to use the more subtle techniques of neutralizing overt political opposition, they have also been prepared to take restrictive or punitive actions. Threats designed to create a climate of fear and to ensure conformity have occasionally been employed. Preventive detention acts, censorship and control over the press, limitations upon public demonstrations and public criticisms of the regime, and other means have been used to maintain "law and order" and to ensure control over oppositional behavior. In general, highly visible punishments such as imprisonment or deportation have been meted out only as a last resort. Punishment has been used as much to impress latent or potential opposition with the consequences of overt dissent as to inflict retribution for the act of opposition.

The second major category of activity in the uniparty consolidation process is the effort by ruling party elites to draw in all forms of existing associations. The intensity, the comprehensiveness, and the determination with which this objective has been pursued have varied considerably. In Mali . . . the Union Soudanaise has systematically sought the total integration of all associations, including those formed by the important groups of youth and women. In the Ivory Coast, leaders have been less compulsively centralizing in their approach; associations such as the Syndicat des Chefs Coutumiers have not been structurally integrated into the PDCI, although they have been deferential to its primacy. Despite these variations, however, the general trend has been toward the creation of single nationwide interest associations closely linked to the dominant party. . . .

The third type of consolidation activity comprises electoral and constitutional changes instituted by leaders of dominant parties in order to strengthen the legal position, if not to establish the constitutional preeminence, of their parties. One of the most common and effective innovations has been the single-list electoral system by which all members of a national legislature are elected on a single slate covering the entire country. In the many French-speaking states where this system has been used, the victorious party has won all the seats in the legislature. A second development has been the progressive strengthening of the executive power. This has been particularly marked in French-speaking states and in Ghana and Tanganyika, and certainly represents a general trend. The French-speaking states modeled their constitutions on that of the Fifth French Republic, which clearly provided for the undisputed preeminence of the executive power. In Ghana, President Nkrumah's program of centralization and solidarity has been reflected in constitutional changes introduced since the achievement of independence in 1957. For example, the constitution of July 1, 1960, fused the functions of president and prime minister into a single, powerful executive endowed with full legal control over all structures of authority in the state. This constitutional ratification of the *de facto* consolidation of unitary power unquestionably enhanced the legal position of the CPP in the Ghanaian political system. The final step in the consolidation process . . . was the January 1964, referendum formally making Ghana a one-party state. Similarly, the Tanganyika African National Union has used constitutional means to bolster its position, and the tendency is visible in most other new states where one party has undisputed control.

Fourth, in order to consolidate uniparty systems, African party leaders have put forward a theoretical defense, a rationale, for the new type of polity. Their speechs and writings on this topic reflect a fairly common stock of ideas, although eclectically drawn from many sources and experiences. Collectively these ideas constitute a rather amorphous and unsystematic, but nonetheless extremely illuminating, African political theory. This loose mélange of ideas, which we will call the theory of unipartyism, is a mixture of defensive explanations and categorical postulations. In it one finds the ever-present and irrepressible sentiment of anticolonialism, a frequently romanticized African traditionalism, and a buoyant progressivism. Like most political ideologies, it serves primarily to rationalize and legitimate a particular political state of affairs, which in this instance is postcolonial unipartyism.

A key element in the theory of unipartyism is that the staggering problem of nation building and modernization requires a central and unitary organization of power within the state, and that Africa's parties are the only structures available for this purpose. Nkrumah has described the situation as "almost analogous to a state of war and national emergency which is always met in the older established countries by the formation of coalition or national governments." Multiparty systems are regarded as forms of "institutionalized factionalism" which not only divide the national will and dissipate national energies, but also threaten internal stability. Thus, *raison d'état* is the primary and most obvious rationale for unipartyism.

Another common theme is that a uniparty form of government is not only rooted in, but is a modern expression of, certain aspects of traditional political culture. It is argued that traditional African culture was communal in character, and that the individual had no identity apart from his group. Decisions were made only after unanimity had been achieved through institutionalized "talking it out" in a "village palaver"; because such decisions embodied the collective will, the idea of a permanently organized opposition was not only alien, but intolerable. It does not follow that traditional societies were autocratic; on the contrary, there were, it is argued, constitutional checks upon the arbitrary exercise of political authority, as well as direct popular involvement in decision making. Nkrumah, a leading spokesman for African unipartyism, has declared, for example, that Ghanaian society is by "form and tradition fundamentally democratic in character."

The theory also connotes the absence of sharp differentiation into classes, either in traditional or in contemporary African societies. Because most African leaders lean heavily upon Marxian theory, including the assumption that parties are solely a reflection of class interests, it is argued that the lack of class differentiation in Africa renders competing parties unnecessary. In traditional African societies, it is reasoned, the transcendent influence of highly diffuse communal and familial rights and duties prevented or retarded differentiation into distinct classes. President Julius Nyerere of Tanganyika, in expounding the communal basis of African socialism, adopts essentially this position:

> In traditional African society *everybody* was a worker. There was no other way of earning a living for the community. Even the Elder, who appeared to be enjoying himself without doing any work and for whom everybody else appeared to be working, had, in fact, worked hard all his younger days. The wealth he now appeared to possess was not *his*, personally; it was only "his" as the Elder of the group which had produced it. He was its guardian. The wealth itself gave him neither power nor prestige.[5]

In modern African societies, uniparty theorists assert that class differentiation has not yet occurred on a significant scale; accordingly, there are no capitalist or proletarian classes, and hence no social bases for competing parties....

---

[5]Julius Nyerere, *Ujama: The Basis of African Socialism* (Dar es Salaam, 1962). This argument is fairly common among uniparty spokesmen. Sékou Touré, for example, has claimed that traditional African society is essentially "communau-cratique." For these and similar arguments see Rupert Emerson, *Political Modernization: The Single-Party System*, University of Denver Monograph Series in World Affairs, No. 1 (Denver 1964), page 26ff. For a debate between two anthropologists on the traditional basis for unipartyism, see Robert F. Gray, "Political Parties in New African Nations," *Comparative Studies in Society and History*, V (July 1963), 449-461, and Lucy Mair's comments thereon, pp. 462-465.

The proposition that traditional African society was essentially egalitarian cannot be uncritically rejected as political romanticism. Lloyd Fallers has argued, for example, that one of the distinctive features of traditional African society, even the larger kingdoms, was a rather pervasive egalitarianism. Tendencies toward crystallization of rigid horizontal strata were checked by a fairly common pattern of kinship and family structure (exogamous unilineal descent groups) and by the "absence of literary religious traditions, which might have provided the basis for more clearly differentiated elite subcultures" ("Equality, Modernity and Democracy in the New States," in Clifford Geertz, ed., *Old Societies and New States* [New York: Free Press of Glencoe, 1963], p. 180).

A more affirmative theme in the theory of unipartyism, not entirely congruent with the foregoing, is that the highly differentiated (i.e., pluralistic and heterogeneous) character of the social base of the new states manifestly makes a one-party structure the best form of governmental organization. It is both an integrative and stabilizing structure which can fuse the diverse groups together into a new sense of community in order that they may realize their common potentialities. It provides an organizational means for conflict resolution, as well as for representation of all interests in society. In short, the structure of the single party, with its network of branches and allied functional associations, is seen as the most appropriate and effective "African" way of organizing society and governing a state. Indeed, the party and the state are one.

Sensitive to, but defiant of, the fact that their behavior as a governing class is being watched closely and is being judged by democratic norms of the West, African uniparty theorists place special emphasis upon the essentially democratic character of African one-party politics. The leaders of the TANU, for example, have declared that one-party democracy under a strong president is not only more appropriate to African conditions, but more readily understood by Africans. The repeated and overwhelming TANU majorities in Western-style democratic elections clearly demonstrate, it is claimed, that Tanganyikans neither require nor desire more than one party. Intraparty democracy is all that is required, and this they believe is assured in African uniparty systems. A variant of this theme is found in Nyerere's assertion that "where there is *one* party—provided it is identified with the nation as a whole— the foundations of democracy can be firmer, and the people can have more opportunity to exercise a real choice, than where you have two or more parties."[6] Other statements reflect the persistent effort made to establish the fact that African one-party polities are functionally democratic, even though structurally they do not conform to the classical Western model. Nkrumah has declaimed that "we in Africa will evolve forms of government rather different from the traditional Western pattern but not less democratic in their protection of the individual and his inalienable rights."[7] In the same vein, Tom Mboya of Kenya argues that the "countries of Africa emerging from political subjection are entitled to modify, to suit their own needs, the institutions of democracy as developed in the West. *No one has the right to cavil at this so long as*

---

[6]Quoted approvingly in Tom Mboya, "The Party System and Democracy in Africa," *Foreign Affairs*, XLI (July 1963), 655.
[7]Kwame Nkrumah, *I Speak of Freedom: A Statement of African Ideology* (New York: Praeger, 1961), p. 58.

*all citizens—irrespective of their social, tribal or religious affiliations—
are treated alike."*[8] Here one finds that interesting mixture of defensiveness and assertiveness employed by African leaders to interpret and justify postcolonial political institutions in terms of the external standards by which they feel they are being judged, while at the same time affirming their right to develop political forms that are distinctively African.

Although the foregoing aspects of the process of one-party consolidation represent a general tendency in all new states, there are significant differences in the emphasis given them by those states oriented toward the revolutionary-centralizing pattern, on the one hand, and states leaning toward the pragmatic-pluralistic type on the other. The differences are both structural and psychological. Structurally, the revolutionary-centralizing uniparty regimes seek to absorb and control all forms of associational life in the country; psychologically, they endeavor to create a climate of full and continuous involvement and commitment on the part of the population regarding party-state goals. In contrast, pragmatic-pluralistic regimes are structurally far less pervasive and all-embracing, for they tolerate considerable associational and traditional pluralism (providing it does not threaten the integrity of the party or the tenure of the governing elite); psychologically, they are far less demanding.

These contrasting orientations are very real; nevertheless, various factors and forces operate to narrow the differences between them. The realities of African conditions—ethnic and regional disunities, serious shortages of trained high-level manpower, limited financial resources and a variety of other incapacitating circumstances—have exerted a powerfully sobering and temporizing influence upon leaders of the compulsive revolutionary-centralizing persuasion. The almost insuperable obstacles they have confronted since independence have compelled them to be more pragmatic and pluralistic in practice, even though they may persist in their declamatory revolutionary-centralizing position. Similarly, the regimes in the pragmatic-pluralistic uniparty states have been rather firmly urged by younger and more militant elements to adopt a more revolutionary and centralizing position with respect to such issues as obstructive traditionalism, accelerated Africanization, and vigorous pursuit of African socialism.

These two countervailing forces—the deterrents to and the limited capabilities for the establishment of a totalitarian state, balanced against the presence of a frustrated younger generation driven to con-

---

[8]Mboya, *op. cit.*, p. 658. Italics added.

summate the "African Revolution"—are among the critical determinants
of the future development of African polities. And further evolution
there will be. The one-party syndrome described . . . does not necessarily
represent the end of the line in the political evolution of the new African
states. Indeed, the triumph of one-party rule, the emergence of the dominant party as the political center of gravity immediately after independence, may prove to be no more than a transitional phenomenon.

In addition to other factors already mentioned, at least three
generic features of the postcolonial situation could affect, if not determine, future patterns of political change in African one-party states:
(1) the ideological and structural vulnerability of the single party under
the radically altered circumstances created by independence; (2) the
strain toward primacy and autonomy of the formal institutions of government; and (3) changes in the social structure brought about by
the modernization, processes launched or accelerated by independent
statehood. These three factors are obviously interrelated. Their impact
upon the course of change will be highly variable. Yet in all new states,
in one way or another, they will introduce stresses and tensions that
will continually challenge the primacy, unity, and omnipotence of the
single party.

We have seen that certain aspects of the immediate postcolonial
situation facilitate the consolidation of one-party dominance. Other aspects, however, render the governing party highly vulnerable to popular
disenchantment and unmask its inherent weaknesses. Most obviously,
the attainment of independence means the abrupt loss of the party's
main *raison d'être,* indeed, the loss of its ideology. "Defending a revolution," as Foltz puts it, "is always a less exciting and onerous task than
making it"; moreover, secondary goals—for example, external ventures
in support of the liberation of the African continent or Pan-African
unity, the elimination of residual colonial influences and of continued
unbalanced dependence upon the former metropolitan country (neocolonialism), or the pursuit of some purely internal goal such as economic
development—neither generate the emotional commitment nor provide
the mobilizing power which characterized the drive toward national independence.[9] There is no ideological substitute of equal integrating and
purposive force, and a single party without an ideology is critically
handicapped.

Independence also means shifts in the forms and goals of political action: the shift from vilification and agitation against government

[9] William J. Foltz, "Building the Newest Nations: Short-Run Strategies and
Long-Run Problems," in Karl W. Deutsch and William J. Foltz, *Nation-Building*
(New York: Atherton Press, 1963), p. 122. [Reprinted in this reader, p. 293.] For three

to its support and defense; the shift from mobilization and maximization of grievances to their containment, sublimation, or projection onto some new internal or external enemy; the shift from the stimulation of exaggerated hopes to the inculcation of duty, sacrifice, and postponed rewards; and the shift from the image of the party as an instrument of liberation to its role of coercion, repression, and self-aggrandizement and enrichment of the elite. In short, independence may become the watershed at which the revolution of rising expectations becomes the revolution of rising frustrations, and the single party has the glory and the stigma of being, respectively, the vanguard of both.[10]

Governing single parties are vulnerable not only because of the psychological deflation produced by independence, but also because many of them, at the outset, were organizationally weak and faction-ridden, and lacked a mass base. The harsh realities of the immediate postcolonial period have made this increasingly clear. Nationalist rhetoric, the romantic predisposition of most persons to believe that an oppressed people struggling for freedom and modernity must have a single-minded purpose, and the high visibility of those few parties possessing a strong national organization and a mass base (for example, the PDG in Guinea, the Union Soudanaise in Mali, and the TANU in Tanganyika)—all these elements combined to create the belief among most persons that the single party was one of monolithic unity and widespread popular commitment.[11] The reality is often very different. . . . The single party, with few exceptions, has been the end product of a

other highly perceptive essays on the changing role of the party in new African states see Pierre de Briey, "Notes on a Conference: The Institutions of the New States," *Civilisations*, XIII, No. 3 (1963), 227–249; Immanuel Wallerstein, "Political Parties in Post-Independence Africa: Recruitment and Participation," and Rupert Emerson, "Political Parties and National Integration in Tropical Africa" (papers presented at the Conference on Political Parties and Political Development held at Frascati, Italy, Jan. 6–9, 1964, under the auspices of the Committee on Comparative Politics of the Social Science Research Council). Both these essays will be published in a forthcoming volume edited by Joseph La Palombara and Myron Weiner, to be entitled *Political Parties and Political Development*.

[10]Tucker has noted that this dual role is a generic phenomenon of nationalist revolutionary movement-regimes, which "show a definite tendency to spend their revolutionary force rather early. In some cases this happens soon after the achievement of the original revolutionary goals and prior to the completion of the revolutionizing of the old society. In other words, the national movement-regime is peculiarly the prey of the phenomenon of 'extinction'" (*op. cit.*, pp. 286–287). A study group of INCIDI put the idea in these terms: "Independence . . . usually brought disillusionment. . . . The narrowed horizons of the nationalist struggle after independence and the difficulty of implementing the promises and hopes of the leaders have led to a certain estrangement of the masses. In the period following independence a large part of the population has broken away from the leaders, ignored the new institutions and sunk into almost complete apathy" (de Briey, *op. cit.*, p. 237).

[11]Rupert Emerson points out, as a characteristic element in the nationalist rhetoric of one-party apologists, the tendency to assert that the single party is an expression of an existent national unity, while at the same time arguing for it as an essential instrument to achieve national solidarity (*op. cit.*, pp. 24–25).

succession of amalgamations in which preëxisting pluralism and competition were not necessarily extinguished, but merely subsumed under a more inclusive organizational label. In effect, competing parties within an emergent state often became competing factions within a one-party state.

Governing single parties in new states were further weakened immediately after independence by the diversion of key party personnel to other activities. As Foltz points out, "Talents that once were available for the crucial work of party organization may now be preoccupied with running a ministry or government bureau.... Unless new sources of loyal organizational and administrative talents can be found immediately, the party's organization—and, therefore, the major link between the regime and the masses—is likely to be weakened."[12] The effect of this leadership mobility upon party continuity or survival was frequently demonstrated during the preindependence agitational period, when the transfer to other activities of only a few central party figures bore devastating results, partly because of the highly personalistic—frequently charismatic—quality of revolutionary leadership, and partly because of the small size of leadership cadres. In any event, both the attractions and the requirements of high bureaucratic office have brought a rather marked shift from emphasis on party roles to emphasis on new governmental roles.

The factors that weaken the single party at the very moment it is establishing its supremacy are also affected by the increased prominence of formal bureaucratic structures. The major element in the colonial legacy to the governing party elite in a new African state has been a centralized administrative system. Indeed, colonial rule in Africa was bureaucratic authoritarianism—the "administrative state"—in its purest form. This "machinery of government" has been indispensable to the party elite in maintaining governmental continuity during the transfer of power, as well as in consolidating its hold over the country. Preindependence hostility toward the government as a structure of "alien imperialist domination" and as a haven of antinationalist "Uncle Toms" tended to be quickly dissipated after independence, for a centralized administrative system was manifestly necessary to a modern state. Party control of that system, coupled with accelerated Africanization of all positions, progressively endowed the public service with legitimacy and made it a truly national structure. Operating simultane-

---

[12]Foltz, op. cit., pp. 123–124. Also see Wallerstein (op. cit., p. 8), who notes that a party official's governmental responsibilities increasingly diminish the amount of time available for party work. Also, once the single party has consolidated its position, there seems to be less need for party activity, a psychological consideration of no little significance.

ously, other factors—the organizational and administrative requisites of accelerated modernization, the weakness of the private sector and the statist orientation of the new elites, and the patronage pressures upon party leaders for jobs for loyal party members—have everywhere led to a vast postindependence expansion in the public service.

The acceptance, legitimation, and expansion of the bureaucracy should be a source of strength, rather than of weakness, to the governing party. Yet the classic theory of bureaucracy, as well as actual developments on the African scene, suggests that formal structures of government tend to assert their autonomy, indeed, their primacy. Carl Beck has summarized this theory as follows:

> The establishment of a legal-rational system is the end product of the process of modernization. As society becomes rationalized, a specialization of roles takes place. Specialization of roles requires the development of formal rules and a hierarchical structure for the enforcement of these rules and the settlement of conflicts. *These pressures cluster together to dictate a bureaucratization of society with an increased power position for members of the formal bureaucracy.* As this occurs, the nonrational (ideological) components of the political milieu tend to be dissipated. The political style tends to become pragmatic.[13]

Foltz argues that a trend of this sort in the new African states is both likely and already discernible. Moreover, if modernization is given priority by party elites, the new managerial and technical elites required to carry it out are bound to become ever more powerful and assertive, as happened in Senegal.[14]

Modernization not only requires and begets new managerial and technical elites; it also brings about fundamental changes in the social structure and unleashes a host of politically destabilizing forces.[15] These are both short- and long-run forces, and all pose a threat to the stability and the survival of a ruling single party, or of any other type of regime.[16] In the contemporary African scene the most immediately

---

[13]Carl Beck, "Bureaucracy and Political Development in Eastern Europe," in Joseph La Palombara, ed., *Bureaucracy and Political Development* (Princeton: Princeton University Press, 1963), p. 270 (italics added). Beck states the theory simply to refute its relevance to Eastern European experience since World War II.

[14]*Op cit.*, pp. 124 ff.

[15]These are reviewed in Mancur Olson, Jr., "Rapid Growth as a Destabilizing Force," *Journal of Economic History*, XXIII (Dec., 1963), 529–552; Ronald G. Ridker, "Discontent and Economic Growth," *Economic Development and Cultural Change*, XI (Oct., 1962), 1–15; James C. Davis, "Toward a Theory of Revolution," *American Sociological Review*, XXVII (Feb., 1962), 5–19; and Bert F. Hoselitz and Myron Weiner, "Economic Development and Political Stability in India," *Dissent*, VIII (Spring, 1961), 172–179.

[16]It should be stressed that the implications of many of the changes discussed here are not peculiar to one-party regimes but would challenge or threaten any type of government. It is theoretically possible that a one-party regime can cope with them more effectively, under certain circumstances, than could alternative institutional forms.

visible, potentially dysfunctional, demographic categories produced by the modernization process are the unemployed primary-school leavers and the frustrated second-generation university students. The former constitute an anomic potential available for exploitation by rival leadership; and the latter are presumptively disposed to assert such leadership.[17] In the long run, modernization means ever-greater differentiation and functional specialization, heightened demands and claims upon government, and a pluralization of the social bases of new centers of power and influence.

In the light of the inherent weaknesses and the vulnerability of a one-party regime, the increasing strength and the strain toward primacy of the bureaucracy in developing societies, and the destabilizing consequences of the modernization process itself, what are the likely patterns of future development of the single or dominant party in the new states of Africa? There are many possibilities, including the final emergence of a stable competitive party system. Because the latter possibility seems somewhat remote at this stage, we will focus upon two tendencies more clearly discernible within the one-party syndrome: the drift toward a "no-party state," and the consolidation of a "party-state."

The no-party state would reflect the culmination of what Wallerstein has called the trend toward inanition, that is, the progressive decline of the party as the center of power and decision making. This outcome would represent a victory for the first two of the three major generic trends discussed above. The most extreme development possible in this direction would be the emergence of a purely administrative state (not unlike the preindependence colonial situation), with the party being kept alive by the governing elite for purely symbolic, ceremonial, legitimating, and community development purposes. In addition to the factors previously mentioned, two others could contribute to this trend. One is the tendency in all African one-party regimes for one dominant personality finally to emerge in states where unitary leadership was not initially established. The other is the already discernible potentiality of the new military elites.

The broad tendency in all movement-regimes (and most African mass single parties fall into this category), Tucker argues, "is oligarchical rule by the top leadership of the ruling party under the over-

---

[17]On the primary-school leaver problem, see Archibald Callaway, "Unemployment among School Leavers," *Journal of Modern African Studies*, I (Sept., 1963), 351–372. Also see Philip J. Foster, "Secondary Schooling and Social Mobility in a West African Nation," *Sociology of Education*, XXXVII (Winter, 1963), 150–171, and J. P. N'Diaye, *Enquête sur les Etudiants noirs en France* (Paris: Editions Réalités Africaines, 1962), pp. 223–239.

all direction of a dominant personality."[18] In some instances there is a further tendency toward "fuehrerism," that is, a tendency for the dominant personality to emancipate himself from the control of the party oligarchy and to subordinate the party to the state, with the latter, as personified in the leader, displacing the party as the supreme symbol. In this process the party is eclipsed and downgraded; it becomes only one of several instrumentalities employed by the leader.[19] The eclipse of the governing party in this manner is only a potentiality in Africa's one-party states, but it is one way in which there could be a movement toward an administrative state.

The potential role of the military in the future political life of Africa's new states has already been vividly demonstrated. Military rule in the Sudan, as well as the use of armed groups at crisis points in the Congo, Togo, and Senegal, is an illustration. The capture of political power in Zanzibar by an armed band of hastily recruited malcontents, and the serious challenge presented by army "strikes" throughout East Africa in early 1964, are even more dramatic evidence of the enormous advantage possessed by even the smallest armed group, especially in the circumstances of extreme institutional fragility and organizational weakness. The monolithic governing party (TANU) of Tanganyika, East Africa's most self-conscious one-party state, was helpless in the face of a few hundred disgruntled soldiers striking for higher pay and accelerated promotions. That the military has not been even more prominent in Africa's political evolution may be attributed partly to the fact that most new states commenced their existence about 1960 either without an army or with only an embryonic one, and partly to the fact that in countries (Sudan excepted) where the military did intervene, its leaders sought relief of specific grievances rather than political power.[20]

The foregoing situation has presented African leaders in single-party states with an extraordinary opportunity to create a military establishment, almost from scratch, along lines that might guarantee the continued supremacy of the party and the loyalty of the new military elites. Such loyalty, however, could be only transitional. The army, like

---

[18]*Op. cit.*, pp. 288–289.

[19]Merle Fainsod has pointed out that under Stalin the party "declined in vitality, and its apparatus became simply one of several channels through which he communicated his commands," whereas Khrushchev "has poured new life into the party and lifted its apparatus to a central position in his structure of direction and control" ("Bureaucracy and Modernization: The Russian and Soviet Case," in La Palombara, *op. cit.*, p. 258).

[20]See James S. Coleman and Belmont Brice, Jr., "The Role of the Military in Sub-Saharan Africa," in John J. Johnson, ed., *The Role of the Military in Underdeveloped Countries* (Princeton: Princeton University Press, 1962), pp. 359–406; William Gutteridge, *Armed Forces in the New States* (London: Oxford University Press, 1962); and *Africa Report*, VIII (Jan., 1964), 4–21.

all institutional groups, tends to develop and to assert considerable autonomy. Although the Sudan is atypical in many respects, its experience has shown that the authoritarian rule of the military, in conjunction with a civilian bureaucracy, is not necessarily an ephemeral arrangement; indeed, it may be a substitute for party government. It may be the "no-party" administrative state par excellence.

A second possible pattern of future party development is the "party-state," a fully developed one-party state in which the dominant party remains supreme in the face of generic forces tending to weaken it. Structurally there would be effective fusion of party and government hierarchies at all levels. Neither the party nor the state would "wither away." This form of polity, the immediate goal of all revolutionary-centralizing parties, has been most closely approximated where the party, such as the PDG in Guinea, has had the opportunity (the mass exodus of French civil servants in 1958) and the determination (as reflected in a strong ideological compulsion) to build, *ab initio*, parallel party-state hierarchies fused at all levels through dual office holding.[21] Those recruited into the two hierarchies came from the same social strata and had the same political orientation. The incomplete fusion in Ghana, on the other hand, reveals the failure to move from a one-party-dominant state to a party-state, despite the rhetorical claim that "the CPP is Ghana and Ghana is the CPP."

The creation of an isolative rather than a fused relationship between the bureaucracy and the party in Ghana stems from a number of factors, including earlier educational development, and, consequently, greater Africanization of the public services during the terminal colonial period; the development of a national university, insulated for more than a decade from party penetration or manipulation, which produced a substantial number of new entrants into the state administrative hierarchies; and a protracted period of diarchy (roughly 1952–1957) during which merit criteria and a neutral public service commission, and not party membership or loyalty, determined recruitment to bureaucratic office. During this same period the CPP recruited most of its activists from entirely different social strata. The consequences of this isolative pattern are tension and conflict between the bureaucracy and the party. . . . One might anticipate a similar development if a revolutionary-centralizing party were to emerge and attempt to establish a party-state in a country where there had been differential recruitment to the dominant party, the bureaucracy, and the military.

---

[21]Fusion of party-state structures has also occurred in the Northern Region of Nigeria, where the hierarchy of the dominant party (NPC) has been fused with a preëxisting indigenous administrative hierarchy. In this respect, however, northern Nigeria is *sui generis* in contemporary Africa.

What is the likely fate of the one party states of the pragmatic-pluralistic pattern? Many will probably move in the direction of variant forms of the no-party state, for the reasons already discussed. Others, however, losing their revolutionary momentum, drifting toward bureaucratic stagnation, and spawning new militant leadership groups determined to complete the revolution, could be catapulted in the opposite direction toward the party-state.

What is the survival capacity of the party-state type of regime? Can it survive the assertiveness of new bureaucratic and technical elites, and the pluralization and social restructuring consequent upon modernization? Experience in the Soviet Union and in Eastern European bloc countries, one-party states that serve as the prototype of the revolutionary-centralizing states, does not support the assumption that increased bureaucratization of a modernizing society necessarily produces extraparty managerial and technological elites who inevitably establish their primacy.[22] Nor does their experience support the proposition that the emergence of new functional groups as a result of industrialization necessarily pluralizes authority or creates a constitutional system of regularized competition among factions and parties.[23] Once these experiences are noted, however, there remains the question of their relevance for the contemporary African scene. It is most unlikely, as Apter has argued, that African one-party states will enter an industrial phase in the predictable future.[24] Not having to confront the destabilizing pluralism created by industrialization, the capacity of the single dominant party to survive should presumably be enhanced. On the other hand, it does confront all the other challenges of state formation and nation building previously discussed. Moreover, none of the African single parties have yet approximated the degree of monolithic unity and ideological cohesion characteristic of their Eastern bloc prototypes. In short, at this stage of Africa's development we must be extremely cautious in calculating future probabilities on the basis of experience elsewhere.

Survival of the one-party regime will be primarily determined by the extent to which the parties concerned can overcome the inherent

---

[22]Beck (op. cit., pp. 296–298) notes that the new managerial class that has emerged in the Eastern European countries is represented in the key administrative and political hierarchies of the state, that the political systems have been successful in "absorbing these changes without creating a bureaucratized administrative system," and that, in any event, there is little evidence to support the view that members of the new class "must be a different type of political man than those now in power."

[23]"Nor should one be unduly beguiled by that special variety of technological determinism which assumes that those who possess important technical skills in a society inevitably transmute these skills into political power. There is no iron law which prevents dictators from presiding over the destinies of highly industrialized societies" (Fainsod, op. cit., pp. 262–263).

[24]David Apter, "Political Religion in the New Nations," in Geertz, op. cit.

weaknesses they suffer in the postcolonial situation. Wallerstein has argued that success here will depend partly on the explicitness of party ideology, and partly on the degree to which they mobilize and train middle-level party cadres to replace those absorbed by bureaucratic and other structures of the new state.[25] It will also be determined by the effectiveness with which they perform certain crucial political functions. The single party can continue to play a critical role in the processes of political socialization, political communication, and national integration.[26] To the extent that it preserves a measure of its aura of legitimacy, the party can also continue to facilitate the legitimation of the formal institutions and processes of government. Insofar as dynamic and revolutionary pressures within the party continue to be the main stimulus for accelerated modernization, the party can infuse the bureaucracy with a sense of national purpose, thereby helping to overcome propensities toward conservatism and routinization. The party can also be an effective extrabureaucratic instrumentality in the hands of governing elites for mobilizing human resources throughout the society in the task of national development. Indeed, all these functions, and probably others, can be performed by the single party in an African one-party state. But it is not preordained that they must do so, or that other structures or institutional arrangements, which are even more effective, and certainly more democratic, will not emerge in time.

FOR FURTHER READING

DOUGLAS E. ASHFORD, *The Elusiveness of Power: The African Single-Party State* (Ithaca: Center for International Studies, Cornell University, 1965)

HENRY L. BRETTON, "Current Political Thought and Practice in Ghana" (*American Political Science Review*, LII, 1, March 1958, 46–63)

GWENDOLEN M. CARTER, ed., *African One-Party States* (Ithaca: Cornell University Press, 1962)

RUPERT EMERSON, *Political Modernization: The Single-Party System* (Denver: University of Denver, Social Science Foundation, Monograph No. 1, 1963–64)

THOMAS HODGKIN, *African Political Parties: An Introductory Guide* (Harmondsworth: Penguin, 1961)

---

[25] *Op. cit.*, p. 16.

[26] These functions must be performed by the national party in most one-party states irrespective of their ideological orientation. See Clement Henry Moore, "The Neo-Destour Party of Tunisia: Structure for Democracy," *World Politics*, XIV (April, 1962), 461–482; L. Vincent Padgett, "Mexico's One-Party System: A Re-evaluation," *American Political Science Review*, LI (Dec., 1957), 995–1008; and Beck., *op. cit.*, p. 281.

MARTIN KILSON, "Authoritarian and Single-Party Tendencies in African Politics" (*World Politics*, XV, 2, January 1963, 262–294)

TOM MBOYA, "The Party System and Democracy in Africa" (*Foreign Affairs*, XLI, 4, July 1963, 650–658)

CLEMENT HENRY MOORE, "The Neo-Destour Party of Tunisia: A Structure For Democracy?" (*World Politics*, XIV, 3, April 1962, 461–482)

RUTH SCHACHTER MORGENTHAU, *Political Parties in French-Speaking West Africa* (Oxford: Clarendon Press, 1964)

RUTH SCHACHTER, "Single-Party Systems in West Africa" (*American Political Science Review*, LV, 2, June 1961, 294–307)

ARISTIDE R. ZOLBERG, *Creating Political Order: The Party-States of West Africa* (Chicago: Rand McNally, 1966)

POLITICAL MODERNIZATION AND THE AFRICAN MILITARY

Claude E. Welch, Jr.

Most tropical African states gained independence through constitutional negotiation rather than armed struggle. Colonial control over the African military was surrendered only after the achievement of self-government—and it appeared that the armed forces did not threaten governmental stability. The sudden eruption of the military and its effects on political modernization in tropical Africa are the themes of this selection.

From mid-1965 to the end of 1969, more than a dozen coups d'etat rocked tropical African states. The armed forces, which had remained on the sidelines during the press toward independence, suddenly became the pivot of power, the agency that could all too readily unseat civilian governments.

Many factors brought about these seizures of control. Although it is not possible to provide an exhaustive list—nor to go to the opposite extreme and cite a single, overarching "Cause" of intervention—eight factors seem especially important.

1. *Declining legitimacy of political parties.* Within a relatively brief period after independence, most African states were ruled by single-party governments, the party having arisen from the nationalist movements that hastened self-government. Winning independence, as Foltz notes elsewhere in this book, "is only the first and perhaps easiest step in building a nation . . . . the very factors making the mass party such an effective tool in the struggle for independence and permitting it to take

Adapted from *Soldier and State in Africa: A Comparative Analysis of Military Intervention and Political Change*, edited by Claude E. Welch, Jr. (Evanston: Northwestern University Press, 1970), by permission of Northwestern University Press.

over governmental power may be weakened by the day-to-day exercise of governmental responsibilities and by the nation-building process itself."[1] Political parties turned increasingly to the use of force, an action that undercut their legitimacy. With uncertainty about who had the right to govern, few checks precluded the usurpation of control by the army.

2. *Schism among prominent politicians.* The development of the single party was usually accompanied by increasing power in the hands of one man. In some instances, however, army intervention resulted from the inability of politicians to decide who was number one. For example, in the Congo, Colonel Joseph Mobutu temporarily deposed both President Joseph Kasavubu and Prime Minister Patrice Lumumba late in 1960, when the two politicians attempted to dismiss each other; in Dahomey, three years later, Colonel Christophe Soglo attempted, after his seizure of control, to force squabbling politicians to form a single party.

3. *Limited likelihood of external intervention.* Most African states retained substantial numbers of European officers and close military ties with the former colonial power after independence. The presence of expatriate officers seemingly diminished the likelihood of coups, as did the possibility of counter-intervention by other countries. If plotting African military leaders felt that their actions would not invite retribution by the former colonial power (as occurred in Gabon early in 1964), they were emboldened to press ahead.

4. *"Contagion."* Success in one coup leads to the desire for similar success elsewhere. Three weeks after soldiers assassinated President Sylvanus Olympio of Togo, the commander of the Liberian National Guard was arrested for allegedly planning a coup d'etat. "If only 250 Togolese soldiers could overthrow their government," he is reported to have said, "a Liberian Army of 5000 could seize power easily."[2]

5. *Unstable social situations.* Primordial sentiments have been part of almost all military coups in tropical Africa, either in their execution or in their interpretation. When members of the armed forces see the government as dominated by members of a hostile ethnic group, grievances based on tribe or region may quickly erupt into violence. Even if such grievances did not spring directly from tribal factors, a seizure of power may be seen as ethnically inspired. For example, the Nigerian coup d'etat of January 1966 was viewed as a scheme by Ibo officers to achieve the hegemony of their ethnic group.

---

[1]William J. Foltz, "Building the Newest Nations: Short-Run Strategies and Long-Run Problems," reprinted in this reader, pp. 293; quote from p. 296.

[2]Helen Kitchen, "Filling the Togo Vacuum," *Africa Report*, VII, 2 (January 1963), 9.

6. *Widespread corruption.* Corruption ranks high among the accusations leveled against civilian governments by their military successors. General Joseph A. Ankrah, chairman of the National Liberation Council that emerged after the ouster of President Kwame Nkrumah, accused Nkrumah of bringing Ghana "to the brink of economic disaster by economic mismanagement, waste, and unwise spending."[3] Cleansing the political system of its corrupt elements is a favored reason (or rationalization) for military intervention.

7. *Economic stagnation.* Independence held extraordinary promise for the emerging African nations. Standards of living would rise, education would become widespread, prices of agricultural produce would jump, imported goods would be readily accessible, taxes would fall—for the exploiting colonial government had departed. But the expectations went far beyond reality. To meet demands for increased social services, African governments found it necessary to raise, not lower, taxes. Agricultural prices often fell. Deficit financing brought inflation. The "revolution of rising expectations" became a revolution of rising frustrations. Particularly among the relatively privileged urban workers and civil servants, fiscal retrenchment enhanced discontent and helped form the background for military seizure of control.

8. *Military awareness of its power.* If members of the armed forces accept civilian supremacy, the possibility of military intervention does not arise. Once they distinguish, however, between the "national" interest and the policies followed by the government in power, what S. E. Finer calls the "disposition to intervene" exists.[4] And, if predisposed to intervene, members of the armed forces possess unique resources: centralization, hierarchy, discipline, a special communications system, *esprit de corps,* and above all armed might. The disposition to intervene then awaits an opportunity to seize control—and the disposition can develop rapidly, because of the previously mentioned factors.

Once the civilian government has been ousted, coup leaders seek to justify their seizure of control by pointing to the economic, political, and social problems politicians failed to resolve. Only a period of military rule, the new rulers argue, can purge the political system of its inadequacies. Their rhetoric must not be confused with the likelihood of action, however. Military-based governments cannot necessarily cope more successfully with the difficulties civilian regimes confronted. I shall argue that military-based governments in Africa will find it extremely difficult

---

[3]*Africa Research Bulletin,* III, 2 (February 1967), Col. 467C.
[4]S. E. Finer, *The Man on Horseback: The Role of the Military in Politics* (New York: Praeger, 1962), pp. 23–60.

to achieve legitimacy and hence that their prospects for successful governance remain uncertain.

The introductory chapter in this reader set forth three aspects of political modernization:

1. an increased centralization of power in the state, coupled with the weakening of traditional sources of authority;
2. the differentiation and specialization of political institutions;
3. increased popular participation in politics, and greater identification with the political system as a whole.

Let us examine the ways in which military-based governments fit these aspects theoretically, look at Kemal Ataturk's transformation of the Turkish political system, and conclude with specific observations on the relative success of military-based governments in Africa.

I. ASPECTS OF POLITICAL MODERNIZATION

Centralization of Authority

As organizations, armed forces are characterized by centralization, discipline, hierarchy, communication, and *esprit de corps*. To function well, they require a clearly defined chain of command, with adequate communications to ensure that orders are carried out and with means of disciplinary control. Effective military organization, almost by definition, demands a high degree of centralization.

Many scholars have equated "modern" government with centralized and highly organized government. Samuel P. Huntington has argued, "Political modernization . . . involves the rationalization of authority: the replacement of a large number of traditional, religious, familial, and ethnic political authorities by a single, secular, national political authority . . . It means national integration and the centralization or accumulation of power in recognized national law-making institutions."[5] Centralized power is a pattern of organization familiar to the military. Hence, seizure of power by the armed forces usually results in greater control from the center.

But can this control be converted into authority? Authority may be defined as the acceptance by the people that certain individuals or offices possess a legitimate right to leadership.[6] The exercise of authority

---

[5]Samuel P. Huntington, "Political Modernization: America vs. Europe" (*World Politics*, XVIII, 3 April 1966), 378.

[6]Carl J. Friedrich, ed., *Authority* (Cambridge: Harvard University Press, 1958).

presupposes "a community of opinions, values and beliefs, as well as of interests and needs."[7] Applied to military intervention in politics, the question of authority centers on the act of seizing control: is this regarded as usurpation, or as a rightful act?

Writing in the troubled years of Charles II, Thomas Hobbes compared politics with a game of cards. In both, he suggested, the participants must agree on what constitutes legitimate power, what is authority—which cards are trumps. If no card is accepted, then clubs—force of arms—become trumps. Where confusion prevails over the source of authority, the possibility of military intervention increases significantly; and should intervention occur, leaders of the coup must convert their power into authority.[8]

Centralization of control is not sufficient, in other words. There must be an accompanying development, namely increasing belief that the central government, even if under military auspices, exercises legitimate authority.

To replace traditional, religious, familial, and ethnic political authorities by a single, secular, national political authority obviously requires time, favorable conditions, communications based upon similar values, and a growth in mutual confidence, among other factors.[9] In the absence of favorable conditions, attempts at centralization may touch off major countervailing forces. Tensions may be exacerbated; would-be centralization can bring disintegration. Accordingly, I hesitate to agree fully with Guy Pauker, who (writing about Southeast Asia) asserts that the officer corps can become "temporary kernels of national integration, around which the other constructive forces of the various societies could rally, during a short period of break-through from present stagnation into a genuine developmental takeoff."[10]

---

[7]Carl J. Friedrich, *Man and His Government* (New York: McGraw-Hill, 1963), p. 244. Robert Dahl defines authority as the influence of a leader clothed with legitimacy; legitimacy is the belief that structures, procedures, acts, decisions, policies, officials, or leaders of government possess "the quality of 'rightness,' propriety, or moral goodness and should be accepted because of this quality." Robert A. Dahl, *Modern Political Analysis* (Englewood Cliffs, N.J.: Prentice-Hall, 1963), p. 19.

[8]Dahl, pp. 31–32.

[9]Karl W. Deutsch *et al*, "Political Community and the North Atlantic Area," reprinted in *International Political Communities: An Anthology* (Garden City: Doubleday, 1966), 1–91. Deutsch and his associates list nine essential conditions for the creation of an "amalgamated security-community:" (1) mutual compatibility of main values; (2) a distinctive way of life; (3) expectations of stronger economic ties or gains; (4) a marked increase in political and administrative capabilities of at least some participating units; (5) superior economic growth on the part of at least some participating units; (6) unbroken links of social communication, both geographically between territories and sociologically between different social strata; (7) a broadening of the political elite; (8) mobility of persons, at least among the politically relevant strata; and (9) a multiplicity of ranges of communication and transaction. The authors note that three other conditions may be essential: (10) a compensation of flows of communications and transactions; (11) a not too infrequent interchange of group roles; and (12) considerable mutual predictability of behavior. *International Political Communities*, 37–38.

[10]Guy J. Pauker, "Southeast Asia as a Problem Area in the Next Decade," *World Politics*, XI, 3 (April 1959), 339.

Differentiation and Specialization

In a traditional setting, as pointed out earlier in this book, the many functions carried out within a society may be "fused."[11] A modern setting, on the other hand, is characterized by differentiation among these functions and by the development of particular structures (institutions) for their accomplishment. Clearly, the armed services epitomize such differentiation of function and specialization of structure. A modern army is not a temporary band of marauders or a disorganized militia. Its *raison d'être* is the rational use of violence; its organization reflects the application of modern techniques.[12]

The high degree of specialization within the armed services contrasts not only with the "fused" traditional social setting, but also with other "modern" groups. Few political parties in Africa, for example, can match the centralization, discipline, hierarchy, *esprit de corps*, and speed of communication of even the smallest professional army on the continent. Qualitatively, the organizational strength of the military sets it apart from other groups. Command of weaponry is not the sole distinguishing factor of African armies vis-à-vis civilian organizations; the very organizational characteristics of armies are distinctive.

Many commentators on the role of the military in developing countries have focused upon the impact of army training on both officers and recruits. Extended military service, under particular conditions, will weaken an individual's primary identification with his village and ethnic group. An African soldier must likely learn a new language, serve in areas hundreds of miles from his home, and associate with men of different ethnic backgrounds. He may acquire technological skills unknown to the average villager. Specialized training courses for officers (particularly those taken outside Africa) further remove them from the traditional setting. Lucian W. Pye argues in this fashion:

> The good soldier is also to some degree a modernized man. Thus it is that the armies in the newly emergent countries come to play key roles in the process by which traditional ways give way to more Westernized ideas and practices. . . . the acculturative process tends to be focused on acquiring technical skills that are of particular value for economic development. . . . Politically the most significant feature of the process of acculturation within the army is that it usually provides some form of training in citizenship. [13]

---

[11]Fred W. Riggs, *Administration in Developing Countries: The Theory of the Prismatic Society* (Boston: Houghton Mifflin, 1964), p. 23.

[12]Lucian Pye notes, for example, that "modern armies are essentially industrial-type entities." Lucian W. Pye, "Armies in the Process of Political Modernization," in J. J. Johnson, ed., *The Role of the Military in Underdeveloped Countries* (Princeton: Princeton University Press, 1962), p. 76.

[13]Pye, p. 80–83.

Morris Janowitz mentions that the military offers training in technical and administrative skills, as well as basic literacy and citizenship.[14] Lerner and Robinson note that the Turkish army became "a major agency of social change" precisely because it"spread among [Turkish rural youth] a new sense of [national] identity—and new skills and concepts as well as new machines."[15] But can the personality changes wrought by army service bring long-range changes in African states, in the face of pronounced ethnic and regional tensions that may affect the armed forces? And, more fundamentally, is the functional specialization of the armed services conducive to political modernization? We shall return to these questions in the concluding section.

Popular Participation and Identification

The extent of political participation can be altered by military regimes; the degree of popular identification with the political system is not susceptible to easy manipulation.

In the creation of political systems, perhaps the most important task is that of fostering popular identification. People who physically are members of a given political system should feel psychologically that they are members of the system.[16] Analysts often presume that increased political participation indicates greater psychological identification with the system as a whole. However, as Clifford Geertz comments, enhanced opportunities for participation may stimulate

> an obsessive concern with the relation of one's tribe, region, sect, or whatever to a center of power that, while growing rapidly more active, is not easily either insulated from the web of primordial attachments, as was the remote colonial regime, or assimilated to them as are the workaday authority systems of the "little community." Thus, it is the very process of the formation of a sovereign civil state that, among other things, stimulates sentiments of parochialism, communalism, racialism, and so on, because it introduces into society a valuable new prize over which to fight and a frightening new force with which to contend.[17]

Popular identification cannot be legislated into existence.[18] To be certain, the overthrow of an unpopular civilian dictator may bring

---

[14]Morris Janowitz, *The Military in the Political Development of New Nations*, reprinted in Wilson C. McWilliams, *Garrisons and Government: Politics and the Military in New States* (San Francisco: Chandler, 1967), p. 74; *cf.* Pye. "Armies in the Process of Political Modernization," 76ff.
[15]Daniel Lerner and Richard D. Robinson, "Swords and Ploughshares: The Turkish Army as a Modernizing Force," *World Politics*, XIII, 1 (October 1960), 19–44.
[16]Sidney Verba, "Comparative Political Culture," in Lucian W. Pye and Sidney Verba, eds., *Political Culture and Political Development* (Princeton: Princeton University Press, 1966), p. 529.
[17]Clifford Geertz, "The Integrative Revolution: Primordial Sentiments and Civic Politics in the New States," reprinted in this reader p. 198.
[18]Morroe Berger, *The Military Elite and Social Change: Egypt since Napoleon*, reprinted in McWilliams, *Garrisons and Government*, p. 225.

great initial credit to the perpetrators of military intervention; installation of a genuinely popular army member as head of state similarly may result in public approbation. The vagaries of popular opinion and the threat of ethnically based parochialism, however, make widespread popular identification with a new regime an unlikely direct product of military intervention.

Let us recapitulate the three major aspects of political modernization. As organizations, the armed forces of African states illustrate centralized control and functional specialization. Seizure of power by the military may result from confusion over the source of authority within the state. There is no guarantee that the new leaders resulting from a coup d'etat will be viewed by the people as exercising *legitimate* authority —a possibility that, in Hobbes's terms, opens the way for further disputes and use of force. The growth of identification with the political system may well depend on factors largely outside the area of direct government control. Despite the changes in individuals through military training, there is no guarantee that the concepts of national unity brought by this training will affect, in the short run, the perceptions and behavior of most inhabitants of the state. Political modernization requires a combination of skillful leadership, fortuitous circumstances, national unity, and political capacity unlikely to coexist simultaneously in any state. However, brief examination of the Ataturk period in Turkey shows that effective transformation can occur if political institutions are carefully fostered.

II. POLITICAL MODERNIZATION IN TURKEY: AN EXAMPLE FOR AFRICA?

The success of Kemal Ataturk frequently is cited as evidence that military rule can bring transformations that a civilian regime was unable to bring about. "Be like Ataturk," the adage seems to run, "and our country will prosper." However, to assume that installation of a military government brings about political modernization is incorrect. The experiences of Turkey under Ataturk ("Father of the Turks") show the severe limitations of military rule *unless* it leads to the development of effective political institutions.

At the close of World War I, the once glorious Ottoman Empire lay in ruins. The hegemony of the Sublime Porte, which had been exercised over an area extending from the Balkans throughout the Near East, had been effectively broken. The government of the sultan, confronted with the ineluctable fact of military defeat, was forced to concede to the Allied Powers what little remained of its Near Eastern territories. However, the surgery performed by the victorious Allies, coupled with effective leadership by a former Army general, appear to have cured the "Sick Man of Europe."

Turkish forces did not distinguish themselves during the war, with the major exceptions of the Gallipoli campaign in late 1915 and the defense of Aleppo in October 1918. In both these campaigns, Ataturk was the leader; he was the sole Turkish military leader to enhance his reputation during the war.[19] The capitulation of the sultan's government to humiliating terms and subsequent occupation of Istanbul and parts of Anatolia stirred great discontent. Ataturk, under the guise of supervising the disarming and demobilization of remaining Turkish forces, established a base in northern Turkey, from which he defied the subservient Istanbul government and challenged the invading Greek armies. His Anatolian nationalists extended control over the civilian administration. Military success against Armenian, French, and Greek forces resulted, by 1922, in a new armistice and a treaty recognizing the independence of Turkey within the 1918 armistice lines (Istanbul and Asia Minor).

It is not my purpose to summarize Turkish history since 1918 or to repeat the arguments of Szyliowicz, printed above. However, five basic points deserve note.

1.   The multi-national Ottoman Empire, whose leaders were torn among conflicting objectives of Pan-Ottomanism, Islamic Solidarity, or Turkish nationalism, faced insuperable obstacles. Ataturk departed from Ottoman policy by recognizing the "necessity for shrinking the Ottoman Empire down to a small, culturally more homogeneous and politically more viable Turkey . . . "[20]

2.   The military in Turkey had long played a basic role in introducing new techniques and "Western" ideas.[21] Ataturk thus continued—and expanded—trends that characterized the Ottoman military establishment.

3.   Ataturk envisaged nothing less than a total transformation of Turkish society. He did not intend to intervene briefly to ameliorate a few minor ills; his objectives were revolutionary. On the other hand, he failed to include the rural peasantry, whose involvement increased only with the growth of competitive party politics after World War II.

4.   Turkey benefited from Ataturk's relatively long rule. Continuity of leadership, combined with relative domestic tranquility after 1923 and the absence of international pressures, eased the long-range changes with which Ataturk was concerned.

---

[19]Richard D. Robinson, *The First Turkish Republic: A Case Study in National Development* (Cambridge: Harvard University Press, 1963), p. 24.

[20]Robinson, p. 22.

[21]Robert E. Ward and Dankwart Rustow, eds., *Political Modernization in Japan and Turkey* (Princeton: Princeton University Press, 1964), pp. 352–388.

5. Despite his military background, Ataturk "civilianized" himself and his regime as rapidly as feasible. His official portrait, to take one example, showed him in white tie and tails, not military regalia, reflecting his "determination to civilianize the Turkish Republic that cut wide and deep."[22]

Ataturk's inimitable foresight rested essentially on a clear recognition of the need for effective political institutions. His was not a self-serving military clique or junta, but a government that built popular support for government by means of economic development, gradual mobilization of support (as through the Houses of the People), and the charisma of Ataturk. The pragmatic Kemalist policy was founded on populism and *etatism*—on an astute combination of limited popular participation and centralized control within a gradually changing social framework. As Lerner and Robinson note, "Central political control was essential to regulate institutional innovation—so that changes would occur fast enough, but not so fast that social mobility would undermine political stability."[23] Or to quote a similar assessment by Janowitz, Turkey under Ataturk "represented the one case in which military oligarchy under an enlightened leader made fundamental contributions to social and economic modernization. The process of modernization in Turkey was gradual and built on evolving institutions."[24] The example of Turkey thus shows that political modernization depends on effective political institutions with sufficient capacity to bring about purposeful change.

III. POLITICAL MODERNIZATION AND INSTITUTIONAL CAPACITIES

An understanding of political modernization requires an understanding of the capacity of political institutions to meet the demands on them—demands emanating both from popular expectations and from the tasks of transformation set by government leaders. Capacity depends on numerous inter-related variables, the combination of which alters over time. At the risk of oversimplification, however, capacity depends on the legitimate organizational strength of government organs, sufficient resources to carry out tasks, and effectiveness, each of which merits closer examination.

It was noted earlier in this chapter that many African states suffered from the declining legitimacy of political parties before the armed forces seized control. Marked government ineffectiveness in the face of

---

[22]Lerner and Robinson, "Swords and Ploughshares," p. 19.
[23]Lerner and Robinson, p. 25.
[24]Morris Janowitz, "The Military in the Political Development of New Nations," p. 271.

mounting popular pressures helped prompt military intervention. Resources obviously were meager; witness the widespread government deficits of Ghana before Nkrumah's overthrow. In brief, military intervention occurred without popular protest because the civilian organs of government largely had lost the legitimacy gained through achieving independence. The issue remains whether military-based governments can regain legitimate authority.

Political institutions exercise authority by exercising control that is seen as rightful, correct, or legitimate. Authority implies a recognition of common purposes and a belief in the inherent rightness of the leadership. Most citizens must be willing to bridle private or personal impulses for the sake of general social objectives. Rapoport comments cogently that this organizational strength characterizes both civilian and military life: recognition of a "rule of law" in the civilian realm and discipline in the army channel individual desires toward a common good.[25]

In many states, both Western and non-Western, nationalism provided cohesiveness and purpose. A sense of unity was enhanced by historical ties, defense against an external enemy, commonality of tradition, language, and territory, and the "intimate interconnections"[26] of state and nation. A sense of community emerged. Governments were recognized as legitimate; their authority rested not on coercion and force of arms, but on expectations of compliance and obedience.

In the nineteenth century, one would be hard pressed to uncover traces of such nationalism in the Ottoman Empire. The Sublime Porte ruled over a territory suffering from a "refractory set of ingredients for a modern nation-state: it stretched over parts of three continents, lacked racial, religious and linguistic homogeneity, included peoples with separate and competitive traditions and aspirations, and possessed few natural frontiers."[27] However, World War I reduced the Ottoman Empire to little more than its Anatolian heartland. The repatriation or repression of the Greek and Armenian minorities further enhanced ethnic homogeneity. Islam (though regarded by Ataturk as retrograde in its impact) reinforced other common bonds. Ataturk added his personal prestige and magnetism to the institutions of the Turkish Republic. But the key factor in Ataturk's effort was the stimulation of nationalism. "Geographical and political nationalism was the device to which Kemal turned,"

[25]David C. Rapoport, "A Comparative Theory of Military and Political Types," in Samuel P. Huntington, ed., *Changing Patterns of Military Politics* (New York: Free Press, 1963), p. 79.
[26]Rupert Emerson, *From Empire to Nation: The Rise to Self-Assertion of Asian and African Peoples* (Cambridge: Harvard University Press 1960), p. 104.
[27]Ward and Rustow, *Political Modernization in Japan and Turkey*, p. 438.

Robinson comments. "There was a deliberate and sustained effort to weld together a Turkish nation."[28]

The necessity for a similar effort confronts African political leaders. It has frequently been stressed that African states are riven with differences arising from conflicting "primordial sentiments." As the subtitle of a recent book inquired, should Nigeria be considered in terms of tribes, people, or race? These differences are often expressed in the antinomy of "tribalism" and "nationalism"—admittedly inadequate and possibly misleading terms to characterize complex phenomena. More appropriately, one should say that ethnic loyalties for most Africans are not yet fully complemented by identification with a nation: Aizo, Fon, Bariba rather than Dahomey; Bamileke, Bassa, Bulu rather than Cameroon; Hausa, Ibo, Yoruba rather than Nigeria. Recognizing the limited extent of "national" loyalties, or, in somewhat different terms, the low level of national political integration, African political leaders have often viewed the state, or a dominant party, as the "architect" of the nation.[29] However, between concept and implementation, theory often goes astray. The inefficiency of the government and the decay of the dominant party into little more than a machine for distributing spoils reduced the necessary element of institutional strength. More significantly, the process of social mobilization in ethnically heterogeneous African states often reinforced particularistic tendencies.[30] "The African nationalist still has before him almost the entire task of creating the nations in whose name he professes to speak," Emerson comments.[31] Nigeria has been established —but not Nigerians. Accordingly, to build political authority on the shallow foundations of Nigerian, Dahomeyan, or any other "nationalism" in Africa runs serious risks.

Obviously, it would be preposterous to assert that nationalism as a factor underlying political authority in African states cannot be enhanced. The major question, rather, is whether African governments *under military auspices* will have greater likelihood than their civilian predecessors of developing nationalism as a basic support for political authority. Are the problems of a type that army-dominated governments can better resolve? To provide tentative answers to this question, let us return briefly to the example of Turkey and then analyze the action of African military regimes since their assumption of control.

[28]Robinson, *The First Turkish Republic*, p. 84.

[29]Leopold Sedar Senghor, *Nation et Voie Africaine du Socialisme* (Paris: Presence Africaine, 1960), p. 24.

[30]Karl W. Deutsch, "Social Mobilization and Political Development," *American Political Science Review*, LV, 3 (September, 1961), 493–514. [Reprinted in this reader, p. 153.]

[31]Emerson, *From Empire to Nation*, p. 94.

The Turkish example seems inapplicable to contemporary Africa in two respects. First, Turkey, after the establishment of the Republic, manifested a degree of ethnic, linguistic, and religious homogeneity more extensive than most African countries. The multi-national Ottoman Empire suffered social cleavages that negated the efforts of the Young Turks. Their vision of a modernized empire caused considerable upheavals among both Christians and Muslims, and eventually stimulated Arab nationalism —all of which defeated the vision.[32] Reduction of the empire to its Turkish heartland preceded the effective implementation of nationalism.[33] Arguing by analogy (though hardly the most defensible form of argument), the development of nationalism as a foundation for political authority in Africa seems to require building on existing ethnic foundations, rather than creating a divided and weak multi-ethnic state. Secondly, to call Ataturk's regime "military" seriously misrepresents the facts. His policies of civilianization, previously alluded to, established a clearer division between military and civilian aspects of government than existed in the Ottoman period.

If the ethnic divisions of African states impede the growth of political legitimacy based on nationalism,[34] are there other bases on which military-dominated governments might seek to achieve legitimacy? The jubilation that accompanied the overthrow of Nkrumah and other unpopular politicians appears to indicate widespread approbation for those coups. In the words of Roger Murray, the leaders of intervention profited from "popular exhaustion and tacit or active support for the dismantling of sclerosed political institutions."[35] By removing venal and autocratic rulers, whether by incarceration, assassination, or exile, the military rulers emphasized the break with the past. Political parties were banned on the basis of the corruption and authoritarianism of their leaders. One may ask, however, whether this distaste for politicians and support for the military persists for more than a few months.

No group of rulers can long base their claims for legitimacy on acrimony and memory of previous injustices. If the new military governors of African countries intend to remain in power for an extended period, they must build the capacity and legitimacy of governing institutions. There are three, interlocking ways that African military rulers

---

[32]Kemal H. Karpat, *Turkey's Politics: The Transition to a Multi-Party System* (Princeton: Princeton University Press, 1959), p. 24.
[33]Ward and Rustow, *Political Modernization in Japan and Turkey*, p. 438.
[34]I am distinguishing here between nationalism and anti-colonialism. This distinction has been criticized by some writers on African affairs and neglected by many others. However, the contrast between unity based on opposition to an imposed, foreign regime and unity based on a sense of shared participation within an historic entity must not be forgotten.
[35]Roger Murray, "Militarism in Africa," *New Left Review*, No. 38, p. 57.

might seek to achieve legitimacy: (1) build effectiveness over an extended period; (2) avoid recourse to excessive use of force; and (3) gain or create a social and political basis of support.

Given the contemporary characteristics of both African states and their military establishments, none of these means will likely bring about legitimacy. "Prolonged effectiveness over a number of generations," Lipset notes, "may give legitimacy to a political system. In the modern world, such effectiveness means primarily constant economic development."[36] This pathway to legitimacy does not appear feasible for governing African juntas, for the timespan emphasized by Lipset suggests that short-run effectiveness will not *ipso facto* be translated into widespread support for military governments.

The tendency to resort to violence exists in all military-dominated governments—after all, how else did the military gain control? As Parsons and Zolberg have demonstrated, the use of force quickly erodes the basis of legitimate authority on which governments are based.[37] Devised to use force in the most efficient manner, armies have a natural proclivity to turn to violence rather than bargaining, to repression rather than compromise. In thrusting aside politicians, military leaders may scorn the techniques well-known to politicians, such as the artful ethnic balance. Military life does not necessarily provide relevant, simple formulae for a viable political system; army leaders must learn politics through experience.[38] Let me cite one example from the ill-fated Nigerian regime of General Aguiyi-Ironsi. The abortive attempt to implement Decree No. 5 in May 1966, "to remove the last vestiges of the intense regionalism of the recent past, and to produce that cohesion in the governmental structure which is so necessary in achieving and maintaining the paramount objective of the National Military Government, and indeed of every true Nigerian, namely, national unity," bore witness to haste, a lack of political realism, an assumption that the centralized structure of the army could be transplanted simply into a complex government. Elemental prudence would dictate that army leaders minimize using their specialization— effective utilization of violence—for the methods of compromise and negotiation developed by politicians.

---

[36]Seymour Martin Lipset, *Political Man: The Social Bases of Politics* (Garden City: Doubleday, 1963), p. 70.

[37]Talcott Parsons, "Some Reflections on the Place of Force in Social Process," in Harry Eckstein, ed., *Internal War: Problems and Approaches* (New York: Free Press, 1963), p. 44; Aristide R. Zolberg, "The Structure of Political Conflict in the New States of Tropical Africa," *American Political Science Review*, LXII, 1 (March 1968), 73–77.

[38]Morris Janowitz, *The Military in the Political Development of New Nations: An Essay in Comparative Analysis* (Chicago: University of Chicago Press, 1964), pp. 104–105.

The most feasible means of building legitimacy rests in careful cultivation of a strong basis of popular support. Military rulers, like their civilian predecessors, must construct a coalition of supporting groups, create political parties with widespread appeal, develop strength among significant parts of the population. Many coup leaders have sought legitimacy by naming civilian advisory councils, often in response to mounting discontent with policies imposed by the miltary governments. Unless a firm commitment has been made to restoring civilian rule, such alliances smack of expediency, however.

Of necessity, army-dominated African governments have worked closely with civil servants.[39] Military governments, having eschewed the politicization of civil services that often had been enforced under single-party regimes, have enhanced the role of civil servants. Indeed, it is tempting to assert that the technocratic orientations and organizational hierarchies of army officers and civil servants bring both groups into natural alliance. An alliance of selected civilians, civil servants, and the military may well lack the "identific" element of sympathy from the population, on the other hand.[40]

Military leaders have other options. Rather than draw on the ranks of former politicians and highly-placed civil servants, they can create new political parties under their direct auspices to foster legitimacy. In other words, instead of drawing on the support given to politicians participating in an elite coalition, army officers may seek their own foundations of popular support. For example, General Joseph Mobutu of Congo Kinshasa announced, in April 1967, his intention of creating and leading the "Movement populaire de la Révolution," intended to organize the popular masses for education, instruction, and training. But the prospects for the rapid creation of a strong party structure are negligible. In the face of widespread apathy, attempts to build legitimacy through persuasion, party activity, and economic development involves huge expenditures of effort without significant short-run impact. The series of failures to create a broadly-based political movement in the United Arab Republic, despite intensive efforts by President Nasser, and the indifferent success of Ataturk himself in developing party support among the peasantry,

[39]Chief Awolowo has expressed this affinity strongly: "It has been said that governments may come, and governments may go, but the Civil Service remains forever. It is a most merciful thing indeed that the Civil Service remains largely unaffected by the vicissitudes of politics. What a tragedy, for instance, it would have been if the recent reverses in the fortunes of politicians had hit the civil servants more or less equally! The smooth take-over by the army would have been impossible. There would have been a chaotic collapse of public administration, with harsh and injurious effects on the welfare of people." Obafemi Awolowo, *Thoughts on Nigerian Constitution* (Ibadan: Oxford University Press, 1966), p. 73.
[40]Claude Ake, "Political Integration and Political Stability," *World Politics*, XIX, 3 (April 1967), 491.

clearly indicate the difficulties of building legitimacy through party auspices.[41]

To rule effectively, once having achieved power, military leaders must develop political organizations of civilian types or work out viable relations with civilian political groups.[42] There are no other paths toward effective political modernization. Military governments will confront the same problems of ethnicity and economic stagnation that confronted civilian governments. The centralized authority and functional specialization of armies may promote intervention, but they do not enhance the possibilities for effective governance based on legitimate governmental strength. The military rulers of Africa often lack bargaining skills. Their impatience with politicians—their "politics of wanting to be above politics"[43]—leads them to distrust the slow, difficult process of coalition-building. Having banned political parties, and usually lacking the abilities to build parties afresh, the African military deny themselves fundamental bases of support. They cannot build legitimate political institutions through the use of force; they cannot transplant their organizational style to the civilian realm; they are not equipped to bring stability, modernization, or political participation; they lack sufficient flexibility and innovativeness to govern effectively.[44] Political decay thus seems to await those who substitute violence for authority—a lesson the African military has yet to take to heart.

FOR FURTHER READING

HENRY BIENEN, *The Military Intervenes: Case Studies in Political Development* (New York: Russell Sage Foundation, 1968)

EDWARD FEIT, "Military Coups and Political Development: Some Lessons from Ghana and Nigeria" *(World Politics,* XX, 2, January 1968, 179–93)

KENNETH W. GRUNDY, "On Machiavelli and the Mercenaries" *(Journal of Modern African Studies,* VI, 3, October 1968, 295–310)

WILLIAM GUTTERIDGE, *The African Military and Politics* (London: Methuen, 1969)

WILLIAM GUTTERIDGE, *Military Institutions and Power in the New States* (New York: Praeger, 1965)

GEORGE H. HADDAD, *Revolutions and Military Rule in the Middle East: The Northern Tier* (New York: Speller, 1965)

KEITH HOPKINS, "Civil-Military Relations in Developing Countries" *(British Journal of Sociology,* XVII, 2, June 1966, 165–182)

---

[41]P. J. Vatikiotis, *The Egyptian Army in Politics; Pattern for New Nations?* (Bloomington: Indiana University Press, 1961).
[42]Janowitz, *The Military,* p. 1.
[43]Janowitz, p. 65.
[44]Herbert J. Spiro, "The Military in sub-Saharan Africa," in McWilliams, *Garrisons and Government,* p. 266.

MORRIS JANOWITZ, *The Military in the Political Development of New Nations: An Essay in Comparative Analysis* (Chicago: University of Chicago Press, 1964)

JOHN J. JOHNSON, ed., *The Role of the Military in Underdeveloped Countries* (Princeton: Princeton University Press, 1962)

J. M. LEE, *African Armies and Civil Order* (New York: Praeger, 1969)

WILSON C. McWILLIAMS, ed., *Garrisons and Government: Politics and the Military in New States* (San Francisco: Chandler, 1967)

DOROTHY NELKIN, "The Economic and Social Setting of Military Takeovers in Africa" *(Journal of Asian and African Studies, II, 3–4, June-October 1967, 230–244)*

AMOS PERLMUTTER, "The Praetorian State and the Praetorian Army: Toward a Taxonomy of Civil-Military Relations in Developing Polities" *(Comparative Politics, I, 3, April 1969, 382–404)*

P. J. VATIKIOTIS, *The Egyptian Army in Politics: Pattern for New Nations?* (Bloomington: Indiana University Press, 1961)

CLAUDE E. WELCH, JR., ed., *Soldier and State in Africa: A Comparative Analysis of Military Intervention and Political Change* (Evanston: Northwestern University Press, 1970)

INDEX OF CONTRIBUTING AUTHORS